THE AEPCO PROJECT

Volume II

Dos Condado to Apache Survey
and
Data Recovery of Archaeological Resources

by

Deborah A. Westfall
Kenneth Rozen
Howard M. Davidson

with contributions by

Jon S. Czaplicki
Gerald K. Kelso

Cultural Resource Management Section
Arizona State Museum
The University of Arizona

December 1979

Archaeological Series No. 117

ABSTRACT

The Arizona Electric Power Cooperative, Inc., contracted with the Cultural Resource Management Section of the Arizona State Museum for an intensive survey of the right-of-way corridor and access roads of a proposed transmission line system between Safford and Cochise, Arizona. This was the second phase of the AEPCO Project, the first phase being concerned with that section from Greenlee Substation near Morenci, to Safford, Arizona (Simpson and others 1978). The AEPCO II survey located 27 sites within the proposed corridor; none were found on access roads. Six of these sites were recommended for inclusion in the National Register of Historic Places. Data recovery was carried out at 11 sites. Due to the surficial nature of the investigated sites, problems of culture history could not be confidently answered, although several sites indicated occupation by Amargosa or Cochise culture groups during the Archaic period; one site had material indicating occupation by early Mogollon or Hohokam groups. Study was focused, instead, on describing site activities as they related to biotic and abiotic resource procurement and processing within specific environmental zones.

ACKNOWLEDGEMENTS

This report on the final phase of the AEPCO archaeological investigations is possible because of the cooperation and support of numerous individuals. Special thanks are due to the Arizona Electric Power Cooperative, Inc. for the opportunity to conduct research in southeastern Arizona. Don Powell, Right-of-Way Agent, has been outstanding in his patience and efforts in coordinating archaeological studies with AEPCO's construction requirements and schedules. Ron Black and Bob Doublebower, then of Burns and McDonnell Engineering Company, Kansas City, Missouri, are also thanked for their technical and personal assistance during all phases of the AEPCO II field investigations.

The ASM field crew is to be commended for their diligent work and consistent good humor while under a tight time schedule. They are: Howard Davidson (Assistant Supervisor), Anne Baldwin, Bonnie Dement, Kate Quinn, Anne Rieger, Ken Rozen, and Steve Weber (crew members). Jeanette Dickerson was Laboratory Supervisor and was assisted by Debbie Confer.

Gay Kinkade of the Safford District Office, Bureau of Land Management, deserves special praise for his assistance in consultations with AEPCO and in the nomination of sites to the National Register of Historic Places. Alfred Dewal, USDA soil scientist of the same office provided helpful advice and unpublished environmental reports.

Mr. Ben Travis, Willcox Superintendent of Schools, and Willcox Scout Troop 409 are thanked for allowing us to use the Willcox Scout Troop Headquarters for the field laboratory. Conklin Contractors of Willcox provided a backhoe and operators for our test excavations.

Appreciation is extended to several individuals of Safford and Willcox who granted permission for access to sites and allowed us to conduct investigations on their properties: Ms. Terry McEuen of Safford; Mr. G.L. Moore, Mr. E.B. Riggs, Mr. G. Clump, and Mr. W.D. Wear, Jr., all of Willcox.

Our colleagues in the Cultural Resource Management Section and Department of Anthropology, University of Arizona, aided us in solving problems during analysis. Among them, Dr. Emil W. Haury and W. Bruce Masse aided in ceramic identification, and Dr. A.J. Jelinek provided advice and guidance for the lithic analysis. Several students in the Professional Internship Program also helped in the lithic analysis. Kim Rossback is thanked for her able assistance with a part of the lithic analysis.

Dr. Robert O'Haire, Arizona Bureau of Mines, University of Arizona, helped to identify lithic raw materials. Roberta Hagaman assisted in our statistical analyses. Lynn S. Teague, Section Head, and Jon Czaplicki, Project Director provided guidance and assistance throughout all phases of this study.

Those involved in producing this report deserve special citation. Marcia Petta drafted the site maps, and Ken Rozen did a fine job of lithic artifact illustration. Esther Walker undertook the onerous job of typing final copy. Any report combining the diverse writing styles of several authors presents a challenge for any editor. Gayle Hartmann and Diane Dittemore are gratefully acknowledged for pulling these chapters together into a coherent whole.

TABLE OF CONTENTS

LIST OF FIGURES

LIST OF TABLES

CHAPTER 1

BACKGROUND TO THE PRESENT STUDY

Introduction

The Arizona Electric Power Cooperative, Inc. (AEPCO), a Rural Electrification Administration generator and transmission cooperative, is adding generating units and associated transmission segments to augment their present system in southeastern Arizona. The AEPCO construction project is a two-phase undertaking: (1) the construction of three new substations and transmission line from the vicinity of Morenci to Safford, Arizona, and (2) dismantling an existing 115-kV line and replacing it with line running from the Dos Condado Substation, southeast of Safford to the Apache Electric Station southwest of Willcox, Arizona. The archaeological investigations were coordinated with these two phases and are referred to as AEPCO I and II, respectively.

Construction Considerations

AEPCO is building two new generating units at their existing Apache Electric Station, located in Section 10, T16S, R24E in Cochise County approximately 6.5 km southwest of Cochise, Arizona (Figure 1). The construction project involves building three new substations: Greenlee in Section 29, T5S, R30E near York, Greenlee County; Morenci in Section 20, T5S, R30E, approximately 12 km southeast of the town of Morenci, Greenlee County; and Hackberry, located in Section 20, T6S, R26E, about 12.8 km northeast of Safford, Graham County. The northern transmission segment terminates at the existing Dos Condado Substation in Section 31, T7S, R26E, approximately 11.2 km southeast of Safford.

Construction of related facilities includes building 105 km of new 230-kV transmission line (the Greenlee-Dos Condado segment), building two 345-kV lines (the Tucson Gas & Electric - Greenlee Substation loop and the Vail-Bicknell line) and replacing 102 km of 115-kV line with 230-kV line (the Dos Condado-Apache segment). Volume I of the AEPCO Project report (Simpson and others 1978) dealt with survey and data recovery on sites affected by the three new substations, the new 230-kV line from Greenlee to Dos Condado, and the TG&E - Greenlee 345-kV loop. The Vail-Bicknell line was reported by McClellan (1976). The remaining Dos Condado-Apache segment is the subject of this volume.

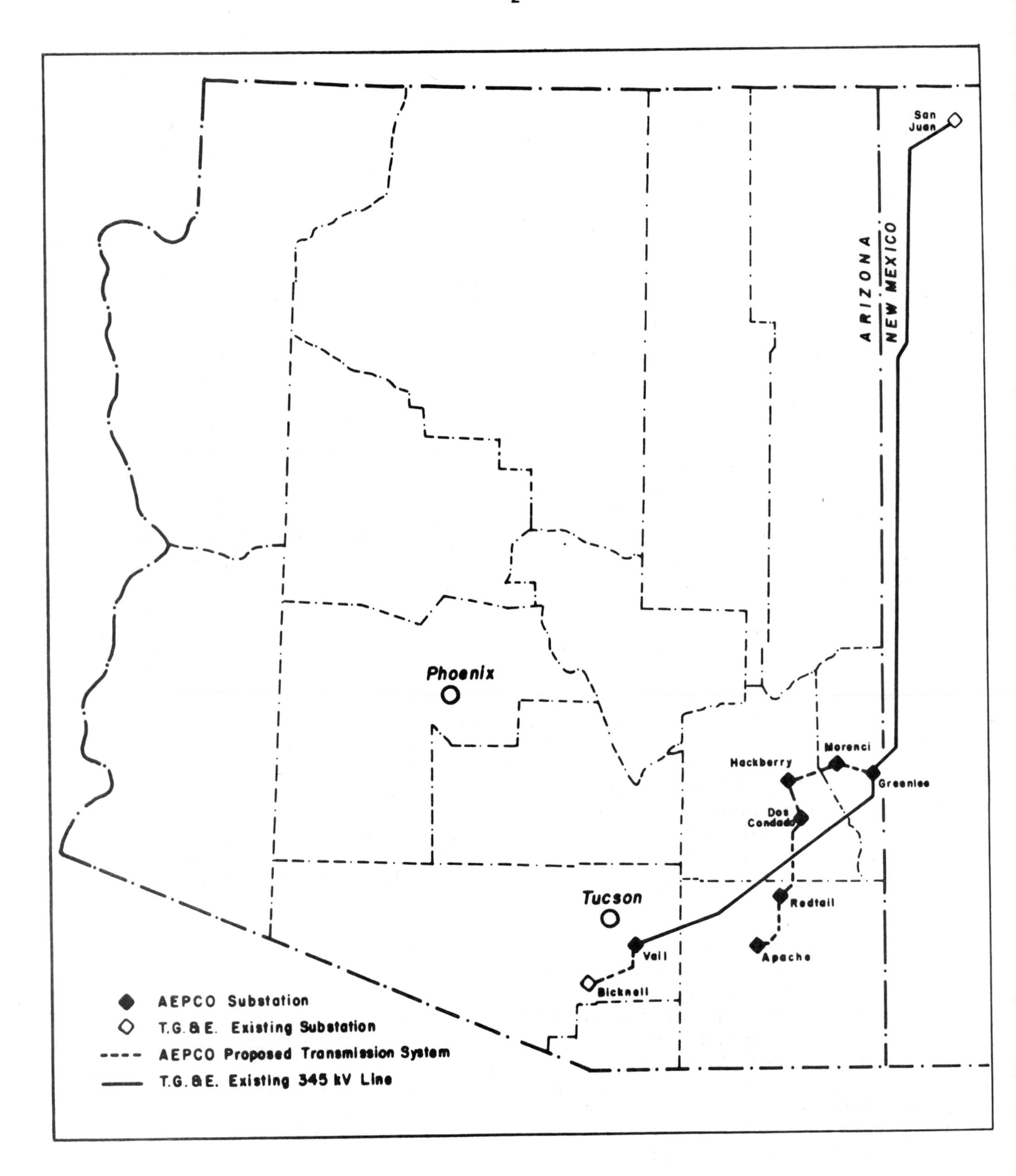

Figure 1. Location of AEPCO project area, southeastern Arizona.

The Northern Segment

The first segment of the new 230-kV line will begin at AEPCO's proposed Greenlee Substation located immediately north of the existing TG&E Reactor Substation (Figure 2). AEPCO will tap the TG&E 345-kV line and extend a 2.4 km 345-kV "shoo-fly" line to connect with the AEPCO Greenlee Substation. The 230-kV line will exit from there and extend west-northwest 15.7 km to the proposed AEPCO Morenci Substation. It will then run southwesterly approximately 40 km to the proposed Hackberry Substation. A 230-kV mine service line will extend north-northwest from Hackberry for 12.8 km, terminating at the Phelps-Dodge Safford mine on the Gila Mountains' lower bajadas. The main 230-kV transmission line will connect the Hackberry Substation to the existing Dos Condado Substation 11.2 km to the south-southeast.

The Southern Segment

The Dos Condado Substation is joined to the Apache Electric Station by a 115-kV line routed to the existing Redtail Substation in Section 35, T12S, R25E, approximately 11.5 km northeast of Willcox in Cochise County (Figure 3). The line then exits Redtail, terminating at Apache. The 115-kV line will be de-energized and "retired", and the new 230-kV line constructed within the original 115-kV line corridor. It is not feasible to use the existing structures due to additional stress and clearance factors; the 230-kV line will require new, larger structures. Span length (distance between towers) varies with terrain. Towers are generally placed 153 to 305 m apart, and average five structures per kilometer.

Identification of Impact Areas —Dos Condado to Apache

The direct impact zone of the transmission line is the proposed 30 m wide right-of-way (R-O-W) corridor. Primary impact within the R-O-W is twofold, involving removal of towers carrying the existing 115-kV line and erection of new towers to carry the 230-kV line. Secondary impact considerations are access roads for construction equipment. Maximum impact will occur at existing and proposed tower locations.

Retirement of the existing 115-kV line involves removing the conductor, dismantling the crossarms of the structure, and removing the upright tower poles from the ground. The impact of these procedures will vary with structure locations. For example, a level ground base may have to be built on the steeper slopes in order to provide an adequate footing for pole removing equipment. In most cases a crane mounted on a rubber-tired vehicle will be used to rock and then uproot the structures from the ground.

Aside from providing access to the structure locations, uprooting and erecting poles, and possibly blading bases for the crane, ground disturbance is expected to be moderate to minimal, particularly in view of the fact that the R-O-W and the area immediately around the base of existing towers were disturbed when the 115-kV line was constructed. Construction

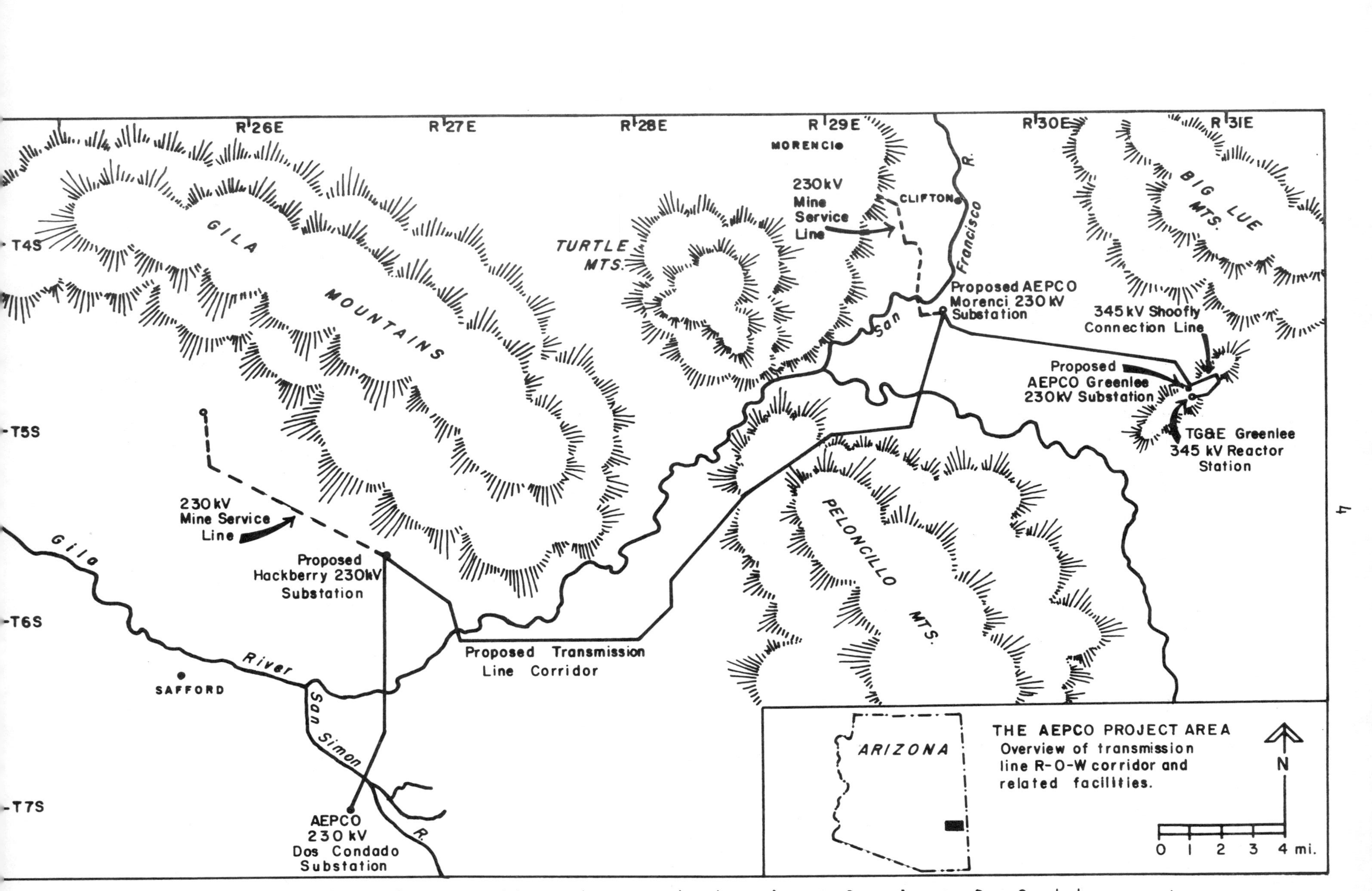

Figure 2. The AEPCO right-of-way corridor and proposed substations: Greenlee to Dos Condado segment.

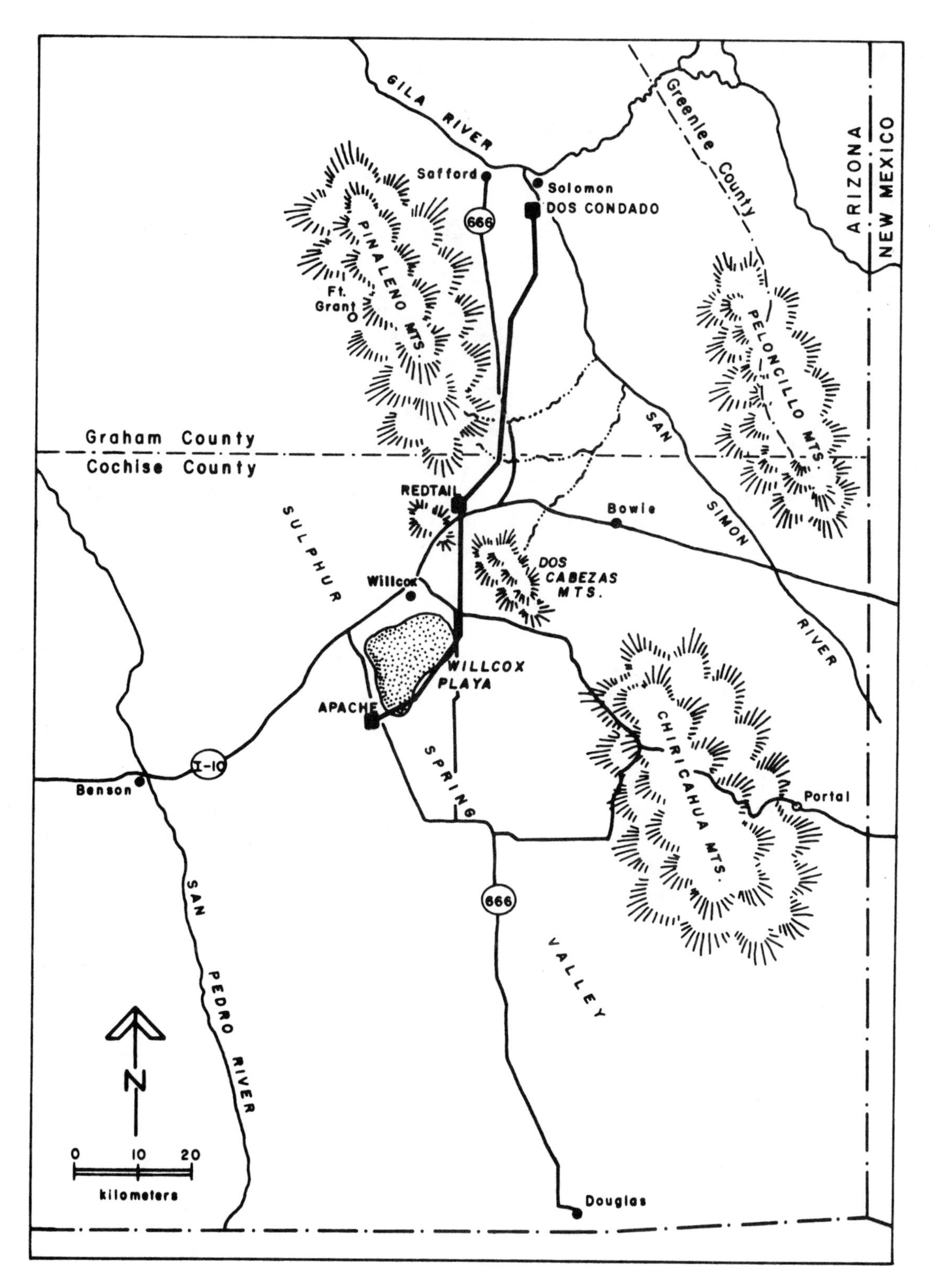

Figure 3. The AEPCO right-of-way corridor and substations: Dos Condado to Apache segment.

of the 230-kV transmission line is expected to have the greatest destructive impact on the archaeological resources for two reasons: (1) the proposed structures are generally located in previously undisturbed areas, and (2) heavy equipment is required during this phase of construction. An auger mounted on a D-8 Caterpillar will be used to drill holes for the upright; a Caterpillar will also be used to string the conductor. This type of equipment will cause greater surface and subsurface disturbance than would vehicles with rubber tires. Less severe disturbance will be caused by the crane used to erect the towers.

Dirt access roads will be built to existing and proposed structures with a blade mounted on a D-8 Caterpillar. Disturbance will range from shallow cutting and filling on existing jeep trails and dirt roads in the basin and bajada zones to cutting through bedrock in the rougher terrain near the Pinaleño and Dos Cabezas mountains.

Summary of Archaeological Investigations

On September 24, 1976 AEPCO contracted with the Cultural Resource Management Section of the Arizona State Museum (ASM) to survey and evaluate the cultural resources of the proposed transmission line R-O-W corridor and access roads for the northern portion of the system (AEPCO I). The survey was conducted from October 12, 1976, to December 15, 1976. Following this survey, recommendations were made by ASM for protection of archaeological resources through a combination of site protection, site monitoring, and partial data recovery on selected sites. These contracts were in accordance with the National Environmental Policy Act of 1969 which states that it is the "continuing responsibility of the Federal Government to use all practical means, consistent with other essential considerations of national policy, to improve and coordinate Federal plans, functions, programs and resources to the end that the nation may...preserve important historic, cultural, and natural aspects of our national heritage." Guidelines for archaeological research in areas affected by federal land modification are provided by Title 36 CFR 800, issued by the Advisory Council on Historic Preservation pursuant to the National Historic Preservation Act of 1966.

The AEPCO I survey discovered 72 archaeological sites in the R-O-W corridor and 17 sites on proposed access roads. Three of these were recommended to the Bureau of Land Management, acting as lead agency, for nomination to the National Register of Historic Places. Adverse effects on the other sites, primarily lithic scatters, were mitigated by a program of research and data recovery which was begun February 28, 1977, and ended April 15, 1977. Thirty sites were investigated and two additional sites nominated to the National Register were mapped. Between April 17 and December 1, 1977, survey findings were analyzed and written. The results of the AEPCO I investigations constitute Volume I of this series.

On January 20, 1977, AEPCO contracted with the Arizona State Museum (ASM) to survey the southern portion of the proposed transmission system from Dos Condado Substation to the Apache Electric Station (AEPCO II) as a continuance of the program instituted for the northern segment. The survey was conducted from March 7 to April 15, 1977. Twenty-seven sites were recorded along the transmission line R-O-W; none were found on the proposed access roads. Six of these sites were later recommended for inclusion in the National Register of Historic Places. On July 13, 1977, ASM was authorized to implement a program to mitigate adverse effects on sites within the impact zone. Conservation and protection of cultural resources, following the precedent set by AEPCO I, was a major concern of the program. Data recovery was carried out at 11 sites that could not be avoided. Archaeological field investigations began August 29 and ended October 7, 1977. Analysis and report writing commenced immediately upon completion of the field investigations.

Aims and Goals of the Dos Condado-Apache Survey

The AEPCO II survey was a continuation of the AEPCO I survey despite a hiatus resulting from data recovery that was required to expedite construction on the line from Greenlee to Dos Condado. The survey of the Dos Condado-Apache segment was conducted simultaneously with archaeological data recovery along the Greenlee-Dos Condado segment. Construction schedules dictated that data recovery be initiated as soon as possible after completion of the AEPCO I survey, pending approval of stipulations by legal agencies. This resulted in some overlap of field investigations. It was imperative to maintain in AEPCO II the orientation set forth by the AEPCO I survey in order to minimize discrepancies and confusion in site recognition and recording. The basic goals that both the AEPCO I and AEPCO II surveys were required to accomplish were (Simpson and others 1978):

1. description of the biophysical and culture-historical aspects of the area examined and their relationship to the project,
2. mapping of the area including project boundaries,
3. inventory and description of archaeological resources within the R-O-W corridor,
4. interpretation of the significance of the identified resources and their potential for contributing information about archaeological problems in the area,
5. identification of sites in the project area which appear to meet criteria of the National Register of Historic Places (36 CFR 800.10),
6. providing of cost estimates to completely excavate, study and report each of the significant archaeological resources affected by the project,
7. development of research design for a realistic program to mitigate adverse effects resulting from the project, including research recommendations, cost estimates, and a sampling design,
8. identification of alternative action to avoid or reduce impact on cultural resources, and
9. description of survey procedures.

The following chapters detail the biophysical and cultural background of the project area. Following this, operational survey procedures and results, and steps toward the development of a research design for archaeological investigations are presented.

CHAPTER 2

THE BIOPHYSICAL AND CULTURAL BACKGROUND

Introduction

The following chapter is a summary of the environmental features of the project area, including both the biophysical and culture-historical setting. The primary goal of the AEPCO project is to reconstruct natural resource exploitation systems through the interpretation of material culture remains in the context of site specific environments. This chapter provides background information on the modern and prehistoric environmental settings and a summary of the results of past archaeological and historical research. An integration of certain environmental characteristics with known cultural patterns results in a tentative model of resource exploitation behavior.

The Biophysical Environment

The AEPCO Project area is located in southeastern Arizona which is roughly bounded by 31°-33° North Latitude and 109°-110° West Longitude (UTM Zone 12, Easting 590000-680000, Northing 3580000-3640000) (Figure 4). It is assumed that extinct cultural systems existed in areas both within and outside of the immediate vicinity of the transmission line corridor. In this study it is necessary therefore, to consider the broader regional environment as well as more specific intra-regional variations. However, southeastern Arizona encompasses over 18,648 km^2 and it would be unnecessarily time consuming as well as redundant to characterize the entire area at the same level of specificity. Therefore, prime consideration is given to a smaller area (less than 9,324 km^2) surrounding the AEPCO project area. Data pertinent to features outside this area are included where important. Elements considered are the present and past physiography, geology, soils, hydrology, climate, flora, and fauna.

Physiography

The entire region is situated in the Mountain, or Mexican Highland, division of the Basin and Range Province. This is characterized by "numerous mountain ranges which rise abruptly from broad plain-like valleys or basins" (Wilson 1962:90). The study area contains the highest and widest mountains of this province. The ranges are roughly parallel, trending in a south-southeast to north-northwest direction. Although most peaks do not exceed

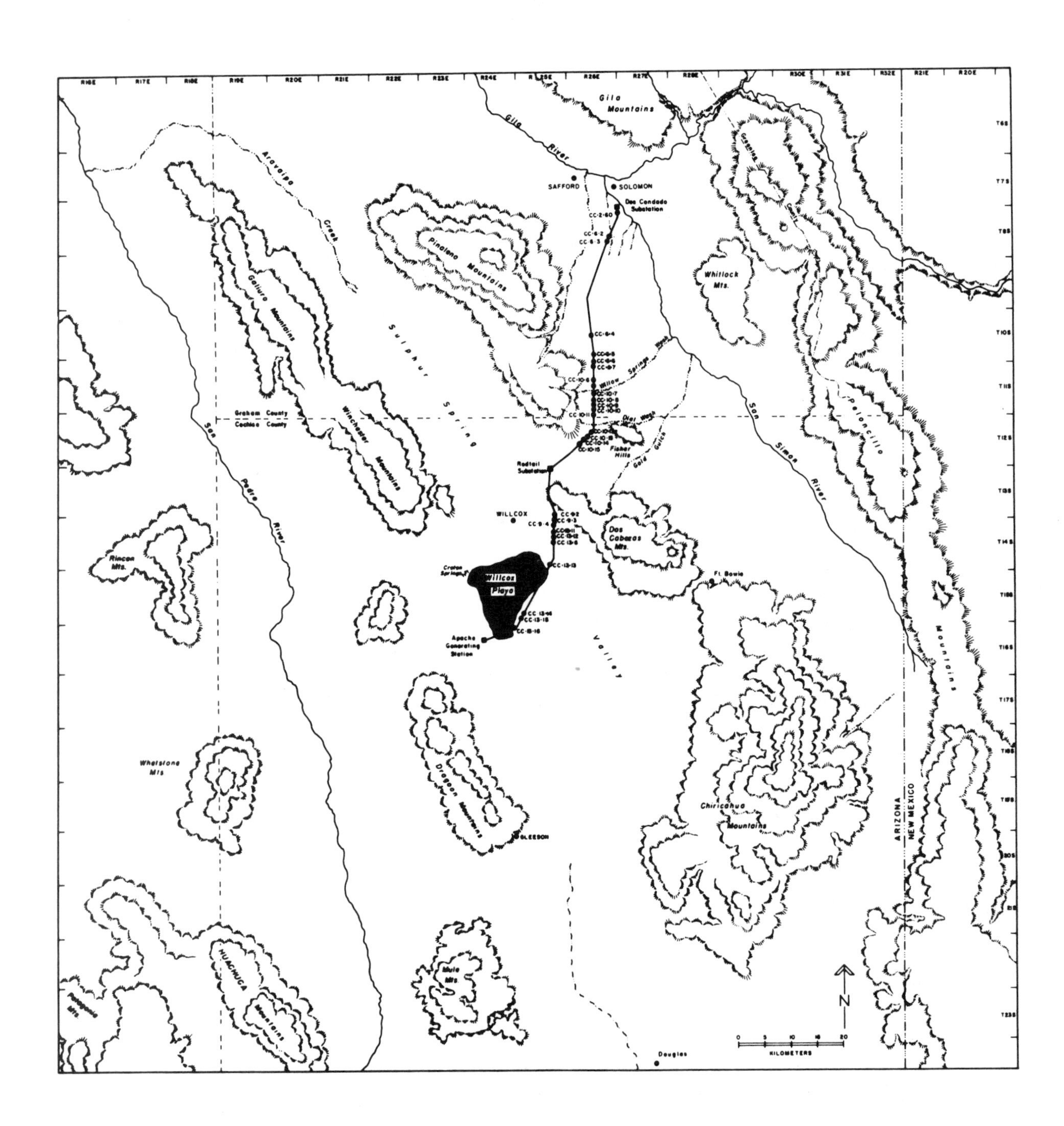

Figure 4. The AEPCO project region and important physiographic features.

2,438 m, 64.75 km^2 of the Chiricahua Mountains and 90.65 km^2 of the Pinaleño Mountains lie above this elevation (Shreve 1915). Mt. Graham, at 3,265 m, is the highest peak in southeastern Arizona.

Intermontane valleys, or basins, range in width from 16 to 48 km. Intermediate between the mountain peaks and valley floors are pediments, or bajadas. These are upward sloping, concave surfaces that occur along the margins of many of the ranges (Tuan 1959).

Under primary consideration are the central and lower San Simon Valley and the central Sulphur Spring Valley, which are separated by the Pinaleño, Dos Cabezas, and Chiricahua mountains. The Peloncillo Mountains to the east, and Winchester and Dragoon ranges to the west, along with the upper Gila River Valley and other regions of the two main valleys will be of secondary interest.

The San Simon Valley extends 136 km north from the headwaters of San Simon Creek to the Gila River and Gila River Valley (Schwennesen 1917). Bounded by the Chiricahua, Peloncillo, Dos Cabezas and Pinaleño mountains, it is only 16 km wide in the south. It opens to 56 km in the center, and in the north (lower) portion averages 40 km wide. The valley axis elevation grades from 1,432 m in the south to 899 m at the Gila River-San Simon Creek confluence, for an average gradient of 378 m/km. Pediments are located along the slopes of the mountains forming the San Simon Valley. These almost meet the axis in the south where the valley is narrow, and in the center and north they gradually merge into a near-level alluvial plain. An illustration of the variety of valley piedmont (axis to mountain base) relief values is presented below.

Relief values for selected San Simon Valley piedmonts:

Chiricahua Peak	22.7 m/km	(120 ft./mi.)
Dos Cabezas Peaks	9.5 m/km	(50 ft./mi.)
Stein's Peak	21.9 m/km	(116 ft./mi.)
Pinaleño Peak "A"	18.9 m/km	(100 ft./mi.)
Thumb Butte	13.2 m/km	(70 ft./mi.)
Mt. Graham	11.3 m/km	(60 ft./mi.)

Mountain peak elevations range from 1579 m (Stein's Peak) to 3265 m (Mt. Graham). The western ranges are significantly higher and broader than the Peloncillo Mountains. Relief values of these mountain slopes (base to peak) greatly contrast with those of the relatively level valley piedmonts. These are listed below.

Note: All relief values presented are based on Tucson, Nogales, Silver City and Douglas AMS series (1:250,000 maps). Elevations are computed from points on a line perpendicular to the axis and intersecting the peak. The values illustrate relative, not absolute relief.

Relief values for selected San Simon mountain slopes:

Chiricahua Peak	94 m/km	(499 ft./mi.)
Dos Cabezas Peaks	131 m/km	(694 ft./mi.)
Stein's Peak	59.2 m/km	(313 ft./mi.)
Pinaleño Peak "A"	83.3 m/km	(440 ft./mi.)
Thumb Butte	66.4 m/km	(351 ft./mi.)
Mt. Graham	221.4 m/km	(1169 ft./mi.)

Access into the valley is open on the north and south ends. Numerous breaks or low spots in the Peloncillo Mountains allow easy passage from the east, but access is considerably more restricted along the massive western ranges. Major routes into the Sulphur Spring Valley are through Apache Pass, Railroad Pass, and Stockton Pass.

The upper Gila River Valley adjoins the San Simon Valley on the north (Knechtel 1938). It is also an intermontane trough, and is bounded on the south by the Peloncillo Mountains and on the north by the Gila Mountains. It commences 12.87 km east of Safford where the Gila River emerges from a narrow gorge. This upper section is 16 to 32 km wide and slopes at a grade of 1.8 m/km along its axis. An almost imperceptible structural or topographic break causing differentiated drainage patterns separates the upper Gila Valley from the San Simon Valley. On the north, the Gila Mountains' piedmont slopes to the river at 26.1 m/km. Webber Peak mountain slope relief is 189.3 m/km. This very steep slope is a characteristic of the lower, smaller mountains in the Basin and Range Province. It is evident from the above values that there is no perfect correlation between peak elevation and relief.

The Sulphur Spring Valley is the other main physiographic unit in the region. This broad debris-filled valley is characterized by internal drainage (Meinzer and Kelton 1913). It shares a common mountain ridge boundary with the San Simon Valley. On the west, smaller ranges prominently define the valley, effectively separating it from the San Pedro Valley further west. It extends 149 km north from an arbitrary southern boundary at the international border to Aravaipa Valley. Ranging from 24 km wide in the northern and southern sections to over 48 km in the valley center, the entire drainage basin averages 80 km wide. Although a portion of the valley drains to the south through Douglas (1188 m), of prime concern is the internal drainage system. There are two axis gradients into the central Willcox Playa: 1.5 m/km from the north and 0.56 m/km from the south. Both are lower than values for the San Simon and Gila valleys, and demonstrate the extreme flatness of the Sulphur Spring Valley. The relatively constant elevation is expressed also in the piedmont relief values as listed here.

Relief values for selected Sulphur Spring valley piedmonts:

Chiricahua Peak	10.6 m/km	(56 ft./mi.)
Mt. Glenn	14.7 m/km	(78 ft./mi.)
Dos Cabezas Peaks	12.5 m/km	(66 ft./mi.)
Reilly Peak	13.4 m/km	(71 ft./mi.)
Mt. Graham	14.2 m/km	(75 ft./mi.)

The homogeneity of the Sulphur Spring Valley features such as cross-section also extends to the bordering mountains. While the western ranges are less massive than the eastern, relief values are relatively similar throughout the valley, as listed below.

Relief values for selected Sulphur Spring mountain slopes:

Chiricahua Peak	183.7 m/km	(970 ft./mi.)
Mt. Glenn	83.1 m/km	(439 ft./mi.)
Dos Cabezas Peaks	212.3 m/km	(1121 ft./mi.)
Reilly Peak	178.5 m/km	(943 ft./mi.)
Mt. Graham	180.3 m/km	(952 ft./mi.)

Upon examining the values for the mountain slopes common to the San Simon Valley, differences are seen. The greater relief on the western side of the Dos Cabezas mountains is attributed to a shorter horizontal distance from the base to peak; the lower values (Chiricahua Peak, Mt. Graham) are a function of the higher basal elevation in the Sulphur Spring Valley.

Mountain ranges in the project region share similar physiographic features, while remaining essentially distinct landmarks. The Peloncillo Mountains define the eastern boundary. The longest single range in the region (193 km), it has three discrete sections. As described by Gillerman (1958), the southern unit is uniformly narrow and peaks along one main ridge while the northern section is much wider and irregular with numerous isolated peaks forming a broken ridge. Both have relatively low, rounded hills. The more elevated central section has several parallel ridges with bolder topography. Projecting well into the San Simon Valley on the west are the Whitlock Hills. In all areas the mountains rise 304 to 457 m above the valley floor.

The Pinaleño Mountain range is the msot massive in this region. Only 48 km long, its topography varies from the low, irregular southern peaks 304 m above the valley to the alpine group around Mt. Graham, which towers 4349 m above the San Simon-Gila valleys. This range is separated from the Dos Cabezas Mountains by Southern Pacific Railroad Pass. The steep, narrow Dos Cabezas Mountains extend for 32 km and rise to 2549 m, averaging 457 to 609 m above both the San Simon and Sulphur Spring valleys. Apache Pass separates the Dos Cabezas Mountains from the geologically similar Chiricahua Mountains (Sabins 1957). The southern range of the central Chiricahua Mountains is one of the widest and highest in the region, with peaks projecting 609 m above the valleys. Its slopes are more dissected by canyons than any other nearby range (Meinzer and Kelton 1913).

On the western boundary of the project area are two of the smallest ranges. The 40 km long Dragoon Mountains are actually composed of two physically discrete units: the Dragoon Mountains proper and the Little Dragoon Mountains to the northwest. The former are significantly higher, extending 457 m above the valley, while the latter reach a maximum of 304 m. Both are characterized by low, disconnected ridges (Meinzer and Kelton 1913). The major Southern Pacific Railroad Divide separates these two ranges from the northern Winchester Mountains. The Winchesters are also low and irregular, with maximum elevation of 304 m above the northern Sulphur Spring Valley.

Geology

Generally similar historic geological events have occurred in all areas of the project region, which have resulted in comparable composition and structure of geographic features. Some areally specific events have also occurred. Major features of the entire region will be discussed; locally important events will also be considered.

The monoclinal ranges and rock troughs found in the area are a result of fault-block deformation and erosion in pre-Quaternary eras (Wilson 1962). Pre-Cambrian sedimentation, deformation, volcanism, and metamorphism established basal granite, gneiss, and schist deposits over much of the area. These are most visible in the Dos Cabezas and Pinaleño mountains. Inundated during much of the Paleozoic, the area experienced widespread sedimentation resulting in numerous limestone deposits (Gilluly, Cooper, and Williams 1954; Quaide 1951). Cherts are locally common in some of these but are rarely as either pure nodules or beds. Sandstone and shales are locally present, while quartzites are characteristic of the Dos Cabezas and Dragoon mountains (Sabins 1957; Enlows 1939). Post-Carboniferous deformation, volcanism, and erosion altered the landscape and changed drainage patterns. These and later volcanic processes have concealed the sedimentary limestones over much of the area. Mesozoic rocks are represented in all areas, but only the Chiricahua and Dragoon mountains experienced volcanism in the Triassic and Jurassic periods. During these two eras, granitic and other intrusive crystalline rocks were formed from acidic lavas (Sabins 1957). Later, Cretaceous sedimentation resulted in the formation of shales, limestone, and sandstones which have in some regions been metamorphosed to phyllite and schist (Gilluly 1956).

A majority of the rocks in the area are the result of extensive Tertiary volcanism (Arizona Bureau of Mines 1958, 1959; Cooper 1960). During the Miocene and Pliocene, basalt, rhyolite, andesite, and granite were formed. Deformation and erosion of older deposits also occurred. Quaternary volcanism was localized in the central Peloncillo Mountains, extreme southern Sulphur Spring Valley and the Winchester Mountains. The San Simon and Sulphur Spring valleys are filled with alluvial gravel, sand, and silt of the Quaternary period ranging in depth from several hundred to several thousand feet.

The lower San Simon and Gila valleys experienced similar depositional and erosional conditions during the Quaternary. The Gila Conglomerate formation (Knechtel 1936) is of combined stream and lake origin. Its stratified clays and silts are intermixed with tuff and marly limestone which grade into a lower, coarser fanglomerate with 0.30 m diameter boulders. The upper terrace of this formation is a dissected remnant with a calichified gravel capping. During the first lowering of the Gila River in the Pleistocene this terrace eroded and a new terrace formed. Subsequent river entrenching produced the current terrace configuration. Alluviation of this trench has occurred and the floodplain of the Gila River is now expanding (Burkham 1972).

Erosion has also affected the central San Simon Valley. The present valley surface is primarily a result of aggradation after the last channel lowering. The San Simon Creek is now becoming entrenched in a well-defined channel and the valley surface is being eroded. Part of this eroded material is being deposited in the Gila Valley.

Because the Sulphur Spring Valley has an internal drainage system, it was not affected by these major erosional events. Here, deposits of clay, silt, sand and gravel in a lime carbonate matrix are believed to approximate the Gila Conglomerate (Meinzer and Kelton 1913). However, the stratified lake and alluvial deposits have not been subjected to major degradation. The Willcox Playa formed as a result of blockage of the through-flowing stream by alluviated bajadas (Long 1966).

To summarize, the geology presents a varied distribution of naturally occurring rock types. Igneous rocks predominate, especially in the Pinaleño and Peloncillo mountains. The Dos Cabezas Mountains and the Chiricahua Mountains have significantly more abundant chert and quartzite; the Peloncillo Mountains have jasper and agates (United States Department of Interior 1978).

Erosional forces have acted in two manners: rocks have been transported downslope and along the valley axes. In the Sulphur Spring Valley floor all surface rocks are a result of downslope erosion. While several rock types are available in the surrounding mountains, igneous rocks predominate and undoubtedly represent the majority of redeposited rock. In the San Simon Valley, downslope and downstream erosion has transported materials. Conglomerate deposits, covered by Quaternary alluvium are being cut into by recent erosional processes. While characterizations regarding the prehistoric availability of raw materials made on the basis of current distribution are tenuous, there have been enough erosion-deposition cycles in the recent past to assume that similar processes operated prehistorically. This means that rocks locally available may not correspond directly to those types forming the geologic structure of a specific area. Thus, rocks available in any one area may be a product of erosion from nearby or far away, or they may be a product of original geologic processes. The AEPCO project area is covered with rocks resulting from this bedrock outcrop fracturing. A smaller portion of the project area is located on alluviated areas where rocks were transported a long distance and may or may not be covered by alluvium.

Hydrology

Several distinct processes operate which affect the nature of groundwater availability in the San Simon, Gila, and Sulphur Spring valleys. These are precipitation, runoff, evaporation, and infiltration. The region is characterized by intermittent drainage, with only the Gila River flowing year round. (Historic changes in the nature and availability of groundwater will be discussed later in the context of environmental change.) At present, surface water is available in the Gila River and intermittently in arroyos, springs, cienegas, and the Willcox Playa. Most streamflow is a product of summer rains when localized storms produce high rate/unit volumes which become, for the most part, runoff. This short lived phenomenon contrasts with the less dramatic winter (November-June) streamflow which is a result of frontal storms, snowmelt, and groundwater outflow (Burkham 1972). Springs contribute to flows in both seasons. While there are numerous localities where spring water has been available historically, the nature and distribution of this water source is not adequately documented. One of the most prominent is Croton Springs, west of Willcox Playa. The San Simon Cienega, on the eastern margin of the project region, is an example of another permanent water source. Willcox Playa, a major lake during Pluvial conditions, is, for the most part, dry, as only two streams on the northwest side feed into it (Pine 1963). It does occasionally contain some water as a result of direct precipitation and spring flow. Little is known as to the present availability of surface water in Willcox Playa.

Groundwater in southeastern Arizona follows slope gradients. Thus, in the San Simon Valley it flows into the trough while in the Sulphur Spring Valley it flows toward Willcox Playa. Ten percent of the precipitation in the mountains becomes runoff, and 50 percent of this (or five percent) becomes recharged to the ground water reservoir (Arizona Bureau of Mines 1969). Very little precipitation directly reaches the water table through penetration of piedmont soils. Most precipitation is evaporated or transpired. The groundwater level is closest to the surface near the valley margin. Where areas have been deeply dissected or where structural situations exist, groundwater may be close to the surface also. The slope of the groundwater table is less than, but close to that of the valley surface (Arizona Bureau of Mines 1969).

Soils

Soils indirectly affect man's environment by placing limits on certain features with which man directly interacts. The relationship between soils and vegetation is of prime importance. Certain features of soil-plant relationships are discussed by Lowe (1959) and Yang and Lowe (1956). As soils directly affect potential vegetation, and thus floral resources, so do they affect faunal distribution through determination of habitat conditions. Because soils are a complex topic, a detailed description of all aspects is well beyond the scope of this research. The following will, however, be included: (1) a general description of soils in the project region and (2) a more detailed consideration of soils at individual sites.

In defining soils as the product of natural processes acting on accumulated or deposited geologic material, five important factors of soil formation can be isolated. These are: parent material, relief, climate, living organism, and time (Gelderman 1970). One or more of these factors may be especially important in the formation of any one soil type. In the Safford area relief and parent material are important (Gelderman 1970). Here, soils are near-level in bottom lands and on gently sloping terraces. They result from erosion of granitic material located in the Pinaleño Mountains, rhyolite in the Gila Mountains, and alluvium in the valley bottom.

Climate is considered to be a dominant factor in soil formation in the Willcox area (Richmond 1976). During the Pleistocene, soil near the center of the basin formed in lacustrine material from pluvial Lake Cochise (Willcox Playa). The soils on surrounding pediments derive from local rock types such as basalt, andesite, rhyolite, and limestone.

The presence of lime influences soil composition in both the San Simon-Gila Valley and the Sulphur Spring Valley. The most recent alluvium and the sloping pediments are considerably more free from the detrimental salts and alkali. Generally, the region contains loamy, mixed thermic soils. The soils of the San Simon-Gila Valley are coarse deposits compared to those of the Sulphur Spring Valley. Both areas contain soils suitable for agriculture as well as sections unsuited for various reasons. While this particular mapping is not in perfect agreement with other association-level maps (USDI 1978; Richmond 1976; Gelderman 1970), a few general comments about the associations can be made (USDA 1973). The northernmost section (A1) has fair to good topsoil and is considered very good to good for irrigation agriculture. There are some soil deficiencies, and dry agriculture potential is low due to an inadequate water supply. The next association (C2) has a shallow, gravel to cobble topsoil that limits its use for irrigation agriculture. It is erodible and only fairly well suited for rangeland. The C1 association is similarly shallow and coarse and likewise not well suited for agriculture. The small portion of the F6 association is very gravelly and shallow and only fairly well suited for rangeland or woodland due to soil deficiencies and erodibility. D1 is similarly steep, shallow and gravelly but is generally well suited for rangeland with some soil deficiencies. The next small section (F4) is of fair potential for rangeland. The last section (B1) has a generally alkaline topsoil and is of limited use for irrigation or dryland cultivation (USDA 1973). Specific soil types will be presented in Chapter 4 in the context of stratum environmental descriptions.

Climate

Climate factors have an important influence on man's adaptation to a particular environment. Human survival depends on an adequate response to the constraints imposed by nature. Weather affects man directly as it affects other biological organisms; wind, precipitation, and temperature all influence the function of life systems. Indirectly, nature affects man by creating and transforming flora and fauna. Adaptation is both physiological anc cultural; our concern is to better understand man's cultural adaptation to the environment of southeastern Arizona. In order to accomplish this, it is necessary to describe the climatic attributes, specifically precipitation and temperature, which heavily influence environmental composition. Detailed climatic records only extend back to the late 1800s in southeastern Arizona. But, a picture may be drawn of present climate, and in a later section, with the aid of paleoenvironmental data, these conditions will be compared with past environments.

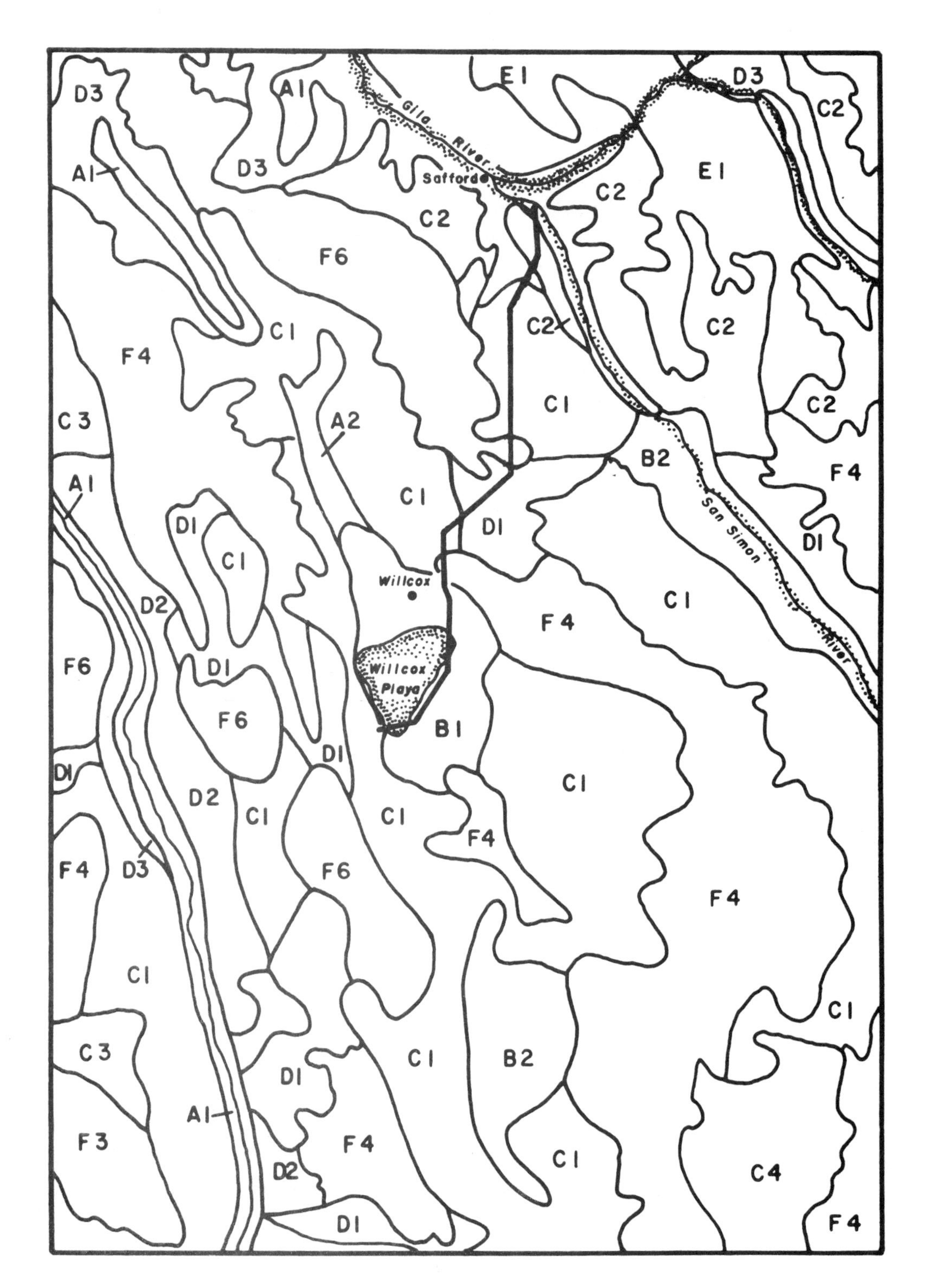

Figure 5. Major soil associations in the AEPCO project region.

Southeastern Arizona is an arid landscape with summer-dominant precipitation and low and high mean monthly temperatures between 0°C (32°F) and 30°C (86°F), respectively (Meigs 1953). This macroclimate extends beyond the limits of the project area. General weather conditions affecting precipitation and temperature will be described first, and then specific climates discussed in relation to one another within the general pattern.

Currently, the precipitation in southeastern Arizona is biseasonally distributed, with 50 to 75 percent falling in the summer (Table 1). Annual totals are illustrated in Figure 6. The majority of the project area receives between 20 and 40 cm annually while the nearby mountains accumulate up to 88 cm. Winter precipitation is frontal, with prevailing west and southwesterly winds bringing storms from the Pacific. Precipitation is generally of light to moderate intensity and falls as either rain or snow depending on temperature and elevation (Table 2).

Table 1. Mean monthly precipitation in southeastern Arizona

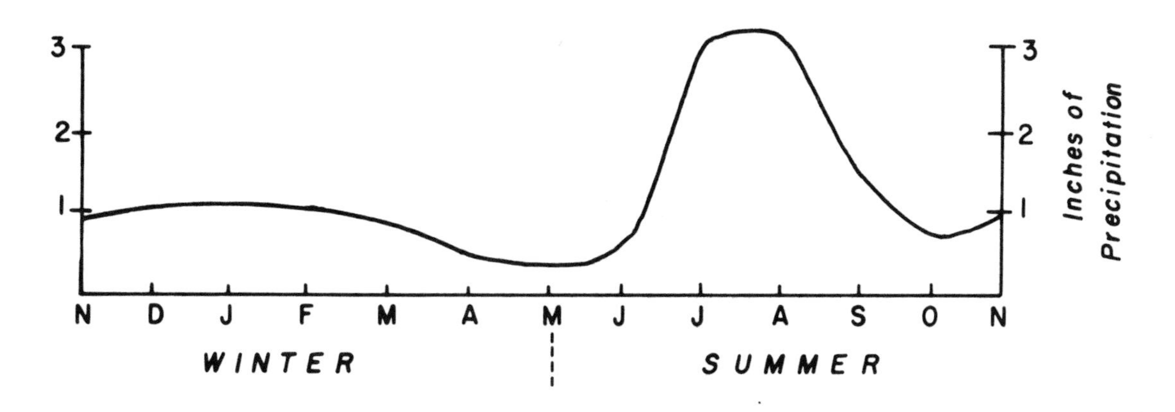

Table 2. Mean daily precipitation in southeastern Arizona

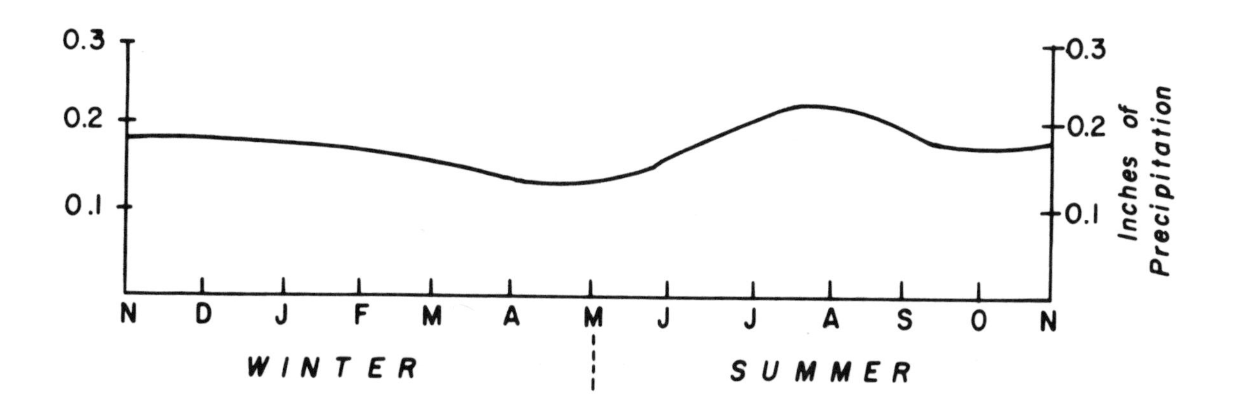

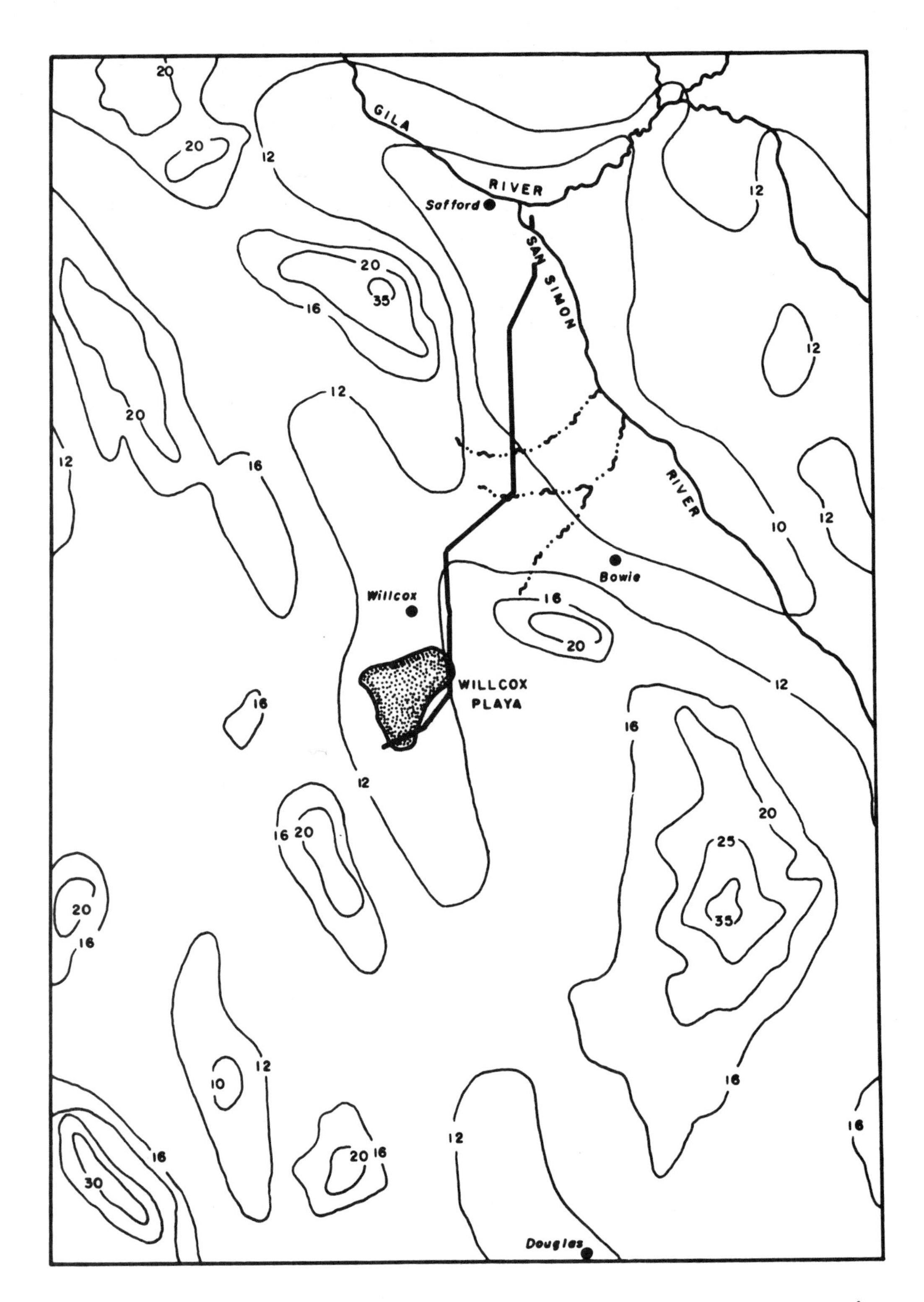

Figure 6. Mean annual precipitation in the AEPCO project region.

Summer storms are convective, bringing moisture from the Gulf of Mexico. This pattern sometimes changes in September or October when storms originate from the Pacific Region and Gulf of California (Sellers and Hill 1974). In general, summer rain is reliable from year to year, but seasonal and spatial variability is high (McDonald 1956). Over 90 percent of summer storms have diameters of less than 5 km (Martin 1963:3). Rainfall intensity and frequency are higher in summer (Table 2). Some storms produce rain at more than 25 cm/hour (Martin 1963). Drought can occur virtually any place during any season. There are no spatial, seasonal, or cyclical drought patterns.

Daily temperatures in the AEPCO region range from January averages of 4° to 7°C (40° to 45°F) to July values of 18° to 30°C (65° to 85° F). Summer values vary about 1°F/235 feet elevation (Sellers and Hill 1974:32). Wind values are variable, commonly between 1 to 10 knots and only rarely over 17 knots (Burns and McDonnell 1974:A-41). Wind direction is also variable with any origin possible in a given season. However, prevailing winds in the project region are from the south, west, and southwest (Meinzer and Kelton 1913:39; USDI 1978). Only in the summer are east or southeast winds common. Wind direction in relation to project physiography orients storms obliquely to valleys and ranges. Usually the larger storms cross these obstacles. Sometimes a storm will remain in a valley, changing course to travel along the valley axis.

A combination of factors such as precipitation, wind speed and direction, and temperature affect evaporation.The potential evaporation rate of the project region is 60 cm/year (Long 1966).

Some of the environmental attributes of specific locations in the project region are illustrated in Table 3. While these conditions reflect more refined environmental conditions, they are not valid generalizations about the region surrounding each locale. As can be seen, they occasionally contradict the generalization that temperature varies inversely and precipitation directly with elevation. Explanations can be advanced for these anomalies.

Table 3. Environmental attributes of selected localities (Based on data in Sellers and Hill (1974)

		Temperature (°C)				Annual Precipitation	
Station	Elevation (m)	Mean Annual	Low	High	Minimum Growing season	Mean (cm)	Range (cm)
Safford	884	17.9	-12.8	46.7	200 days	21.3	9.6-45.0
San Simon	1100	16.6	-16.6	43.3	195 days	22.3	10.4-38.6
Bowie	1151	17.3	-15.6	46.7	220 days	25.1	22.8-42.6
Willcox	1272	15.0	-18.3	43.7	155 days	28.4	14.7-47.5
Ft. Grant	1486	16.4	-16.6	41.1	200 days	31.7	16.5-58.4
Chiricahua	1615	14.6	-18.3	41.1	180 days	45.2	24.9-66.5

Both Safford and San Simon are located in the shadow of high mountains to the southwest. As storms--especially winter ones--approach from the southwest, mountain masses produce orographic lifting, thereby reducing precipitation on the lee side. Summer storms which often move up and down valleys are the source of a majority of the rain at these locations. Bowie, also on the lee side, is granted partial immunity because a pass between the Pinaleño and Dos Cabezas mountains reduces the orographic effect.

Bowie and Ft. Grant, both located on bajadas immediately below mountain foothills, have slightly warmer temperatures as cold, dense air has a tendency to move downslope and settle in lower valley elevations. All listed locations have adequate growing seasons for most crops, especially those known to be important prehistorically.

The actual distribution of precipitation is varied. Analysis of data in Sellers and Hill (1974) shows relative homogeneity with respect to percent chance of no rain in summer season (Table 4).

Table 4. Percentage reports of no rain in summer at selected localities

Month	Safford	San Simon	Bowie	Willcox	Ft. Grant	Chiricahua	Average total
May	41	48	50	32	33	16	37.7
June	20	16	22	7	18	12	16.0
July	0	3	2	0	0	0	1.0
August	0	0	2	0	0	0	0.3
September	12	6	10	5	11	8	9.0
Average total	14.6	15.1	17.3	10.5	12.7	7.2	

However, the actual percentage varies by location. For example, Willcox exhibits one of the lowest frequencies of no rain in May and the lowest frequency of no rain in June. Bowie is the only location which shows evidence of no rain in either June, July or August. Table 4 illustrates frequencies of rainfall with respect to months when it is hypothesized that horticulture (dry-farming) would be practiced. It is not, however, intended as an explanatory device for proving horticulture did not occur in certain areas.

Interpreting Sellers and Hill's (1974) data further, we find that specific reports of no rain in May or June are localized by station/year. It is highly probable that one, two, or even three stations will report no rain in May or June of the same year, but only 6 percent of the reports show all stations receiving no rain in May and only 2 percent in June. Only in two reports have all stations reported no rain in May and June of the same year.

Generally, there is a high chance of any one station reporting no rain in May, a moderate chance in June or September, and a low chance in July or August. Specifically, Bowie has the highest frequency of no rain and Chiricahua has the lowest. In fact, Bowie is the only station to have reported three or four consecutive summer months of no rain (May, June, July, August, 1940). Precipitation is important for floral development as are proper soils and other factors.

This discussion has not intended to illustrate where or why horticulture would be possible, but to illustrate precipitation variability in time and space and thereby show that horticulture could fail in any area where precipitation alone supplies moisture.

Vegetation

The vegetation of southeastern Arizona is a complex mixture of plant species which form plant communities in certain associations. Various units of vegetational analyses have been employed by investigators (Shreve 1951; Nichol 1952; Lowe 1964; Lowe and Brown 1973, USDI 1978). Unfortunately, not all investigators use the same criteria (dominant plants) for distinguishing between units. While units are helpful in identifying general associations of plants and horizontal and vertical distribution of zones, individual plant species often have wide ranges that cross cut zones or units of analysis. Conversely, certain flora have very restricted ranges and are characteristic of only one unit (zone). In the discussion below, the classifications of Lowe and Brown (1973) will be employed, and characteristic or dominant unit flora from this source as well as others will be listed. The nature of species-zone overlap cannot be thoroughly evaluated and presented.

It is of importance that units <u>per se</u> are not the major consideration in discussing vegetation, but rather the specific plants. Man utilizes natural resources at the species level without regard to vegetational units. Also, modern vegetation is not isomorphically related to past resources. Specific issues of vegetational change will be discussed later in this report.

Several factors influence the distribution of plants. Floral composition and structure (species, density, combinations) are determined by interoperative factors of temperature, precipitation, wind, sunshine, and soil (Lowe 1964). While each factor exerts a limiting influence, all are related to topography and exposure (aspect).

Soil type is of extreme importance as Yang and Lowe (1956) point out: "different soil attributes characterize and are intimately associated with different and major climax vegetation types existing with the same macroclimate" (Yang and Lowe 1956:542). Soil moisture in any one macroclimate is partly a factor of soil texture. Yang and Lowe (1956:542) state: "available soil moisture during critical dry seasons determines the occurrence of one vegetation type over the other."

Vegetation is also a function of elevation. The vertical zonation of plants in Arizona has been extensively studied (see Lowe 1964). Because the mean annual temperature decreases approximately 1°C/160 m elevation increase, the generalized vertical distribution in the Basin and Range Province is quite apparent. It may be stated generally that mesophytic species are located at higher elevations than xerophytic plants. However, more immediate topographic features such as slope exposure also condition specific environments.

In any given region climate extremes are more significant than means in controlling plant distribution (Lowe 1959:59). Seasonal variation of temperature and precipitation also affects floral composition. Critical limits affect different southeastern Arizona plants in different fashions. For example, certain plant ranges are determined by critical minimum temperatures or minimal precipitation values. Other plant ranges might be more importantly fixed by maximum tolerance levels (Shreve 1915). But while floristic spatial variability is commonly a species response to environmental factors, most often more than one species of any vegetation type is affected. The generalized and specific environmental factors affecting vegetation enumerated above will be further presented during the discussion of vegetational change.

The use of the term climax has been debated in American ecology. This paper adopts Whittaker's (1953) usage and identifies desert (climax) vegetation as representing genetic climax in both mosaic and continuum patterns. The modern vegetation may or may not represent true climax types; if they are disclimax states, climax vegetation may still be present in certain areas.

The present vegetation in southeastern Arizona has been described at the ecological formation level (Lowe 1964; Lowe and Brown 1973; Brown 1973). This system uses the biotic community as a basic unit. The AEPCO II project region will be discussed within this system, and supplemental data on finer levels of distinction, such as associations, will be considered when the individual strata are described. The region considered and zones discussed are presented in Figure 7. Three main formations--desertscrub, grassland, and woodland--are present in the AEPCO region. Tables within the text list most perennial plants found in specific zones (Tables 5, 6, and 7).

Desertscrub. Components of two of the four North American deserts are represented in the AEPCO II region. Both Sonoran and Chihuahuan deserts contain desertscrub communities. The Sonoran desert units are the Arizona upland and the lower Colorado subdivisions (Lowe 1964; Lowe and Brown 1973). The former is typified by mixed cactus and tree-scrub association. This desertscrub is the most structurally diversified vegetation type in the United States (Lowe and Brown 1973). The paloverde-saguaro (*Cercidium Cereus*) community is dominated by arborescent species with understories of mixed and dwarf shrubs, cactus, and grasses. Generally found below 1300 km on coarse soils of volcanic origin, especially granite, this community contains abundant wild vegetal foods. Table 5 presents an inventory of Arizona upland species.

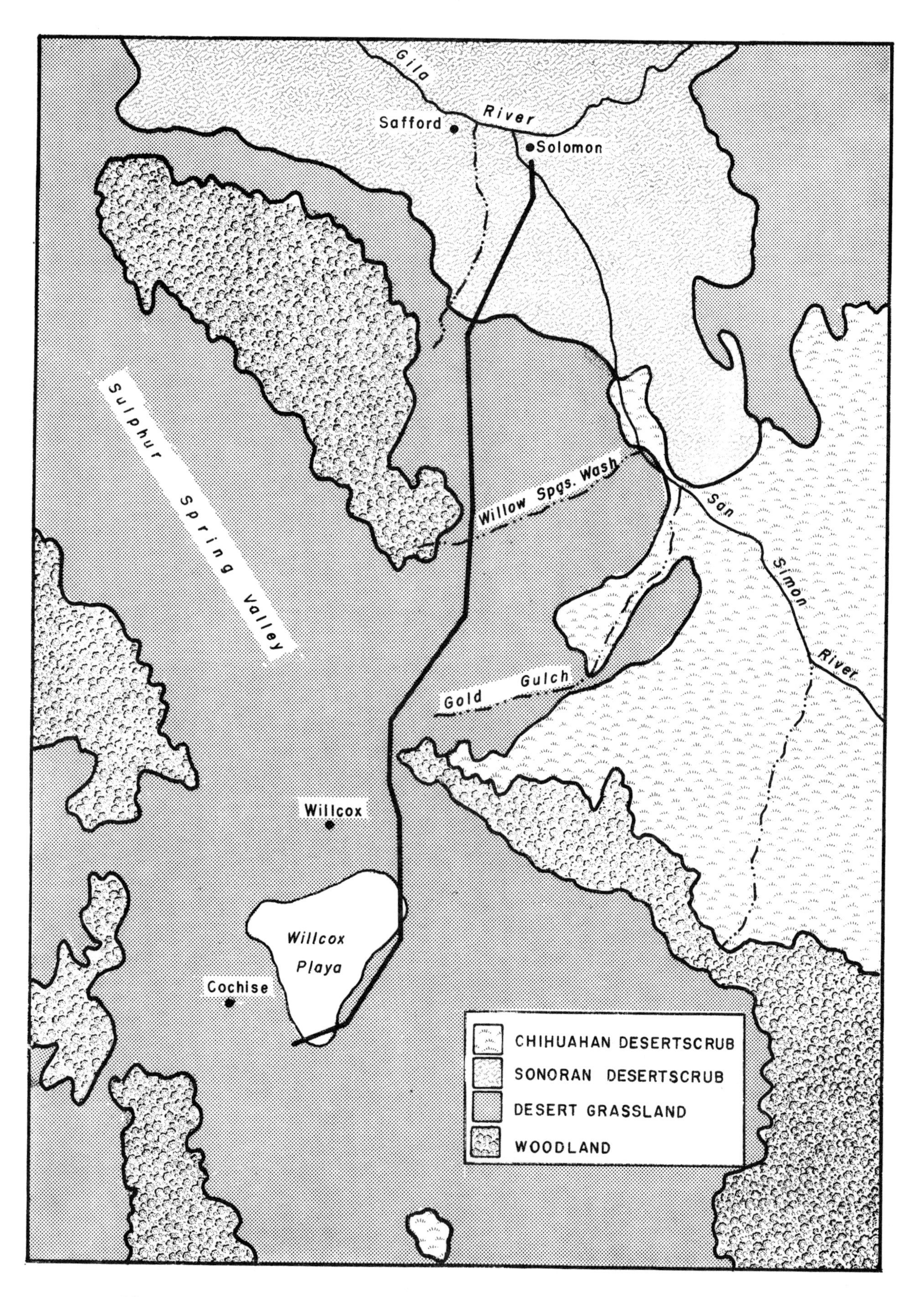

Figure 7. Major vegetation zones in the AEPCO project region.

Table 5. Arizona upland Sonoran desertscrub species in southeastern Arizona

foothill paloverde	Cercidium microphyllum
saguaro (giant cactus)	Cereus giganteus
triangle bursage	Ambrosia (Franseria) deltoidea
brittlebush	Encelia farinosa
jojoba	Simmondsia chinensis
ironwood	Olneya tesota
creosotebush	Larrea divaricata
ocotillo	Fouquieria splendens
ratany	Krameria grayi, K. parvifolia
deer buckwheat	Eriogonum wrighti
crucifixion-thorn	Holocantha emoryi
elephant tree	Bursera microphylla
organ-pipe cactus	Lemaireocereus thurberi
senita cactus	Lophocereus schotti
barrel cactus	Ferocactus wislizeni
cane cholla	Opuntia versicolor
jumping cholla	Opuntia fulgida
Christmas cactus	Opuntia leptocaulis
prickly pear	Opuntia phaeacantha
hedgehog	Echinocereus fendleri
fish-hook cactus	Mammilaria microcarpa
blue paloverde	Cercidium floridum
velvet mesquite	Prosopis juliflora
catclaw	Acacia greggi
white thorn	Acacia constricta
desert willow	Chilopsis linearis
netleaf hackberry	Celtis reticulata
desert hackberry	Celtis tala
desert fluff grass	Tridens pulchellus
bush muhly grass	Muhlenbergia porteri
Rothrock gramma	Bouteloua rothrocki

The creosotebush-bursage (Larrea-Franseria) community is a more xeric example of Sonoran desertscrub. It is dominated by shrubs and dwarf shrubs, with trees almost absent and cactus and grass less abundant than in the paloverde-saguaro community (Table 6).

Table 6. Lower Colorado Sonoran desertscrub species in southeastern Arizona

creosotebush	Larrea divaricata
white bursage	Ambrosia (Franseria) dumosa
big galleta	Hilaria rigida
desert saltbush	Atriplex polycarpa
four-wing saltbush	Atriplex canescens
desert holly	Atriplex hymenelytra
quelite-salado	Allenrolfea occidentalis
desert thorn	Lycium macrodon, L. andersoni

Table 6. Lower Colorado Sonoran desertscrub species in southeastern Arizona (continued)

white-thorn	*Acacia constricta*
velvet mesquite	*Prosopis juliflora*
screwbean mesquite	*Prosopis pubescens*
catclaw	*Acacia greggi*
tamarix	*Tamarix pentandra*
desert lavender	*Hyptis emoryi*
smoketree	*Dalea spinosa*
elephant tree	*Bursera microphylla*
fan palm	*Washingtonia filifera*
tree-nolina	*Nolina bigelovi*

This community is located below 1000 m elevation in less rocky and more level habitats, where it is also drier and warmer.

The Chihuahuan desertscrub is slightly more elevated than its Sonoran counterpart. Characteristic of large areas of northwestern Mexico, it reaches its northwesternmost limit in southeastern Arizona. Essentially a shrub and dwarf shrub desert, the Chihuahuan desertscrub contains species also common to Sonoran desert (Table 7).

Table 7. Chihuahuan desertscrub species in southeastern Arizona

tarbush	*Flourensia cernua*
white-thorn	*Acacia constricta*
sandpaperbush	*Mortonia scabrella*
mariola	*Parthenium incanum*
shrubby senna	*Cassia wislizeni*
whitebrush	*Lippia wrighti*
desert zinnia	*Zinnia pumila*
little coldenia	*Coldenia canescens*
allthorn	*Koeberlinia spinosa*
ocotillo	*Fouquieria splendens*
banana yucca	*Yucca baccata*
Palmer agave	*Agave palmeri*
prickly pear	*Opuntia laevis*, *O. phaeacantha*

It is characterized by shrubs with succulents and grasses intermixed. Trees are rare and cacti are not common in the Arizona portion although both are widespread further south and east in Mexico. Giant cacti are absent. Primarily located between 1200 to 1600 m elevation on valley soils, it is more highly diversified in its southern ranges.

Riparian associations occur in all desertscrub communities and include both riparian woodland species as well as desert riparian species. Both habitats support species adapted to more mesic environments than those found in the immediate vicinity (Table 8).

Table 8. Desert and woodland riparian species in southeastern Arizona

banana yucca	*Yucca baccata*
desert hackberry	*Celtis pallida*
Wright's buckwheat	*Eriogonum wrightii*
Fendler bush	*Fendlera rupicola*
Apache plume	*Fallugia paradoxa*
canyon grape (vine)	*Vitis arizonica*
chuparosa, desert honeysuckle	*Anisacanthus thurberi*
brickellia	*Brickellia* spp.
snakeweed	*Gutierrezia* spp.
seep-willow, batamote	*Baccharis glutinosa*
Arizona baccharis	*Baccharis thesioidies*
arrow-weed	*Pluchae sericea*
rabbit-brush	*Chrysothamnus nauseosus*
cottonwood	*Populus fremontii*
coyote willow	*Salix exigua*
arroyo willow	*Salix lasiolepis*
Goodding willow	*Salix gooddingii*
Bonpland willow	*Salix bonplandiana*
Arizona walnut	*Juglans major*
thinleaf alder	*Aluns tenuifolia*
Arizona alder	*Aluns oblongifolia*
net-leaf hackberry	*Celtis reticulata*
Texas mulberry	*Morus microphylla*
Arizona sycamore	*Platanus wrightii*
Gila chokecherry	*Prunus virens*
honey mesquite	*Prosopis juliflora* var. *velutina*
inland boxelder	*Acer negundo*
salt cedar	*Tamarix pentandra*
velvet ash	*Fraxinus velutina*
tree tobacco	*Nicotiana glauca*
desert willow	*Chilopsis linearis*

Grassland. Desert grassland is abundantly represented in southeastern Arizona. The majority of the AEPCO II project area transects this zone (Figure 7).

The Chihuahuan desert grassland is of a highly diverse grass-scrub type where woody shrubs and succulents are intermixed with varied perennial grass species; cacti also are occasionally present (Table 9).

Table 9. Desert grassland species in southeastern Arizona

blue grama	*Bouteloua gracilis*
black grama	*Bouteloua eriopoda*
sideoats grama	*Bouteloua curtipendula*
tobosa grass	*Hilaria mutica*
three-awn	*Aristida divaricata*
palmilla	*Yucca elata*
sotol	*Dasylirion wheeleri*
beargrass	*Nolina microcarpa*
velvet mesquite	*Prosopis juliflora*
catclaw	*Acacia greggi*
Mexican crucillo	*Condalia spathulata*
burroweed	*Aplopappus tenuisectus*
snakeweed	*Gutierrezia sarothrae*
cane cholla	*Opuntia spinosior*
buckhorn cholla	*Opuntia acanthocarpa*
prickly pear	*Opuntia phaeacantha*, *O. chlorotica*

Specific landscapes trend from extensive pure grass stands to shrub-tree dominated areas with grass understory. Common to southeastern Arizona are mixed communities in undulating valley habitats between 1200 and 1600 m elevation.

Woodland. The evergreen-oak woodlands in southeastern Arizona are related to these more fully developed in the Sierra Madre Occidental of northwestern Mexico. There are three community types; oak woodland, encinal, and Mexican oak-pine woodland. They are all dominated by oaks in association with other trees, shrubs, and grasses in varying combinations (Table 10).

Table 10. Oak woodland species in southeastern Arizona

scrub oak	*Quercus turbinella*
sugar sumac	*Rhus ovata*
buckthorn	*Rhamnus californica*, *R. crocea*
mountain mahogany	*Cercocarpus betuloides*
bricklebrush	*Brickellia californica*
Chihuahua pine	*Pinus leiophylla*
Apache pine	*Pinus engelmanni*
Mexican pinyon pine	*Pinus cembroides*
alligator-bark juniper	*Juniperus deppeana*
Emory oak	*Quercus emoryi*
Arizona oak	*Quercus arizonica*
Mexican blue oak	*Quercus oblongifolia*
silverleaf oak	*Quercus hypoleucoides*
netleaf oak	*Quercus rugosa*
madroño	*Arbutus arizonica*
Arizona cypress	*Cupressus arizonica*
little bluestem	*Andropogon scoparius*
sideoats grama	*Bouteloua curtipendula*

Located between 1300 and 2300 m, the communities overlap ranges but are generally situated in the order described above with oak woodland at the lowest ranges.

Characteristic chaparral evergreen shrubs such as manzanita (Arctostaphylous and mountain mahogany (Cercocarpus), and dry-tropic shrubs and succulents such as agave (Agave), mesquite (Prosopis), and yucca (Yucca) also occur. Cacti and grasses fill out the understory.

In the encinal and Mexican oak-pine woodland of the AEPCO project area live a mixture of chaparral and woodland species. Upslope are evergreen woodlands. The available data do not specify exactly which species are present.

Fauna

The abundance and distribution of fauna is a culturally important environmental attribute, especially for populations that heavily exploit wild resources. Even sedentary horticultural groups such as those who lived in southeastern Arizona relied upon animal foods. Therefore, an examination of faunal data for the AEPCO region is included in this report.

It is commonly accepted that modern man has affected the natural habitats and ranges of animals in southeastern Arizona, but the degree of change is difficult to determine with certainty. The nature of known and potential changes will be discussed later, but it is important first to examine present-day faunal distribution and abundance so that previous conditions and subsequent changes can best be understood.

Researchers have established faunal areas in Arizona not unlike the previously discussed vegetation zones. These are geographic regions where the distributional ranges of several animal species are similar, and where many reach their maximum occurrence. Within any region there are characteristic species (Lowe 1964). There is no direct correlation between the faunal and vegetation zones, but remembering that man relates to resources at the species level, it is useful to consider the distribution of individual animals with regard to vegetation.

Ecosystems in the project region are almost infinite in variety due to interrelationships of vegetation, physiography and climate. The complexity of territorial habitats provide for abundant fauna. While there are no accurate total population estimates, 16 species of toads and frogs, 5 species of turtles, 32 species of lizards, 41 species of snakes, 26 species of mammals, and over 200 species of birds are present in the AEPCO region (USDA 1973).

Certain floral zones and microzones provide superior animal habitats. Regardless of species, riparian vegetation is the most suitable habitat in Arizona (Jahn and Trefethen 1972), as the greater density and diversity of flora supports more diverse wildlife activity. The other vegetation zones in the region all support a variety of fauna except for the monotypic creosotebush unit where both diversity and quantity are low (USDI 1978). The type and availability of water sources are important for all species, especially semiaquatic and aquatic birds, reptiles, amphibians, and other mammals. Most desert species can survive for long periods without "free" water, as plant foods generally provide sufficient moisture (Kendeigh 1964). Many species compensate for dry desert conditions by adopting behavior patterns which maximize water conservation.

In general, habitats of all animal species will crosscut environmental zones. However, specific individuals migrate very little; the home range of virtually all animals is restricted. In addition, certain mammals such as squirrels and turkeys are restricted to specific vegetation types as habitats.

Particular species and their distribution in southeastern Arizona are discussed below. Only those known to be culturally important, primarily as food sources are mentioned.

Figure 8 illustrates the distribution of some large mammals and birds in the project region. While mule deer (Odocoileus hemionus) inhabit all zones, oak-pine woodland is preferred because evergreen browse is a dietary mainstay. In the desertscrub fruits and seeds of cacti and leguminous shrubs are eaten. White-tailed deer (Odocoileus virginianus) habitat ranges from grassland to woodland, with primary range above 1900 m. During the drier spring and fall months when forage is scarce deer are likely to be closer to permanent water sources.

Javelina (Pecari tajacu) range from river bottoms to oak-woodlands with the preferred habitat near water in the foothill zones where prickly pear and other vegetal foods are most abundant. Herd size is normally less than 15 individuals, but groups of 30 have been reported. Pronghorn (Antilocapra americana) prefer flat and rolling grasslands, but also range upward and downward occasionally. Herds average 30 individuals. Currently, pronghorn distribution is severely restricted due to environmental change. Other large mammals such as black bear (Euarctos americanus), mountain lion (Felis concolor) and desert bighorn sheep (Ovis canadensis) have low frequencies and very restricted ranges, all of which lie considerably outside the AEPCO project vicinity. Bison (Bison bison) and elk (Cervus canadensis) are not present.

Of the small mammals, rabbits enjoy the widest distribution and largest population. Both desert cottontail (Sylvilagus audubonii) and black-tailed jackrabbit (Lepus alleni) rely on vegetation for a majority of their water needs. While not forced to range near prospective water sources, this is still their preferred habitat. Cottontails prefer a more heavily vegetated understory, and avoid the open desert lowlands which are preferred by the jackrabbit. Numerous rodents are present, including desert pocket mouse (Perognathus penicillatus), Merriam's kangaroo rat (Dipodomys merriami) and Yuma antelope squirrel (Citellus sp.). The black-tailed prarie dog (Cynomys ludovicianus), once common in the grasslands of southeastern Arizona, is now extinct.

Several species of birds are present in the region also (Figure 8), quail being the most abundant. Of three varieties, Gambel's quail (Lophortyx gambelli), scaled quail (Callipepla squamata), and Mearn's quail (Cyrtonyx

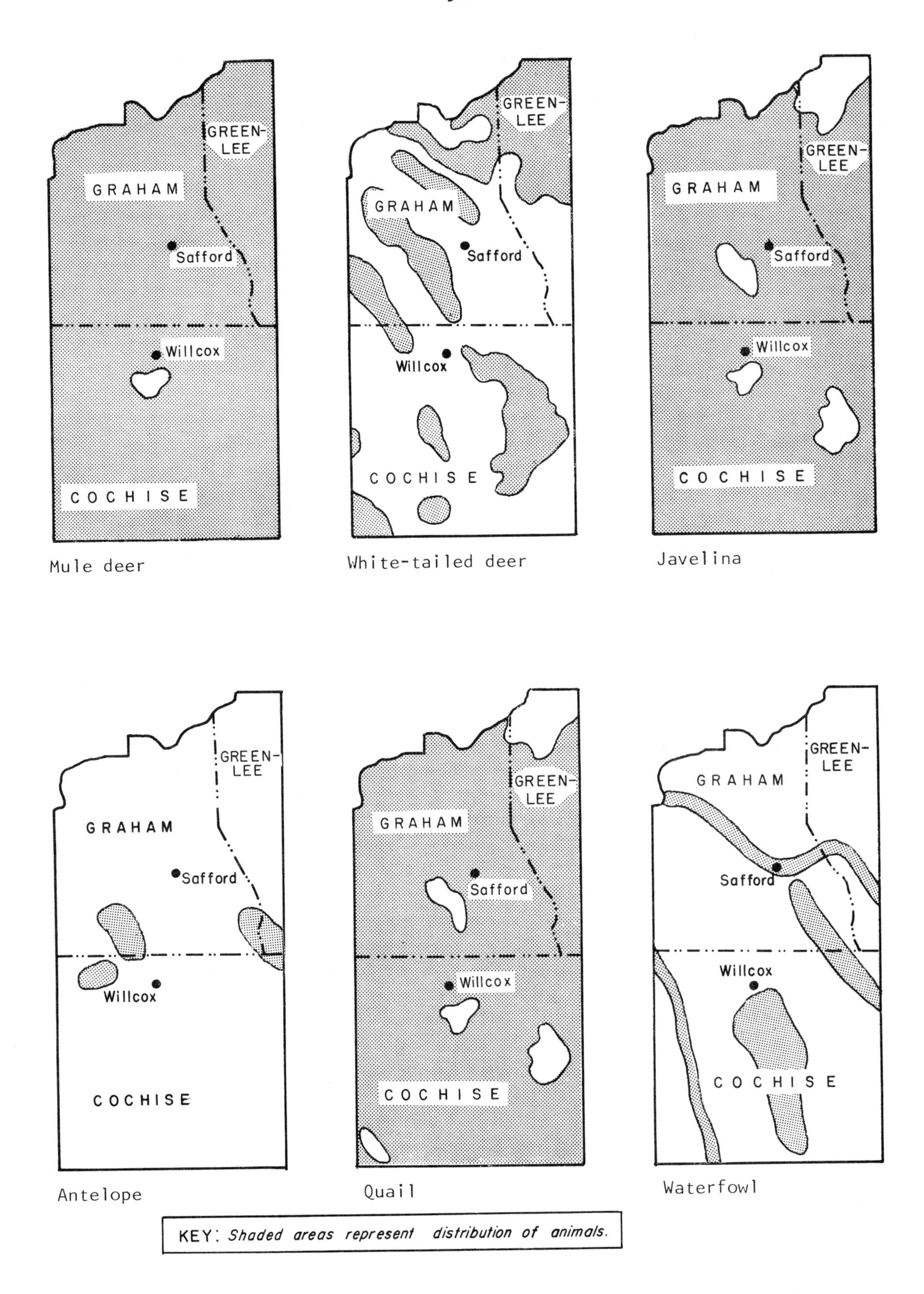

Figure 8. Distribution of certain wildlife species in southeastern Arizona.

montezumae), Gambel's quail is the most widespread, primarily occupying more densely vegetated, wetter habitats. Scaled quail are abundant in grasslands and desertscrub, and Mearn's quail are located somewhat higher in the grasslands and woodlands. All are uncommon in the creosote-saltbush vegetation. The white-winged dove (*Zenaida asiatica*) and mourning dove (*Zenaidura macroura*) are the next most common birds. While doves can be sighted in most zones, the preferred habitat is the Sonoran desertscrub, including the wetter and riparian associations. Like quail, doves nest most commonly on the ground, or less frequently in mesquite. The mourning dove, along with most waterfowl, is a migratory species.

Waterfowl habitats are not abundant nor of high quality. Intermittent water is available in the Gila River and near most springs and drainages, but this latter source is unreliable and too small to support large numbers of birds. Thus, most of the water birds are migratory. The most common species include green-winged teal (*Anas carolinensis*), mallard (*Anas platyrhynchos*), shoveller (*Spatula clypeata*) and ruddy duck (*Oxyura jamaicensis*).

After birds, amphibians and reptiles are the next most common animals in the project region. Both terrestrial and semi-aquatic species have sharply limited tolerances to extreme environmental factors and are habitually sedentary. Commonly observed are various toads and frogs (*Scaphiopus* spp., *Bufo* spp., *Rana* spp.) in riparian areas, whiptail (*Cnemidophorus* spp.) and spiny (*Sceloporus* spp.) lizards and the western diamondback rattlesnake (*Crotalus atrox*) in the desertscrub. In the grasslands are found the western box turtle (*Terrapene ornata*), collared (*Crotaphytus collaris*) and greater earless (*Halbrookia texana*) lizards, and Mohave rattle snake (*Crotalus scutulatus*). The Texas (*Phrymosoma cornutum*) and short-horned (*P. douglassi*) lizards and black-tailed rattlesnake (*Crotalus milossus*) occur in the woodlands.

Thirteen native species of fish were identified in southeastern Arizona (McKinley 1973). Over the past 100 years several native species have disappeared and 15 species have been introduced. The Gila River is the major fish habitat.

Environmental Change

This section encapsulates some of the environmental changes which have occurred in all major environmental categories since the Pleistocene, and which may have affected prehistoric occupation of the region.

Wind and water are the primary agents of erosional change in the AEPCO project region. Since the Pleistocene several processes have been operating on geologic and physiographic features. They are:

1. weathering and stream erosion in mountains, on the uppermost part of piedmonts, and some on the lower part of these slopes;
2. stream deposition in lower valley areas;
3. stream erosion in certain lower valley areas;
4. formation of caliche on slopes and alkalai on flats;

5. wind erosion, including enlargement of the Willcox Playa; and
6. deposition of aeolian deposits, especially northeast of the Playa.

(after Meinzer and Kelton 1913:78).

Bryan (1925), Miller (1958) and Knechtel (1938) discuss different aspects of the major erosion-deposition periods in the western United States. Martin (1963) summarizes these by concluding that while the deformational episodes are generally synchronous they are more accurately described as being localized. Several cycles have occurred since the Pleistocene. Currently the AEPCO project region is experiencing a cutting episode (Bryan 1925).

Of the different locales in the project region, the San Simon Valley and Gila Valley have experienced the most drastic physiographic alteration. Repeated lowerings of the Gila River have caused erosion of the Gila Valley terraces and the San Simon pediments, and recently, the entrenchment of the San Simon River. From historical records, it appears that there was no trenching in the San Simon Valley prior to 1880 (Hastings 1959:33). Now the Gila River channel is also in a minor erosional phase (Burkham 1972).

As a result of this erosion, the soils in the floodplain are the region's youngest and least developed. Though new soils have formed in the postpluvial period, soils change very slowly under the present climatic regime (Gelderman 1970:60). Wholesale erosion and replacement of soils is possible but has not been recorded historically in the San Simon Valley (Alfred Dewall, USDA soil scientist, Safford District).

Hydrologically, the AEPCO project region has changed considerably. Since the retreat of the glaciers approximately 10,000 years B.P., relatively dry conditions have existed in southeastern Arizona. Pluvial Lake Cochise (Willcox Playa) has dried and been subjected to wind erosion. Only on occasion does water now stand in the lake bed. Prior to channel cutting in the 19th century, extensive cienagas and shallow, impermanent streams existed. Groundwater was closer to the surface year-round than at present (Martin 1963:3). Due in great part to a dam downstream, the San Simon Cienaga is not greatly changed (Hastings 1959:129). While Croton Springs west of the Playa still flows, Dragoon Springs, along the Butterfield Stage route, and Sycamore Spring at the north end of the Dos Cabezas Mountains have dried (Hastings 1959:30). Of course the drying of those water sources cannot be attributed merely to erosion but must be considered in relation to climate change.

Extensive climatic reconstruction for southeastern Arizona has been completed only once (Martin 1963). Martin develops a general macroclimatic picture which holds for the period of human occupation. A more refined chronologic correlation of minor shifts is not currently available. The following discussion draws heavily from Martin (1963) and also from Whalen (1971), who presents a broader treatment of relationships of climate and man during this period. Evidence of more recent climatic shifts to the north of the project area will be considered as it relates to southeastern Arizona.

The postglacial (postpluvial) period in southeastern Arizona features three main periods. They are included in Antevs' (1955) Neothermal which actually is more applicable to areas to the northwest (for example, the Great Basin). Martin (1963) disputes Antevs' reconstruction for southeastern Arizona and develops a similar scheme with significantly different natural-cultural implications. Martin's (1963) three divisions and their respective climates are:

I.	Present - 4,000 B.P.	warm, arid
II.	4,000 - 8,000 B.P.	warm, semiarid
III.	8,000 - 10,000 B.P.	warm, arid

Period III was similar to the present. The annual distribution of precipitation changed from winter dominant to summer dominant during the transition from Period III to Period II. Period II experienced temperatures similar to Period III but with increased precipitation especially during the summer monsoons. When the intensity of the monsoons declined in Period I, the precipitation pattern became biseasonal. Perhaps two short periods, one around 2000 B.P. and the other around 1000 B.P., also had a summer dominant rainfall. Otherwise, temperatures and precipitation from 4000 B.P. to the present have been similar. In recent years, summers account for more than one-half of the annual rainfall but the distribution has not approached the dominant monsoon patterns of the past.

Martin (1963) concludes that there have been no climatic shifts significantly affecting biota in the past 4,000 years. Nevertheless, minor fluctuations have occurred, and these may have affected native biota at a finer level than has been investigated. Evidence suggests that for the northern Southwest changes have occurred during the last 2,500 years which have had at least minor effects on native populations. Schoenwetter and Dittert (1968), Hevly (1964), and Karlstrom, Gumerman and Euler (1976) present data from three separate locales and achieve similar but not consistently identical results. It is clear that the data are not entirely appropriate for establishing broad climatic patterns for the AEPCO project region. However, there is some agreement among the three which will be summarized and applied to southeastern Arizona.

From approximately 500 B.C. to A.D. 200 conditions were slightly moister and cooler. These conditions appear to wane and then reappear around A.D. 400 to 600. The period between A.D. 700 to 900 undoubtedly experienced a decline in moisture. After a period from A.D. 900 to 1100 which was similar, or slightly more moist than the present, another 200 years of drier weather followed. Then from A.D. 1300 to 1500 moister conditions existed. Beginning around 1850, and continuing to the present, conditions with summer rains have predominated. The exact nature of the climate of Period I and its impact on the cultures is not well understood (Schoenwetter and Dittert 1968; Plog 1974). There is agreement that climate did not drastically change available biota; however, certain fluctuations in the upper and lower limits of plants and animals occurred. The greatest impact was on agricultural economies which were already in a delicate ecological equilibrium. The effect of similar climatic conditions in southeastern Arizona undoubtedly corresponds to those in the northern Southwest. Similar subsistence systems could be affected in similar ways, although population responses may vary. The effect of climatic variability on other natural environmental features is discussed more fully below.

By the Pleistocene the current major Southwest vegetation patterns had been established, and while various migrations (zonal expansions and contractions) have occurred and are still occurring, major habitat differences have been maintained over time (Hastings 1959). Martin (1963) has described paleoenvironmental conditions for southeastern Arizona and concludes that by 10,000 years B.P. the desert grassland had returned to this area (1963:60). Mehringer and Haynes (1965) support this by concluding that desert grassland existed before 11,000 years B.P. (1965:23). Van Devender (1977), however, feels that woodlands existed in the Southwest while postpluvial conditions were gradually receding and resulting in a drier environment.

Martin (1963) describes this grassland during the later, mesic altithermal as exhibiting "a richer cover of perennial (grama, sacaton, needlegrass) grasses and...blue oaks, Emory oaks and Chihuahan pines" (1963:68). It probably resembled the belt of grassland and encinal found today in Mexico east of the Sierra Madre. During this period animal and plant species of these southern regions migrated northward into Arizona (Martin 1963:68). Since 4,000 years B.P. modern vegetation patterns have existed.

Vegetation change has also occurred in southeastern Arizona during the historic period. Though more data on change exist for this time than for the preceding era, it is still not clear exactly what the nature of the changes has been and why the changes have occurred. However, there is agreement that the structure and floral composition of vegetation types has been altered. A sketch of events since the early 1800s can help to better understand environmental conditions in the AEPCO project region.

Terrestrial ecosystems were in a state of natural equilibrium before the arrival of the Spanish in southeastern Arizona (USDI 1978). The complex and varied plant communities which were found prior to 1905 do not now exist; vegetation change is no longer cyclical with preexisting conditions. This change has been analyzed thoroughly by Humphrey (1958) and Hastings and Turner (1965).

> [The] extent to which the vegetation of the desert region has changed in the past eighty years is...almost startling. Changes of this order are not at all to be expected as part of the normal course of events (Hastings and Turner 1965:274).

The most common pattern of change is upward displacement of plant ranges along a xeric to mesic gradient, but this is not consistent throughout the region. All records indicate that grass has decreased in quantity and that various other woody plants such as mesquite, creosote, burroweed, snakeweed and *Opuntia* sp. have been the principle invaders (Humphrey 1958:56).

In the riparian areas, broadleaf species such as ash, sycamore, and cottonwood have given way to mesquite, salt cedar, seepwillow and seepweed. Where marshes have dried as a result of arroyo cutting the cottonwood is now making inroads (Hastings and Turner 1965).

Compared to other vegetation types in the project region, the desertscrub has exhibited fewer dramatic changes. Those that have occurred appear somewhat random. Small semiwoody perennials such as bursage, brittlebush, and desert zinnia have declined in number, and larger woody plants such as mesquite have shifted their range upward. Locally, species may be increasing or decreasing. Even the drought-resistant creosotebush has exhibited a decline in certain localities, though in dense communities in the project region it has remained fairly stable (USDI 1978). Grass is also on the decline in the desertscrub areas.

The grassland has experienced the most dramatic and profound changes. Hinton (in Humphrey 1958) describes the Sulphur Spring Valley in 1869:

> This vast area is...covered to a great extent with fine grass. The soapweed, the cactus, the sagebrush and the greasewood are but little found here...Approaching Sulphur Springs from the east, the road lies for miles through a dense growth of saccatone grass, of far less value than the shorter grama that fairly covers the ground at the springs. (Humphrey 1958:18)

Though still a grassland, the area now supports mesquite, acacia, burroweed, and rabbitbrush (Humphrey 1958:18). Similar descriptions exist for the San Simon Valley, where snakeweed and creosotebush are also invading the grassland (USDI 1978). Elsewhere in the grassland, 21 different woody species (shrubs and trees) are growing in number as grass decreases (Hastings and Turner 1965:182).

Change has also been recorded in the woodland zone. There appears to be a general decline in the oak population accompanied by an upward retreat of the woodland. In some higher elevations oak population has increased. The grass understory has receded and other woody plants have invaded. Mesquite especially dominates the lower woodland zones now (Hastings and Turner 1965).

The reasons for change are difficult to fully assess. Climate, fire, grazing, rodents, and plant competition have all been offered as explanations, and there is agreement that all of these factors can affect vegetation. It is evident from annual vegetation fluctuations illustrated in Figure 9 that change can be dramatic in a short time. The inclusion of this illustration is not to prove that change occurs, but to show the potential for yearly differences in vegetation availability. This short term change could be locally random or widespread. Both this and diachronic change could drastically alter existing nature-culture balances.

Changes in climate and vegetation also produces changes in native faunal density and distribution. Some of the documented change in fauna in the AEPCO project region will now be considered.

The earliest documented human occupation in southeastern Arizona was with Pleistocene megafauna (Haury, Sayles, and Wasley 1959; Lance 1959). The transition to modern fauna was relatively rapid in geological time, accelerated no doubt by man's exploitation of mammoth, bison, horse, camels, and tapirs (Haynes 1966; Van Devender 1977).

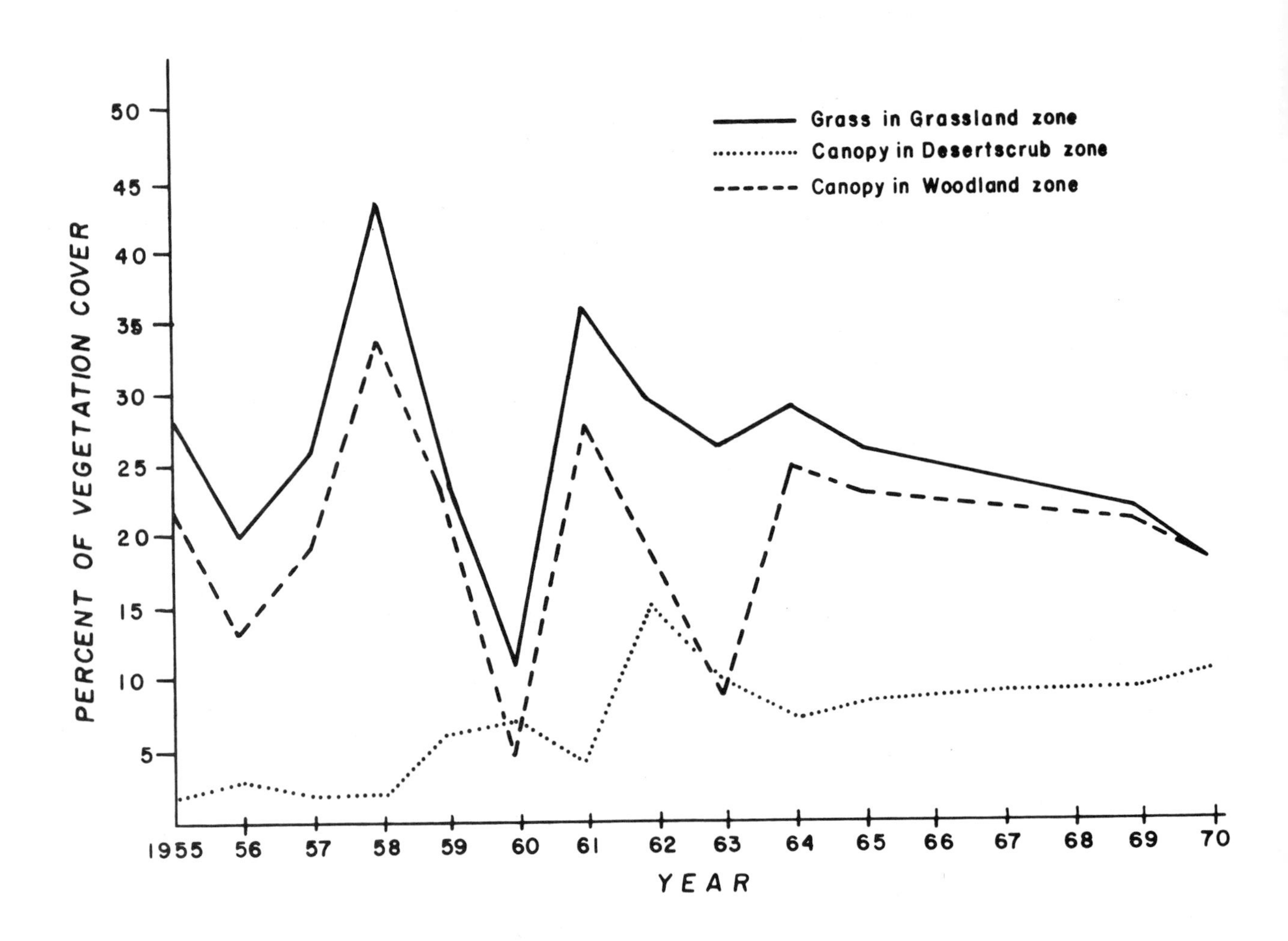

Figure 9. Change in vegetation cover in southeastern Arizona.

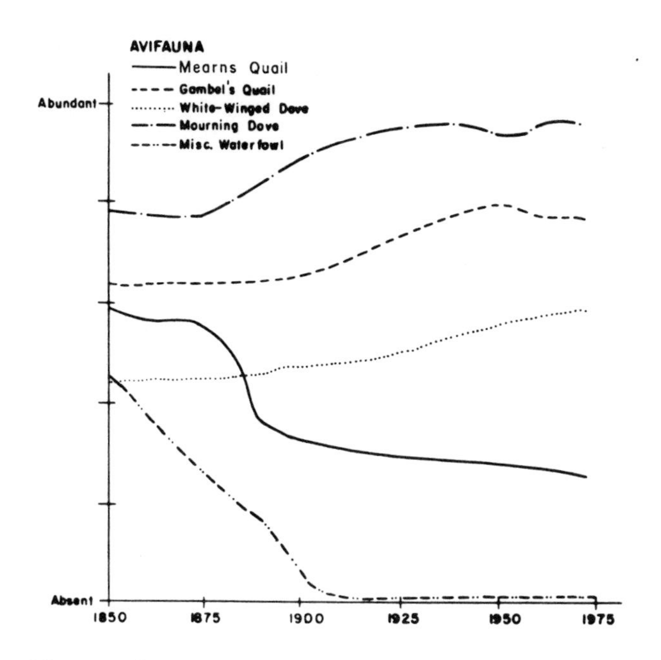

Figure 10. Relative abundance of certain avifauna in southeastern Arizona.

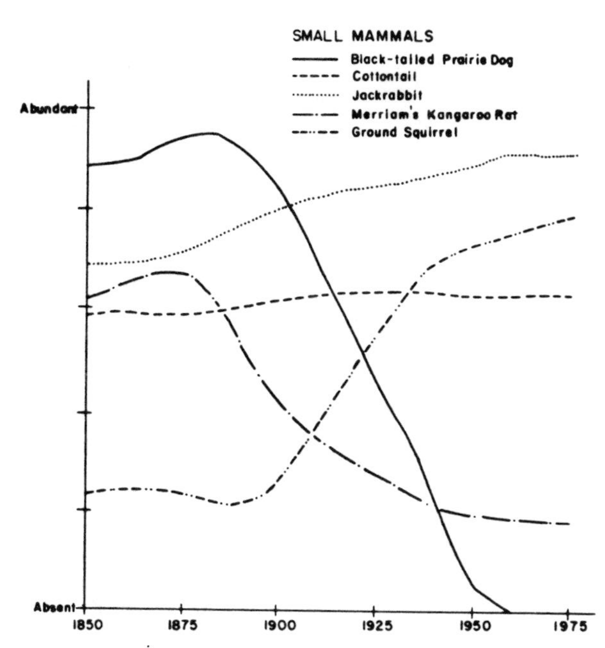

Figure 11. Relative abundance of certain small mammals in southeastern Arizona.

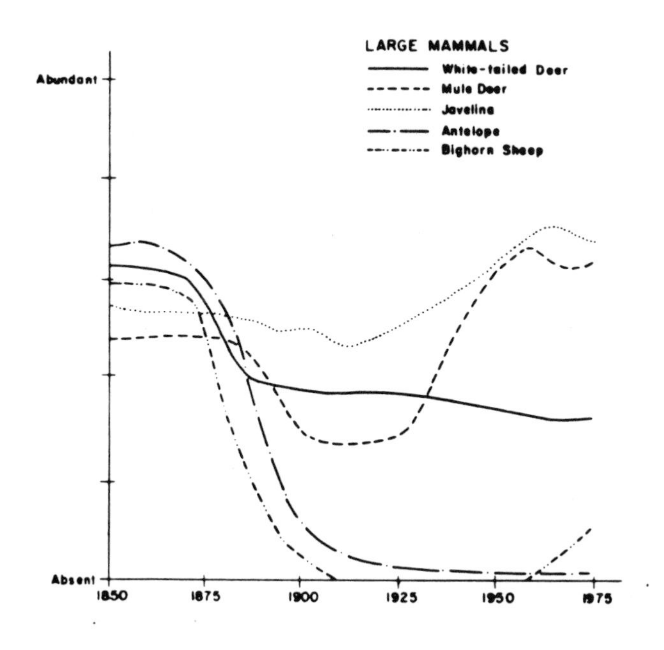

Figure 12. Relative abundance of certain large mammals in southeastern Arizona.

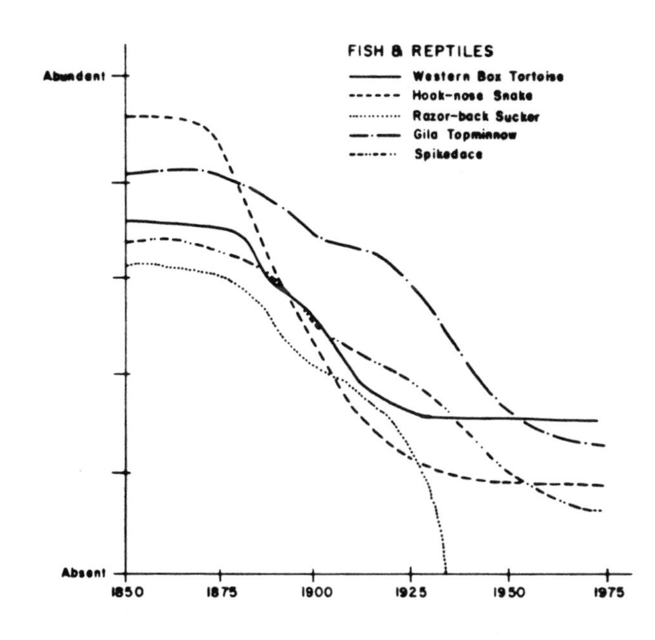

Figure 13. Relative abundance of certain fish and reptiles in southeastern Arizona.

Data on historic change are more plentiful. All records indicate that the various species have reacted differently to environmental change. While it is true that natural changes in habitat indirectly affect species distribution there has been a significant change in the abundance and distribution of fauna in the AEPCO project region since the mid-1800s (Davis 1973; USDI 1978). Hunting, livestock grazing, and land modification are key forces in this change. Grazing has changed the food resources through the reduction of or elimination of palatable flora upon which species (such as prairie dog, pronghorn and Mearn's quail) are dependent (see Figures 10, 11, 12).

Large mammals such as mountain sheep have been drastically reduced (Figure 12), while similar reductions have affected water-dependent species such as fish and certain reptiles, and avifauna (Figures 13 and 10). Some species, however, benefit from the changes associated with grazing (Dick-Peddie 1976). The jackrabbit and kangaroo rat are two such species (see Figure 11).

All of these changes, and others, have created a significantly different modern environment than that which existed during the pre-Spanish period.

The Cultural-Historical Background

Previous Archaeological Investigations in the Project Area

Previous archaeological investigations in southeastern Arizona include the Gila Pueblo surveys and excavation projects of the 1930s, followed by small projects undertaken by various institutions since that time. Early investigations tended to focus on single village sites, high density activity loci, or unique paleontological remains, and gave but cursory treatment to smaller, low density, limited activity sites. The goal of these early investigators was to define cultural groups in time and space by identifying diagnostic artifact assemblages and site characteristics, and to integrate them into chronologically distinct cultural stages. These efforts, based on trait comparisons, were useful in establishing a general cultural-historical framework for the region. However, small scale intrasite variability is not as easily understood and the application of the commonly used trait comparison approach is not always useful.

In assessing previous archaeological research in the project area, it is difficult to draw the line as to what is relevant to the region. Southeastern Arizona has no clear cut cultural boundaries. In general, a great deal of interaction between and among Hohokam, Mogollon, Salado, and perhaps a local indigenous group is evident. Also, prehistoric cultural remains of the much earlier Archaic period have been found to occur on the same surface with those of a later cultural group. Local variation on major Southwestern cultural themes is a consistent attribute of these sites, and as a result recent research has focused on attempting to understand this variability.

For purposes of this report, research in the Upper Gila, San Simon, and Sulphur Spring valleys will be presented and research peripheral to the immediate project zone referred to as it applies to common problems of cultural-historical reconstruction.

An inventory of known sites and associated research in the San Simon district was compiled by Quinn and Roney (1973). The Bureau of Land Management, Safford District Office, has compiled an inventory of previous archaeological research and cultural resources on lands within its jurisdiction (USDI 1978). Much of the following data presented in Table 11 that follows has been excerpted from these reports.

Table 11. Previous research in the AEPCO project region

Date	Personnel/ Institution	Project
1897	J.W. Fewkes W. Hough	Reconnaissance survey of Pueblo Viejo (Safford Valley). Recorded 15 prehistoric sites; carried out test excavations. (Fewkes 1909; Hough 1907)
1929	Sauer and Brand	Reconnaissance survey throughtout SE Arizona. Recorded 37 prehistoric sites: Mogollon, Salado, Hohokam. (Sauer and Brand 1930)
1931	Oscar Tatman	Partial excavation of the Buena Vista site in the Safford Valley. (Brown 1973)
1934-1938	W.S. Fulton Mus. of the Amer. Indian	Excavation of five sites in Texas Canyon, near Benson, Arizona. (Fulton 1934, 1936, 1938)
Prior to 1935	Gila Pueblo	Informal surveys and reports by amateurs (Quinn and Roney 1973)
1935	B. Cummings ASM	Reported discovery of oldest known artifacts in the Southwest, near Double Adobe in the Sulphur Spring Valley.
1935-1941	Haury, Sayles, Antevs Gila Pueblo	Reconnaissance and intensive survey of the San Simon Valley and Whitewater Draw in the Sulphur Spring Valley; search for sites to define extent of Cochise culture location and for promising sites for future excavation.
1939-1941	Sayles and Antevs Gila Pueblo	Excavations at Cave Creek and San Simon Village and excavation at one Cochise site. (Sayles and Antevs 1941; Sayles 1945)

Table 11. Previous research in the AEPCO project region (continued)

Date	Personnel/ Institution	Project
1940	Fulton and Tuthill Amerind Found.	Excavation of the Gleeson Site, Sulphur Spring Valley, Arizona. Definition of "Dragoon Complex". (Fulton and Tuthill 1940)
1940-1949	Mills and Mills (amateurs)	Nine Mile Ruin excavations. Salado-type compound south of Bowie, Arizona. (unpublished; MS on file at Amerind Foundation, Inc., Dragoon)
1947	Danson and Woodbury Peabody Mus.	Upper Gila Expedition. Several Mogollon sites recorded in Gila River Valley. Subject for Ph.D. thesis. (Danson 1957)
1947	Wendorf SMU	Reported sites in the Black Hills district. (Teague 1974)
1947	Tuthill Amerind Found.	Excavations at the Tres Alamos site, north of Benson, Arizona, on the San Pedro River. (Tuthill 1947)
1950s	Sayles and others Gila Pueblo	Revisited sites in the San Simon and Sulphur Spring Valley. Recorded a few new sites. Purpose was to update the Cochise culture sequence. (Sayles and others n.d.)
1953-1966	Haury University of Arizona	Seminar field trips throughout the Safford district. Reconnaissance survey. (Quinn and Roney 1973; Teague 1974)
1958	Tuohy ASM	Survey of Gila River from east of Safford to Buttes Dam Site. Excavation of two sites. (Tuohy 1960; Vivian 1970)
1969	Kayser and Fiero ASM	Salvage excavation of San Simon Mogollon-Hohokam-Pueblo site near Willcox, Arizona. (Kayser and Fiero 1970)
1969-1970	Brown University of Arizona	Reconnaissance survey and excavation in the Safford Valley. Ten large sites recorded, one excavated. Subject of Ph.D. dissertation on extent of the Salado culture. (Brown 1973)
1970	Windmiller ASM	The Fairchild Site near Double Adobe, Sulphur Spring Valley. Excavation of extinct mammoth remains and a Cochise culture site. (Windmiller 1971, 1973)

Table 11. Previous research in the AEPCO project region (continued)

Date	Personnel/ Institution	Project
1972	Huckell ASM	Excavation of the Gold Gulch Site, a Cochise culture specialized limited activity site near Bowie, Arizona. (Huckell 1973)
1972	Doyel and others ASM	Clearance survey of the TG&E San Juan to Vail 345 kV line R-O-W, from Clifton to near Tucson. Recorded three sites, one a possible San Simon site northeast of Willcox. (Doyel 1972)
1975	Kinkade ASM	Clearance survey of Foote Wash - No Name Wash. Thirteen sites recorded, all limited activity sites. (Kinkade 1975)
1975	Scott EAC	Field school, Eastern Arizona College, Thatcher. Partial excavation of a Salado village south of Safford, Arizona. (USDI 1978)
1975-1977	Kinkade BLM	Reconnaissance survey of approximately one million acres in Safford-Aravaipa District. Recorded about 60 prehistoric and 40 historic sites. (USDI 1978)
1976	Fitting Commonwealth Associates	Foote Wash - No Name Wash Project. Mitigation. Surface collection and test excavation at limited activity sites recorded by Kinkade (1975). (Fitting 1977)
1976	Scott EAC	Field School, Eastern Arizona College, Thatcher. Partial excavation of a Salado village near Safford, Arizona. Report in preparation. (USDI 1978)
1977	Simpson and others	Arizona Electric Power Cooperative, Inc. Clearance survey for 56 miles of R-O-W for 230 kV line, from near Morenci to south of Safford, Arizona. Seventy-six sites recorded. (Simpson and Westfall 1978)
1977	Simpson and others ASM	Arizona Electric Power Cooperative, Inc. Clearance survey of access roads to 230 kV line R-O-W. Seventeen sites recorded. (Simpson and Westfall 1978)
1977	Simpson and others ASM	Arizona Electric Power Cooperative, Inc. Mitigative activities on 21 sites in 230 kV line R-O-W from Morenci to Safford. (Simpson and Westfall 1978)

Regional Culture History and Research Problems

Paleo-Indian and the Desert Culture. The archaeological record documents the presence of man in the Southwest for at least 11,000 years (Whalen 1971:2). The earliest known prehistoric groups were those of the Paleo-Indians, recognized as being in the Southwest as early as the end of the Pleistocene. Paleo-Indian subsistence was based on hunting now extinct migratory megafauna, smaller game, and gathering wild food resources. Paleo-Indian sites in southeastern Arizona include Ventana Cave (Haury 1950), Murray Springs (Haynes and Hemmings 1968; Hemmings 1968), Lehner (Haury and others 1959), and Naco (Haury 1953). Such sites are recognized by the presence of lanceolate projectile points, sometimes in association with remains of extinct mammals. With the extinction of the large Pleistocene mammals around 9000 B.C. (Whalen 1971:3), these early Indian groups shifted their subsistence pattern to more intensive wild food gathering and hunting of smaller species of game. Out of this developed the Desert culture (Jennings 1957). It is viewed as a cultural adaptation to changing environmental conditions across much of the American Southwest.

Several important problems have developed since the origin of the Desert culture concept and its application to certain physiographic regions within the greater American Southwest. They will be mentioned here, as sites found along the Dos Condado-Apache transmission line lie in the region defined by Sayles (1941) as having been occupied by the Cochise culture, a variant of the Desert culture. In a recent review, Jennings (1973:1) says:

> The term Desert Culture was first suggested...as a label that would provide a meaningful referent for a coherent pattern of life that could be recognized in the scores of reported archaeological sites scattered over the arid West....The concept implied a modest core of shared artifacts, a cluster of tools and technologies in a complex geared to the special environment of the West and a stable cultural longevity over a period of 5 or 6 millenia beginning about 7000-7500 B.C. ...The original intent was to emphasize a basic and pervasive unity of lifeway implied by the artifacts all over the Great Basin and environs, minimizing local/regional variations in the artifact inventories from place to place. At the same time the fact of regional or sub-areal variation was recognized and the eventual delineation of such areas as internally cohesive cultural units, marked by distinctive artifacts and subsistence patterns closely geared to local resources, was predicted.

Since its formulation, the Desert culture concept has been applied by various researchers in their studies to determine its validity as a cultural tradition. Some authors have developed alternate models to describe and explain characteristics of this time period, often referred to as the Archaic period (Heizer 1966; Swanson 1966). Controversy notwithstanding, Jennings (1973:4) observed that "many authors merely accept the idea as useful in helping them order their data, or in establishing the wider framework where their findings have relevance."

Research has tended to substantiate the general idea and also to create an awareness of multiple regional variants of the Desert culture. In southern Arizona, cultural groups falling within the time-space limits of the Desert culture are those of the Cochise culture (Sayles and Antevs 1941; Sayles and others n.d.), the occupants of Ventana Cave (Haury 1950), and the Amargosa (Rogers 1958; Rogers 1966; Hayden 1970).

In the 1930s and 1940s Gila Pueblo (under the direction of Harold S. Gladwin) undertook numerous areal surveys in southeastern Arizona, southern New Mexico, and western Texas. This was done, in part, to balance out the great amount of research that had been conducted in the Four Corners area. The primary intent was to describe and organize the diverse cultural traditions in the general southern desert region of the southwest. One result of these efforts was the identification and description of the Cochise culture (Sayles and Antevs 1941).

A distinctive aspect of Cochise culture sites was a high frequency of milling stones in the artifact assemblage. Sayles interpreted this as a dependence on wild food gathering and processing, when elsewhere sites of this time indicated an emphasis on hunting. Since the publication of the first report on the Cochise culture (Sayles and Antevs 1941), additional research has been carried out, data reviewed and reassessed, and several misunderstandings have been clarified (Sayles and others n.d.). While the results of this study have yet to be published, permission has been granted to cite here several examples that clarify certain problems pertaining to the Cochise cultural pattern as originally outlined by Sayles. The original information will be summarized below. Problems will be discussed, then reviewed in light of the new data.

Sayles and Antevs (1941:8) originally postulated three chronological stages for the Cochise culture based on typological changes in artifact assemblages and geologic-climatic dating:

Sulphur Spring stage	? to 8000 B.C.
Chiricahua stage	8000 to 3000 B.C.
San Pedro stage	3000 to 500 B.C.

Habitation sites have not yet been identified for the earliest two stages. The sites investigated in the 1930s were high-density artifact scatters. Sayles suggested that a seminomadic seasonally based lifeway was characteristic of the early inhabitants of southeastern Arizona. The Sulphur Spring stage was characterized by an artifact assemblage consisting of one-hand manos (handstones) which were unmodified or only slightly modified river cobbles, flat slab metates (milling stones) and percussion-flaked stone tools. Ground stone tools outnumbered chipped stone tools, and no projectile points were found in sites of this stage, creating problems regarding site function. Sayles postulated that during this stage food gathering and processing was a primary subsistence effort, with hunting, as evidenced by the presence of burned and broken animal bone, of secondary importance. Given the hunting based subsistence pursuits of the earlier Paleo-Indian tradition and the occurrence of projectile points in later Cochise stages, the absence of projectile points in the succeeding Sulphur Spring stage appears to be in contradiction to the pattern.

Sites of the Chiricahua stage are characterized by trash middens and hearths; no habitation features have yet been identified. During this stage the diversity of tool types increases, suggesting exploitation of a greater variety of natural resources. Sayles (1941:17) describes the cultural material of this stage thus:

> The artifacts identified with this stage possess certain characteristics which distinguish it from both earlier and later stages. These artifacts consist of handstones and milling stones, tools made by percussion-flaking, both plano-convex and biface, and intrusive artifacts made by pressure-flaking.

More specifically, the handstones tend to be small, wedge-shaped, multifaceted one-hand types, a distinction from the earlier Sulphur Spring small unifaceted pebble handstone. Metates show a trend from the flat slab type to a more basin-like shallow grinding facet. The chipped stone assemblage of the Chiricahua stage consists of:

> ...handaxes, blades of the plano-convex and biface types, knives, scrapers, hammerstones, and spokeshaves. The axes are of the plano-convex variety, some chipped along one edge only, others over the entire upper surface. All the blades are of the thick, sinuous-edge type, without retouching. The knives were fashioned from primary flakes, some retouched along a single edge, others along both edges, occasionally over the entire surface...
>
> The scrapers consist of both thin and thick primary flakes, retouched along the edge, ranging into the type called flake knives or side scrapers (Sayles 1941:18).

According to Sayles (1941), the changing form of the ground stone tool kit is indicative of the growing importance of grinding in the Cochise economy, and is possibly related to increasing dependence upon primitive maize.

The San Pedro stage was identified by Sayles (1941:21) at sites near Fairbank, on the San Pedro River west of the Sulphur Spring Valley. Excavations at Benson 5:10 revealed a number of pits and hearths, but no habitation features. There were fewer ground stone tools than chipped stone implements, a reversal of the pattern of the earlier Chiricahua stage. A peculiar feature of the chipped stone industry of the San Pedro stage is the frequency of pressure-flaked pieces in addition to percussion-flaked tools. The deep mortar and pestle also make their appearance in this stage, and a diagnostic San Pedro projectile point style is also found. Along with changes resulting from cultural continuity, a shift in the subsistence is suggested for this stage. According to Sayles' (1941:25) interpretation of the San Pedro stage data, hunting became a more important activity than was apparent for the preceding stages. Haury (1962:115), however, suggests that the prehistoric hunters and gatherers were becoming more sedentary and adapting to agriculture, and by the end of this stage semipermanent pit house villages had become established along streams and wet meadows (cienagas) of mountain slopes (Windmiller 1971:6).

Cochise culture settlement-subsistence patterns were not clearly delineated by the early researchers who merely pointed out that gathering superceded hunting as the major subsistence activity. The emphasis on aspects of the ground stone assemblage and a somewhat cavalier attitude toward chipped stone analysis beyond identifying "diagnostic" tool types resulted in some misunderstanding of the data. For example, Bryan and Toulouse (1943:278) find the Chiricahua stage Cochise to be "wholly food gatherers," a regrettable error. Haury (in Sayles and others n.d.) aptly notes the unfortunate tendency to classify prehistoric cultural groups by the dominant activity represented in the artifact inventory, for example, "Clovis big game hunters" and "Cochise gatherers." For it is most likely that Clovis people exploited plant foods and Cochise hunted an appreciable amount of game.

Using new data, the revised report on the Cochise culture (Sayles and others n.d.) addresses itself to several of these problems. The main intent of the report is to provide a fuller description of tool types and infer subsistence behavior therefrom, and to assess the chronological framework. Understanding the necessity and desirability of further investigations regarding the Cochise culture, Sayles conducted additional field excavations, surveys and artifact analyses. Research elsewhere also contributed information (Agenbroad 1970; Whalen 1971). Ventana Cave (Haury 1950) yielded artifacts of a type and age comparable to the Chiricahua and San Pedro stages. Radiocarbon dating provided substantial chronological data and the original Cochise temporal sequence was correspondingly refined. Sayles also identified a fourth stage transitional between the Sulphur Spring and Chiricahua stages, which he termed the Cazador (Sayles and others n.d.; Whalen 1971:68). The revised chronological sequence is as follows:

Sulphur Spring stage	10,500 B.C. to 9000 B.C.
Cazador stage	9000 B.C. to 6000 B.C.
Chiricahua stage	6000 B.C. to 1500 B.C.
San Pedro stage	1000 B.C. to A.D. 1

While the Cazador is weakly represented, Sayles distinguished it on the basis of geologic context, and the occurrence of projectile points, biface blades, and milling stones. Some authors have disputed the existence of Cazador as a separate stage. Quinn and Roney (1973), citing Whalen (1971), view the Cazador as an aspect of the Sulphur Spring stage. Whalen (1971:69) notes that:

> Other types of chipped stone tools are present in the Cazador stage and are comparable to those identified with the Sulphur Spring stage. Some of the milling stones are likewise similar to those identified with the Sulphur Spring stage; in addition there are modified types comparable to those found in the later stages.

Whalen suggests that the absence of projectile points in the Sulphur Spring stage sites may be due to sampling error, and that Cazador may represent the hunting, and Sulphur Spring the gathering aspect, of a single stage. In the revised Cochise report (Sayles and others n.d.) radiocarbon dates, geologic context, and the occurrence of modern faunal bones (contrasted with bones of extinct mammals in the Sulphur Spring stage sites) substantiate the distinctness of the Cazador stage.

Whalen's statements were based on an assessment of incomplete and unverified data. Consequently, the information provided in the revised Cochise report does not support Whalen's interpretation.

Sayles maintains that the absence of stone projectile points in the Sulphur Spring stage continues to pose a problem (Sayles and others n.d.), although he acknowledges the probability of points made from bone or wood. Haury (in Sayles and others n.d.) favors tempering the negative evidence, suggesting that the investigated Sulphur Spring stage sites reflect specialized activities oriented toward plant processing and are but one component of a diversified subsistence base. Irwin-Williams (n.d.) similarly suggests a mixed foraging system.

One of the more vexing problems was Sayles' original contention that pressure-flaking and projectile points were introduced into the Chiricahua stage as an intrusive element. Later analysis (Sayles and others n.d.) resulted in modification of this position, and pressure flaking came to be recognized as an integral component of the Cochise lithic industry.

The specific research problems of the Cochise culture discussed above provide little information about subsistence pursuits. In that regard, Hayden (1970:88), following a line of reasoning first postulated by Jennings (1957), views the Cochise culture as an adaptation of Desert culture groups (Amargosa) to a high desert grasslands environment. Discussion of the Amargosa follows this section. Whalen (1971:202) considers the Cochise subsistence pattern not as an adaptation to specific environmental zones and their respective resources, but rather to certain plants and animals that crosscut zones, for example, mesquite, agave, deer, and rabbits. Further, Whalen proposes that during later Chiricahua and San Pedro stages these prehistoric groups exploited plant and animal resources in a seasonal cycle. Whalen's basic model of Cochise settlement and subsistence is as follows (1971:204):

> The deployment of large and small sites...in which maintenance and extractive tasks were conducted on base camps and on work camps connotes a society utilizing a wide range of biotic resources in a rotational cycle of seasonal exploitation through effective use of a settlement pattern of mobile encampments. Frequent migration from one camp to another followed the exhaustion of culturally acceptable food resources in one area and the maturation of the same and other resources elsewhere.

Investigations elsewhere (Huckell 1973; Windmiller 1973; Agenbroad 1970) at Cochise culture sites indicate that a similar system of semipermanent camps and sites are characterized by variability in the material culture. Artifacts do not always therefore correspond to the Cochise basic pattern set down by Sayles. Problems concerning the relationship of Cochise to the Desert culture are explored more fully in the section on site significance.

One aspect of Cochise subsistence that is not fully understood is the role of maize in the Chiricahua and San Pedro stages. Popcorn has been found in Bat Cave (Dick 1965) in a stratigraphic level given a date of 2500 B.C., coeval with the Chiricahua stage Sayles (1941) and Whalen (1971) both note an apparent slowness on the part of the Cochise people to accept maize agriculture when it first appeared in the Southwest at this time. Cited in support of this observation are certain characteristics of Cochise sites and associated tool kits. Sayles and Haury (Sayles and others n.d.) note that agriculture is commonly associated with permanent settlements, and only in the late San Pedro stage have pit houses been found. The formal, shaped trough metate and accompanying two-hand subrectangular mano commonly found with agriculturally-based sites have not been found earlier than 300 B.C. It would appear that the Cochise, with their well-developed milling stone industry would readily adapt to agriculture, but the data do not bear this out. Whalen (1971) suggests that the reason may be due to environmental factors; corn from Mesoamerica was adapted to growing at higher elevations, with more moisture requirements. He suggests that not until around 300 B.C. with the coming of the Hohokam and the development of hybrid corn did the Cochise settle down to pit house living and agriculture. However, corn does adapt to changed conditions quite rapidly. It would appear that more intensive botanical and paleoenvironmental studies are necessary to solve the problems of the beginning of agriculture in this part of Arizona.

By the late San Pedro stage, the Cochise culture as a recognizable semi-nomadic hunting and gathering tradition had ceased to exist. Martin and Antevs (1949) postulate that eventually the Cochise developed into the Mogollon culture, discussed below.

Recent and current research in southern Arizona prehistory has paid little attention to the presence of the San Dieguito and Amargosa cultural patterns, originally defined by Rogers (1939) and discussed by Haury (1950) and Hayden (1970). While much literature exists on such early aboriginal groups in the lower Colorado basin, relatively little information is available regarding their role in general pan-Southwestern culture history. Since the time of Rogers' 1939 publication, certain revisions in chronological and cultural continuities have been made (Haury 1950). Rogers' original sequence was modified on the basis of new information derived from the stratigraphic record at Ventana Cave (Haury 1950). Based on the Ventana Cave excavations, parallels between Cochise and Amargosa are so apparent that the issue deserves further consideration.

San Dieguito is well represented in the Great Basin and in Baja California and occurs less commonly in southwestern Arizona. Rogers (1958) conducted a survey along the Pantano drainage near Tucson and identified San Dieguito materials on ancient terrace remnants and Amargosa materials in canyons nearer the mountains. This pushed the San Dieguito-Amargosa range farther east. No stone projectiles or ground stone have yet been found at a San Dieguito site. On the basis of the lithic industry, characterized by scrapers, core tools, and choppers, Rogers (1958:11) postulates a subsistence economy focusing on hunting and limited gathering. He further notes that chipped stone implements of San Dieguito I and Sulphur Spring stage Cochise are nearly identical.

Amargosa has been subdivided into three time periods and correlated with Cochise by way of Ventana Cave (Haury 1950; Rogers 1966):

Amargosa I		5000 B.C. to 3000 B.C (approx-
Amargosa II	Chiricahua stage	3000 B.C. to 2500 B.C. imate
Amargosa III	San Pedro stage	2500 B.C. to A.D. 1 dates)

Hayden (1970:88) notes that:

> Rogers (unpublished field notes 1958) traced the Amargosa complex across southern Arizona into the southeastern part of the state and found both Phase I and Phase II diagnostic materials associated with Medithermal land forms and deposits. In southeastern Arizona, these are termed the Chiricahua and San Pedro phases of the Cochise culture; while there are some areal differences between the two complexes, Rogers seems to have been persuaded that they had a common origin. It may be that adaptation of the Amargosans to the high grasslands of this portion of Arizona, and contacts with cultures to the east and north, caused these differences.

Briefly, the Amargosa artifact assemblage is characterized by numerous chipped stone tool types: bifacially flaked choppers, pulping planes, scrapers, and a wide variety of projectile point styles. Points characteristic of Pinto Basin (Campbell and Campbell 1935) and Gypsum Cave (Harrington 1933) occur primarily during Amargosa II, and have been found in Ventana Cave. Ground stone, consisting of flat slab metates (Rogers' "pigment slabs") and hand-stones absent in the San Dieguito, occur in low frequencies. On the basis of site distribution and artifact assemblage, Irwin-Williams (n.d.) suggests that: "The derivative Pinto Basin (Amargosa II) assemblages of southern California and Western Arizona evidently represent groups with a mixed foraging economy adapted to lake edge, river valley, and succulent desert environments..."

Haury (1950) goes to some length in discussing the co-occurrence of Cochise and Amargosa type artifacts in Ventana Cave, yet maintains a basic distinction between the two. Hayden (1970) suggests that Cochise and Amargosa are but examples of regional adaptation to different environmental areas by segments of a widely dispersed population. This is borne out by basic similarities in the chipped stone tool kits. The fact that more ground stone artifacts are found in Cochise is seen as a factor of specialized adaptation to the grasslands environment of southeastern Arizona. But, while differences existed, a basic unity of lifestyle pervaded much of the desert Southwest, geared to exploitation of available natural resources.

Mogollon. As was discussed in the AEPCO I report (Simpson and Westfall 1978), the project area is situated in a region known to demonstrate a mixture of recognized prehistoric culture groups. Many late sites in the region display an array of cultural traits common to the Mogollon, Hohokam, and Salado of Arizona and New Mexico and occasionally to the prehistoric inhabitants of parts of Chihuahua (Sauer and Brand 1930). The Greenlee-Dos Condado segment passed through this cultural interface zone; the Dos Condado-Apache segment passes through the periphery of the postulated Mogollon cultural sphere and into the recognized Cochise and Hohokam cultural areas, although Mogollon traits are still strong. The postulated transition from late Cochise culture to Mogollon (Sayles 1945; Whalen 1971) is not well defined in the Mogollon core area. Martin and Plog (1973:82) suggest that the first inhabitants of the Mogollon area may have expanded into the area from the south.

Few sites of the period 2000 B.C. to A.D. 1 have been reported and so it is not possible to say with certainty that Mogollon did, indeed, derive from the Cochise culture; nor is there sufficient data to postulate settlement and subsistence patterns for this time in order to find a possible correlation.

The following information on the Mogollon is derived from the AEPCO I report with some supplemental data included.

The Mogollon were originally defined as a puebloan people who inhabited the mountain and mountain-lowland transition zones of east-central Arizona and western New Mexico (Wheat 1955). Mogollon culture history lacks a synthesis at the current moment, since research has focused primarily on single site analysis and on the derivation of explanations for variations within the basic Mogollon cultural pattern. Consequently, several branches or subgroups of Mogollon are currently recognized in different geographical areas but their relationship to each other is by no means clearly defined. Some of these branches are: Mimbres, in the Mimbres Valley of New Mexico; San Simon in the San Simon Valley near Safford and Willcox, Arizona; Forestdale and Point of Pines near Showlow, Arizona; Pinelawn in the Reserve area of western New Mexico; and Little Colorado in the drainage of that name in east-central Arizona (Wheat 1955). Elements of the San Simon and Mimbres branches lie within the project area, so they will be discussed as relevant cultural-historical problems.

The San Simon branch as defined by Sayles (1945) was based on investigations at two sites in the San Simon VaLley: San Simon Village and Cave Creek Village. Sayles (1945:vi) suggests that it would be appropriate to refer to the San Simon culture as Mogollon, but he cautions against inferring any strong relationships. However, Gladwin (1957:224) regards the San Simon branch as an eastern subgroup of Mogollon. This association has persisted to the present day despite the lack of research to further substantiate the cultural affiliation of the San Simon. As will be seen below, DiPeso (1958) suggests that San Simon Village may represent a site of the Ootam culture.

The established cultural sequence for the San Simon branch is: Peñasco phase (300 B.C. to A.D. 100), Dos Cabezas phase (A.D. 100 to 400), Pinaleño phase (A.D. 400 to 650), Galiuro phase (A.D. 650 to 850), Cerros phase (A.D. 850 to 950), and Encinas phase (A.D. 950 to 1200?) (Wheat 1955). The Cave Creek Village site shows a direct superposition of Peñasco phase pottery on the earlier nonceramic San Pedro Cochise horizon. Throughout the sequence there is a trend from the oval/circular Peñasco pit house towards the rectangular Encinas pit house type. Above-ground pueblo architecture has not been found at San Simon branch sites, although rock-lined and masonry-lined rooms do occur. Pottery types recognized for the San Simon branch are Dos Cabezas Red-on-brown, Pinaleño Red-on-brown, Galiuro Red-on-brown, Cerros Red-on-white, and Encinas Red-on-brown, each of which corresponds to the respective phase designation of the San Simon branch. The dominant plainware is Alma Plain. It is interesting that sherds of Mimbres Black-on-white and those of Hohokam Red-on-buff have been found as intrusives at San Simon branch sites, yet San Simon branch pottery is not intrusive at sites of other cultures, although it has occasionally been found at sites near the Tucson Basin and along the San Pedro and Santa Cruz rivers (Swanson 1951; Greenleaf 1975; Tuthill 1947; DiPeso 1956). Ground stone artifacts in the earlier phases of the San Simon branch include slab and shallow basin metates, ovoid one-hand manos, mortars, and pestles. Ground stone artifacts of later phases evolved into the rectangular flattened mano and trough metate. The description of the chipped stone assemblages from the Cave Creek and San Simon villages tends to be somewhat generalized, but there is a tendency for higher frequencies of tools made for expedient use than formally produced tools. No diagnostic projectile point style has been isolated for the San Simon branch, although points do fall into two basic categories: a heavy, lateral and diagonally notched type and a lighter, serrated triangular type (Sayles 1945:51). Due to lack of data Sayles does not indicate any temporal distinctions between projectile point styles; however, he remarks that the heavy projectiles are similar to those found in Mimbres branch sites of the upper Gila River and in the vicinity of Gleeson, Arizona (Fulton and Tuthill 1940). The small triangular type resembles that of the Sacaton phase of the Hohokam. The ceramic evidence indicates that during the early phases there was interaction between the Hohokam and San Simon branch. However, the two groups maintained essentially distinct developments until the Cerros phase, when Hohokam traits, such as cremation burial, shell ornaments, and pottery design styles began to appear in the San Simon cultural pattern.

Strong interaction with the Mimbres branch began in the Dos Cabezas phase and continued through the Encinas phase, indicating the Mimbres influence probably played an important role in the development of the San Simon branch. By the Encinas phase, sites are characterized by a blend of Hohokam and Mimbres cultural traits with only minor traces of the San Simon branch pattern persisting (Quinn and Roney 1973:19).

Mimbres branch sites are found along the Mimbres, middle and upper Gila, lower San Francisco, and lower Blue rivers. Sauer and Brand (1930) recorded several Mimbres sites in the San Simon Valley and Mimbres pottery has been found in sites in the Sulphur Spring Valley. The major excavated sites are the Harris Site (Haury 1936b) Mogollon Village (Haury 1936b), Swarts Ruin (Cosgrove and Cosgrove 1932), and Cameron Creek Village (Bradfield 1931), all in the Mimbres drainage. Until approximately A.D. 700 the Mogollon lived in pit house villages in easily defensible mountainous or semi-mountainous locations. After A. D. 700 there was a change to aboveground structures located at lower elevations along valley floors (Martin and Plog 1973).

Phases defined for the Mimbres region are the Georgetown (A.D. 700 to 800), San Francisco (A.D. 800 to 850), Three Circle (A.D. 850 to 900) and Mangus (A.D. 900 to 950). Like the San Simon branch, there is a trend through time from circular to rectangular pit houses. Important ceramic developments include, among others, the appearance of red-on-brown pottery (Sayles 1945; Bullard 1962). Mimbres branch sites appear to be common in the Gila Mountains area (Danson 1957:27, 97-106). Classic (Mangus phase) Mimbres sites have also been found in the Old Hot Springs area 11.2 km south of Safford. These tiny pueblos are the farthest downstream Mimbres sites known (Sauer and Brand 1930:428-29). On the terraces above the Gila

River, Tularosa phase black-on-white pottery known from the Reserve area of New Mexico occurs, and small pueblos with about a dozen rooms have been found in association with mountain redwares dating to around A.D. 1200. Some sites in the San Simon area have been classified as pure Mimbres (Sayles 1945:2), although without further study this can only be considered an initial impression.

Mogollon subsistence patterns have not been the focus of much in-depth research except for investigations at Tularosa Cave in New Mexico (Martin and others 1952). Analysis of vegetal and faunal remains from this site indicate that the Mogollon exploited a wide variety of natural biota on a scale nearly equal to that of domesticated crops. However, San Simon branch sites occur in upper Sonoran and Chihuahuan desert ecosystems, with resources very different from those available in the mountainous Mogollon core area. It would be interesting to discover whether desert adaptation partly determined the basic cultural pattern of the San Simon branch. Sayles (1945) found no direct evidence for agriculture at the two San Simon branch sites he investigated, but inferred such from the presence of numerous ground stone tool kits and habitation features (indicating some permanency). He could not, however, determine the relative importance of agriculture and wild food gathering.

By the 14th century much of the Mogollon area was abandoned while the remaining inhabited portions showed a strong mixture of Mogollon-Hohokam and Mogollon-Anasazi characteristics (McGregor 1965). These influences were already appearing in the Mogollon area by A.D. 100. Johnson (1965) interprets this as the disappearance of the Mogollon and emergence of the "Western Pueblo culture," a syncretism of the three co-traditions. The Bylas sites, AZ V:16:8 and AZ V:16:10, have all been tentatively identified as variants of this culture (Johnson and Wasley 1966).

Hohokam. The Hohokam culture, partially contemporaneous with the Mogollon, developed west of the study area, primarily in the middle Salt and middle Gila valleys. Two basic variants of the Hohokam cultural pattern, based on differing subsistence patterns, have been suggested by Haury (1950): Riverine Hohokam and Desert Hohokam. The former inhabited the major river valleys, practicing canal irrigation agriculture; the latter existed primarily as food gatherers in the desert regions of the Papaguería, with dry-farming agriculture as a secondary pursuit. Safford has been viewed as the easternmost extent of the Riverine Hohokam (Gladwin and Gladwin 1935), with Hohokam occupation evident only in the Gila floodplain where sites are thought to be of Colonial-Classic age (A.D. 700 to 1000) (Tuohy 1960).

From its earliest manifestations around 300 B.C. (Gladwin and others 1937), the Hohokam was a distinctive semiagrarian culture adapted to the arid Southwest desert, occupying much of the Salt and Gila drainages for approximately 1700 years. The material culture of the Riverine Hohokam is characterized, except during the latest Classic period, by permanent habitation sites with a dispersed ranchería settlement pattern, wattle and daub construction, platform mounds, ball courts, irrigation systems, cremation of the dead, red-on-buff painted pottery, full trough metates, and a great array of projectile points. Few small formal tools have been found; rather the trend is toward large cutting, chopping or scraping tools (Haury 1976).

Early research at Hohokam sites in the Gila Basin established a chronological sequence based on correlation with the northern Anasazi and Mogollon chronologies, using tree-ring-dated intrusive pottery. Subsequent work at Snaketown (Haury 1976) and at the Classic period Escalante Ruin (Doyel 1974) has resulted in minor revisions of the original chronology:

Pioneer period	300 B.C. to A.D. 500
Colonial period	A.D. 500 to 900
Sedentary period	A.D. 900 to 1150
Classic period	A.D. 1150 to 1400 or 1450

The origins of the Hohokam culture have been the focus of some controversy. Haury (1976) feels that the Hohokam represent a group pf Mesoamerican immigrants that brought with them the knowledge of irrigation agriculture and that they had no known antecedents in the American Southwest. The primary concentration of the Hohokam was in the Gila and Salt river valleys. However, Hohokam occupation has been found north of the Salt-Gila basin along the Agua Fria and Verde rivers, as far as Flagstaff, east to Safford, west to Yuma and along the Santa Cruz river south of Tucson (Gladwin and Gladwin 1935). It is in the Salt and Gila valleys that the largest permanent habitation sites are found. By the time of the Sedentary period these are marked by large trash mounds and an increasingly sophisticated cultural material assemblage. The Classic period is the focus of a long standing discussion, for it was during this time that widespread adjustments and changes in material culture and settlement pattern occurred. Some of the changes include inhumation of the dead, change from dispersed _rancheriá_ settlements to aboveground stone and mortar contiguous dwellings, compound enclosures, and "great houses" as seen at Pueblo Grande and Casa Grande. The ceramic assemblage is characterized by a shift from red-on-buff pottery to the Saladoan Gila and Tonto polychromes. The most common explanation for this change is that Salado groups from the Tonto Basin moved into the area bearing their own cultural traditions and coexisted with the Hohokam (Haury 1945). Other authors believe there was no invasion or migration. Wasley (1966) and Doyel (1974) view the change as the evolution of forms that the Hohokam were experimenting with in the preceding Sedentary period. Weaver (1972), citing cultural-ecological factors, suggests that change was brought about by the internal evolution of class structure in combination with population pressure and expanded social institutions (Debowski and others 1976:26). Clearly, the issue of cultural change in the Hohokam culture is one that needs further research.

Ootam. The Ootam have been described by DiPeso (1956) and Hayden (1970) as an indigenous population derived from the Cochise culture that inhabited the region of southeastern Arizona and were dwelling in the area when the Hohokam arrived around A.D. 500 (according to DiPeso). DiPeso (1958:5) states that:

> This culture has variously been referred to as the "Red-on-brown culture" or "Dragoon Complex" by Tuthill (1950), the "San Simon Branch of the Hohokam" by Haury....The small village concentrations consisted of individual houses which were generally built, either in pits or as shallow pit houses with or without side entrances. The ceramic tradition consisted of tool polished red-on-brown pottery, brownware and unsmudged redware....The lithic complex was unspecialized and appeared to have certain affinities with the earlier preceramic Cochise Culure...The economy seemed to stress food gathering rather than intensive agriculture and there is no known evidence of the use of complicated irrigation systems such as were utilized by the Hohokam of the Salt-Gila drainage.

After A.D. 1000, the Ootam culture absorbed many Hohokam traits, such as pottery decoration styles and cremation of the dead. Also at this time, states DiPeso, the Ootam were being influenced by the puebloan Mimbres. Around A.D. 1250 to 1300, partly because of climatic factors that disrupted irrigation farming practices, the Hohokam abandoned the area, at which time the Ootam "reasserted" themselves and carried on with a basic culture pattern incorporating elements of Ootam, Hohokam, and Anasazi (DiPeso 1958:567).

The period A.D. 1300 to 1400 was the time of the "great house" builders and a revival of intensive irrigation farming. DiPeso (1958:566) attributes this to a reoccupation by the Hohokam. Regarding the various cultural traits represented at sites in southeastern Arizona, Doyel (1977:6) points out that "it remains to be seen if different groups of people were moving into the area, or the changes in the local culture, whether Ootam or Hohokam, may be explained by participation in a widespread trade and interaction network."

Salado. The upper Gila Valley has many cultural remains identified as Salado. Numerous sites in the San Simon and Sulphur Spring valleys have been investigated that exhibit salient Salado cultural traits,notably the ubiquitous polychrome pottery (Sauer and Brand 1930). Young (1967:81) has noted a "strong concentration of Salado Polychrome that extends out of the Tonto Basin area and up the San Simon drainage toward Chihuahua...." The following information on Salado is drawn from the AEPCO I report (Simpson and Westfall 1978:25-6).

> The Salado complex is a difficult cultural entity to define but the traditional definition includes the following cultural traits: polychrome, black-on-white, polished redware, and corrugated plainware ceramics; puebloan architecture associated with coursed masonry or solid adobe,cliff dwellings, compounds or defense walls; storage pits; sheet rubbish deposition instead of trash mounding; and primary inhumation of the dead (Gladwin 1957:264; Weaver 1976:19). The heartland appears to be the Roosevelt and Tonto Basin region with heavy occupation in Canyon and Cibecue Creeks, the upper Salt River Valley and the Safford Valley. The primary diagnostic trait is the distinctive ceramic assemblage—Pinto, Tonto and Gila Polychromes.

The Salado appeared as a distinct entity by A D 1100 in the mountainous country north of the middle Salt River Valley. By A D 1300 characteristic Salado stylistic traits had appeared in widespread areas of the Southwest.

Much research has concentrated on what constitutes the Salado and its derivations. Opinions have fallen into five main camps (Lindsay and Jennings 1968:4; DiPeso 1974):

1. Western Pueblo: a mixture of Anasazi and Mogollon
2. Mogollon (including Casas Grandes)
3. An indigenous population similar to Sinagua
4. An indigenous population with influences from the Little Colorado cultural tradition
5. An outpost for Casas-Grandes-based _puchteca_.

Salado polychromes have been found on terraces above the Gila River, mainly on sites downstream from Safford. Brown (1973) surveyed 11 sites in the Safford Valley and Pinaleño Mountain foothills (most of them previously known), and excavated within all of them. Brown's research was oriented toward defining the presence and extent of Salado occupation in the Safford region. The results of his research, however, indicated a dominant Point of Pines Mogollon influence at most of the sites, although he found strong influences of Hohokam at the Methodist Church site on th north side of the Gila River. Borwn's study did document the occurrence of Salado Polychromes in the Safford Valley although the reasons for this need to be more fully explored.

Some of the current thinking on Salado links it more closely to Casas Grandes, the large, late prehistoric community in Chihuahua (Young 1967; DiPeso 1974). As LeBlanc and Nelson comment (1976:78), "the founding of Casas Grandes at about A.D. 1150 certainly had enormous effect on much of the Southwest." Gila Polychrome, the hallmark of the Salado culture may have its origin at Casas Grandes, and the dense population of the Safford Valley by A.D. 1300 may have been the result of an exodus from the Casas Grandes area (LeBlanc and Nelson 1976:78).

Apache. For the period A.D. 1400 to 1600, the time between depopulation of the Southwest by the prehistoric inhabitants and the arrival of the Spanish, a gap exists in the cultural record of the area. Few sites are known for this time, during which Apachean groups moved into the area. Although the Spanish explorer Oñate clearly records Apache west of the Rio Grande by 1957 (Wilcox n.d.:20), not until 1680 did the Spanish explorers and missionaries record encounters with the Apache of southeastern Arizona, and even then little was written about settlement and subsistence during this early period. It is known that the Apache were mostly hunters and gatherers, although the Chiricahua Apache in southeastern Arizona did some farming. They moved about seasonally, occupying temporary camps. Therefore, Apache sites characteristically lack traces of architecture or significant numbers of artifacts. They are often recognized solely on the basis of the presence of historic trade goods.

Raiding of sedentary Indians was of prime economic importance (Basso 1971:16), and in the 1750s, with Anglo colonization of the area, Apache raiding and depredations became increasingly violent (Schultz 1964:6).

In 1786 the Apache were brought under control by the Spanish, so that relative peace was maintained until the Mexican War for Independence. After that time, as Spanish control began to break down, Apache raiding and warfare resumed (Schultz 1964).

In 1862 Fort Bowie was established at Apache Pass, between the Dos Cabezas and Chiricahua Mountains. The U.S. Army made peace with the Chiricahua Apache chief Cochise, and the tribes were moved to reservations. However, trouble developed anew with Geronimo, the infamous Chiricahua Apache leader. Sporadic fighting continued until 1886, when Geronimo was captured and sent to prison in Florida, and a large number of Apaches were placed on the San Carlos and White Mountain reservations.

The Apache today are involved in modern economic pursuits, such as forestry and agriculture, although they continue to maintain a tribal social organization.

Euro-American. There are few records of the project area in the 16th and 17th centuries. The first Spanish explorer to pass through the upper Gila area was Coronado in 1540. His army marched from a point near modern Benson, Arizona, northeast to the foot of Eagle Pass, the opening between the Pinaleño and Santa Teresa mountains. At Eagle Pass he discovered the pueblo "Chichilticale."

Coronado was disappointed to find the pueblo destroyed, and a nomadic Gila River tribe living in isolated huts among the ruins. Coronado then crossed a wilderness from Chichilticale to a location near the present town of Bylas and passed through the mountains of eastern Arizona to the Little Colorado River (Wagoner 1975:50-56). There were other Spanish military expeditions into this area, mainly to subdue the Apaches, but these are poorly documunted.

In the early 19th century, American mountain men explored the Gila but they rarely recorded their journeys in great detail (for example, Pattie 1930). During this time, the Apache were fairly peaceful. But in 1833, after a series of disputes with the Spanish, the Apache of eastern Arizona and western New Mexico once again swept down into Sonora. The Chiricahua Trail, used by the Chiricahua, Mimbreño, Mogollonero, Tonto and other Apache bands was a major raiding route. From the Gila River the trail paralleled the San Simon River to the Chihuahua-Sonora boundary line. Because of recurring Apache raids, few Mexicans settled in southeast Arizona (Wagoner 1975:239).

In 1847 the "Army of the West," commanded by General Stephen Kearny, was organized to take New Mexico and California from Mexico. At Santa Fe, the army divided into four parts. One part, the Mormon Battalion led by Lt. Colonel Phillip Cooke, was ordered to open a wagon road to California. This battalion passed through the upper Gila River drainage and south through southern Arizona (Faulk 1973:19). The report of their reconnaissance is the earliest extensive description of the project area (Emory 1848). The battalion reported the Safford Basin to be uninhabited by either Mexican or sedentary Indians. However, by the 1850s and 1860s, Mexicans had become permanent inhabitants of the valley (Poulson and Youngs 1938:3).

The United States Boundary Commission was set up in 1851 to establish the international border between the United States and Mexico. The commission was one of the first organized groups of Americans to enter Arizona for purposes of exploration. A second survey group determined a railroad route through southeastern Arizona between the Dos Cabezas and Chiricahua mountains. At Apache Pass, one member of this expedition stopped to write in his journal his observations of the landscape. These are recorded by Schultz (1964:2):

> ...toward the middle of the plain [are] a series of pools or springs which yield a large supply of water. He found it unpleasant tasting, as it was slightly saline, sulphurous and highly impregnated with decaying vegetation.

Appropriately, the "plain" was named the Sulphur Spring Valley. This valley was once one of the finest stock ranges in the west, but overgrazing and a natural erosion cycle combined to reduce the available forage.

After the Gadsden Purchase was ratified in 1854, Anglo-Apache relations deteriorated rapidly. During the 1860s the upper Gila River was the scene of heavy fighting between Apache and Anglos. In the 1870s Anglos moved onto the original San Carlos Apache Reservation. They took large pieces of the reservation in the Clifton-Morenci area for copper mining, and Mormon farmers pushed into the rich agricultural district of Safford. The new farmers used so much Gila River water that San Carlos Indian farms suffered. During the Geronimo wars, Mormon farmers often were harassed by Apaches passing through the Gila River corridor on their way to raids into Mexico (Williams 1937; Spicer 1962:229-61; Myrick 1975:79).

The railroad and cattle industries were largely responsible for the economic development of the Sulphur Spring and Safford valleys. Willcox began as a railroad camp in 1873 during construction of the Southern Pacific Railroad from Yuma to Deming. In 1880 the railroad reached Deming to meet up with the main SPRR route through the southern United States, and Willcox became an important shipping point for various small towns in the region. The California Gold Rush of 1848 caused a great population influx to the west and with it an increasing demand for beef. Several large ranches sprang up in the Sulphur Spring Valley and southeastern Arizona entered the open range era. Schultz describes the cattle industry that shaped history in the project area (1964:50-1):

> The completion of the Southern Pacific Railroad through the Sulphur Spring Valley in 1880 was a great incentive to the growth of the cattle industry in the area. Not only were the grazing-lands made more readily accessible to prospective cattlemen, but transportation to outside markets was provided. However, beef was in great demand for home consumption at this time. Railroad construction companies, government posts, and mining camps furnished the principal markets in the Territory. Virtually all of the cattle were sold locally or shipped to California until 1885. Between 1881 and 1883 the average price per head advanced from $10 to $30.
>
> Under these favorable conditions, the available range was utilized with amazing speed. Men from all over the United States and from other countries....were attracted to Arizona and during 1883 and 1884 they settled all over the Sulphur Spring Valley, building homes, and stocking the range with cattle.
>
> In 1885 the inevitable happened. The range had been so heavily overgrazed that most of the grass was destroyed and this, combined with the severe drought of that summer resulted in an extremely heavy loss of cattle....The following year ranchers began a new policy--that of selling immature steers to cattle feeders in other parts of the country rather than trying to fatten them on the open range.

The cattle industry generally ebbed and flowed during the years from 1888 to 1905, depending on vagaries of rainfall, Indian raids, and rustlers. By 1911 the open range era ended, when farmers, taking advantage of the 1862 Homestead act, came into the region and obtained restrictions on grazing lands. To summarize:

> During the 85 years of its existence, Willcox has grown from a railroad construction camp, consisting mainly of tents, into a prosperous little city of nearly 2,500 population, with the majority of the growth occurring since World War II. While cattle and irrigation agriculture are the most important industries, mining and the tourist business contribute their share (Schultz 1964:118).

CHAPTER 3

THE SURVEY, RECOMMENDATIONS, AND GENERAL RESEARCH DESIGN

Introduction

As with AEPCO I, the AEPCO II survey was exploratory in nature. The primary intent was to identify and evaluate sites occurring within the proposed transmission line R-O-W corridor. A problem facing all aspects of the survey and mitigation program was the lack of a regional archaeological and ecological synthesis for southeastern Arizona. Previous archaeological research has focused on specific large archaeological sites. Analysis of stratified remains has been the primary concern of past investigations, with attempts made to establish a regional perspective based on inferences from a fairly limited data base. Environmental studies have also lacked a regional perspective because the study area is a mixture of federal, state, and private lands. While detailed data are often available for federal lands, other areas have received little or no attention.

Given this lack of a firm data base on which to develop a research design, the survey used a basic cultural-environmental approach. Objectives were to obtain a complete inventory of site characteristics, vegetation communities, faunal data, and physiographic features for the areas transected by the R-O-W. A full description of the 27 sites recorded on the survey will be found in Volume III of the AEPCO Project report (Simpson and others 1978). A condensed version of this information is presented in Table 12.

Upon completion of the survey, recommendations were submitted to AEPCO and the Safford District, Bureau of Land Management for site protection and data recovery, together with cost estimates for a complete program to mitigate adverse effects on sites. Adjustments in construction design were made by AEPCO to lessen the impact on cultural resources. The Bureau of Land Management drew up stipulations to further protect sites scheduled to be affected by the construction.

Logistics and Methods

The primary concern of the survey was the location, mapping, and recording of all archaeological resources within the 30 m wide R-O-W corridor and in buffer zones around maximum impact areas. The R-O-W corridor and access roads survey began March 8 and ended April 15, 1977. A total of 90.1 km from Dos Condado Substation to the Apache Electric Station was covered. Twenty-seven sites were located; 25 were prehistoric sites and two were early 20th century historic ranch sites. Carol Coe acted as Field Supervisor, assisted by Anne Rieger. Jon S. Czaplicki was Project Director.

The survey was conducted on foot with little difficulty, since the proposed corridor followed the R-O-W of an existing 115 kV line. Access roads were flagged by BLM personnel. Upon arriving in the survey area one vehicle was left at a point the crew felt confident it could reach in a day's walk. A second vehicle was then driven to the point where the previous day's survey had ended. Daily coverage averaged about 9.6 km, depending on terrain, weather, and number, size, and complexity of archaeological resources.

Site Recognition and Recording

The fundamental unit identified at the survey level is the site. A site can be defined as any place, of any size, where there are found traces of human occupation or activity (Hole and Heizer 1965:59). The majority of sites in the project area have low artifact densities dispersed over a deflated surface. Because this type of site was so common in the Greenlee-Dos Condado segment, it was anticipated that similar sites would be encountered on the Dos Condado-Apache segment. Therefore, the criteria for site recognition used for the AEPCO I survey was maintained for AEPCO II. If dispersed artifact scatters had been excluded, investigation would have been limited to large camps or habitation sites. Also, since much information is needed on small, limited activity sites, the survey decided to examine these low density lithic scatters and sherd and lithic scatters as examples of prehistoric human activity in the project area.

To record multicomponent or multifeature sites, the standard ASM site survey form was used; it is designed to accommodate the following questions (Canouts 1975:vii):

1. The cultural and temporal affiliation of the site
2. The past activities represented at the site
3. The nature of site deposits (stratified or surficial)
4. The degree to which past human activities could be determined to have affected the environmental setting
5. The degree and nature of postoccupation site disturbance
6. The elegibility of the site for inclusion into the National Register of Historic Places
7. The relationship of the site to others in the region.

A number of sites encountered on the survey lacked the density and complexity that would warrant recording on the detailed ASM site survey form. Such sites were small surface sherd and lithic scatters and chipping stations. These single component, single feature sites were recorded on a short form developed for the survey (Figure 14).

ARIZONA STATE MUSEUM
Archaeological Survey

Short Form

ASM No.____________________

Recorded by ____________________ Land Ownership________________

Date____________________ Other Map Reference________________

Project____________________ Site Field No.________________

Photographs B/W No(s)____________________ Color No(s)________________

State____________________ County________________

Quad and Series____________________

T________R________S________, ______ ¼ of the ____ ¼,

UTM Zone______ Easting________________ Northing________________

Description of how to get to site:

Elevation____________________ Dimensions of site________________

Boundaries: Natural____________________ Arbitrary________________

Vegatation:

Topography:

Components:

Material Culture:

Disturbance:

Comments:

Figure 14. Arizona State Museum AEPCO survey short form.

Some subjectivity entered into the decision to record a site on the long form, short form, or as an isolated feature or group of artifacts. "Short form" sites were generally small, isolated limited activity sites and isolated artifacts which, while appearing negligible in themselves, are seen as important when viewed as components of a widespread pattern of prehistoric land use. Isolated artifacts and features were marked with a symbol on aerial photographs with pertinent locational information and detailed artifact assemblage descriptions recorded in field journals. These aerial photographs, provided by Burns and McDonnell, Inc., engineers, contained both plan and profile views of the R-O-W centerline. AEPCO did not contract for recording and mapping of sites or site boundaries outside the R-O-W corridor, but it was always noted when site boundaries extended beyond the corridor, and arbitrary (buffer zone) and true site boundaries were carefully distinguished on site maps. Crew members obtained information on natural site boundaries outside the R-O-W when necessary to assess a site's elegibility for nomination to the National Register of Historic Places.

Site Collections

It is the policy of the Arizona State Museum to make few surface collections on an initial survey. Indiscriminate collection could literally remove a site. However, as the cultural traditions present in the project area were so diverse and the crew members were not familiar with all artifact types, samples of possibly diagnostic artifacts were occasionally collected. In such a case, the location of each collected artifact was plotted on the aerial site maps by using a Brunton compass and measuring the distance from a fixed point, usually a proposed or existing tower location. This was done to preserve surface context for future investigations.

Archaeological Resources of the Dos Condado-Apache Segment

The survey crew located and recorded 27 sites within the Dos Condado-Apache transmission line corridor. One site, AZ CC:13:6 had been previously recorded in 1956 by Emil W. Haury for the Arizona State Museum.

Only five sites were found in the 26 km segment from Dos Condado Substation in the San Simon Basin to the lower bajadas of the Pinaleño Mountains. However, many isolated artifacts were found in this segment; these will be discussed in a later section. Twelve sites were found in the 19 km segment crossing the Pinaleño Mountains' upper bajadas, three in the 10 km segment along the Dos Cabezas' lower bajadas, and seven in the 21 km portion from the interface of the Dos Cabezas and the Sulphur Spring Valley to the eastern edge of Willcox Playa. No sites were found in the segment crossing the Willcox Playa to the Apache station. The prehistoric sites could not be easily placed into a definite category since it was not always apparent if, for example, sherd and lithic scatters on the surface were indicative of a short-term camp (limited activity site) or of a more permanent one containing subsurface features (habitation sites). Additionally, the R-O-W corridor sometimes passed through only a small portion of a site, in which case, the area transected would not be representative of the site as a whole. For example, at AZ CC:9:2, the survey crew noted no surface pottery within the R-O-W, which suggested that the site represented a preceramic Archaic occupation. However, during data recovery, several sherds were found immediately outside the R-O-W. Therefore, sites were described by their surface remains (lithic scatter, sherd and lithic scatter, sherd and lithic scatter with ground stone) within the R-O-W, with notations made regarding possible cultural depth. All sites recorded are listed by arbitrary zones in Table 12. A full description of each site may be found in Volume III of the AEPCO Project report (Simpson and others 1978).

Historic Sites

Ranch buildings, evidence of historic Anglo activity, were found particularly in the vicinity of Willcox. Built in the early 20th century, they are now uninhabited and are situated outside the impact zone.

Prehistoric Sites

Habitation Sites

These are characterized by evidence of settlement over an extended period of time with a variety of activities carried out at the location. Habitation sites were defined in the field by evidence of cultural depth and unusually dense, complex artifact assemblages. Three sites were recorded as habitation sites: AZ CC:6:6, AZ CC:6:7 and AZ CC:13:6. Although house structures are not visible on the surface, the presence of sherd and lithic concentrations, deep bedrock mortars, abundant grinding implements, and cultural depth all indicate sites of some permanence. Pit houses could be present beneath the surface, or the sites could be semipermanent camps. However, test excavations would be necessary to determine this.

Limited Activity and Multiple Use Sites

The majority of sites encountered on the Dos Condado-Apache survey are difficult to place into specific functional categories. Many appear to be sites where a number of different activities were carried out, but one cannot state with assurance what these activities were. This is especially true of the larger, dispersed artifact scatters predominantly composed of flaked lithics yet with grinding implements in localized portions of the site. For the most part, sites represented only by a flaked stone assemblage appear to be lithic procurement and tool manufacture sites. However, tool _use_ is also indicated at some of these sites. With the exception of AZ CC:6:6, AZ CC:6:7, and AZ CC:10:6, the majority of sites in the Pinaleño Mountains upper bajadas appear to be locations where the abundant lithic raw materials were exploited. AZ CC:10:11 is a large quarry site noteworthy for its distinctive fine-grained purple-brown felsite. AZ CC:10:12 - 15 are smaller lithic scatters containing discrete concentrations that may be the remnants of chipping stations. Generally these sites in the Pinaleño upper bajadas strongly indicate use of this physiographic zone primarily as a source for lithic raw material.

Table 12. Archaeological Resources: AEPCO Dos Condado-Apache R-O-W Corridor

Site Number	Field Designation	Physiographic Zone	Landform	Type of Boundary	Site Dimensions (in meters)	Site Type	Grinding Implements	Lithic Artifacts			Ceramics		Features				Historic Material
								Flakes	Cores	Tools	Plain	Decorated	Chipping Stations	Rock cluster	Hearth	Bedrock mortars	
AZ CC:2:60	201	San Simon Basin	terrace	natural	1 m	isolated hearth											
AZ CC:6:2	202	San Simon Basin	terrace	arbitrary	95 m x 60 m	lithic scatter		X	X	UF							
AZ CC:6:3	203	San Simon/ Pinaleño baj.	terrace	arbitrary	173 m x 60 m	lithic scatter		X	X	UF, CT							
AZ CC:6:4	204	Pinaleño lower baj.	bajada	natural	5 m x 2 m	lithic scatter		X	X				X				
AZ CC:6:5	205	Pinaleño lower baj.	bajada rdg	natural	20 m x 14 m	lithic scatter		X	X	UFR							
AZ CC:6:6	206	Pinaleño upper baj.	bajada rdg	arbitrary	333 m x 60 m	habitation	X	X	X	PP, CT, UF	X		X			X	
AZ CC:6:7	207	Pinaleño upper baj.	bajada rdg	natural	214 m x 195 m	habitation	X	X	X	UF	X		X			X	
AZ CC:10:6	208	Pinaleño upper baj.	bajada ridge	arbitrary	128 m x 60 m	lithic scatter with ground stone	X	X	X	UF, PP							
AZ CC:10:7	209	Pinaleño upper baj.	bajada ridge	natural	34 m x 90 m	bedrock mortars w/ lithics & sherds	X	X	X	UF	X					X	
AZ CC:10:8	211	Pinaleño upper baj.	bajada rdg	natural	92 m x 104 m	lithic scatter	X	X	X	BF, UF							

Table 12. Archaeological Resources: AEPCO Dos Condado-Apache R-O-W Corridor (continued)

Site Number	Field Designation	Physiographic Zone	Landform	Type of Boundary	Site Dimensions (in meters)	Site Type	Grinding Implements	Lithic Artifacts: Flakes	Lithic Artifacts: Cores	Lithic Artifacts: Tools	Ceramics: Plain	Ceramics: Decorated	Features: Chipping Stations	Features: Rock cluster	Features: Hearth	Features: Bedrock mortars	Historic Material
AZ CC:10:9	212	Pinaleño upper baj.	bajada ridge	natural	54 m x 86 m	lithic scatter (quarry ?)		X	X	UF, UFR			2		X		
AZ CC:10:10	213	Pinaleño upper baj.	bajada rdg	arbitrary	123 m x 60 m	lithic scatter		X	X								
AZ CC:10:11	214	Pinaleño upper baj.	bajada rdg	arbitrary	862 m x 60 m	lithic scatter (quarry)	X	X	X	UF, UFR			X				
AZ CC:10:12	216	Pinaleño upper baj.	bajada rdg	arbitrary	193 m x 60 m	lithic scatter		X	X								
AZ CC:10:13	217	Pinaleño upper baj.	bajada ridge	arbitrary	178 m x 60 m	lithic scatter		X	X	utilized core			X				
AZ CC:10:14	218	Pinaleño upper baj.	bajada rdg	arbitrary	374 m x 60 m	lithic scatter		X	X	BF, UF			5+				
AZ CC:10:15	219	Pinaleño upper baj.	bajada rdg	arbitrary	589 m x 60 m	lithic scatter		X	X	RF, CT	X						
AZ CC:9:2	220	Dos Cabezas lower bajada	lower baj. slope	arbitrary	380 m x 60 m	lithic scatter w/ ground stone (Cochise ?)	X	X	X	PP, BF, Hs, UF							
AZ CC:9:3	221	Dos Cabezas lower bajadas	lower baj. slope	arbitrary	148 m x 60 m	lithic scatter w/ ground stone (Cochise?)	X	X	X	PP, S, Hs BF, UF	X				X		

TABLE 12. Archaeological Resources: AEPCO Dos Condado-Apache R-O-W Corridor (continued)

Site Number	Field Designation	Physiographic Zone	Landform	Type of Boundary	Site Dimensions (in meters)	Site Type	Grinding Implements	Lithic Artifacts			Ceramics		Features				Historic Material
								Flakes	Cores	Tools	Plain	Decorated	Chipping Stations	Rock Cluster	Hearth	Bedrock mortars	
AZ CC:9:4	222	Dos Cabezas lower bajadas	lower baj. slope	natural	225 m x 125 m	Historic ranch w/ lithic scater	X	X	X								X
AZ CC:13:6	CC:13:6	Willcox Playa dunes	high dunes	arbitrary	373 m x 60 m	habitation reported by Haury 1953	X	X	X	PP,Hs, S. BF	X	X		X			
AZ CC:13:11	223	Willcox Playa dunes	low dunes	arbitrary	105 m x 60 m	sherd & lithic scatter	X	X	X	PP,S UF	X	X					
AZ CC:13:12	224	Willcox Playa dunes	low dunes	arbitrary	680 m x 60 m	lithic scatter	X	X	X	BF	X			X			
AZ CC:13:13	228	Sulphur Spring Basin	flat grass-land	natural	130 m x 70 m	Historic ranch											X
AZ CC:13:14	225	Sulphur Spring Basin	flat grass-land	natural	52 m x 35 m	lithic scatter	X	X	X	UF, UFR							
AZ CC:13:15	227	Sulphur Spring Basin	flat grass-land	natural	270 m x 85 m	sherd scatter					X						
AZ CC:13:16	226	Sulphur Spring Basin	low dunes	natural	145 m x 47 m	sherd & lithic scatter	X	X	X		X						

BF = biface
baj. = bajada
CT = core tool
Hs = hammerstone
PP = projectile point
rdg = ridge
RF = retouched flake
S = scraper
UF = utilized flake
UFR = unifacial retouch

Sites in the Dos Cabezas lower bajadas, Willcox Playa dunes, and Sulphur Spring Valley floor exhibit evidence of a greater variety of activities than do the lithic scatter sites of the Pinaleño upper bajadas. AZ CC:9:2 is a unique site that seems to represent a broad range of activities including tool use and refurbishing, gathering and processing of vegetal foods, and hunting. No habitation features were noted within the R-O-W; however, testing is needed to determine if any are present. Sites in the Willcox Playa dunes, AZ CC:9:3, AZ CC:13:11 and 16, contain ceramics and ground stone, but few lithic artifacts. Primary lithic reduction at these sites is not indicated, possibly because of the paucity of suitable raw material in the immediate vicinity, or because of sample bias. Gathering activities, plant processing, and perhaps some hunting may have occurred at these sites. Sites on the Sulphur Spring Valley floor, AZ CC:13:14 and 15, occur in what was formerly desert grassland. These are characterized by sparse, dispersed sherd scatters with few lithics and little ground stone. The extent of hunting at these sites is uncertain; they probably were primarily locales of plant gathering and processing.

Isolated Artifacts

Lithic cores, flakes, and tools, seemingly randomly distributed, were found primarily in the segment from Dos Condado to Redtail Substation. The transmission line corridor begins at San Simon Basin, transects the lower and upper bajadas of the Pinaleño Mountains, and curves around the southern end of the Pinaleños to Redtail Substation, which is situated on the lower bajada of the Dos Cabezas just above the the Sulphur Spring Valley. Very few isolated artifacts were found in the R-O-W corridor from Redtail Substation to Apache Electric Station but instead were largely confined to a small portion of the Dos Cabezas lower bajadas. None were found within the R-O-W in the Sulphur Spring Basin or Willcox Playa. For ease in recording, isolated artifacts were listed as they occurred between tower spans (for example, "between Towers B-36 and B37") and their location pinpointed on aerial photographs. The artifact types, frequencies, and locations are tabulated in Volume III of this series (Simpson and others 1978).

A total of 176 isolated artifacts were recorded on survey. In gross categories, there were 67 cores, 41 debitage flakes, 17 miscellaneous worked pieces, and 51 tools (Table 13). The last category includes unretouched but utilized flakes, utilized cores, flakes with unifacial or bifacial retouch, and projectile points. The majority of items (68.8 percent) were made from fine-grained materials such as chert, chalcedony, agate, jasper, and quartz. Rhyolite comprised 11.9 percent, basalt 3.4 percent, quartzite 4.0 percent, obsidian 1.1 percent and unidentified types 10.8 percent (Table 14).

The artifact total was arbitrarily stratified according to occurrence in basic physiographic zones (San Simon Basin, Pinaleño lower bajadas [near Redtail], Pinaleño upper bajadas, Pinaleño lower bajadas [along Route 666], and Dos Cabezas lower bajadas) to determine if a correlation existed between artifact/material type and environmental setting. No obvious patterning could

Table 13. Isolated artifacts: Frequency by artifact type

	Cores	Flakes	Tools	Misc.	Total
San Simon Basin	17	4	8	3	32
Pinaleño lower bajadas (Route 666)	28	21	25	14	88
Pinaleño upper bajadas	19	13	12	0	44
Pinaleño lower bajadas (Redtail area)	2	2	3	0	7
Dos Cabezas lower bajadas	1	1	3	0	5
Totals	67	41	51	17	176

Table 14. Isolated artifacts: Frequency by material type

	Silicates	Rhyolite	Basalt	Quartz-ite	Obsidian	Uniden-tified	Total
San Simon Basin	26	4	0	1	1	0	32
Pinaleño lower bajadas (Route 666)	55	11	2	4	0	16	88
Pinaleño upper bajadas	35	6	2	0	0	1	44
Pinaleño lower bajadas (Redtail area)	3	0	1	1	1	1	7
Dos Cabezas lower bajadas	2	0	1	1	0	1	5
Totals	121	21	6	7	2	19	176

be discerned; the distribution of artifacts and material types was relatively consistent across physiographic strata. However, the total number of artifacts in two zones was so low (Pinaleño-Redtail: 7, Dos Cabezas: 5) as to negate a statistically valid interpretation. However, these zones exhibited a high frequency of tools comprising 29 percent of the observed isolated artifacts. These were, for the most part, flakes with a minimum of modification, apparently fashioned for expedient use at a given time.

While little can be said regarding the isolated artifacts, they are considered significant because they are evidence of geographical continuity of prehistoric groups in the area. The absence of sites along the segment from AZ CC:6:4 to AZ CC:6:5 may be explained in part by the restricted path of the narrow R-O-W transect (sites may occur outside the R-O-W), and the comparatively poor availability of lithic resources in this particular geographic area. The occurrence of isolated artifacts does, however, indicate a broad-based pattern of land use by the prehistoric inhabitants at one time.

Significance of the Archaeological Resources

The concept of archaeological significance involves consideration of both research and resource management problems. For this study, three areas of significance are considered: legal, historic, and scientific significance.

Legal Significance

The federal government has established one important measure of significance in the "Procedures for the Protection of Historic And Cultural Properties" developed by the Advisory Council on Historic Preservation (U.S. Department of the Interior, National Park Service 1974):

> The quality of significance in American history, architecture, archeology, and culture is present in districts, sites, buildings, structures, and objects of State and local importance that possess integrity of location, design, setting, materials, workmanship, feeling and association and:
> (1) That are associated with events that have made a significant contribution to the broad patterns of our history; or
> (2) That are associated with the lives of persons significant in our past; or
> (3) That embody the distinctive characteristics of a type, period, or method of construction, or that represent the work of a master, or that possess high artistic values, or that represent significant and distinguishable entity whose components may lack individual distinct-tion; or
> (4) That have yielded, or may be likely to yield information important in prehistory or history.

This definition, particularly the fourth clause, is used to determine the elegibility of archaeological remains for nomination to the National Register of Historic Places. Six of the sites recorded in the AEPCO II survey were recommended to the Bureau of Land Management, Safford District office for nomination to the Register. These are AZ CC:6:6, AZ CC:6:7, AZ CC:10:6, AZ CC:9:2, AZ CC:13:6, and AZ CC:10:11. The first five are large, stratified (or shallow, but complex) habitation sites evidencing occupation by early desert Archaic groups. Some also have indications of occupation by later Hohokam and Mogollon groups. Their significance lies in the fact that limited research has been done on early Cochise period sites, and the available evidence has provided an incomplete knowledge of subsistence and settlement adaptations through time. We have limited data on which to base premises of why the Cochise culture evolved as it did from the general southwestern desert culture, and even less is understood of the presumed development of Cochise into Mogollon. Additionally, much of the debate regarding indigenous groups in southern Arizona before the appearance of the Hohokam cultural pattern hinges on the assumption that Cochise groups became these indigeneous people. Since several of the large habitation sites contain buried Cochise materials underlying surface deposits of pottery, they have the potential for contributing information to help resolve these problems of prehistoric cultural development.

The significance of AZ CC:10:11, a large quarry site, lies in its uniqueness; no other major quarry sites have been recorded for this general area in southeastern Arizona. The site's enormous size, density, and complexity of remains indicate continuous use over a long period of time. The site has the potential to supply information on the lithic technology of desert Archaic groups and later groups in southern Arizona, an area of research that only recently has been intensively studied (see Huckell 1973).

A determination of legal significance in part rests upon a determination of the historic and scientific significance of a site (or sites), which are discussed below. Legal significance, in itself, is not an expression of qualities inherent in archaeological resources, but a reminder that such qualities affect the management strategies appropriate to those resources.

Scientific and Historical Significance

Historical significance concerns the potential of cultural resources for providing information on specific cultural patterns and periods. Scovill, Gordon, and Anderson (1972:20) state that "cultural resources are historically significant if they provide a typical or well-preserved example of a prehistoric tribe, period of time, or category of human activity." Scientific significance is the "potential for using cultural resources to establish reliable generalizations concerning past societies and cultures and deriving explanations for the differences and similarities between them (Scovill, Gordon, and Anderson 1972:20).

In this respect, every archaeological entity is significant, not simply because it is unique and non-renewable, but because it forms part of a sample or data base necessary for testing anthropological generalizations. The assessment of scientific worth is dependent on such factors as:

> (1) the relative abundance of the resources to be affected; (2) the degree to which specific resources and situations are confined to the project area; (3) the cultural and environmental relationship of the archaeology of the project area to the surrounding culture province or provinces; (4) the variety of evidence for human activities and their environmental surroundings that is confined in the project or program area; (5) the range of research topics to which the resources may contribute; and (6) specific deficiencies in current knowledge that study of these resources may correct (Scovill, Gordon, and Anderson 1972:21).

The 27 sites found on the AEPCO II survey fulfill the criteria for historical significance in that they have potential to yield information that may fill numerous gaps in our knowledge of patterns of settlement and subsistence during the desert Archaic period and the later Mogollon and Hohokam occupation. Several research problems pertinent to the historical and scientific significance of the AEPCO II cultural resources are discussed below

Significance of the AEPCO II Archaeological Resources

The study area is one of intercultural contact among several major prehistoric southwestern traditions. Such an area offers an excellent opportunity to study processes of culture change through time. The area lacks a comprehensive culture-historical framework integrating the various manifestations of cultural traditions. The presence of Hohokam, Salado, and Mimbres influence is well documented for the area, yet the precise nature of this influence has not been determined. Quinn and Roney (1973:41) make pertinent observations:

> Another significant aspect...is an apparent superposition of Hohokam and Mimbres branch traits upon an indigenous base. The indigenous people were certainly subjected to strong outside influence, but the form of that influence and reasons for acceptance of various aspects of Hohokam and Mimbres branch cultural elements are unexplored. To date, archaeological research in the Southwest has focused upon "core areas" of major cultural groups. Little is known of the cultural processes operative in peripheral areas.

While it is generally recognized that a strictly historical approach is inadequate for modern research, all studies of cultural process rest on control of culture history. It is known that different groups inhabit the region at different time periods but contemporaneous occupation has yet to be proven. In the absence of datable wood and clear-cut ceramic styles that enable precise coordination of temporal and spatial relationships (as for example, in the Anasazi region), other methods of determining these relationships must be developed. Current knowledge about the region's prehistory has been gathered in bits and pieces over the decades and only now is research attempting to accomplish systematic studies of prehistoric settlement and subsistence patterns, resource exploitation, and general cultural ecology. This approach emphasizes functional and behavioral considerations as described by Binford (1962), in contrast to distinctions based on trait comparisons. Such lines of inquiry are applicable to sites encountered in the AEPCO transmission line R-O-W, since the majority are surface scatters of lithic debris with few or no diagnostic artifacts. With the absence of recognizable traits, analysis must then focus on functional studies. A review of previous archaeology reveals a dearth of detailed information needed to reconstruct the entire range of activities at a site. If it is possible to identify and define specific tasks at limited activity sites (for example, lithic reduction to produce tools), it may be possible to correlate these with activities at multiple activity sites (large camps and habitations) that do contain diagnostic attributes, for eventual synthesis into a cultural-historical tradition. This then permits more sophisticated interpretation of geographically and temporally broad patterns of behavior.

Although the culture history of the area has been outlined, several important questions remain unanswered, attesting to the archaeological significance of sites in the region. A major problem is cultural continuity. Little is known of the transition from the Paleo-Indian period with its postulated economic reliance on big game hunting to the Cochise period with emphasis on gathering wild foods and hunting smaller game. Sayles and Antevs (1941) postulate a heavy reliance on wild food resources during the earliest (Sulphur Spring) stage, since the majority of artifacts were milling stones and no projectile points were found. The analysis was largely limited to a consideration of variation in artifact inventories, through time, with little attempt at reconstructing prehistoric behavior beyond the inferential level. Sayles' study was significant because it provided a starting point and frame of reference for later studies. However, specific questions about the reasons for site variation both in time and space remain to be explored. Quinn and Roney (1973:39) suggest that the Cochise culture followed a pattern of transhumance, carrying out different activities at different sites throughtout the year. The resulting pattern of site variability could be related to seasonal exploitation of various ecological niches.

A second research problem is the previously discussed role of maize in the Cochise culture, as pointed out by Whalen (1971). The questions of why the Cochise people apparently did not take advantage of maize when it was first introduced, and what the degree of dependence upon agriculture was compared to hunting and gathering in the later stages remain unanswered. Pit house villages are commonly associated with agriculture. Sayles (1941) notes that pit houses did not appear until the later San Pedro stage, when, based on changes in the ground stone tool kit, the Cochise culture appears to have settled down to a more sedentary way of life with an economy based on agriculture. Cochise culture sites have been observed near the Gila River in the vicinity of Safford and within the San Simon and Sulphur Spring valleys, yet no Cochise agricultural site is known to have been investigated.

In the revised Cochise culture report (Sayles and others n.d.), no attempt was made to point out specific analogies between the Cochise culture and other groups identified with the Desert culture other than the relationship with Ventana Cave where the Californian San Dieguito-Amargosa sequence is present (Haury 1950). Since the genesis of the Desert culture concept, several authors have tried to maintain a regional perspective when considering preceramic cultural remains (Irwin-Williams (1967, n.d.; Rogers 1958; Haury 1950). They recognized the fallacy of considering one geographical area as culturally distinct from another because of a lack of corroborating "hallmark" artifact types. As was mentioned in the previous chapter, environmental adaptation produces distinct artifact assemblages that do not always conform to basic cultural patterns. The "Cochise Basic Pattern" described by Sayles and Antevs (1941) lists certain artifact and site characteristics that should identify a site as Cochise. Many of the investigated sites in the AEPCO I R-O-W, however, do not conform to this basic pattern. Further, specific chronological or cultural affiliations could only be tentatively defined on the survey. On the one hand, many of the sites found in the R-O-W contain only a few "hallmark" artifacts of Cochise culture, on the other hand, they exhibit many characteristics of the Amargosa material culture found in Ventana Cave (Haury 1950). It is hoped that study of the artifact assemblages from the AEPCO II sites may shed some new light on the problem of Cochise-Amargosa relationships and the concept of the Desert culture.

The transition from a postulated hunting and gathering based economy to one based on agriculture forms the basis for the hypothesis that the Cochise culture developed into Mogollon (Sayles and Antevs 1941). Quinn and Roney (1973:40) observe that:

> ...there is evidently an unbroken development from a simple hunting and gathering economy to a relatively complex agriculturally based economy. A number of important adjustments are expected to accompany this transition (Martin and Plog 1973:271). As agricultural resources became important subsistence items, major changes in patterns of environmental exploitation and settlement would probably result. Decreasing emphasis on gathering activities would reduce the need for seasonal migration and result in the development of permanent or semi-permanent settlements.

Related to this problem of cultural transition is the question of the identity of the ceramic-producing people that developed from the Cochise culture. We have already discussed the possibility of Mogollon development out of this base. Gladwin (1957) suggests that the Cochise people became the Mogollon, and that knowledge of pottery-making was brought in by Mexican groups from the south. DiPeso (1958) feels that Cochise developed into the indigenous Ootam of the region. This discussion demonstrates how problems dealing with cultural transition are some of the most difficult to solve.

Another problem concerns the San Simon branch. As indicated previously, aspects of the San Simon branch cultural pattern need to be clarified and explained. Sites found along the Dos Condado-Apache segment near the Dos Cabezas Mountains occur near the San Simon Village type site (Sayles 1945). A few of the sites encountered (for example AZ CC:13:6 and 11) contained a few San Simon branch type sherds in addition to a scattering of lithic debris. Such sites as well as others with no diagnostic ceramics appear to be locations of limited activity rather than permanent habitation (except AZ CC:13:6). The activities performed at these locations and their relationships to the village sites are not clearly understood. It is possible that some of these may represent Cochise sites, considering their proximity to the Gold Gulch site (AZ CC:10:2) (Huckell 1973).

With the end of the Encinas phase of the San Simon branch (about A.D. 1200), a multiplicity of transitional, shifting elements are again present, including both Salado and Casas Grandes traits. There is question as to whether this presence is due to migration, trade, or diffusion of ideas. But since none of the sites encountered in the Dos Condado-Apache survey seem to contain evidence for any of these phenomena, little further consideration can be given to this problem.

Finally, there is no substantial archaeological or historical information for the period between the postulated Salado presence in the area and the settlement of the area by Apache and Europeans. Simpson and others (1978:47) state: "research on this time gap, particularly on the entrance of the Athapaskan peoples into the area, would be valuable, not only from a cultural-historical standpoint, but would also provide information on culture change, stability, abandonment, and interaction between groups."

Due to the nondiagnostic nature of the majority of sites found on the survey, the contribution towards finding answers to cultural-historical questions may not be substantial. Research is focused on understanding the functions of sites with lithic scatters and sherd and lithic scatters, as well as more complex artifact assemblages. Localized studies of resource exploitation may be the key to understanding such sites. Analysis focusing on lithic reduction and tool manufacture, evidence of tool use, and availability of raw materials can be used to understand site specialization. Data on the availability of plant and animal resources also contribute to this understanding. It may be possible to isolate discrete technological traditions, postulate their cultural affiliation, and thereby draw general conclusions concerning cultural processes through time. Defining temporal attributes and sequences at sites is crucial to studies concerned with cultural processes. Due to the restricted nature of the data base such an ambitious task may not now be possible, but by contributing to the existing body of data such a synthesis may eventually be realized.

Recommendations for Site Preservation and Data Recovery

Following completion of the survey, recommendations for site protection and data recovery were developed based on an evaluation of site significance and an assessment of direct and indirect construction impacts. These recommendations were submitted to AEPCO and the Safford District BLM archaeologist in order that immediate decisions could be made regarding mitigation of adverse impact to cultural resources. These recommendations and the rationale for selection of sites for data recovery are summarized below.

Recommendations for sites found during the R-O-W survey were made with two major goals in mind: (1) the preservation of those sites considered to be in themselves highly significant cultural resources and (2) the preservation of information through avoidance or data recovery from a sample of sites representing the range of variability found on the survey. Four options were considered for each of the 27 archaeological sites (Coe 1977:12). These and site-specific data are listed in Table 15: (1) testing/minimizing construction impacts/data recovery/monitoring, (2) data recovery, (3) no data recovery/monitoring, (4) no data recovery/no monitoring.

Testing/Minimizing Construction Impacts/Data Recovery/Monitoring

This option was considered for five sites recommended for inclusion on the National Register of Historic Places: AZ CC:6:6 and 7, and AZ CC:10:6, AZ CC:9:2, and AZ CC:13:6. (A sixth site AZ CC:10:11 was later added to this list, when the true complexity of the site was assessed during the data recovery phase). These all have dense surface cultural remains which are suggestive of long-term use or habitation (Coe 1977:12). To allow AEPCO to arrive at a realistic management decision, testing, in order to more completely assess site significance and excavation cost, was recommended prior to making mitigation plans. Surface collection and backhoe trenching were performed at each of these sites. The tests revealed extensive subsurface cultural deposits at AZ CC:6:6 and 7. AZ CC:10:6 and AZ CC:9:2 revealed little or no artifact depth within the R-O-W, although the density of the artifact scatter and discrete concentrations of artifacts outside the corridor indicate a strong likelihood of intensive prehistoric utilization elsewhere on the sites. Testing at AZ CC:13:6 revealed no cultural depth within the corridor, although intensive occupation of the dune crest immediately west is apparent. Additional recommendations for avoidance, construction restrictions, and site monitoring

Table 15. Recommendations for minimizing impact on cultural resources

Field Number	ASM Number	Data Recovery	No Data Recovery	Monitor	No Monitor	National Register
201	AZ CC:2:60		X		X	
202	AZ CC:6:2		X		X	
203	AZ CC:6:3	X				
204	AZ CC:6:4		X		X	
205	AZ CC:6:5		X		X	
206	AZ CC:6:6					X
207	AZ CC:6:7					X
208	AZ CC:10:6	X				X
209	AZ CC:10:7		X		X	
211	AZ CC:10:8			X		
212	AZ CC:10:9			X		
213	AZ CC:10:10		X		X	
214	AZ CC:10:11	X				X
216	AZ CC:10:12		X		X	
217	AZ CC:10:13	X				
218	AZ CC:10:14	X				
219	AZ CC:10:15	X				X
220	AZ CC:9:2	X				X
221	AZ CC:9:3			X		
222	AZ CC:9:4		X		X	
223	AZ CC:13:11	X				
224	AZ CC:13:12			X		
CC:13:6	13:6	X				X
228	AZ CC:13:13		X		X	
225	AZ CC:13:14	X				
227	AZ CC:13:15	X				
226	AZ CC:13:16	X				

---

were drawn up for these five sites and submitted to AEPCO and the Safford District BLM. As a result, AZ CC:6:6 and 7 were avoided completely by construction, and heavy equipment was restricted to the R-O-W corridor at AZ CC:10:6, AZ CC:9:2, and AZ CC:13:6.

Data Recovery

Based on survey recommendations eight sites were originally selected for data recovery (Coe 1977:13). After testing at the aforementioned five sites, three of these were also slated for data recovery, since it was not feasible to alter AEPCO's construction plans. These sites represent the more significant archaeological resources within each of the physiographic stratum defined for the survey. Along with the five sites recommended for the National Register of Historic Places,they provide a representative sample of the cultural resources found within the R-O-W corridor. These sites will be directly affected by construction since at least one existing or proposed structure is located within or on the site boundaries. The probability of finding subsurface materials was lower at these eight sites, consequently costs of adequate data recovery were expected to be less than the cost of re-engineering the transmission line to avoid them.

No Data Recovery/Monitoring

No data recovery was undertaken at sites that were sparse or spatially contained surface scatters (AZ CC:9:3 and AZ CC:10:9), very light scatters with possible deposition (AZ CC:13:12) or very significant sites with dense materials outside the R-O-W (AZ CC:10:8). Monitoring was stipulated to prevent construction damage to existing cultural resources. Data recovery was not recommended for AZ CC:10:8 and 9, since sites AZ CC:10:11, 13 and 14,which occur in the same physiographic setting,would provide adequate information on cultural resources in the Pinaleño Mountain upper bajadas (Coe 1977:14).

No Data Recovery/No Monitoring

Ten sites were not recommended for data recovery. It was expected that data recovered from those sites (Table 15) would be similar to that of more significant sites found in the same physiographic settings. In addition, many of these sites will be only slightly affected by construction. No towers are located within the boundaries of AZ CC:2:60 and AZ CC:6:5. A chipping station, AZ CC:6:4, was collected during the survey. The main features of AZ CC:10:7, a site consisting of two outcrops of bedrock mortars and a few sherds and lithics and those of AZ CC:9:4, a historic ranch with a light prehistoric lithic scatter which may have been brought in by ranchers, are outside the AEPCO R-O-W corridor. AZ CC:13:13, a historic ranch, is also outside the corridor.

Research Design for Data Recovery and Analysis of Archaeological Resources

Introduction

In order to maintain continuity, the research orientation for AEPCO II does not diverge from the cultural-ecological approach of AEPCO I. The nature of prehistoric land use in the study areas of both phases has been investigated. Goodyear states that human societies are directly and indirectly linked to their biophysical and social environments. "In other words, all societies have an ecology; they are each part of an ecological system" (Goodyear 1975:25). Human ecology provides a useful framework for understanding prehistoric human behavior. However, due to the limited AEPCO II data base, questions about past man-land relationships are correspondingly restricted.

A major research problem is why sites are located where they are (Gumerman 1971). AEPCO project objectives were to determine what activities were carried out at project sites and to relate these activities to available natural resources. This research design is based on the assumption that each site is a discrete part of the local prehistoric pattern of adaptation to the environment, and that certain procurement and processing activities are components of a larger system of subsistence-related behavior (Teague 1975:7). Data collection and analysis focused on reconstructing and interpreting prehistoric behavior and integrating the results into an overall subsistence pattern.

Methodological Problems

One of the overriding concerns in developing a research design for the entire AEPCO project was the nature of the project impact zone—a narrow, linear corridor. Goodyear (1975) describes the problems of doing research within such narrowly restricted limits. Linear transects, he claims, prevent "...generating reliable statements about the proportions or ratios of various activities in a given society's exploitative range. This will be true since we can never get the necessary spatial dispersion which will insure adequate statistical representation of microenvironments and their associated exploitatative activities" (Goodyear 1975:11).

However, the long range of a linear transect in itself constitutes a virtue. "As transects cross-cut several environmental zones it seems inevitable that distributions of a regional or paleoecological nature will be suggested, many of which will ultimately be demonstrated and tested by subsequent projects with less geographical restraints" (Goodyear 1975:11). Despite the problems of doing archaeological research within a spatially restricted area and limited by contract restraints, investigations may still be carried out with an eye towards eventual regional synthesis.

Another problem facing the AEPCO archaeological research was that of bias. Goodyear (1975:16) cites the need to study <u>all types</u> of cultural remains within a defined area if the full range of prehistoric behavior is ultimately to be understood. The priority given to preservation of the more individually significant sites, and the cost-benefit considerations of the AEPCO project that resulted in avoidance of the sites by tower construction ruled out testing certain site types (for example, large habitation sites). Site types that were chosen for data recovery were surface scatters of chipped stone debris, sherds, and ground stone, with no visible architectural features, occupying a relatively restricted area. These appear to be short-term limited activity sites. A second general type of site contains similar materials that were dispersed over a wide area on the flatter, lower mountain pediments. These appear to be longer-term multiple use base camps or overlapping series of subsites. In the end, then, only certain types of sites could be investigated within the diversity of microenvironmental settings. Thus, rather than attempting to infer regional, or even subregional cultural patterns, the research orientation favors intensive analysis at the single site level.

Criticisms directed at single-site analysis are based in part on the shortcomings of early archeological research that emphasized describing stylistic traits of artifacts, comparing these, and inferring their functions. Such studies focused on a few diagnostic artifact types, with little consideration for the total range of cultural material and the corresponding range of activities it may represent. Only recently has research tried to encompass a broader range of problems in conjunction with environmental studies to develop hypotheses concerning a wider range of prehistoric behavior (Whalen 1971; Huckell 1973; Windmiller 1973).

With the problem of bias in mind, we chose to focus analysis on some aspect common to all sites in the corridor. One fundamental characteristic of the prehistoric sites investigated in AEPCO I was that all were lithic scatters. The AEPCO I analysis then considered several problems basic to lithic technology. Before understanding general site function, the material culture assemblage must be described as explicitly as possible, not only in terms of form and frequency, but in order to determine stages of procurement, manufacture, use, and discard of particular artifacts. Only with a solid data base and an understanding of the relationships among its various components can one begin to make inferences about prehistoric human behavior, and relate these to processes of cultural adaptation and change. The original intent of the AEPCO I study was single site analysis and subsequent intersite comparison. However, given the opportunity to test generalizations about prehistoric land use in various physiographic zones, the research focus shifted slightly to accommodate a broader range of problems. This reassessment of research priorities influenced the direction of the AEPCO II analysis, as will be discussed below.

Research Problems

Developing hypotheses prior to data collection is particularly difficult in a contract situation, since avoidance of sites by a sponsor reduces the data base usable in testing hypotheses. It may, indeed, be impossible to test hypotheses since the data that inspired them may no longer be available for examination (Goodyear 1975:7). This is especially true when an attempt is made to relate the available data to existing general problems and models of human behavior. A cautionary note is provided by Jelinek (1976:20):

> Given full artifact recovery, we should ideally be able to recreate systems of exploitation and processing within a prehistoric culture....Unfortunately, the archaeologist seldom recovers more than a small, highly selected portion of the material culture of a prehistoric population. With these limited materials he is seldom able to validate his hypotheses.

Thus, given limited and often biased data, it is necessary to wring out every possible bit of information from an artifact assemblage. But, since total information retrieval is restricted by contract and budget concerns, one must determine what, within reason, the data can yield and how well they can be related to general research problems.

In order to understand these lithic sites, then, we first postulated discrete activities that were carried out, integrated these into specific tasks, and finally integrated the specific tasks into a general pattern of subsistence-related behavior. This method allowed us to postulate a few general problems for the AEPCO study area.

Site Specific Considerations. The first question is why sites are located in certain environmental contexts (for example, bajadas and valley bottoms) and what resources may have been exploited. Presumably, activities at the AEPCO sites were ultimately directed toward obtaining and processing wild food resources. It is necessary then, to describe potential resources and determine which of these could have been used by prehistoric peoples. Thus, data collection included recording biotic and abiotic resources that are available in the general region (mountains, river valleys), those in the general vicinity of sites (such as, the Pinaleño Mountain bajadas) and those available on or near a site.

Since it is assumed that sites are located with respect to availability of resources, it is necessary to identify the specific activities, (for example, tool manufacture) related to specific tasks (for example, plant processing) at each site. Environmental and archaeological data are both required for the investigation of this problem. The question is what are the potential resources at the site and what methods were used to procure and process them. To answer this question, detailed analysis of cultural remains is necessary to reconstruct basic site activities, from initial procurement of raw material, to tool manufacture, use and eventual discard. This basic sequence—procurement, manufacture, use and discard—is applicable to the three major types of non-perishable artifacts: chipped stone, ground stone, and pottery.

After identifying specific site activities it is necessary to determine if these activities are part of a single set of tasks oriented to a specific subsistence pursuit, or if they reflect a wider variety of tasks. If there is variation, can it be traced to different subsistence practices and related to the seasonal availability of resources, or to differences of a social nature? In other words, is site variability due to environment, culture, or a combination of both?

Intersite Level Considerations. Proceeding from the site specific level, it is necessary to determine if relationships exist between sites and what factors account for similarities and differences between them. For example, do sites within a specific environmental context show similar resource use, or if differences exist, what accounts for them?

Interstratum Level Considerations. The major objective of AEPCO I was to determine if differences in material culture would correspond to differences or similarities in different enviornmental zones. It was assumed that similarities might be due to a single culture having exploited the resources; if there were differences, these could be explained by variation either in exploitation strategies or cultural practices. The data showed that at least two different lithic technologies were present; it was, therefore, suggested that these may represent two cultural traditions. Unfortunately, the AEPCO II data cannot be used for tests at the interstratum level as was done for AEPCO I due to the small number of sites in each environmental stratum. The AEPCO II data base is simply too small for valid comparisons with AEPCO I. Therefore, differences between sites, as related to the enviornment will be studied instead. The AEPCO I objective of determining variability or uniformity within different environmental contexts and of finding what accounts for such trends, can be maintained for AEPCO II. But such studies will be conducted at the more specific intersite and intrasite level.

Regional Considerations. As discussed previously, regional problems can seldom be resolved when dealing with a low number of sites in a narrow corridor. Only tentative suggestions about the cultural identity of sites found in the northern segment could be made because no substantial diagnostic artifact assemblages were recognized in the analysis (Simpson and Westfall 1978). It was observed however, that two distinct lithic reduction technologies were present, which may be related to the desert Archaic and Mogollon traditions. The sites found in the southern segment contain more complex artifact assemblages as well as diagnostic artifact types. It is hoped that the AEPCO II data may yield some information regarding known and postulated cultural groups in the area. Diagnositic artifact types such as projectile points and decorated pottery are helpful to this end. However, such indicators must be treated with caution, as mixing of material on a single deflated surface is common. Cultural identification can therefore only be tentative, but artifact occurrence and distribution in time and space can be important in recognizing cultural adaptation through time.

CHAPTER 4

DATA RECOVERY AND SITE DESCRIPTIONS

Introduction

Pursuant to recommendations made, data recovery was carried out at 11 sites. While this number represents 40 percent of the 27 sites found on survey, the actual number of sites is low when compared to the 26 sites investigated on the AEPCO I project. In the interest of maintaining continuity with AEPCO I, several guidelines used during AEPCO I were retained for AEPCO II. One of these is the use of arbitrarily established environmental strata.

Corridor Environmental Strata

Due in part to the large number of sites dealt with by AEPCO I for which management decisions had to be made, arbitrary environmental strata were set up to organize data recovery and analysis. During the AEPCO I analysis, the cultural material of these strata was compared. The comparisons indicated that internal zone heterogeneity and external zone homogeneity exist among the recovered materials. That is, the various recovered artifact types crosscut strata (Simpson and Westfall 1978). Certain theoretical and methodological problems exist with this approach, however, so the results must be considered tentative.

Since it was possible to avoid destruction of most of the 27 sites found during AEPCO II, the number of investigated sites is low. No sampling was required and thus the strata are merely convenient units to group material for analysis. Again, these strata will be compared, but the main research problems deal with site-specific activities.

Archaeological sites were recorded in six arbitrarily defined strata during the R-O-W survey. Due to avoidance of certain sites, those in only five strata were subjected to data recovery. These strata, described below, are based on generalized environmental criteria such as elevation, topography, proximity to major physiographic features, soils, and vegetation (Table 16). These strata descriptions are valid only for the environments immediately surrounding investigated sites. They do not apply to other, similar environments transected by the R-O-W where investigations were not conducted.

Table 16. Attributes of corridor environmental strata

Environmental Feature	Stratum 1	Stratum 2	Stratum 3	Stratum 4	Stratum 5
Elevation (meters)	975	1325-1371	1280-1295	1280-1295	1264-1280
Topography	Flat or some slope; shallow washes	Rolling, w/ ridges and entrenched arroyos	Flat or some slope; very shallow runnels	Unstabilized dunes interspersed with small playas	Flat but somewhat dissected or hummocky lake terrace
Soils	Deep, loamy	Shallow, gravelly loam w/ bedrock exposed	Deep, gravelly loam	Deep, sandy loam	Deep, loamy
Mean temperature (degrees C)	18.1	16.5	17.0	15.4	15.4
Mean precipitation (cm)	22.8	35.5	27.9	27.9	27.9
Vegetation (D)=Dominant (C)=Codominant	Creosote (D) Cactus Grasses	Snakeweed (C) Acacia (C) Cactus Grasses Yucca Mesquite	Mesquite Saltbush Snakeweed Russian thistle Grasses	Grasses (C) Mesquite (C) Sage Yucca Burroweed	Alkali Sacaton Grass (D) Cactus
Archaeological Sites	AZ CC:6:2	AZ CC:10:6 AZ CC:10:11 AZ CC:10:13 AZ CC:10:14	AZ CC:9:2 AZ CC:10:11 AZ CC:10:13 AZ CC:10:14	AZ CC:13:6 AZ CC:13:11	AZ CC:13:14 AZ CC:13:15 AZ CC:13:16

1. San Simon Basin-Pinaleño Mountains Lower Bajada Transition Zone

AZ CC:6:3 (AEPCO 203) is located in this stratum. Thus, it is narrowly defined by specific environmental criteria. At an elevation of approximately 975 m, the topography is basically flat with some low, rolling hills (Figure 15). The area is shallowly dissected by arroyos which drain north-northeast into Foote Draw and eventually to the Gila River, approximately 11 km away. Soil data at the series level is not available for this stratum. The available information states that the soils in this area are highly variable in texture and composition. The stratum-specific soil is a shallow loam which contains a high percentage of lime and is subject to wind and water erosion. With a mean annual temperature of 18 degrees C and 22.8 cm of annual precipitation, the Sonoran desertscrub is dominated by creosotebush. Ocotillo, cholla, prickly pear, acacia, desert poppy, and grasses are present in low quantities.

Figure 15. General environment of Stratum 1: San Simon Basin/Pinaleño Mountain lower bajada transition zone. AZ CC:6:3 is in foreground.

2. Pinaleño Mountains Upper Bajadas

This is the largest stratum, with four sites: AZ CC:10:6 (AEPCO 208), AZ CC:10:11 (AEPCO 214), AZ CC:10:13 (AEPCO 217), and AZ CC:10:14 (AEPCO 218), located along a 9.6 km stretch of the R-O-W. The elevation varies from 1325 m to 1371 m, and the terrain is dominated by long, low, wide, and gently rolling east-west or southeast-northwest trending ridges (Figure 16). This zone is close to the Pinaleño Mountains, with the foothills commencing 1.6 km to 4.8 km to the northwest. The sheetwash erosion which affects this area ends in several entrenched washes which drain to the east. The San Simon River is 16 km to 32 km east. In many areas bedrock is either close to the surface or exposed; abundant raw lithic material is a characteristic of this stratum.

The three soil series represented—Chiricahua, Atascosa, and Signal—are similar in several respects. They are all formed from residuum of weathered igneous (granite or rhyolite) bedrock and are gravelly loam to sandy clay loam. The soils have a slow permeability and are subject to moderate runoff.

In a climate where approximately 35.5 cm annual precipitation is accompanied by an approximate mean annual temperature of 16.5 degrees C, desert grassland vegetation predominates. The actual amount of grass cover varies greatly in this stratum, and nowhere is it the dominant vegetation. Woody plants such as acacia, snakeweed, and Aplopappus associations now predominate; cacti and grasses are secondary species.

Figure 16. General environment of Stratum 2: Pinaleño Mountains upper bajadas, showing ridge system. Photo taken from site AZ CC:10:13. View is to the southeast, with the Dos Cabezas Mountains in the background.

3. Dos Cabezas Mountains Lower Bajadas

While Strata 1 and 2 are in the San Simon Valley, this unit and those following are in the Sulphur Spring Valley. Only one of three stratum sites, AZ CC:9:2 (AEPCO 220), was investigated. The other two were avoided by AEPCO. This stratum is situated between 1280 m and 1295 m elevations with the gently sloping level terrain facing west-southwest. Approximately 1.6 km east and northeast are the Dos Cabezas foothills. Deflation and sheetwash erosion into many small shallow stream channels trending in a westerly direction have created a surface littered with gravel. There are no major permanent or periodic drainages in this stratum. The Sonoita series soil is a deep, gravelly, sandy loam which originated from weathered mixed igneous alluvium. Grassland again is the major vegetation type with mesquite-sacaton grass associations predominating. Also common are saltbush, snakeweed, acacia, and Russian thistle. The area has a mean temperature of approximately 17.0 degrees C and precipitation of 27.9 cm annually, values which are intermediate between those for the two preceding strata.

4. Willcox Playa Dunes

This stratum consists of unstabilized sand dunes interspersed with small dry lakes. These postpluvial dunes vary in size, mass, and shape but all are located between 1280 m and 1296 m. Two of the three sites recorded in this stratum, AZ CC:13:6 and AZ CC:13:11, situated near the edge of dunes approximately 4.8 to 6.4 km northeast of the playa, were investigated (Figure 17). The Vinton series soil is a deep sandy loam which has a low water runoff rate but is subject to moderate wind erosion. With annual precipitation and temperature values at 27.9 cm and 15.4 degrees C respectively, the major vegetation is again desert grassland. Grasses are common, but woody species comprise the greater proportion of the vegetation. Sacaton grass—mesquite associations are dominant, with snakeweed, burroweed, squawbush, sage, and yucca are also common.

5. Sulphur Spring Basin

Three of four stratum sites were investigated. They are AZ CC:13:14, 15, and 16, lying between 1265 m and 1280 m on a very level plain less than 1.5 km southeast of Willcox Playa. The area is characterized by a hummocky surface which is subjected to sheetwash erosion. Most of it is undissected. The Crot series soil is a deep, highly alkaline loam formed from alluvium deposited on the terraces of extinct Lake Cochise. It receives an average of 27.9 cm of precipitation with a mean temperature of approximately 15.4 degrees C. Vegetation is predominately alkalai-sacaton grass. Occasional woody species and cactus are present (Figure 18).

Figure 17. General environment of Stratum 4: Willcox Playa Dunes. Taken from vicinity of AZ CC:13:6, showing dense mesquite invasion of dunes, Dos Cabezas Mountains.

Figure 18. General environment of Stratum 5: Sulphur Spring Basin, taken from vicinity of AZ CC:13:15.

Field Methodology

All of the sites chosen for data recovery were characterized by surface artifacts in varying densities and appear to have little or no depth. Of the six sites nominated for inclusion in the National Register, four were partially investigated: AZ CC:10:6, AZ CC:10:11, AZ CC:9:2, and AZ CC:13:6. These sites consist of complex and widely dispersed artifact scatters indicative of multiple discrete and overlapping activity areas. The R-O-W crossed over the perimeter of each of those four sites, with the main site area being some distance away from the impact zone. Sites AZ CC:6:6 and 7 are spatially contained and required only minor engineering adjustments, such that impact could be confined to previously disturbed areas and site preservation ensured. On the other hand, the four other sites were so widely dispersed that major engineering adjustments were not a realistic alternative to minimize impact. Adequate data recovery from the entire sites could not be accomplished with the available time and funding. As a result, preservation and protection of these sites, became the primary concern rather than data recovery. Cultural materials did, however, occur within the R-O-W corridor and these could not be ignored. Thus, tower placement within the R-O-W at these sites was slightly redesigned to confine construction to previously disturbed areas, and data recovery was completed within the R-O-W. While such collections may not be statistically representative of a site's total range of activities, the data are nevertheless useful for deriving inferences regarding activities when general comparisons between sites are made.

Field methodology for all sites involved controlled surface collection, detailed mapping, and testing for cultural depth. Ordinarily, a grid column was laid out in alignment within the 30 m wide R-O-W corridor, and sectioned into standard 5 m^2 grid units for the length of the site within the R-O-W. Grid units were designated according to the Cartesian method, which allows for expansion into any direction from a fixed datum. Permission was obtained from AEPCO and landowners to conduct limited investigations outside the R-O-W where necessary to obtain an adequate sample for analysis. Existing or proposed tower locations usually served as Datum 00 and units took their designation from the northwest corner. Thus a designation of 10N 15W indicates a grid unit as 15 meters west from point 10 m north of Datum 00, encompassing an area 5 m square. Every grid unit was examined, with artifacts from each unit bagged and recorded on field check sheets. At AZ CC:10:11, Locus 2, a 50 percent nonrandom geometric sample was taken.

Some of the smaller, spatially contained artifact scatters were so dispersed that a majority of the units in a grid would be devoid of artifacts. In such a case, the point provenience of each artifact or cluster of artifacts was plotted on the site map and the item(s) then collected. In other examples, the R-O-W perpendicularly bissected the long axis of the site. If this occurred, in addition to laying a grid within the R-O-W, a second grid column was laid down perpendicular to the R-O-W corridor grid column. Several sites in the Sulphur Spring Valley and Willcox Playa dunes were small and well defined enough to warrant gridding of the entire site for surface collections. Such flexibility was necessary to ensure an adequate sample size for eventual statistical analysis enabling comparison of sites. In all cases where a grid collection was used, a 5 m^2 unit was the standard unit size.

Features are commonly recognized as architectural (rooms, pit houses, and storage pits) or as nonarchitectural (roasting pits, hearths, water control features). Many of the investigated sites had neither, yet contained discrete concentrations of artifacts indicating task-specific activity at the site. Such concentrations may be the remains of a lithic chipping station,a broken pot, a cluster of ground stone fragments, or a simple rock pile. Properly, these may be called "loci" (task-specific activity areas); however, this term was ordinarily applied to a subarea within a large site to better define site attributes on a gross scale. For example, at AZ CC:10:11, two distinct lithic use areas within the R-O-W were recognized (based on raw material and artifact types) and were designated Locus 1 and Locus 2. Within these loci, discrete concentrations occur, which may be reconstructable episodes of lithic reduction activity. Such a concentration was designated a feature, mapped, recorded, and collected as a unit.

In the following site descriptions,data recovery techniques are described in more detail. Sites have been placed in order according to their situation in a particular physiographic stratum.

Site Descriptions

Stratum 1: San Simon Basin-Pinaleño Mountains Lower Bajada Transition Zone

AZ CC:6:3

Elevation: 976 to 978 m
Site Size: 173 m along R-O-W by 60 m (arbitrary)
Field Designation: AEPCO 203

The site is situated south of the Dos Condado substation in an area transitional between the San Simon Basin to the east and the Pinaleño Mountains lower bajadas to the west. The site is within a small flat basin-like area with small rises (Figure 19). The surface soils are composed of a loose wind-deposited gray sandy loam overlying a calcareous, gravelly, sandy loam substrate. The surface of the immediate site area is covered by a semipavement of small igneous pebbles. The general landscape surrounding the site is one of west-to-east trending low ridges interspersed with shallow, sandy drainages. Two drainage systems occur in the vicinity. To the west is a system of shallow, sandy, braided arroyos draining northeastward to Foote Draw and thence to the Gila River. On the eastern edge of the site the flat desert pavement slopes gradually eastward into a system of low, sandy gravel hills with braided stream channels draining into the San Simon Valley.

The current vegetation is predominantly creosotebush which is sparsely distributed across the flat central site area, becoming denser in the arroyos. A few ocotillo and sparse grasses also occur, and a lone mesquite grows in one of the drainages.

AZ CC:6:3 is a sparse lithic scatter of mostly small cores and flakes of extremely fine-grained light-colored rhyolite. The survey crew defined the artifact scatter for a distance approximately 25 m east and 75 m west of the R-O-W centerline. Artifacts immediately within the R-O-W were very scarce, averaging approximately three to five items per 5 m^2; however, a noteworthy aspect of the lithic assemblage was the miniscule size of individual artifacts. Flakes and cores seldom exceeded 3 to 4 cm in length.

An access road had been accidentally bladed down the R-O-W prior to data recovery at the site, eradicating all artifacts within the corridor (Figure 20). Thus, field methods focused on recovering data from outside the R-O-W to compensate for the loss of information within the R-O-W. Due to the sparse distribution of material, a 100 percent point provenience collection was made, rather than laying out a grid. Given the uniqueness of the artifact assemblage and obvious discrete clustering of artifact types, more useful information could be obtained by the plotting of specific locational data than by the "lumping" characteristic of a grid collection method. The site area was intensively surveyed by walking transects parallel to the R-O-W corridor. Artifacts were bagged as they were encountered and left in place to be mapped in on the site contour map before they were collected.

Figure 19. AZ CC:6:3, view of main site area. View is to the east, with the San Simon Basin in the distance.

Figure 20. AZ CC:6:3, general view of site, looking south down the right-of-way corridor.

As can be seen on the site map (Figure 21), artifacts were scarce east of the R-O-W corridor and were densest in the central area 30 m west of the R-O-W centerline (Figure 22). Artifacts were concentrated in desert pavement areas; as the desert pavement dissipates outward into a sandy gravel cover surrounding the main site area, there was a corresponding decrease in artifacts. Also, the majority of artifacts in the peripheral area were larger, angular pieces of coarse-grained rhyolite, while most of those occurring on desert pavement were made from small nodular cryptocrystalline silicates and fine-grained chert-like rhyolites.

One mano fragment and one sherd were found in isolated contexts; their relationship to the general artifact assemblage remains uncertain, however. Determining the boundaries of artifact concentrations was difficult. Approximately 205 m from the R-O-W centerline, situated on a low rise sloping from east ot west, was a locus of large cores of coarse-grained rhyolites. Artifacts continued farther west, but this area could not be intensively investigated due to contract restrictions. However, the different nature of the material at this locus strongly indicated a separate activity area from the main site area adjacent to the R-O-W.

Stratum 2: Pinaleño Mountains Upper Bajadas

AZ CC:10:6

Elevation: 1358 m
Site Size: 120 m N/S by 60 m E/W (arbitrary)
Field Designation: AEPCO 208

AZ CC:10:6 is associated with three other Stratum 3 sites (AZ CC:10:11, 13, and 14) by its similar physiographic location although the site area is environmentally distinct. The site is located on an east-sloping ridge with a wash to the north and south. Vegetation is more abundant than at the other sites, but similar plants are present. The most common of these include acacia and snakeweed, with lesser quantities of mesquite, yucca, burroweed, and cactus (Figures 23 and 24). The Chiricahua series soil is formed from granitic residuum and is a shallow, very gravelly to sandy loam with a moderate runoff. Lithic raw materials, principally igneous and metamorphic rocks, are common along the ridge edge and less frequent on the ridge top. Raw material is also abundant along the bench above, and in Willow Springs Wash 30 m south (Figure 25). This entrenched drainage carries water intermittently along its very sandy bottom. Riparian vegetation includes desert willow, walnut, and desert hackberry.

Human disturbance of the site appears to be moderate. The AEPCO transmission line R-O-W is oriented perpendicular to the site's long axis, and previous tower construction and road building have produced the only visible direct impact. Some erosion is caused by small rivulets draining east along the ridgeline or south of the ridgetop into the wash channel. Grazing has had direct and indirect effects on the site.

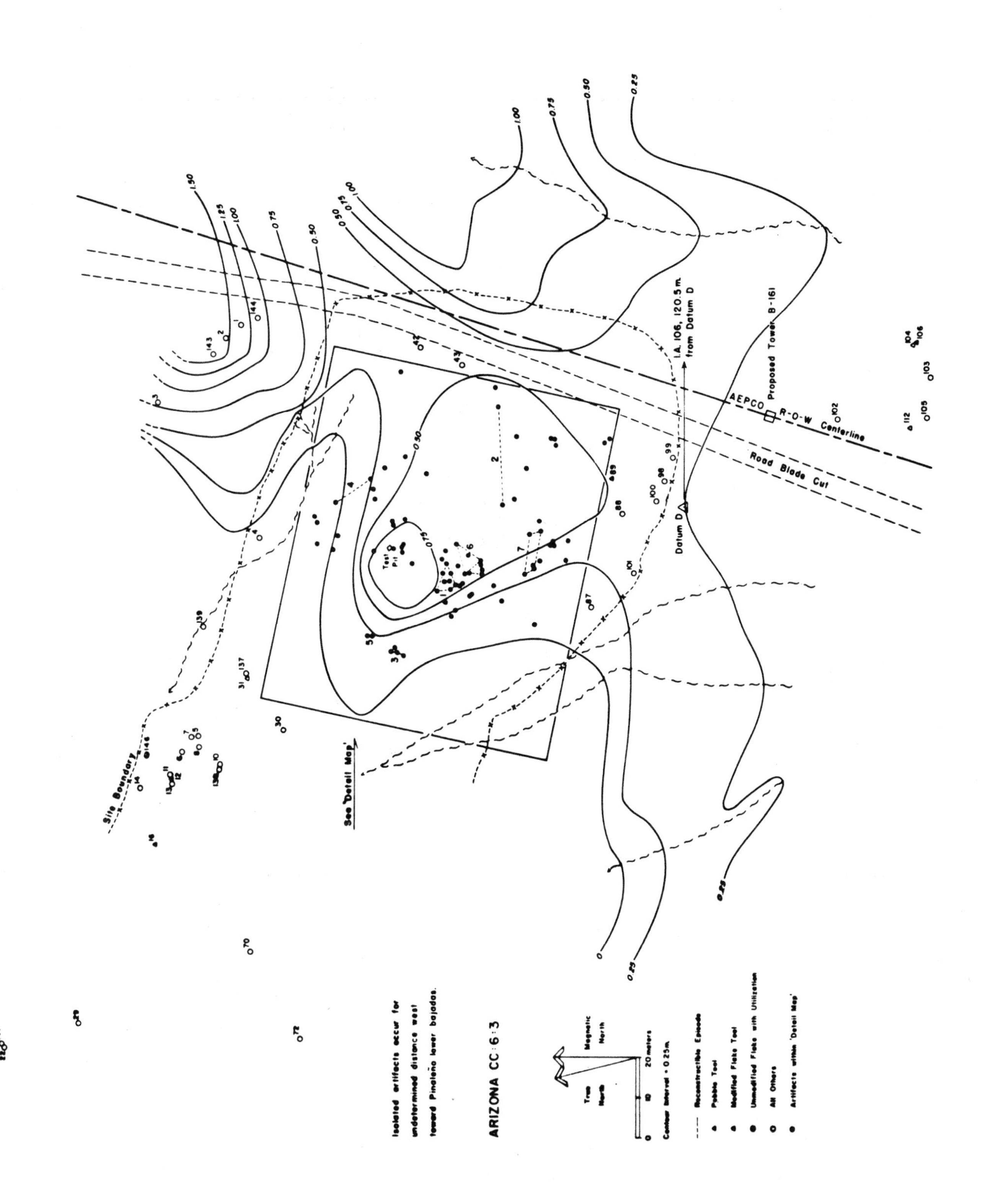

Figure 21. AZ CC:6:3, site map.

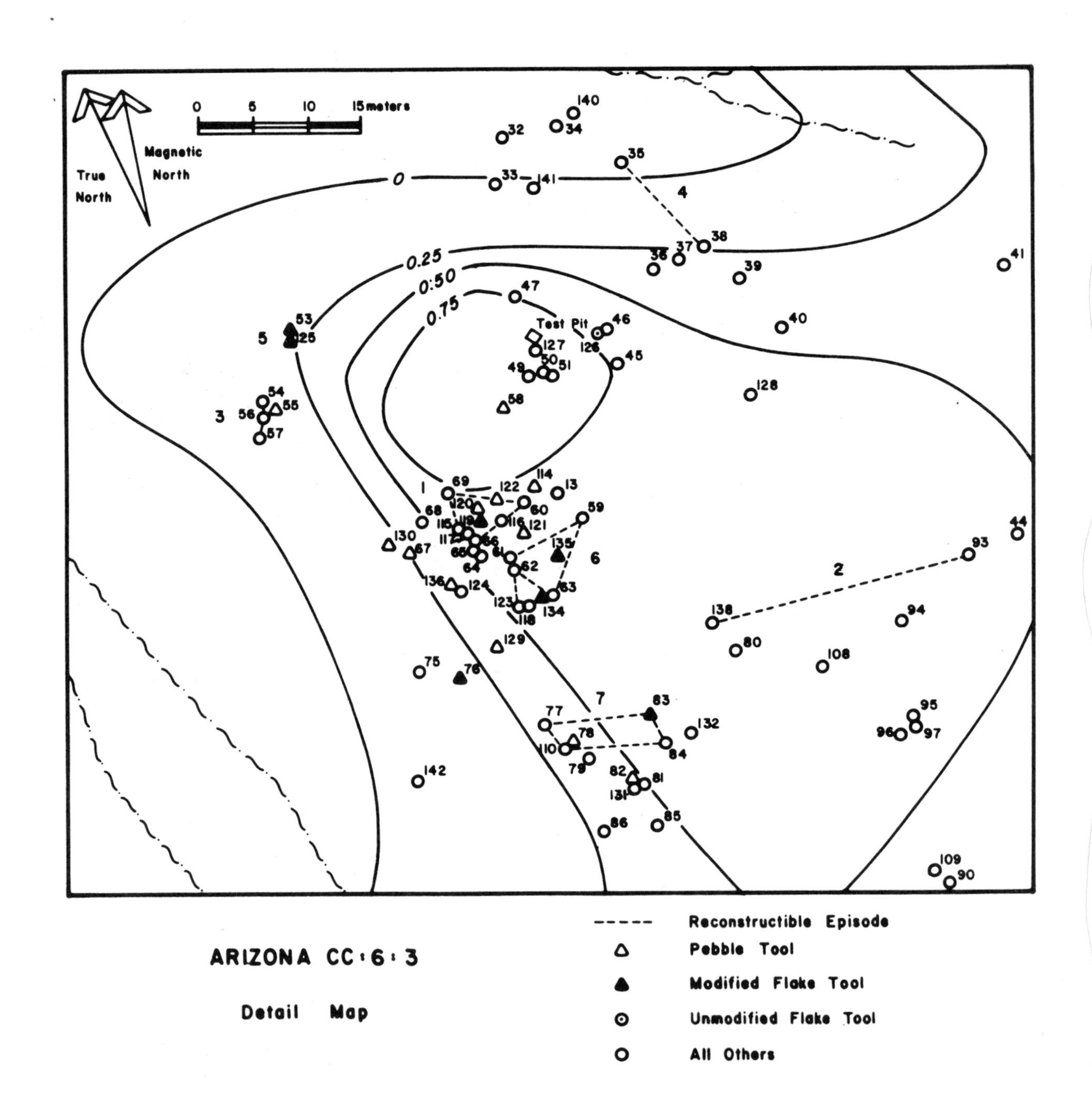

Figure 22. AZ CC:6:3, detail map of main lithic use area.

Figure 23. AZ CC:10:6, general environment of site, showing mesquite. The main part of the site is in the foreground.

Figure 24. AZ CC:10:6, general environment of site, showing yucca, mesquite, and Aplopappus. View is east, San Simon Basin in the distance.

Figure 25. AZ CC:10:6, view of Willow Springs Wash.

The site was originally described as a moderately dense, extensive lithic scatter. The natural site boundaries within the R-O-W were located but its extent to the east and west of the transmission line corridor was simply estimated. The survey crew noted that cultural material extended for at least 235 m east and 50 m west of the R-O-W boundary. A rancher said that artifacts also have been discovered approximately 750 m southwest of AZ CC:10:6 on the opposite side of U.S. Highway 666, but these were determined to be spatially distinct.

One research activity proposed for data recovery was an intensive survey of the general area to locate the natural site boundaries and all features and assess the nature and distribution of artifacts. It was also proposed to record and map in detail certain features outside the R-O-W in addition to completing a 100 percent surface collection of the site within the R-O-W, drafting a detailed site map, and recording all R-O-W features. Finally, subsurface testing was recommended by the survey, and was completed during an earlier project phase (see Chapter 3).

The site was mapped, and the surface collected using 5 m^2 units within the R-O-W (Figure 26). Dense vegetation hindered or prevented this in some areas. A total of 452 artifacts were collected, with chipped stone constituting 98.9 percent of the total, and ground stone 1.1 percent.

During surface collection, certain artifact distribution patterns were discerned (Figure 27). The site boundary was based on the greatest extent of artifacts within the R-O-W. North of the datum artifacts were very sparsely distributed and none were seen north of the mapped area. South of the datum artifacts were scattered downslope to the bench above Willow Springs Wash. The material on this slope and that near the southern boundary was probably redeposited by erosion and road building. The mapped southern site boundary reflects this present distribution and may not accurately represent the original context. No artifacts were seen on the bench directly above the wash.

Another obvious patterning was the higher artifact density above and below the ridge edge. More than 54 percent of the artifacts occurred between 10S and 15N. Compared to a mean overall site density of 3.1 items per grid, the density here is 8.2 per grid. This may represent either an activity area or a trash deposit.

During collection it became apparent that some material was partially buried. Also, the amount of artifacts collected from areas which had been previously investigated (surface collected and backhoe tested) was suspiciously high, indicating that artifacts probably existed below the surface. After surface collecting and mapping were completed two options for further work were considered: (1) additional survey, feature recording and mapping outside the R-O-W, and (2) excavation in the area already surface collected. The advantage of working outside the R-O-W was that a greater amount of data representing more varied activities could be gathered. However, collecting data from the entire site to determine spatial or temporal relationships between this material and that within the R-O-W would have required too much

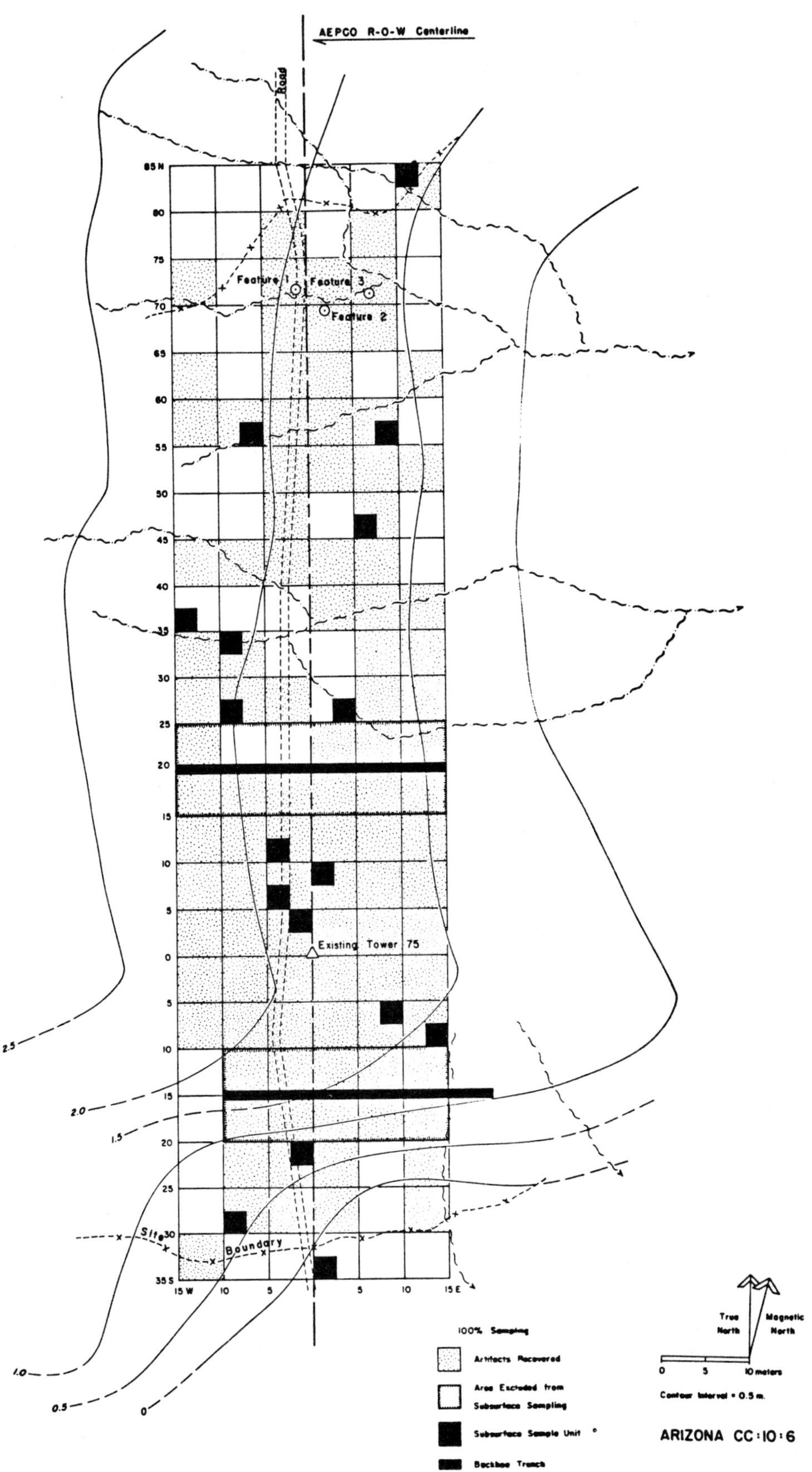

Figure 26. AZ CC:10:6, site map.

SURFACE COLLECTION

	15W–10W	10W–5W	5W–0	0–5E	5E–10E	10E–15E
85N–80N						1
80N–75N			1		1	
75N–70N	1		1	1	1	
70N–65N			5	4	1	
65N–60N	1		3	2		3
60N–55N	2	3	1	3	4	
55N–50N			1	3	1	3
50N–45N		2	1		4	
45N–40N	1	2	1	2	1	2
40N–35N				1	1	2
35N–30N	2	1			2	1
30N–25N	3	1	1	1	1	1
25N–20N	1			4	2	2
20N–15N	1	1	1	4	2	3
15N–10N	13	3	7	8	8	3
10N–5N	7	8	11	8	3	5
5N–0	12	25	11	1	3	4
0–5S	5	4	7	2	4	1
5S–10S		2	1	12	14	5
10S–15S		2	3	4	15	4
15S–20S		3	1	3	3	2
20S–25S		1	5	4		8
25S–30S		2	2	1		7
30S–35S	1					

TESTED UNITS

	15W–10W	10W–5W	5W–0	0–5E	5E–10E	10E–15E
85N–80N						1
80N–75N						
75N–70N						
70N–65N						
65N–60N						
60N–55N		1			0	
55N–50N						
50N–45N					1	
45N–40N						
40N–35N	0					
35N–30N		4				
30N–25N		4		2		
25N–20N						
20N–15N						
15N–10N			4			
10N–5N			24	12		
5N–0			16			
0–5S						
5S–10S					18	4
10S–15S						
15S–20S						
20S–25S			5			
25S–30S		5				
30S–35S				1		

Figure 27. AZ CC:10:6, distribution of artifacts.

time. By confining the investigations to the corridor area more detailed information about specific, areally restricted activity loci could be acquired. Three goals were proposed: (1) to obtain a large artifact collection that would be representative of a wide range of behavior, (2) to determine the horizontal extent of the deposits, and (3) to assess the relationship between the surface and subsurface material and determine if correlations in density and artifact variability existed.

A sampling design was required that matched available time with the proposed goals. Graphing the artifact quantity per grid (Figure 28) revealed a distribution pattern that was useful for devising a sampling plan. A disproportional stratified random sample scheme was chosen (Cochran 1953; Blalock 1972:518). The total population from which a sample could be selected was all the R-O-W grids (144) minus those disturbed by heavy equipment during testing (22), or 122 grids. Three strata were created from the artifact patterning perceived in the above graphs:

Stratum	Artifact Range	Number	Percent
1	0 - 8	110	90.2
2	10 - 17	10	8.2
3	21 - 27	2	1.6

A sufficient sample size for each stratum lay between 10 and 50 percent. Though the 5 m^2 grids were the sample units, the actual recovery spaces were one-quarter (2.5 m^2) of each grid. In the sample, each grid in a stratum was consecutively numbered beginning with the northwesternmost unit, and each quadrant within each grid was also numbered. A table of random numbers was used to select both grid and quadrant units for testing. All quadrants were excavated in 5 cm arbitrary levels which conformed to the surface topography. When possible, all fill was passed through 1/8 inch screen, which allowed recovery of large numbers of small artifacts. All units were backfilled to approximate the original surface contour.

The sampled quantities were: Stratum 1, 2 grids (10 percent); Stratum 2, 5 grids (50 percent); and stratum 3, 1 grid (50 percent), for a site total of 17 grids (13.9 percent). Since the actual recovery spaces were one-quarter of each grid, the total site area tested within the R-O-W was 3.5 percent. The excavation units were:

Stratum 1:
40N 15W, SW quad
35N 10W, NW quad
30N 0E, SE quad
5S 10E, SE quad
25S 10W, SE quad
60N 5E, SE quad
50N 5W, SW quad
30S 0E, SW quad
60N 10W, SE quad
85N 10E, NW quad
30N 10W, SW quad

Stratum 2:
10N 0E, NW quad
5N 5W, NE quad
20S 5W, SW quad
10N 5W, SW quad
15N 5W, SW quad

Stratum 3: 5S 5E, NE quad

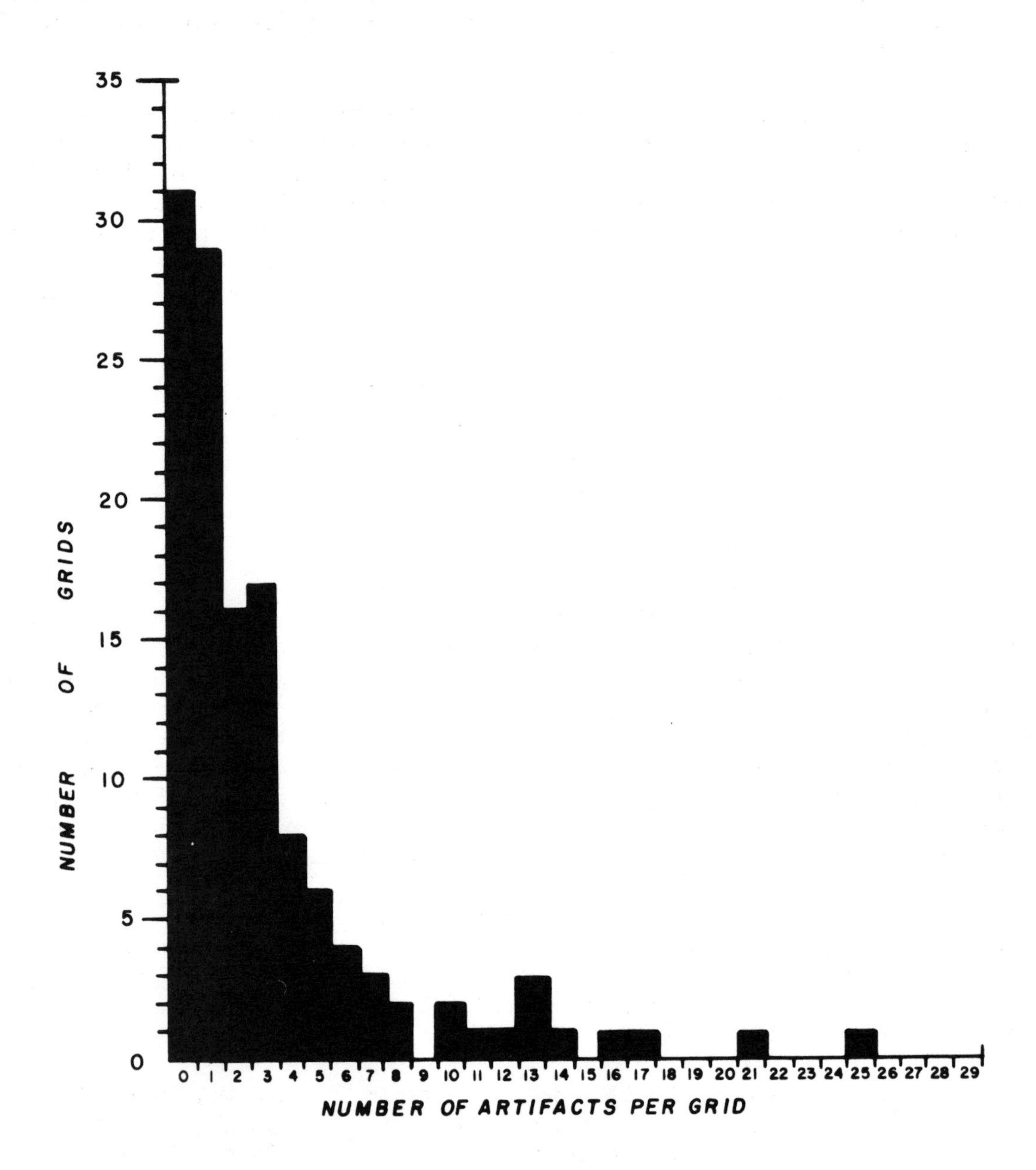

Figure 28. AZ CC:10:6, artifact quantity per grid.

A total of 133 lithic pieces was recovered from the excavations. The densest units were near the ridge edge, and a fair correlation exists between the surface and subsurface artifact density. These tests also confirmed the site boundaries within the R-O-W, but because no excavations were conducted outside these boundaries the hypothesis of surface distribution is not true for the entire site. The subsurface investigation did, however, fulfill proposed research goals.

Features 1, 2, and 3. There were three ambiguous accumulations of rocks which appeared as irregularly shaped rings. The survey crew noted these as either "possible hearths" or "stone circles." Since they are all similar and close to one another, they will be described as a group.

Feature 1 is in 75N 5W and consists of ten medium cobbles partially embedded in the ground in a 20 cm diameter area. Several of the cobbles are cracked, but they are in a shallow, bladed road, and the fractures may be due to recent heavy equipment disturbance. Feature 2 in 70N 0E is comprised of five small cobbles in a 1 m diameter area. Feature 3 is in 75N 5E and consists of seven large cobbles in a 1 m diameter area. All the rocks of each feature are locally available igneous or metamorphic types. The top 5 cm of the soil within and around each feature was examined. There was no evidence of any burning. No artifacts were found in or immediately adjacent to any feature, but lithics were recovered from surrounding grids. The artifact density in this section of the site is very low in both surface and subsurface levels. A single metate fragment was located approximately 15 m west-southwest from this feature group.

The function of these rock features is uncertain. Because there was no evidence of burning, it is doubtful that they are hearths. If they had been temporary hearths, the rocks and soil may exhibit no evidence of heating and the charcoal may have washed away before soil accumulated over it. All are situated next to a small rivulet that may have altered the features.

The rock rings do resemble hypothesized basket supports found archaeologically in the Papago region (Goodyear 1975; Doelle 1976; Raab 1974; Stewart and Teague 1974). A lengthy discussion of their purported function in the saguaro fruit-seed and prickly pear fruit economic subsystems is presented by Goodyear (1975) and Doelle (1976). These interpretations are not strictly applicable to AZ CC:10:6 because the environment around the site does not contain any of these plants. Leguminous seed plants are very common, but rock rings have not been considered as elements in this procurement system. Though the features could have supported containers there is no confirming evidence to assign any cultural role to them.

AZ CC:10:11

Elevation: 1333 to 1344 m
Site Size: 862 m (along R-O-W) by 500 m E/W (arbitrary)
Field Designation: AEPCO 214

This is a large lithic quarry and workshop site situated in a basin-like niche in the Pinaleño upper bajadas. High ridges of granitic formation to the north, east, and west of the R-O-W corridor dominate the topography. At the crests of these ridges are numerous outcrops of rhyolite, felsite, and decomposing granite.

Two main soil series are represented in the site area. The Atascosa series predominates, consisting of shallow, well-drained, moderately permeable soils formed on rhyolite conglomerate and tuff on moderately steep to very steep hills. Slopes are usually 30 to 45 percent and occur west of the site area. Surface soils are shallow, grayish-brown, very gravelly, sandy loam overlying a dark gray gravelly sandy clay loam. Rhyolite conglomerate bedrock is ordinarily encountered at a maximum depth of 22.9 cm. Chiricahua series soils, secondarily represented at the site in the lower elevations, are derived from weathered quartzite, granite, quartz monzonite, granodiorite, phyllite, and gneiss. Slopes are dominantly 8 to 30 percent, and runoff is medium with slow permeability. Surface soils are a light cobbly loam overlying a thick (36 cm) subsoil of reddish-brown gravelly clay loam that rests on quartzite bedrock (National Cooperative Soil Survey 1972). Both the Atascosa and Chiricahua series support grasses and shrubs and are presently used as rangeland.

Due to contract restrictions, the survey crew was unable to determine the true eastern and western extents of the site outside the R-O-W. Within the corridor, however, two distinct loci were observed based on raw material composition of the artifacts. Additionally, in the center of the site within the corridor there is a large cattle tank which has severely affected artifact distribution. This section was excluded from data recovery procedures. Chipped stone debitage and tools were found east of the tank, however, indicating a continuous artifact distribution prior to distrubance. For ease in recording and data recovery, the site was separated into two loci (Figure 29).

Locus 1. This portion of the site is noted for its dense concentration of artifacts of a distinctive waxy, fine-grained chocolate-brown felsite. Locus 1 is situated on a unique landform within the general system of high ridges characteristic of the Pinaleño upper bajadas. The immediate topography is a broad southwest-to-northeast dipping fan of detrital material several meters thick, overlying a base rock of decomposing granite. This fan (Figure 30), composed of material derived from the upper Pinaleño Mountains, forms a broad, unconsolidated terrace-like surface, strewn with an abundance of fine-grained angular, purple and brown felsite cobbles and pebbles. The northeast edge of the fan is gradually eroding into a wide sandy wash. Within the R-O-W corridor, Locus 1 is dominated by a high steep knoll capped with decomposing bedrock outcrops. The soil cover on the slopes of the knoll is quite thin in contrast to the thick deposit at the base of the knoll created by the fan.

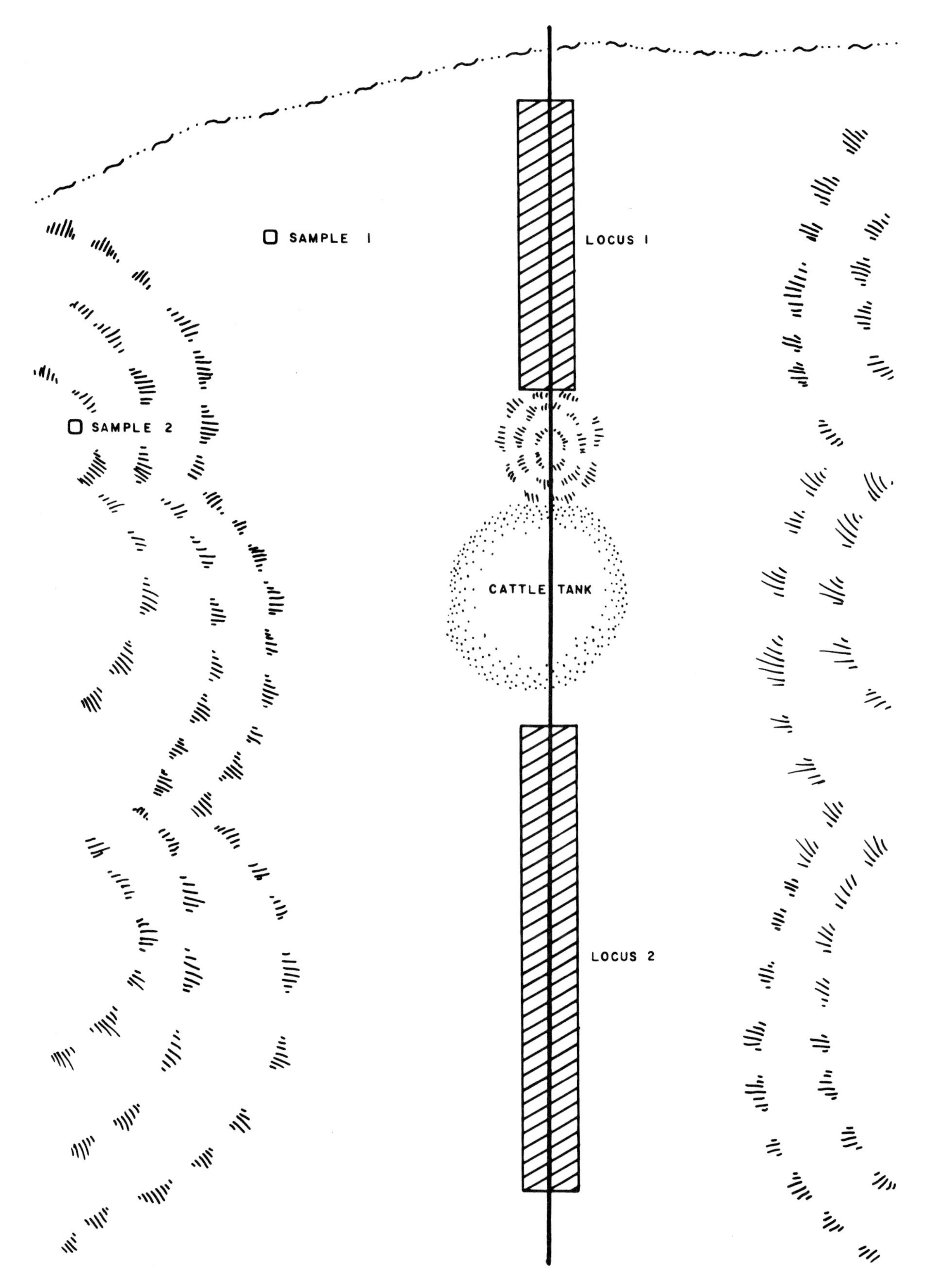

Figure 29. AZ CC:10:11, general site map.

Figure 30. AZ CC:10:11, Locus 1, general view, showing detrital fan on which lithic raw material and knapping debris occur.

Vegetation in the immediate R-O-W corridor and adjacent areas is dominated by yucca, snakeweed, catclaw, and burroweed, with occasional prickly pear, cane cholla, and whitethorn acacia. The wash at the north end of Locus 1 also contains an abundance of mesquite. The major (northern) portion of Locus 1 on the terrace (within the R-O-W) has been disturbed by cattle wallowing; consequently smaller pieces of lithic debitage may have been trampled underfoot. Approximately 100 m west of the centerline, however, the terrace is relatively undisturbed by cattle.

The densest distribution of felsite artifacts extends 80 m north of and 35 m south of proposed tower B-49, for a total length of 115 m. Investigations during data recovery determined that lithic artifacts occur across the entire east-west extent of the terrace (approximately 215 m). Material was also found on the ridge slopes west of the terrace and will be discussed below.

Data recovery at Locus 1 was restricted to the R-O-W when it became apparent that the sheer enormity of the site rendered recovery from outside of the R-O-W impractical. A grid column 115 m long and 30 m wide, sectioned into 5 m^2 grid units, was constructed within the R-O-W corridor (Figure 31). The southernmost 50 m of the grid column covered the lower slopes of the knoll at the southern end of Locus 1. A bedrock outcrop lies at the crest

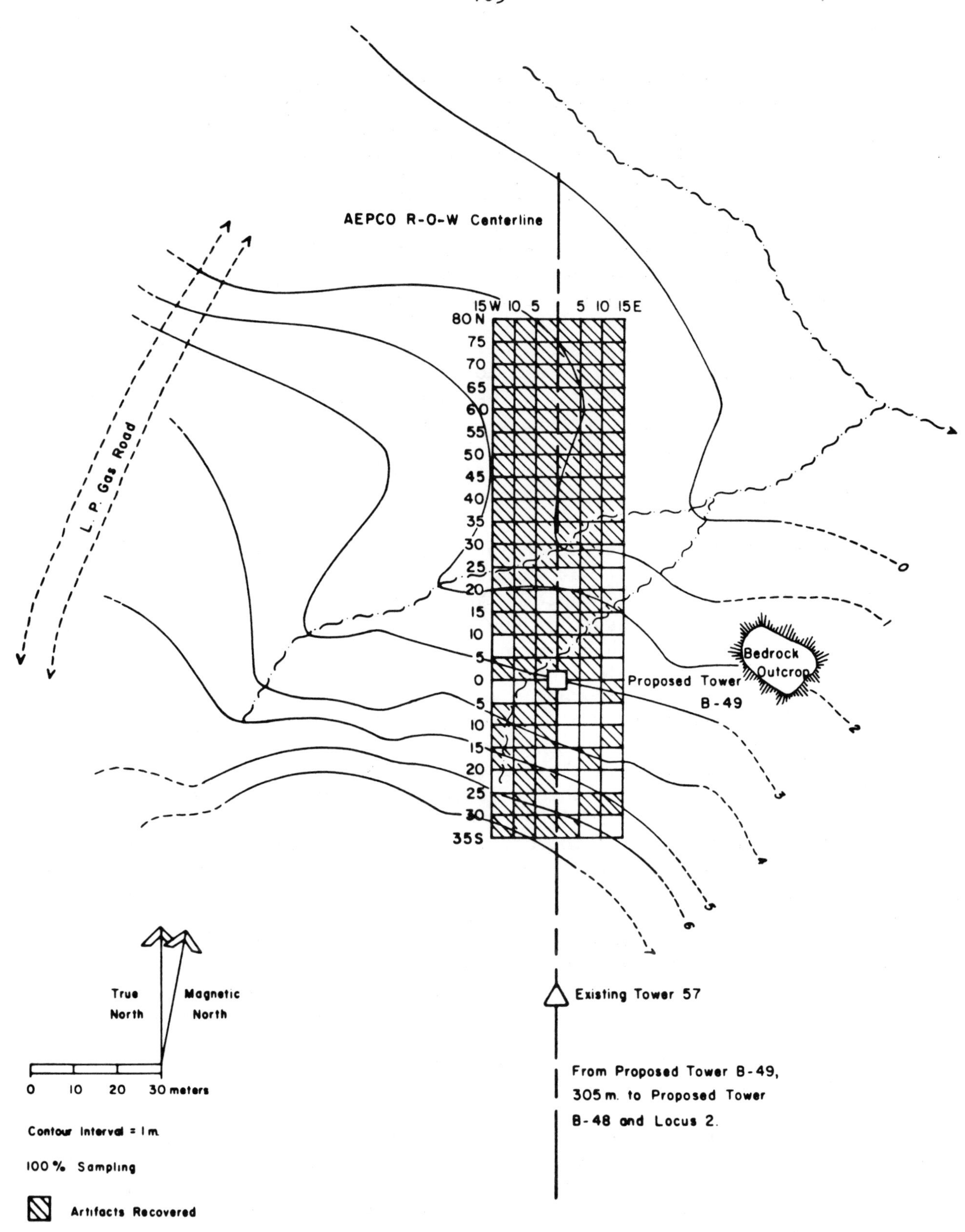

Figure 31. AZ CC:10:11, Locus 1, site map.

of the knoll, but this material was not heavily exploited and hence few artifacts were found. Material on the slope was sparse, consisting of a few isolated cores and flakes of brown felsite and chert. At the interface of the knoll slope and detrital fan, the amount of cultural material increases considerably. The section of the grid 30N to 70N cuts through a field of naturally occurring angular cobbles and pebbles of felsite. Although the basic fine-grained composition of this material would lend itself well to the production of flakes and tools, it contains numerous structural weaknesses and tends to break along planes of natural fracture. It was difficult to differentiate between cultural and natural fracturing. The majority of material collected from the grids was small irregular chunks ranging from 5 to 8 cm, rarely exceeding 10 cm. Flakes occurred in nearly equal proportion to chunks and generally were 2 to 3 cm in size. A small, square slab metate was found in unit 20S 15W. The northernmost end of the grid (70N to 80N) is at the edge of the terrace, just above a wash. At this location, other types of raw material and more "finished" tools were found. It seems that raw material was obtained from stream cobbles in the drainage to produce these artifacts, or that a chronologically distinct event occurred here.

Observations made during the grid collection concerned the behavior of the raw material when it was subjected to weathering, prehistoric knapping techniques, or cattle disturbance. The irregular form of a majority of the chunks seemed to be the result of noncultural forces; however, their sheer number and association with definite artifacts indicated at least that they could be tested cobbles. In order to better understand the nature of artifacts within the R-O-W, a nonrandom sample was collected from a section of the undisturbed western half of the terrace. The intent was to compare this sample with that collected from within the R-O-W to see what differences or similarities existed and how these might be explained. Sample 1 (see Figure 30) was collected from within a 10 m^2 unit, sectioned into four 5 m^2 quadrants. Subsequent reconnaissance of the site revealed that similar raw material, in the form of bedrock outcrops and large angular fragments, occurred on the upper ridges west of the R-O-W, and it was noted that artifact types differed markedly. Intrasite variability could be expected at a lithic quarry/workshop. Due to restrictions during the survey, however, the true extent and complex variability at the site could not be assessed at that time. Therefore, a second nonrandom sample. Sample 2, was collected from the crest of the western ridge adjacent to the terrace in order to quantitatively assess variability. Because of the extremely high density of material this sample unit was arbitrarily restricted to an area 5 m square. The results of comparing the artifacts from the sample units and the R-O-W are discussed in Chapter 7.

Locus 2. This portion of the site extends from the southern edge of the cattle tank south to the Graham County-Cochise County line for a distance of 350 m within the R-O-W. The R-O-W crosses the base of the ridges that border the eastern edge of the site. The general topography at the foot of these ridges is one of low relief with low rises and much deep channel cutting and cattle disturbance. The northern portion of Locus 2 contains a partially exposed bedrock that has a thin soil cover. This bedrock is a distinctive, friable fine-grained gray rhyolite that is subject to extensive natural fracturing. The southern portion of Locus 2 is a shallow basin containing a moderately dense scatter of chert and chalcedony nodules (Figure 32).

Figure 32. AZ CC:10:11, Locus 2, southern extent. General view east showing basin area of chert/chalcedony workshop.

Vegetation in the area, denser than at Locus 1, is dominate by yucca, snakeweed, burroweed, catclaw, and whitethorn.

A grid column was laid down the R-O-W corridor, 30 m wide and 350 m long. This was sectioned into 5 m^2 units (Figure 33). Due to time and logistical constraints, a 50 percent nonrandom geometric sample was collected from within the grid, rather than the standard 100 percent sample.

During data recovery at Locus 2, three dense lithic concentrations were found which appeared to be discrete lithic reduction areas. These were designated Features 1, 2, and 3. The features averaged 3.8 m by 6.5 m in diameter, and contained numerous flakes, shatter, and core fragments. A few tools were also found within the debitage scatter. Each feature was photographed, mapped, recorded, and collected as a unit.

Summary. After completion of the grid collection, the site area to the west and east was examined to better understand the nature of each locus and the extent of the entire site. It was discovered that three distinct types of

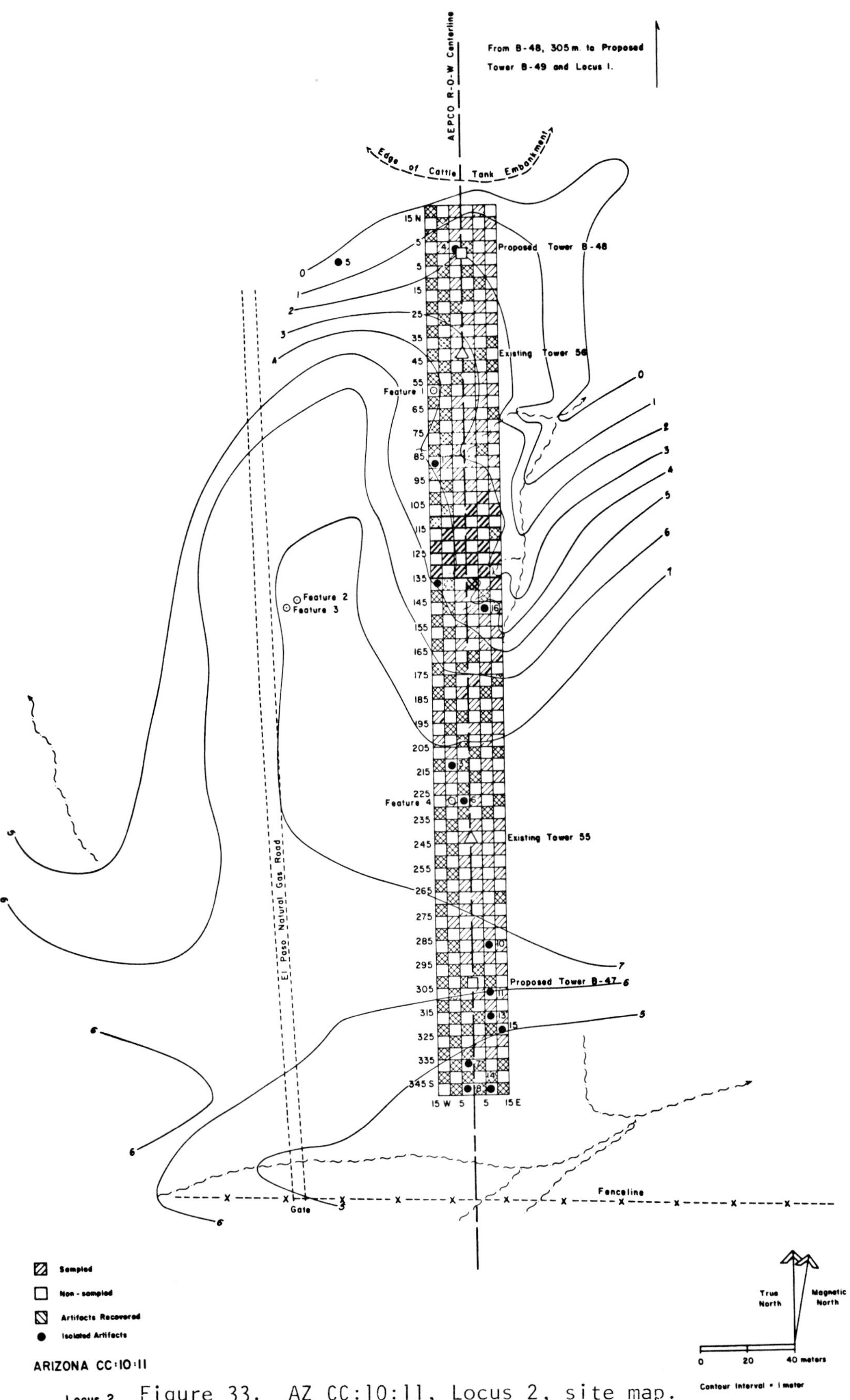

Figure 33. AZ CC:10:11, Locus 2, site map.

raw material were used: a purple to brown felsite ranging from a fine to medium grain; a medium-grained gray to pinkish-gray rhyolite; and cryptocrystalline silicates: chert, chalcedony, agate, and quartz. The geographical distribution of these three types is also distinct although they overlap, indicating possible site continuity.

Locus 1 is but one small section of a vast felsite cobble quarry and series of workshops. Lithic debitage is extremely dense on the east slopes and crests of the western ridges bordering the detrital fan. This carpet of flakes, cores, and tools extends over the ridge crests, down the west slope, and continues up the ridge system toward the upper Pinaleño Mountains. The material begins to thin out with the increase in elevation. Our survey ended at a point approximately 500 m west of the R-O-W, where material becomes increasingly sparse. The furthest western extent remains undefined. The distribution of felsite artifacts tends to occur with the natural distribution of raw material. Hence, felsite artifacts tend to be confined to the detrital fan and the ridges to the west and northwest, although several isolated felsite artifacts were found elsewhere.

Locus 2 essentially comprises two basic lithic areas distinguished by raw material type. A high knoll in the central part of the site west of the cattle tank and outside the R-O-W is composed of gray to pinkish-gray rhyolite. The surface of this knoll, especially at the crest and upper slopes, is strewn with cores, large and small flakes, and tools. In addition, dense concentrations of irregular rhyolite fragments and chunks are found. The second component of Locus 2 is situated in the dish-shaped basin at the southern end of the site. It comprises a series of workshop areas within a dense scatter of siliceous pebbles and nodules which do not occur elsewhere on the site. The grid column crossed only the extreme southeastern periphery of this artifact scatter. The western extent of the siliceous artifact scatter was traced as far as 200 m from the R-O-W centerline, at which point the basin gives way to an elevated system of low knolls on which the artifact scatter becomes sparse. A vesicular basalt mano and metate were found on a rise immediately southwest of the basin; as with the metate at Locus 1, the relationship of the ground stone to the lithic workshop area is uncertain.

The eastern boundary of the site was clearly defined at the base of the ridges that flank the eastern periphery of the site basin. A few isolated artifacts do occur on the lower slopes, but raw material on this ridge system was not utilized as heavily as on the western ridges.

AZ CC:10:13

Elevation: 1345 to 1358 m
Site Size: 178 m along R-O-W by 250 m E/W (arbitrary)
Field Designation: AEPCO 217

This site is a moderately dense lithic scatter on the crest and north and south slopes of west-to-east trending ridge of the Pinaleño upper bajadas (Figure 34). The north slope dips gently to form a broad pediment cut through by a wide sandy arroyo. The south slope, however, is very steep with a correspondingly narrow drainage. Several chipping stations occur on the crest of the ridge within the general artifact scatter. The majority of artifacts are primary decortication flakes of medium-grained brown rhyolite. A lesser number of artifacts are of chalcedony, chert, and basalt. Although few rhyolite bedrock outcrops are on the ridge, there is an abundance of medium to large-sized angular cobbles on the surface. Also many cobbles are exposed on the lower ridge slopes and in the erosional troughs on either side of the ridge. A great deal of natural thermal fracturing has occurred, and it was often difficult to determine natural from cultural flaking on cobbles. In some instances cobbles exhibiting thermal fracture scars also displayed flake scars caused by knapping or use. The site has been disturbed by previous construction of the 115 kV line, cattle grazing and a D-8 Caterpillar driven down the R-O-W.

The general topography of the area is one of massive, rounded, west-to-east trending parallel ridges that finger out from the Pinaleño Mountains. Broad, deep erosional troughs drain between these fingers resulting in a markedly undulating landform. These drainages run into Gold Gulch 7.5 km southeast, and thence to San Simon Creek.

Soils in the area are of the Atascosa, Chiricahua and Signal series (predominantly the two former, which have been described for AZ CC:10:11). These shallow, well-drained soils with moderate permeability formed on weathering igneous bedrock. Signal series soils are more characteristic of the lower ridges of the Pinaleño upper bajadas, occurring on ridge slopes.

Figure 34. AZ CC:10:13, general environmental view. Tower is in center of site. Pinaleño foothills in the background.

The ridge crest on which the site is located is quite flat and even, with a few small knolls. The ridge crest is quite barren of large vegetation, but supports a dense community of bunchgrass, catclaw, snakeweed, and low-growing succulents. Vegetation in the washes bordering the ridges is dense and varied, including such economic plants as mesquite, yucca, desert willow, and catclaw.

Due to the site's conformation, adjustments were made in the data recovery plan. First, a grid column was laid out within the R-O-W corridor, then a second column was laid out perpendicular to and bisecting the R-O-W (Figure 35). Although the site was originally recorded as being 178 m along the R-O-W, materials on the north and south ridge slopes were extremely sparse averaging one item per 10 m^2. Gridding the R-O-W for the total 178 m to pick up so few items was not efficient. It was decided that sufficient information about the site could be obtained by collecting the surface materials from the denser central portion of the site. As such, the grid along the R-O-W corridor is 100 m long; the second, bisecting grid is 25 m wide and extends from 60 m on either side of the centerline. All surface artifacts from within the grid network were collected and a contour map made of the ridge top. Of a total of 210 units sampled, 106 yielded artifacts for a 50.5 percent data recovery of the grid.

During the grid collection, three lithic concentrations, that represent discrete knapping loci, were recorded and designated as Features 1, 2, and 3.

Feature 1.

Dimensions: 3.6 m N/S by 3.3 m E/W
Location: Grid Unit 15N 10E

This feature is a dense concentration of chipped stone of two varieties of rhyolite and may represent two chipping stations. A large rhyolite hamerstone was also found within the lithic debris. One type of rhyolite is a distinctive greenish-yellow color and contains a quantity of low-grade inclusions. The finer material has a chert-like quality, and it appears that the flaking was performed in such a manner as to maximize procurement of flakes of this finer material.

Feature 2.

Dimensions: 3.7 m N/S by 3.15 m E/W
Location: Grid Unit 0S 35E

This feature is a dense concentration of fine-grained brown rhyolite flakes, core fragments, and a large core.

Feature 3.

Dimensions: 3.6 m N/S by 2.4 m E/W
Location: Grid Unit 10N 15W

This feature is a smaller concentration of flakes and cores of a fine-grained gray rhyolite and represents a third chipping station.

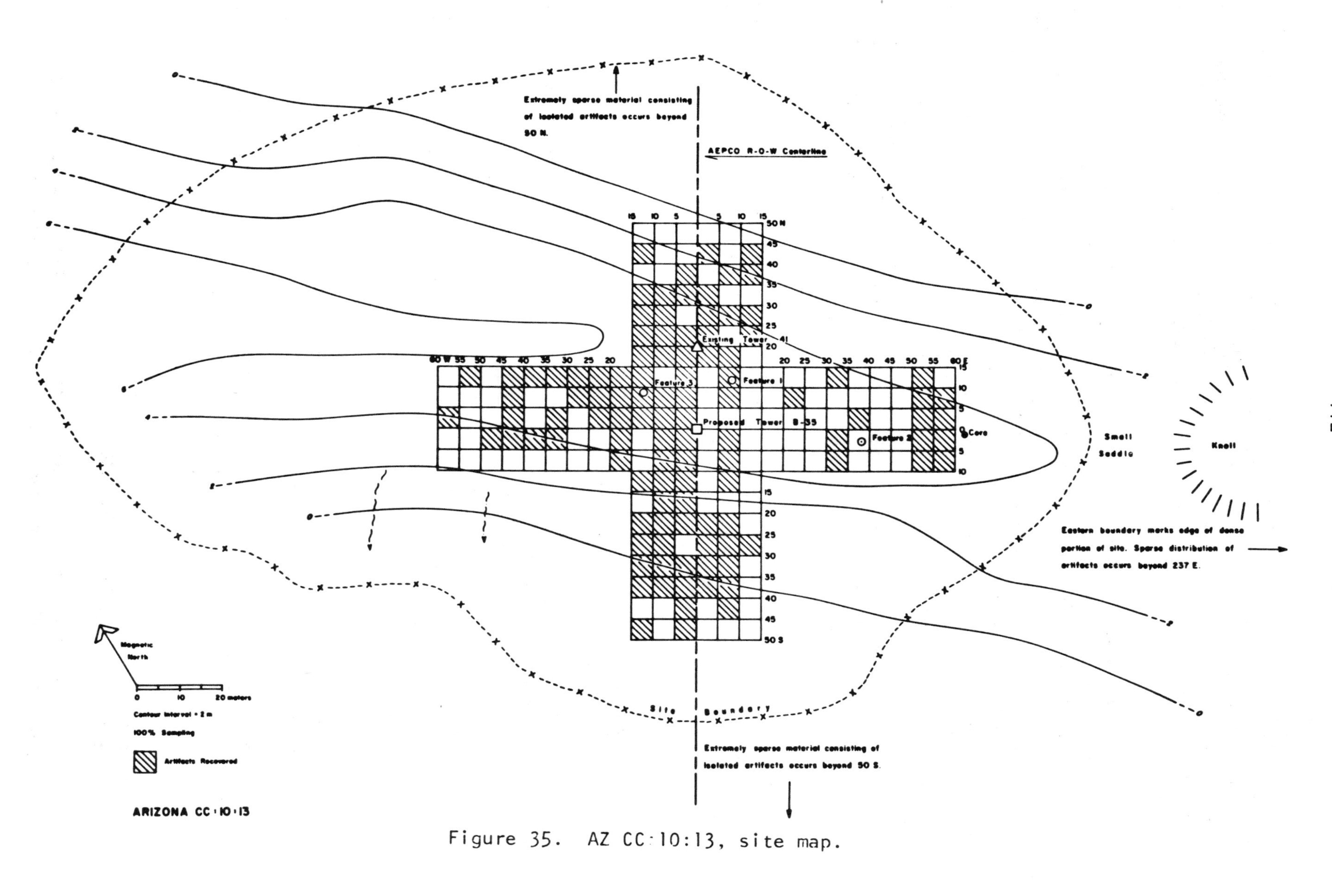

Figure 35. AZ CC:10:13, site map.

Each of the features was mapped and photographed. Analysis and interpretation of the features and the general artifact collection are discussed in Chapter 7.

AZ CC:10:14

Elevation: 1344 to 1362 m
Site Size: 347 m (along centerline) by 230 m (arbitrary)
Field Designation: AEPCO 218

This site is situated 1.10 km southwest of AEPCO 127, in the same physiographic setting. It is a lithic scatter on the crest and upper slopes of a southeast-trending ridge fingering out from the Pinaleño Mountains (Figure 36). Steep, deep erosional troughs parallel the ridge on the north and south, draining in Gold Gulch 7.6 km southeast. The Fisher Hills 6.8 km to the northeast and the Dos Cabezas Mountains 10 km to the south are visible from the ridge crest. The San Simon basin lies approximately 5 km to the east (Figure 37). Local vegetation is dominated by catclaw, snakeweed, burroweed, and whitethorn acacia. Mimosa and rainbow and prickly pear cacti occur occasionally, and are densest at the base of the ridge. Soils in the area are the shallow, well-drained types of the Chiricahua, Atascosa, and Signal series. The surface soils are composed of a loamy sand overlaid with a dense cover of igneous gravels, pebbles, and cobbles. The dominant natural stone is rhyolite, which was used in lithic reduction activities at the site. Few bedrock outcrops occur on the ridge and there are several small, dense concentrations of angular fragments.

Data recovery at this site was similar to that carried out at AZ CC:10:13 due to similarities in artifact distribution along the ridge crest; that is, the majority of the site was concentrated along the east-west ridgetop axis, perpendicular to the R-O-W. Although the survey crew noted that the site extended 374 m along the R-O-W, artifacts on the middle and lower ridge slopes were few and isolated. Indeed, a "trail" of isolated artifacts occurs across the ridges and drainages between AZ CC:10:13 and 14. A decision was made to grid the R-O-W within the area of maximum impact (tower construction) and establish a perpendicular grid bisecting the R-O-W and parallel to the site's long axis. Since five lithic concentrations occur within the general lithic scatter along the ridge crest, three of which are situated outside the R-O-W, it was felt that a more representative sample of site activities could be obtained by recording and collecting these discrete concentrations and the dense lithic scatter in the main site area. For the most part, the lithic concentrations consist of a few cores and core fragments and numerous debitage flakes.

The grid extended along the 30 m wide R-O-W corridor for a distance of 50 m north and 25 m south of proposed tower B-31 (Datum 00). The 20 m wide crosswise grid bisected the R-O-W grid between 15 and 35 m north of Datum 00 and extended 60 m east and 60 m west from the centerline (Figure 38). As anticipated, artifact distribution was sparse with units generally yielding two to five artifacts. These flakes, cores, and tools were predominantly rhyolite, in varying grain sizes. As at AZ CC:10:13, much natural fracturing

Figure 36. AZ CC:10:14, general environmental view, looking west toward Pinaleño foothills. Tower is in center of site.

Figure 37. AZ CC:10:14, general environmental view, looking east from site to San Simon Basin in background. The Fisher Hills are to the left, Dos Cabezas Mountains to the right.

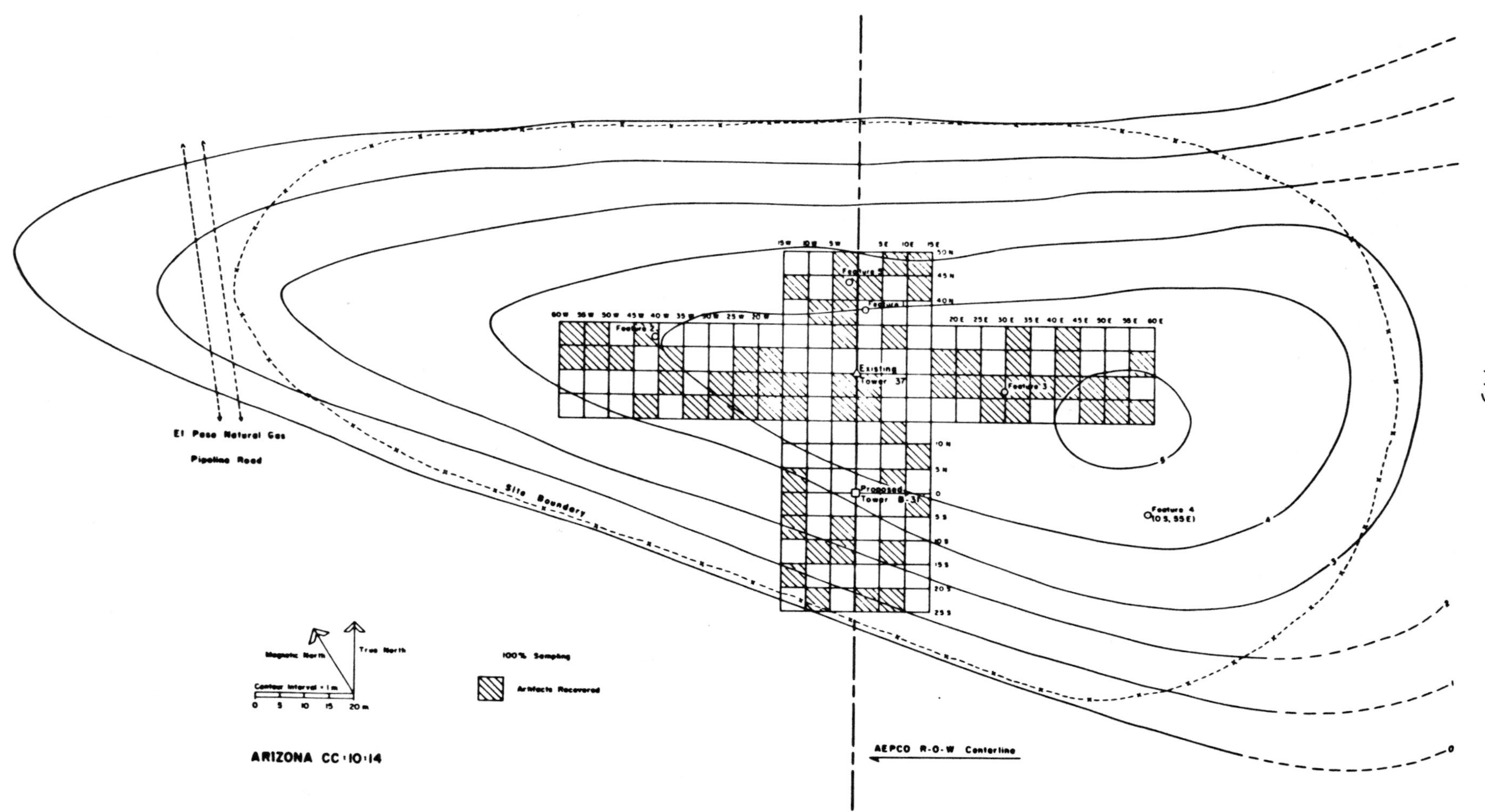

Figure 38. AZ CC:10:14, site map.

and spalling has occurred on large cobbles. A few artifacts made from silicates--agate, chert, and chalcedony--were also found, primarily in the form of secondary flakes and "chunks." Only a few large pebbles of siliceous material occur on the ridge. The low number of silicate artifacts appears to be related to the low availability of this raw material.

Each of the five lithic concentrations was given a consecutive feature number, mapped, recorded, photographed, and collected as a unit. Analysis and interpretation of the lithics contained within each concentration is presented in Chapter 7.

Stratum 3: Dos Cabezas Lower Bajadas

AZ CC:9:2

Elevation: 1284 to 1289 m
Site Size: 380 m (along centerline) by 60 m E/W (arbitrary)
Field Designation: AEPCO 220

This dense, expansive lithic scatter with numerous ground stone artifacts is situated at the interface of the lower bajada of the Dos Cabezas Mountains and the Sulphur Spring Valley floor (Figures 39 and 40). The upper Dos Cabezas Mountains are approximately 2.8 km norhteast and the lake bed shore of Willcox Playa lies 8 km southwest. The topography of the immediate site area is a gently west-sloping broad pediment with low relief, crossed by numerous east-west running small drainages ranging from 4 to 20 cm deep and from 0.2 to 4.0 m wide. Generally, these channels are not arroyos but broad belts of sheetwash erosion. Wind erosion has created numerous blowout areas in which discrete artifact concentrations are found (Figure 41). The effects of natural erosion have been exacerbated by overgrazing, resulting in horizontal displacement of artifacts and features. The site map (Figure 42) illustrates only a few of these drainages to illustrate direction of flow. Dense mesquite greatly hindered site mapping.

As discussed previously, soils in the area are of the Sonoita series, formed in mixed old alluvium from coarse-grained acidic igneous rocks. Dense, small gravels abound on the surface.

Vegetation in the immediate vicinity is dominated by mesquite, with lesser numbers of saltbush, snakeweed, graythorn, and several varieties of grasses. Russian thistle is invading the area as a result of disturbance by overgrazing and chaining.

A significant aspect of this site is its accessibility to a variety of natural resources, which may account in part for the apparent intensity of occupation as indicated by the dense surface artifact assemblage. To the northeast are the mountain resources of the Dos Cabezas; west, south and southwest are the Dos Cabezas lower bajadas with dense mesquite and acacia communities and the Sulphur Spring Valley grassland environment.

Figure 39. AZ CC:9:2, general view of site, looking south down R-O-W. Sulphur Spring Basin in the distance.

Figure 40. AZ CC:9:2, general view of site, looking north down R-O-W. Dos Cabezas Mountains in background.

Figure 41. AZ CC:9:2, erosional channel with scattered artifacts.

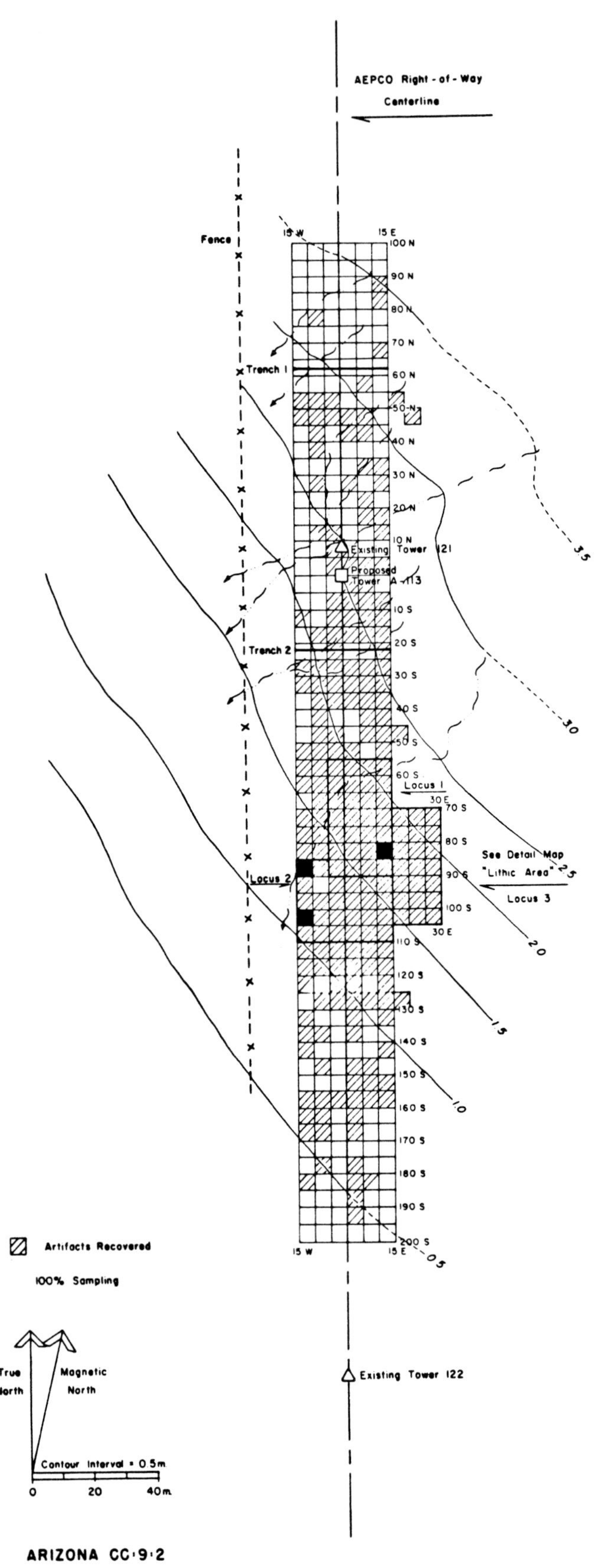

Figure 42. AZ CC:9:2, site map.

North of the site is a pass between the Dos Cabezas and Pinaleño mountains, allowing access to the Pinaleño Mountain lower and upper bajadas and eventually to the Gila River.

Raw material for ground stone implements such as manos and metates is available in the immediate vicinity, since the Dos Cabezas are composed primarily of coarse-grained metamorphic rock. Fine-grained raw material for small chipped stone implements is rare. Surface soils at the site are gravelly sands with few stones larger than fist size. A majority of the small lithic tools and debitage are cryptocrystalline silicates such as jasper, chert, and chalcedony; quartzite and basalt constitute most of the larger artifacts. It is likely that the silicates were brought in from elsewhere, while basalt and quartzite were available in the upper bajada region, less than 1 km east. Obsidian was also noted, undoubtedly obtained from elsewhere.

The presence of certain projectile point types, absence of pottery, and preponderance of one-hand manos recorded on the survey indicated a San Pedro stage Cochise site. However, when the site was revisited during the data recovery phase, a few plainware and redware sherds were found outside the R-O-W. One plainware sherd was found in the R-O-W during data recovery. This is not to dispute the cultural designation of the site, but rather to point out that elsewhere, beyond the R-O-W, there are indications that the site was also occupied at a time later than the San Pedro stage.

The R-O-W corridor transects the present western periphery of the site. Twenty-five m west of the centerline is a fence and west of this the land has been drastically altered by chaining, cultivation, and grazing. A few isolated artifacts found for a distance approximately 50 m west of the corridor indicate the site may have covered an area greater than is now visible, although this cannot now be determined. Eastward from the corridor, the site extends 500 m and terminates at a point where the pediment gives way to the Dos Cabezas foothills. Additional disturbance at the site has been caused by collectors who, according to the leasee of the land, commonly removed points, metates, and pottery from sites in the area.

Data recovery focused on collecting all surface material from within the R-O-W and identifying discrete artifact concentrations within the general artifact scatter so that such areas could be tested for deposition. The 30 m wide corridor was gridded into 5 m^2 units with the general grid column in alignment with the north-south orientation of the R-O-W. Proposed tower A-113 served as Datum 00. The grid extended 100 m north and 200 m south from this datum. The entire column comprised 360 grid units all of which were sampled. Of these, 216 (60 percent) yielded artifactual material.

The general distribution of artifacts tended to be a function of surface conditions. For example, artifacts were quite sparse in the northernmost 100 m of the grid. A heavy growth of mesquite dominates this area and was nearly impenetrable in some places with the dense, low-growing thickets obscuring much of the surface. However, the overall sparseness of artifacts in the northern 100 m of the grid and outside the R-O-W suggests that sparseness is typical for this section. South from Datum 00, artifact density increases considerably; the section from 50S to 130S (total length 80 m) contained numerous and varied artifact types made from diverse raw materials. Within the general artifact scatter were three discrete activity areas, although there is considerable overlap between them. These are referred to as Loci 1, 2, and 3 and were tested.

Original research goals called for defining the true extent of the site, mapping, collecting, and testing within the R-O-W. The main area of the site to the east was not sampled or tested, although additional information was recorded in order to more completely assess the site's eligibility for nomination to the National Register. The purpose of testing was to determine the nature and extent of subsurface cultural deposition. Although the previous backhoe testing indicated no great cultural depth, the density of surface artifacts in areas not trenched suggested that some shallow deposition was present. Examination of artifact concentrations indicated that during the earlier trenching, the impact of the backhoe bucket was so great that it obliterated traces of artifact-bearing levels near the surface. One goal of data recovery was additional testing to determine if the shallow depth of the site was due to cultural or erosional processes. A second goal was to obtain more information on artifact concentrations to determine what activities were conducted at these loci. Much time was taken up during surface collection and mapping due to the large area and complexity of surface remains and difficulty in working within the mesquite forest. Consequently, little time was available for testing. Several methods of sampling were considered but rejected as too time consuming. It was felt that the most useful information about site activities could be obtained from the three loci, and subsequently, test pits were placed in units of highest artifact density.

Locus 1. This area, at 5S to 95S, 5W to 10E (greatest density at 75S to 80S, 0-10E), is a section where several complete and fragmentary projectile points and numerous tiny (less than 10 mm) flakes were found. The vast majority of these artifacts were of chert, jasper, fine-grained basalt, and obsidian and, reviewed as a whole, may be indicative of a specialized task area. Grid unit 80S 10E was selected for testing since it was an area of high artifact density and minimal disturbance. The unit was excavated in arbitrary 5 cm levels with all fill screened through 1/8 inch mesh screen. Cultural material was found to a depth of 20 cm below the surface with very few items found in the lowermost 5 cm. One projectile point, a denticulate tool, one mano fragment, and over 500 tiny flakes were recovered. Interestingly, jasper was commonest on the surface of the unit, yet was rare in the subsurface fill. No discrete concentrations of material were observed during the excavations; all material was homogeneously distributed through all levels. At 20 cm depth a circular charcoal-stained area was encountered which appeared to be a postmold containing charcoal and dark-stained fill. The charcoal was collected for radiocarbon dating; however, additional stripping failed to yield a pit house outline or occupation surface. Nor were the sides of the hole noticeably compacted or burned. This hole may actually be a rodent burrow; these were noted on the surface beyond the tested unit. Although 20 cm is admittedly shallow it is recognized as cultural depth. Cultural deposition has also been influenced by natural erosional processes, but not a great deal of horizontal displacement seems to have occurred.

Locus 2. Locus 2 (Figure 43) is situated in a northeast-to-northwest trending blowout/erosional channel area. The majority of artifacts observed on the surface were broken and, as such, the area appeared to be a trash deposit. However, numerous pieces of ground stone occurred in this area—more than elsewhere within the R-O-W—and it was felt that this could be a discrete activity area where vegetal food processing tasks were carried out. Two test units were opened up to determine the true nature of the artifact deposit (trash area vs activity area) and to test for depth.

Locus 3. Locus 3, situated immediately east of the R-O-W at 70S to 105S, is a slightly water-eroded blowout area containing a well-defined artifact assemblage (Figures 44 and 45). This locus was chosen for detailed mapping and collection of surface artifacts since it was an excellent example of the blowout-exposed, overlapping activity areas so typical in the eastern and central portions of the site. The eastern boundary of Locus 3 was arbitrarily set at the edge of a dense mesquite thicket, yet it obviously overlaps with other activity areas to the north and east. All large artifacts (cores, hammerstones, manos, and metate fragments) and recognizable tools and preforms were mapped by point provenience. Additionally, three features were mapped, photographed, and recorded. The area was then gridded and all remaining material collected (Figure 45). The features are amorphous, disarticulated rock clusters comprised primarily of flat schist cobbles. This is not particularly unusual except that schist rarely occurs on the site and is encountered in quantity only near the eastern periphery of the site near the Dos Cabezas foothills. Some of the cobbles appear to be modified around the edges, but this was difficult to definitely determine because of the friable nature of the material. The rocks do not appear to have been piled in any manner; all are resting on the surface and appear to once have had a circular confromation. Features 1 and 2 contain 12 to 15 schist cobbles in a circular arrangement, each averaging 1 m in diameter. Feature 1 could be remnants of a hearth, since several rocks have been burned. Feature 3 is 2.6 m in diameter and contains quartz and andesite cobbles in addition to schist cobbles. The function of these rock clusters is not known. They occur at sporadic intervals across the site and are invariably found in association with lithics and ground stone. They could be the result of clearing land for agriculture (thus explaining why so few cobbles are found on the site surface), platforms for supporting baskets, stones for heating water (although few exhibited thermal fracturing or burning), "sleeping circles," or small check or diversion dams to control water flow or erosion. This last interpretation is less tenable, however, since a great deal of recent sheetwash erosion has occurred and some clusters may be redeposited disarticulated features.

Interpretations of site activities at AZ CC:9:2 are reserved for Chapter 8, following the analyses of ground stone and chipped stone artifacts.

Figure 43. AZ CC:9:2, Locus 2, eroded trash area. View northeast, with Dos Cabezas in the background.

Figure 44. AZ CC:9:2, Locus 3, blowout area with artifact concentrations. View northeast with Dos Cabezas in the background.

Stratum 4: Willcox Playa Dunes

AZ CC:13:11

<u>Elevation</u>: 1278 m
<u>Site Size</u>: 120 m N/S by 65 m E/W
<u>Field Designation</u>: AEPCO 223

This site is situated on the northeasternmost large dune formed by the prevailing winds which erode the Willcox Playa surface 6.75 km to the southwest. There is a gradual 3 m rise from the site to a crest approximately 175 m east of the transmission line centerline.

The general dune environment is an undulating surface presently covered by dense vegetation (Figure 46). Mesquite is the dominant plant, with grasses subdominant. Other plants are common but none are individually abundant. Among these are yucca, sagebrush, burroweed, and graythorn. Some small scattered areas are completely free of vegetation, giving the area a patchy appearance especially on the ridge and steeper dune slopes.

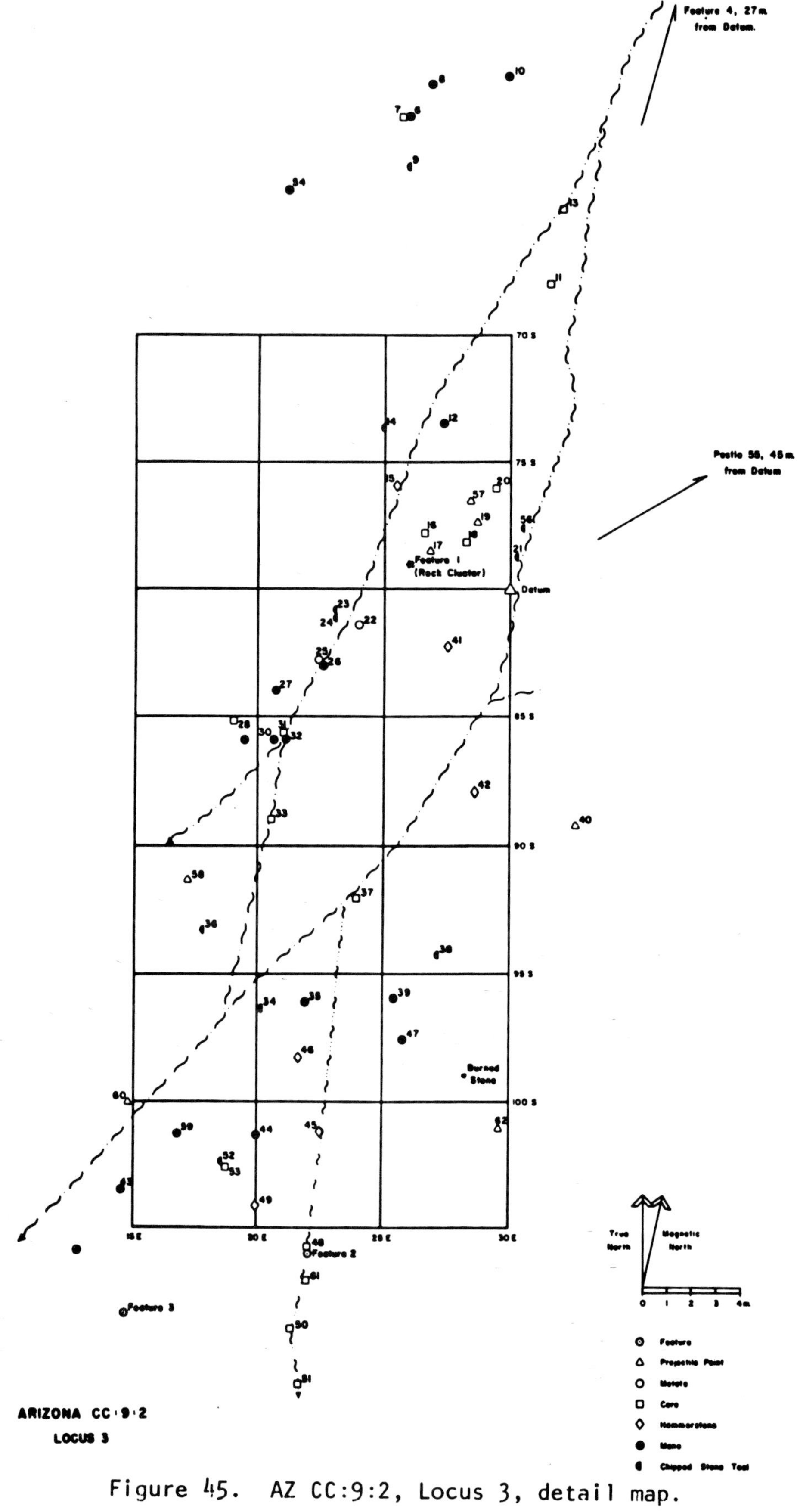

Figure 45. AZ CC:9:2, Locus 3, detail map.

Figure 46. AZ CC:13:11, general environment of site. View is east, looking toward Dos Cabezas Mountains.

Vinton series loamy sand soil is deep and well drained, and is only moderately alkaline to neutral, thus being partly suited to dune dry farming. Although this environmental stratum is characterized by numerous small playas interspersed between the dunes, there are none in the immediate vicinity of AZ CC:13:11, nor was there any other type of drainage or water source apparent. There is no lithic raw material available in the site vicinity.

Both natural and human disturbance have occurred in this area. The primary natural agent has been wind, resulting in the desposition (and to a lesser degree the erosion) of aeolian sand. Rainfall probably accounts for some erosion, and rodent disturbance was also observed. Human disturbance is easier to recognize with transmission line contruction and grazing predominant. The current lessee recalls at least a 40 year history of grazing for this area, and has noticed a gradual increase in the mesquite population. Previous AEPCO construction placed existing tower 108 on the southern periphery of the site, and a shallow, bladed centerline access road almost exactly bisects the artifact distribution on its long axis.

The survey identified the site as a sparse lithic and sherd scatter with two small, well-defined artifact concentrations (Figures 47 and 48). Research recommendations called for 100 percent surface collection, mapping, and testing prior to formal date recovery, but this site was not investigated during the testing phase.

Figure 47. AZ CC:13:11, southern artifact concentration (Feature 1). Flags indicate artifacts.

Figure 48. AZ CC:13:11, northern artifact concentration.

The first task was to clarify the association between the material within the R-O-W (Locus 1) and that outside the corridor on the dune ridge. An abundance of artifacts occur along this ridge; the concentration was designated Locus 2. An intensive reconnaissance revealed a definable area free of surface material, intermediate between the two artifact distributions. Since Locus 2 was well outside the corridor and would not be affected by construction activities, data recovery focused on Locus 1. Locus 2 investigations are described in more detail below.

Locus 1. The surface of Locus 1 was examined, and artifacts were flagged and collected according to a 5 m^2 grid system (Figure 49). Three concentrations were designated features and treated as separate units. Because of the density of vegetation and the artifact sparseness actual grids were not laid out. Rather, artifact provenience was recorded in reference to a set of N/S and E/W axes.

Only one of the artifact concentrations was collected and mapped by point provenience methods. After testing determined the presence of abundant subsurface material the research methodology was revised and the second artifact concentration collected by grid units. The results of the general site surface collection are presented below and illustrated in Figure 50:

Ceramics	110/40.1%
Lithics	110/40.1%
Ground stone	6/ 2.2%
Bone	35/12.8%
Cracked rock	13/ 4.7%
N =	274

The artifact concentration called Feature 1 was arbitrarily limited to two 5 m^2 units, 5N 5W and 5N 10W. Although artifacts were also collected in all adjacent units but one (5N 0E), the density in Feature 1 was much higher and the arbitrary cutoff was made with some assurance that those materials collected in this group would be spatially and functionally related. The overall feature density is 2.9 artifacts per m^2 compared with only 0.6 per m^2 in the densest surrounding unit. The inventory of artifacts by class collected from Feature 1 is:

Ceramics	86/58.5%
Lithics	44/29.9%
Ground stone	2/ 1.4%
Bone	2/ 1.4%
Cracked rock	13/ 8.8%
N =	147

The artifacts are scattered over approximately one-half of the two-grid (50 m^2) area (Figure 51) which is primarily in a slightly depressed area free of vegetation (see Figure 47).

Artifact distribution in Feature 1 has been disturbed by construction of an access road. The eastern one-third of the feature is almost devoid of artifacts. There were virtually no artifacts scattered along the roadway on the south side of Feature 1, but in the unit just north of this feature there was a relatively high quantity of artifacts. The slopes of a large ant hill on the north edge of the feature contained artifacts, primarily minute lithic debris, which probably was transported by these insects. Although the feature appears to be located in a blowout, it is impossible to tell whether erosion or soil deposition and vegetation establishment are occurring.

After Feature 1 was collected and mapped, a 2.5 m^2 test unit was dug in 5N 10W, SE. This unit was selected because it was in the lowest portion of the depression and required the least amount of overburden be removed to

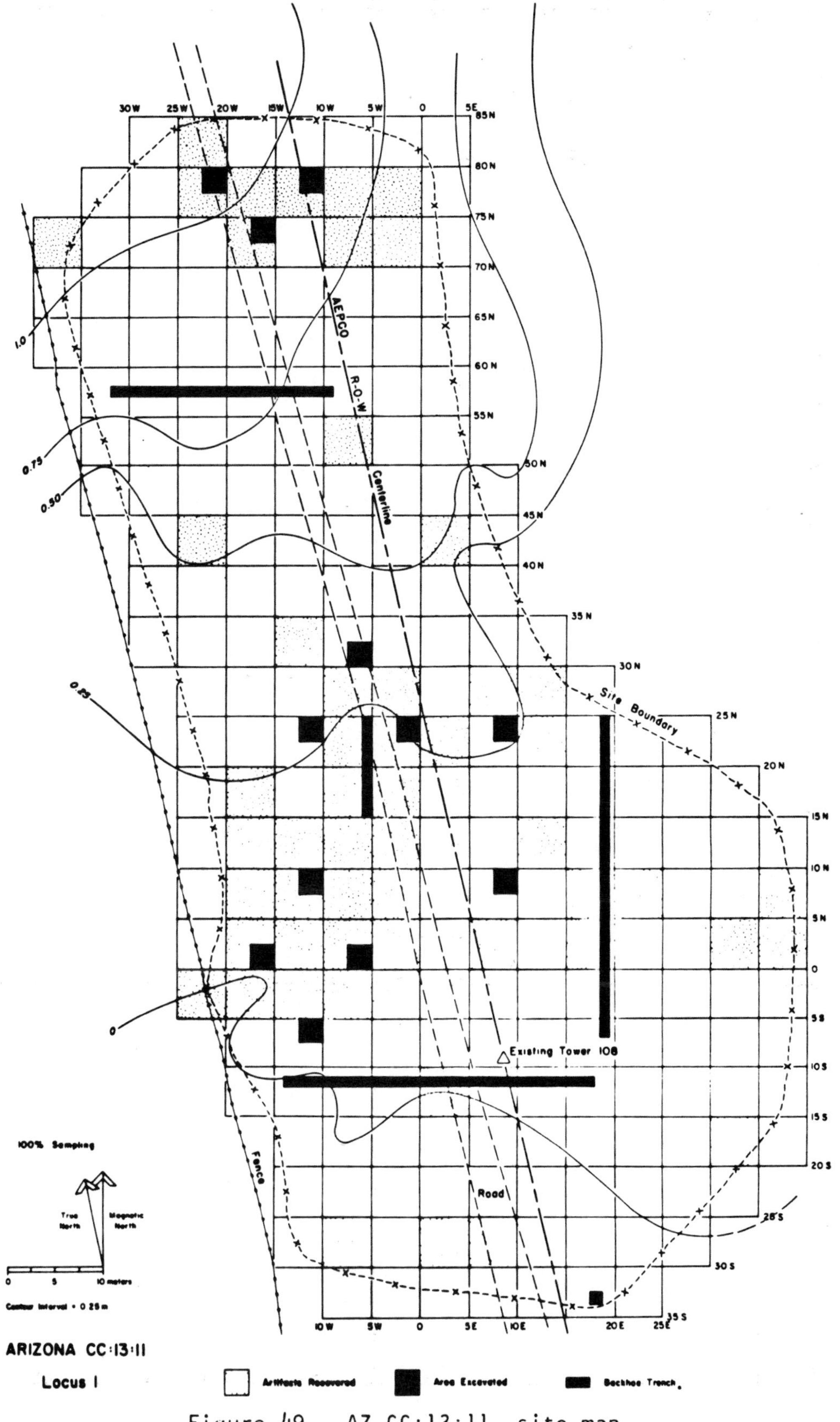

Figure 49. AZ CC:13:11, site map.

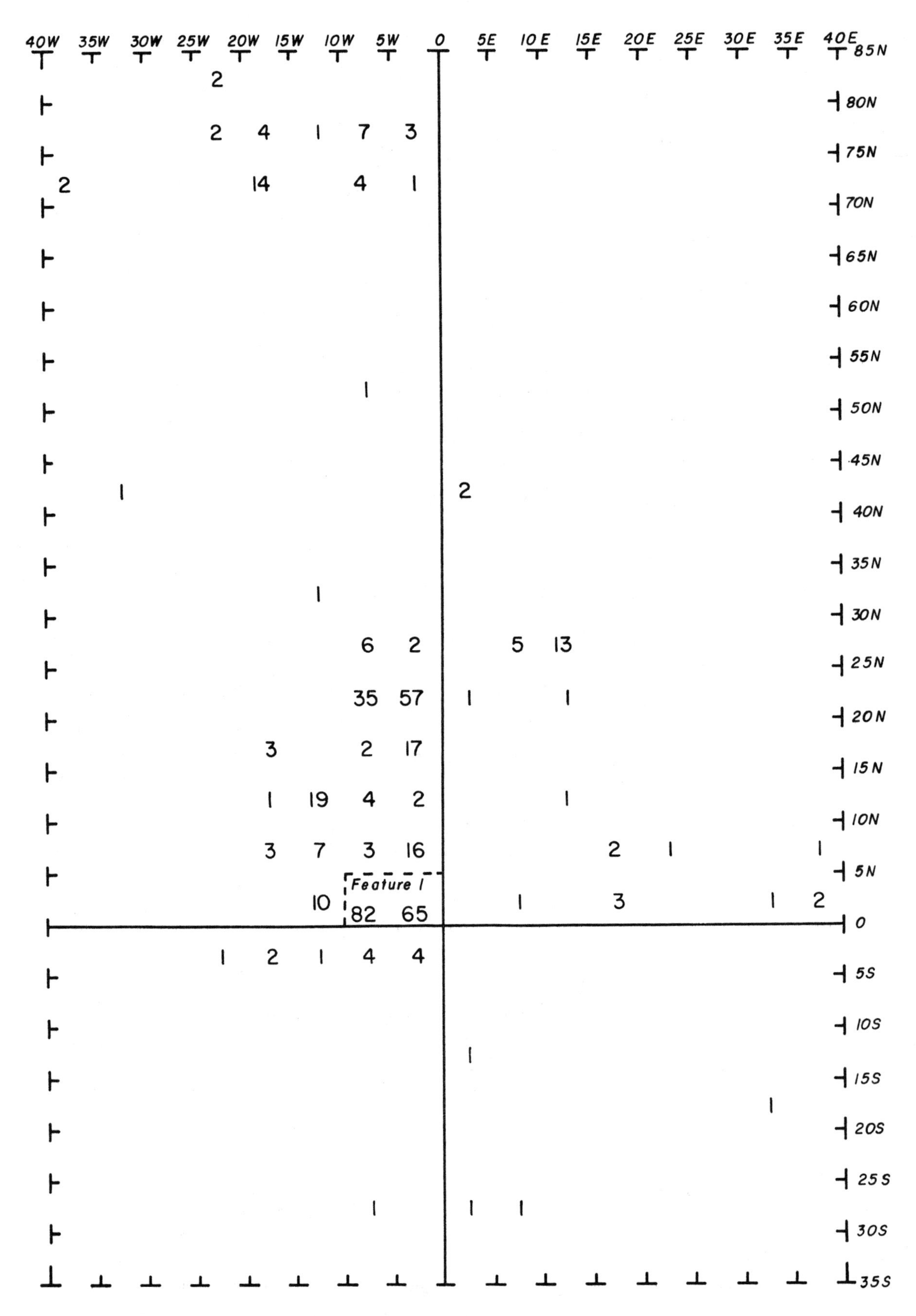

Figure 50. AZ CC:13:11, Locus 1. Artifact frequencies of collected grid units.

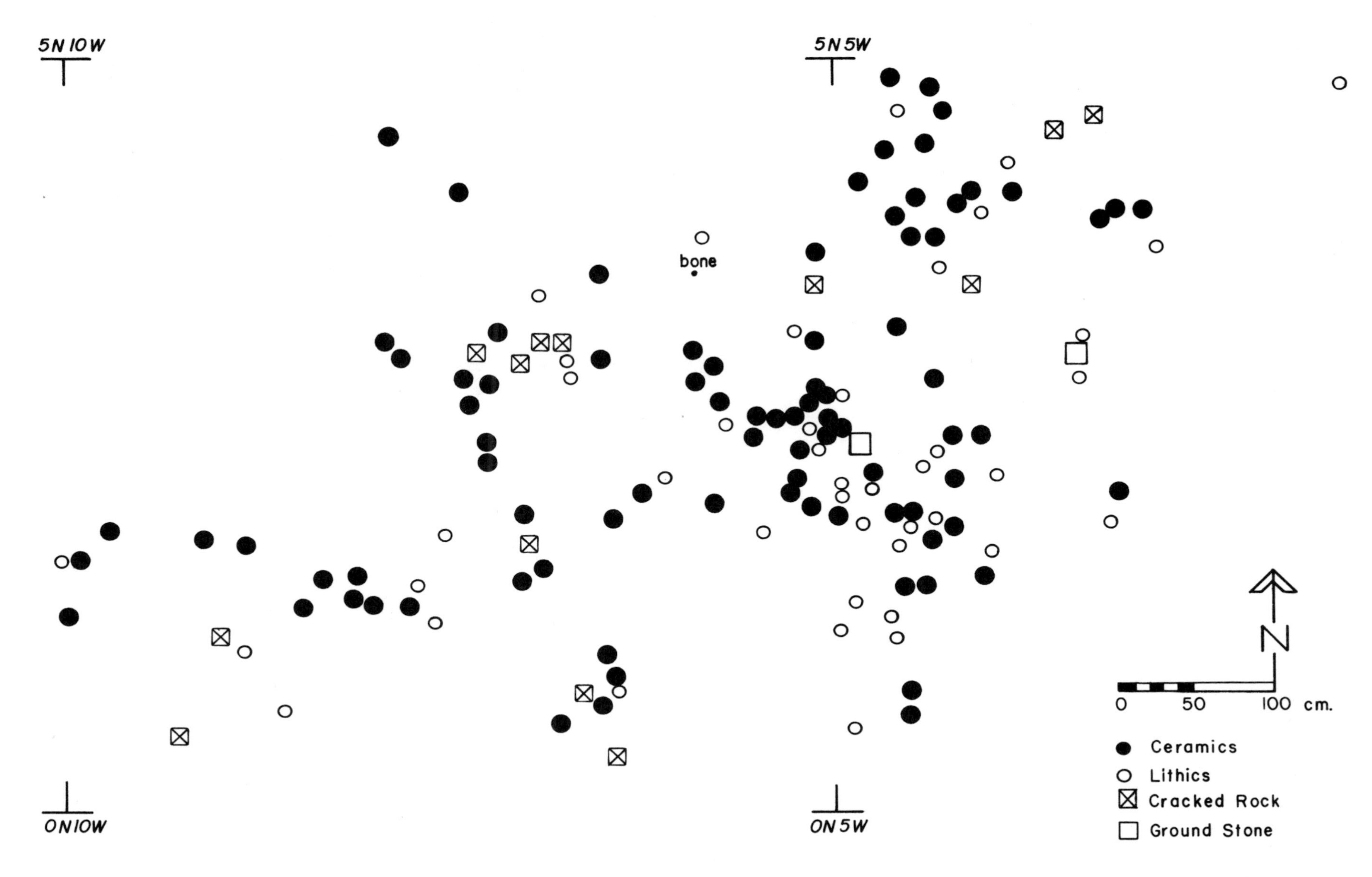

Figure 51. AZ CC:13:11, Feature 1 map.

determine the vertical extent of deposition. All excavation was completed with shovel and trowel and all fill was passed through 1/8 inch mesh screen. The uppermost soil (Level 1) was very fine, loose aeolian sand, and was merely scraped off to expose a moist, firm deposit. Level I varied between 2 and 4 cm, Levels II to VI were arbitrary 5 cm units, and Levels VII to VIII were arbitrary 10 cm units which were dug only in the west half of the test unit to expose stratigraphy.

Levels I to VI contained abundant artifacts which decreased in number with increasing depth. Nothing was recovered in Level VII, but Level VIII had two artifacts. The uppermost six levels consisted of charcoal and ash-stained soil, with a large pocket of charcoal unearthed in a rodent burrow between 26 and 40 cm below present ground surface. The lower two levels were virtually free of this staining. An excavation wall profile was drawn, notes taken, and the area backfilled to approximate the original surface configuration.

The inventory of artifacts by class from the entire excavated unit is:

Ceramics	190/31.1%
Lithics	128/21.0%
Ground stone	2/ 0.3%
Bone	290/47.5%
Cracked rock	0/ 0.0%
N =	610

A comparison of surface artifacts from Feature 1 (421 artifacts) and the general site surface (147 artifacts) indicates that not only are there more artifacts in the excavated unit than on the entire site surface, Feature 1 included, but that there also is a different distribution by class (Figure 52). Thus the test excavation showed that abundant subsurface deposition was likely, and placed the interpretive value of the surface collection alone in question. The very high percentage of bone from the test unit also indicated an emphasis on faunal exploitation which was not evident from survey or surface collection data. The test data strongly suggested subsurface occupation and additional work was conducted after surface investigations were completed.

A concentration of burned bone on the site's southern periphery was designated Feature 2. The majority of the bone was distributed within a 1.25 m^2 area (30S 10E, NW¼ of SE¼). In order to determine the nature of the bone deposit a sample excavation was carried out. All fill within the provenience was removed in two arbitrary 5 cm levels and passed through 1/8 inch mesh screen. All bone and abundant charcoal fragments occurred in the upper 5 cm level, and no artifacts were found. Several charred wood fragments and some rusted wire were found in the adjacent area.

The bone concentration was near a bladed section adjacent to the transmission line access road. A second, smaller bone concentration was located 30 m south of Feature 2, at the road edge. Also, an unburned, partially articulated coyote (?) skeleton was located west of the road, approximately 20 m from Feature 2. It was complete except for the limb bones.

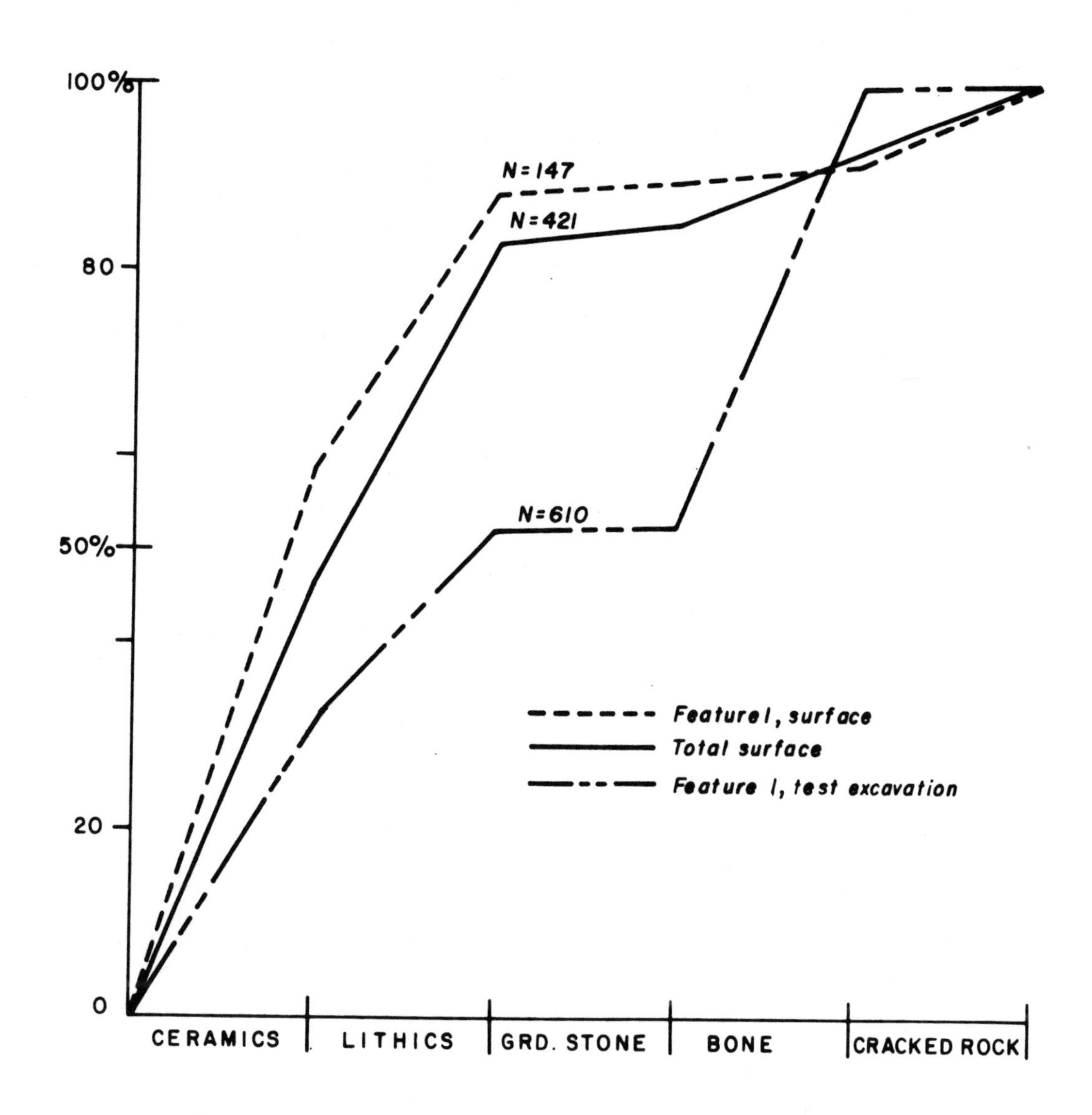

Figure 52. AZ CC:13:11, comparative artifact frequencies.

Analysis of the bone collected from Feature 2 was carried out by Jon S. Czaplicki. The majority was too small to be identified, but several vertebrae and carpal bones of a domestic horse (Equus cabalus) were identified. More detailed results of the bone analysis are found in Appendix 1.

A period of five days was allotted for testing Locus 1. Certain informal goals were established in light of the project research focus and data previously acquired from surface investigations and limited testing. These goals were (1) to determine the vertical and horizontal extent of occupation, and (2) to gather interpretive data on site activities. No refined temporal data were available from work to date, but it was assumed that multiple occupations could be defined in both vertical and horizontal dimensions. The surface artifact distribution (see Figure 51) indicated there were two possible occupation areas, and that the larger southern one had discrete task areas within it.

The site was systematically tested using 2.5 m^2 units. The advantages of this sampling scheme are discussed by Cochran (1953), and there are numerous archaeological examples of its use. Two checkerboard patterns placed over the site's two distinct deposits resulted in a maximum of 26 possible units for excavation. Major obstacles such as trees eliminated some of these from consideration and time constraints allowed only a maximum of 15 units for final consideration. Actual units were selected on a case by case basis, using previous excavation results to select the unit most likely to furnish data. Eleven 2.5 m^2 units and a 1 m by 10 m trench were excavated during this phase of research, which when combined with the Feature 1 test unit yielded approximately 14 excavated units (see Figure 49).

As units were excavated in 10 cm arbitrary levels, the fill was passed through 1/8 inch mesh screen. The topsoil was removed as a separate unit for convenience and to keep possible final occupation separate from earlier, lower cultural material. After each unit was excavated, recorded, and mapped, it was backfilled. Due to equipment and time shortages excavated fill was screened immediately adjacent to the excavated unit. During backfilling there was undoubtedly some alteration of the adjacent surface area, but the overall impact was probably not significant.

On the northern site periphery three units were dug to 13 cm below present ground surface. Twelve artifacts were recovered, the majority coming from the topsoil; no artifacts were found below 8 cm. The non-stained, sterile appearance of the soil and the low artifact density were sufficient criteria for halting excavation at the 13 cm level.

The southern area was similarily tested, but the sample pattern was more dispersed because a larger area was investigated. Unit wall profiles, which were not drawn in the shallow northern units, were mapped in all southern units. For stratigraphic purposes maximum unit excavation was to 80 cm below present ground surface. The greatest depth of cultural deposition appeared to be at the 60 cm level (in grid unit 10N 15W, NE quad), but this lower limit varied from unit to unit between 40 and 60 cm below present ground surface. The majority of material was recovered from the 10 to 30 cm level. Three to six natural or cultural stratigraphic layers could be observed in each unit wall profile, but only with some difficulty as soil texture was a consistent sandy loam. Color was variable but since standard color charts were not available for description and identification, color names were grossly approximated. Light brown to dark gray-brown soil colors predominated, and were judged to be significantly different from the Crot series soil upper horizon which are characteristically pale brown. The excessive darkening is probably due in part to the charcoal and ash scattered throughout the deposits. The coloring was consistent across all excavated units regardless of artifact density, but the densest units and levels did have the darkest soils.

Units 5S 15W, NE quad; 5N 20W, SE quad; and 10N 5E, NE quad produced virtually no artifacts or other evidence of occupation. These units were considered representative of the periphery of activity and partially defined the horizontal boundaries of occupation. In order to save time and to define the lowest occupation level, not all levels were screened; however this did not result in the loss of significant information on the nature and extent of occupation.

The trench and four units (25N 5E, NE quad; 35N 10W, SE quad; 25N 15W, NE quad; 25N 5W, NE quad) yielded a moderate amount of cultural material, with the latter two units having relatively more. The first two units were probably on the fringes of major site activity. Material appeared to be mixed refuse.

Only Feature 1 and unit 10N 15W, NE quad had a high quantity of cultural material. This latter unit was also the deepest and contained the largest variety of artifact types. One large metate fragment was recovered and bagged for pollen wash, and a corresponding pollen sample of contact soil was taken.

A large quantity of artifacts was recovered from all excavations, but represents only a small portion of the total site artifact assemblage. Of a total of 1,183 excavated artifacts, sherds constitute 44.2 percent, lithics 40.1 percent, ground stone 0.6 percent, and cracked rock 15.1 percent. No permanent features were found and no occupation surfaces were conclusively identified during the excavations.

In addition to the hand excavated units, three 1 m wide trenches were excavated by a backhoe. These were placed at subjectively chosen locations in alignment with the grid system. The actual location was determined on the basis of time, primary goals, and data from hand excavation. The locations were: Trench 1, 58N 9-32W; Trench 2, 12S 14W-18E; and Trench 3, 18.5E 7S-25N. The trench depths varied from 1 to 3 m. At some point in each a caliche layer was encountered. Soil samples were collected from each natural layer in Trenches 1 and 2 but they dried before accurate color assessments could be made.

The primary reasons for the backhoe testing were to determine if there was evidence of deep occupation levels and if near-surface occupation could be detected in these areas. The results were not totally conclusive on either point, but the available evidence indicates that there is no deeply buried occupation level. There were no artifacts below 35 cm below present ground surface in any trench and no cultural soil below 125 cm.

The soil characteristics are difficult to interpret. Due to the impact of backhoe excavation, the upper 30 cm in each trench was disturbed. Soils similar to those encountered during a hand excavation were found to a maximum depth of 90 cm in Trench 1. The strongest evidence for cultural soil was found between 10 and 40 cm in all trenches but only one artifact was recovered to substantiate the cultural appearance. This was a sherd in Trench 3 at a depth of 10.5N and 35 cm. Based on all available data it can only be said that no major occupation occurred in the immediate vicinity of the backhoe trenches.

Locus 2. During the R-O-W survey this area was recorded as a locus separate from that designated Locus 1. A goal of the subsequent investigations was to determine the relationship between these loci. As mentioned previously, it was observed that the loci were spatially distinct, but a more accurate assessment of the nature and distribution of cultural material was needed to further distinguish functional and cultural limits of the loci. This would also allow more specific research questions to be formulated if and when additional investigation in this area was planned.

Approximately two man-days were spent defining, locating, and recording artifact concentrations in Locus 2. Concentrations were arbitrarily determined by one main criterion: at least five artifacts occurring in a 2 m^2 area. Due to soil and vegetation conditions and erosional patterns, most but not all concentrations were spatially distinct. Isolated artifacts and small groups which were too dispersed to meet the criterion were not recorded, but these were very few. No material from Locus 2 was collected; since the area was not to be affected by construction, it was felt that preservation of the surface context of the material for future studies would be more appropriate.

Once defined and located, each concentration was inventoried at a class level (for example, sherds, chipped stone, ground stone), and notes were recorded on specific artifact attributes and classes. Figure 53 illustrates the location of specific artifact concentrations. While a similarity exists between the two loci in the percentages of ground stone artifacts, Locus 2 had a greater percentage of lithics and a lower percentage of sherds. This relationship is illustrated in Figure 54. The differences between the artifact classes could reflect differences in activity, or other functionally related aspects of the site. Aspects of site interpretation are discussed in the final chapter of this report.

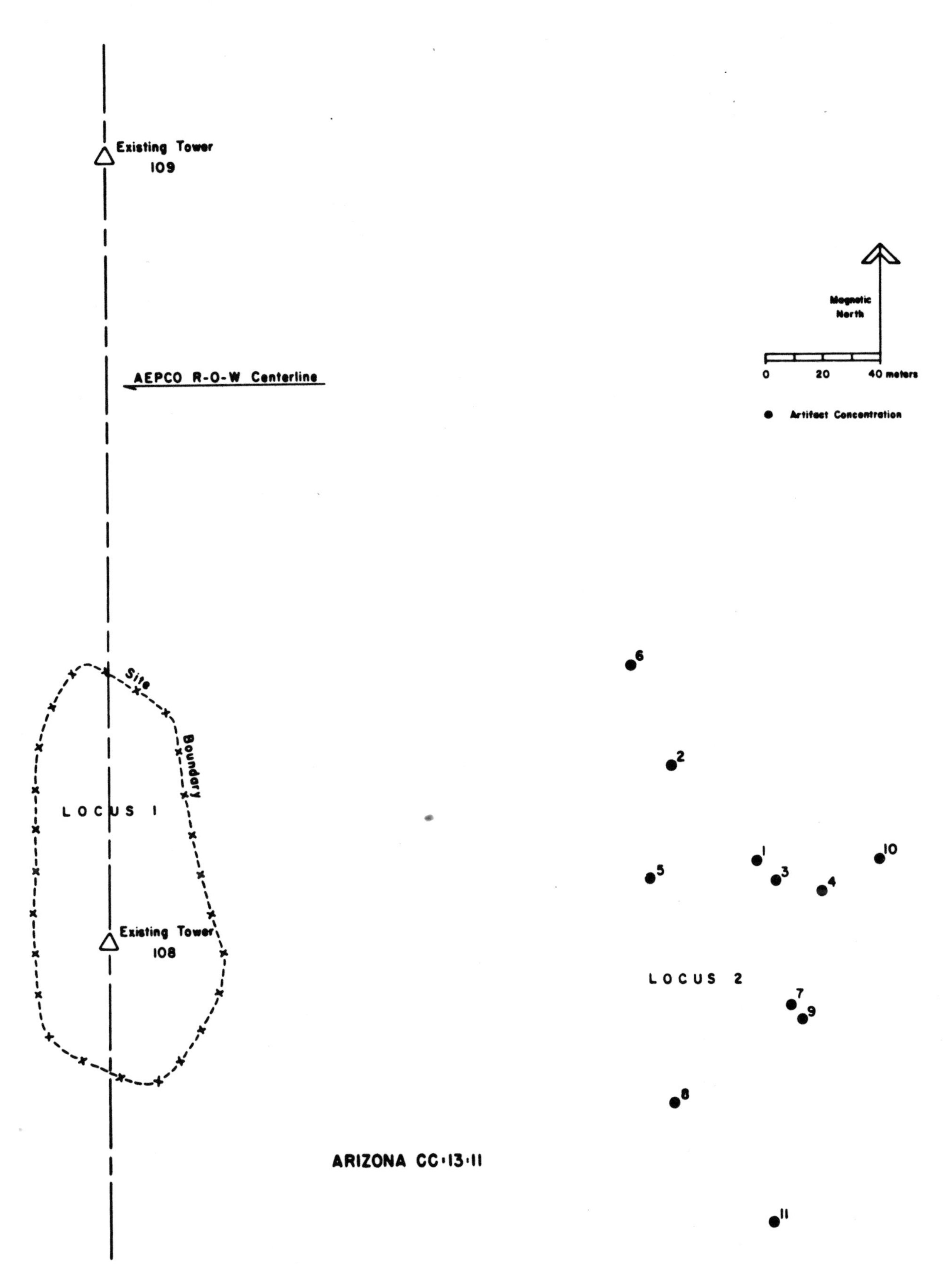

Figure 53. AZ CC:13:11, Locus 2 map.

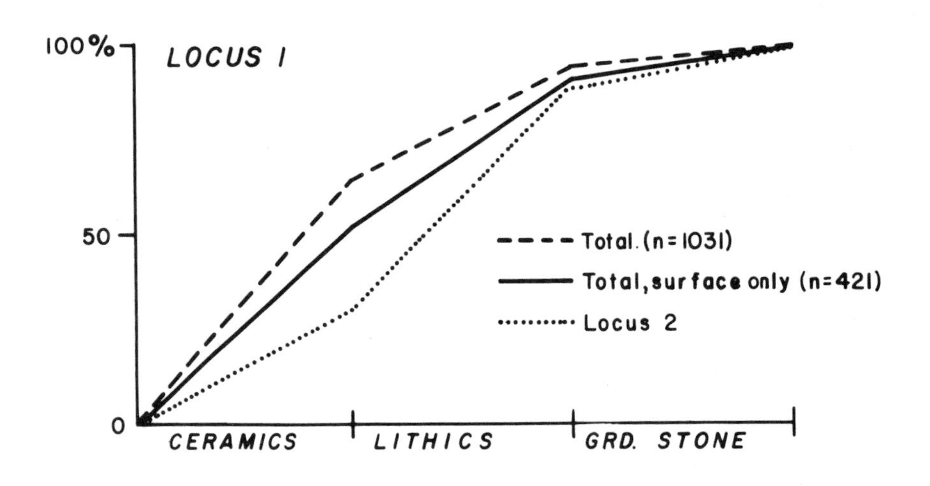

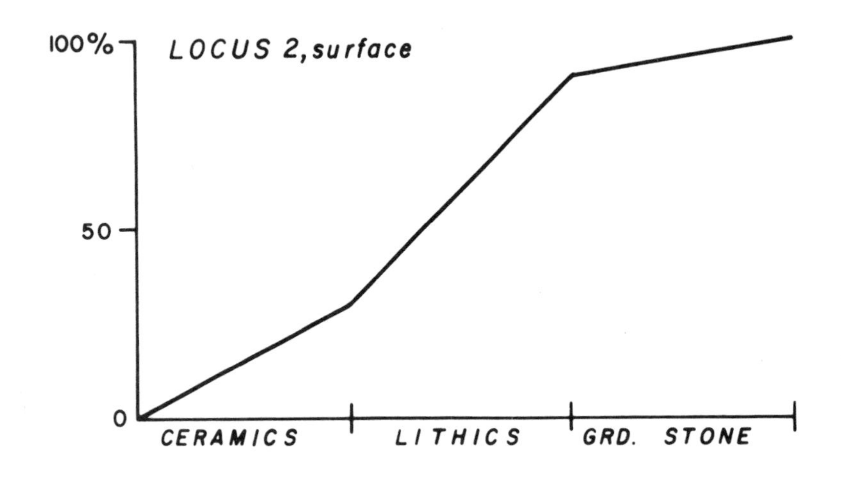

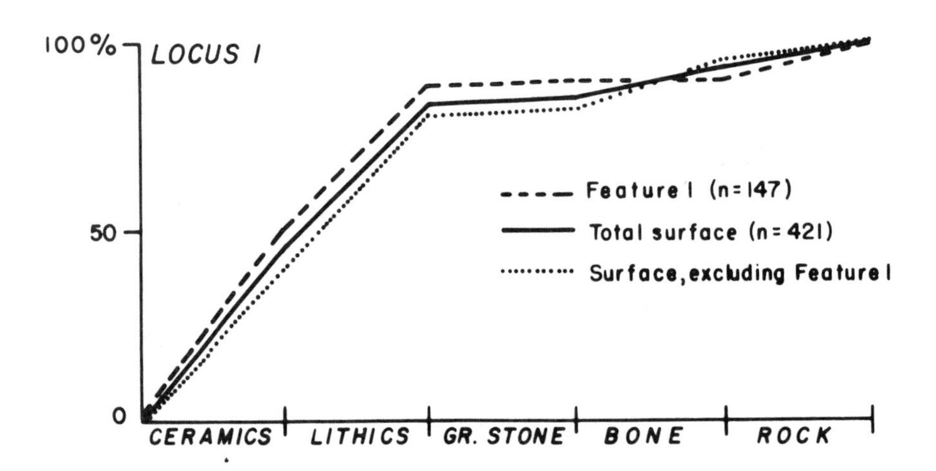

Figure 54. AZ CC:13:11, comparison of Locus 1 and Locus 2 artifact frequencies.

AZ CC:13:6

Elevation: 1283 to 1288 m
Site Size: 373 m (along R-O-W) by 225 m (arbitrary)
Field Designation: AZ CC:13:6

This site, previously recorded in 1956 by Emil W. Haury for the Arizona State Museum, is located on a sickle-shaped series of high dunes 4.2 km northeast of Willcox Playa and 7.5 km southwest of the Dos Cabezas Mountains. According to Haury (Department of Anthropology, University of Arizona, 1977, personal communication), these dunes east and north of Willcox Playa formed in post-Pleistocene times, when pluvial Lake Cochise dried up and the prevailing winds shifted from the southwest thereby piling up lake bed deposits as low, undulating dunes (Figure 55). AZ CC:13:6 is situated on one of the highest and most massive dunes in the area. Soils in the area are Vinton series which were formed on alluvium derived from mixed igneous and sedimentary rocks. In profile the surface layer is pale brown sandy loam averaging 10 cm thick. Below this is loamy sand and fine sand extending to a depth of 168 cm or more. Permeability is moderately rapid with low water availability, such that the effective rooting depth is 152 cm or more (Richmond 1976:28).

The dunes currently are partially stabilized by grasses, shrubs, and mesquite. The extensive range of plants in the immediate site vicinity includes mesquite, alkali-sacaton grass, dropseed, snakeweed, squawbush, fluff grass, yucca, desert holly, Mormon tea and burroweed. Vegetation on the dune crest is dominated by grasses, with a few low-growing mesquite; the east slope base is dominated by a high, impenetrable mesquite bosque. Due to deteriorating soil conditions aggravated by overgrazing, mesquite and burroweed have invaded the area in high densities.

The transmission line corridor passes across the eastern base of the dunes (Figure 56); there are two existing towers, two proposed tower locations, and a dirt road in the R-O-W corridor, otherwise, disturbance by heavy equipment is minimal. The owners of the land on which the site is situated stated that collectors have removed artifacts from the site over the years, particularly complete metates, manos, and projectile points. Deflation constitutes the primary natural erosional distrubance on the tops and slopes of the dune, and arroyo cutting is beginning to severely erode features on the southwestern slope.

The site most likely represents a base camp occupied during late desert Archaic times, based on dune chronology and artifact types such as one-hand manos, slab and shallow basin metates, projectile point types, and paucity of ceramics. The site is an extensive lithic scatter with concentrations of artifacts resting on hardpan exposed in deflated areas across the dune (Figures 57 and 58). Most of these concentrations consist of fractured rocks and broken mano and metates, usually found in assoication with a sparse scatter of lithic debitage. It is not known for certain if this clustering is a function of redeposition caused by deflation and erosion, although certainly these natural processes have partially affected original artifact distribution. Some of these clusters may be disarticulated features such as hearths or piles of rocks which were heated for cooking. It is noteworthy

Figure 55. AZ CC:13:6, general environment. Looking south to Willcox Playa and Dragoon Mountains from dune top.

Figure 56. AZ CC:13:6, general view of site along R-O-W corridor at base of dune. Dark vegetation is mesquite.

Figure 57. AZ CC:13:6, view of dune crest, showing typical deflated areas with artifact concentrations.

Figure 58. AZ CC:13:6, view of northwestern portion of dune with Dos Cabezas in background. Deflated areas in foreground contain artifact concentrations.

that the majority of ground stone artifacts are fragments. Indeed a majority of the artifacts are items that are no longer functional; however, the effects of collecting over the years must be considered as a reason why so few whole artifacts are present. Although no articulated features are visible, the dune area could well have served as a locality for temporary camps. The artifacts are dense and represent a range of activities, with primary emphasis on plant food procurement and processing. The site's environmental situation, affording easy access to both the desert grassland resources of the Sulphur Spring Valley and the mountane resources of the Dos Cabezas, support this assumption.

Artifacts within the R-O-W are very sparsely distributed and appear to be randomly scattered over the surface, although a possible activity area is located immediately south of Existing Tower 98. Here, a few lithic flakes and a basalt core tool were found resting on hardpan in a deflated area. Except for this one instance, deflated areas that are common on the dune crest are absent in the R-O-W corridor. Testing in the R-O-W by means of backhoe trenching revealed no subsurface features or artifacts in the R-O-W, and due to the impenetrable mesquite bosque at the base of the dune, it was not determined whether features exist at the interface of the dune with the valley floor. Because the exposed dune-top features were close to the R-O-W corridor, original mitigation plans called for detailed mapping, collection and testing of these features, since it was felt that the materials in the R-O-W could not be fully understood when analyzed apart from the main body of the artifact assemblage. However, the cost of such an endeavor would have been prohibitive and therefore, stricter stipulations were implemented for site protection during construction. Nevertheless, the materials in the R-O-W, albeit sparse, are substantial representations of the total range of activities at this site, and thus collection of the material within the R-O-W was done in the event AZ CC:13:6 is more completely investigated in the future.

A grid system was established along the 30 m wide R-O-W corridor according to standard procedures, for a total length of 320 m. Mapping of features on the southeast dune, begun during the testing program, was completed (Figure 59). These features are listed below, although it must be noted that this listing is by no means complete. Cultural depth of the recorded features is as yet unknown and additional features may occur on the uninvestigated northwest portion of the dune.

Feature 1. A cluster of small fragments of ground stone (granite and basalt) and lithic flakes of chert and basalt, in an area 90 cm N/S by 70 cm E/W. It rests on hardpan in a blowout area.

Feature 2. A blowout area, 9.5 m N/S by 22 m E/W, containing a slab metate (42 cm long, 25 cm wide, 4 cm thick), with a few lithic flakes in association.

Feature 3. A metate locus; two quartzite slab metates partially set into surface. Metate 1: irregular fragment (distal end) with oval grinding facet; 36 cm long, 31 cm wide, 7 cm thick; metate 2: irregularly rectangular; oval shallow grinding facet; 44 cm long, 30 cm wide, 4 cm thick situated 86 cm SW of metate 1.

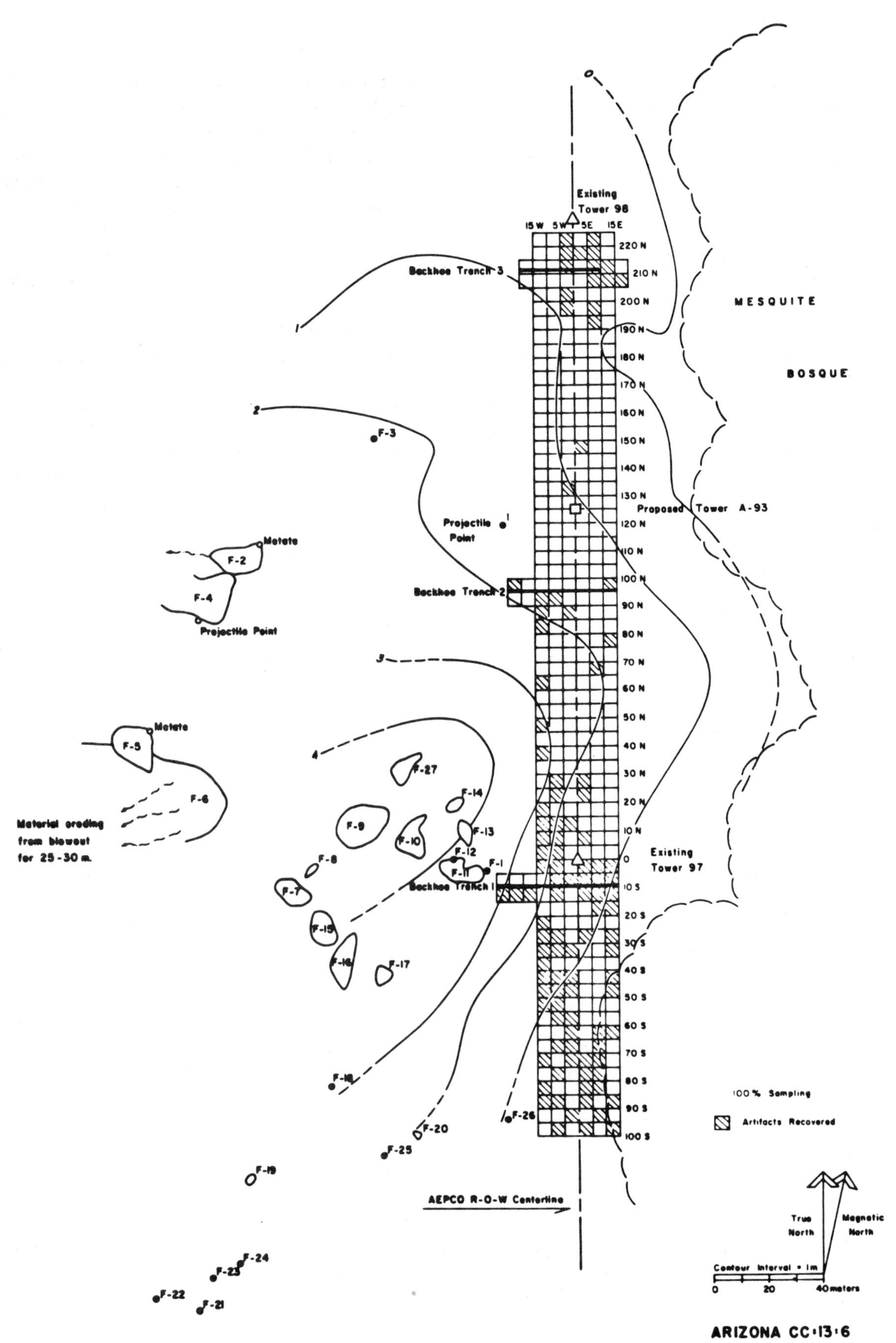

Figure 59. AZ CC:13:6, site map.

Feature 4. A blowout area, 16 m N/S by 15 m E/W (arbitrary) containing flakes of low grade chert, broken stones, ground stone fragments. Western edge of blowout is eroding into arroyo, and lithics have subsequently washed down into drainage. Obsidian projectile point found at southeastern edge.

Feature 5. A blowout area, 29 m N/S by 14 m E/W (arbitrary), badly eroded; artifacts are eroding into an arroyo for some distance. Metate fragment situated in northeast edge of blowout, 32 cm long, 31 cm wide, 3 cm thick. There are also at least five concentrations of lithics, ground stone fragments, cores, and hammerstones, in addition to a sparse lithic scatter.

Feature 6. A blowout area directly east of Feature 5; the western portion is severly eroded and artifacts occur along the drainage for 25 to 30 m. Fractured rock, ground stone fragments, lithic flakes and cores are present. There are concentrations of artifacts on the noneroded exposed hardpan.

Feature 7. A blowout area 9 m N/S by 9.4 m E/W; artifacts are resting on a red soil zone that occurs beneath the hardpan. Artifact scatter consists of cores, fractured rocks, chert, basalt cores, flakes, hammerstones, and two plainware sherds.

Feature 8. A small lithic concentration located 7.5 m northwest of Feature 7. Blowout is 7.1 m N/S by 3.8 m E/W. Lithic flakes, ground stone fragment, core fragment, and a retouched basalt flake were noted.

Feature 9. A blowout area 16 m N/S by 19 m E/W containing a lithic concentration of flakes, cores, ground stone pieces.

Feature 10. A blowout area 15 m N/S by 11.52 m E/W situated approximately 8 m east of Feature 9. Within a sparse lithic scatter is a concenration of basalt flakes, shatter, and ground stone.

Feature 11. A large blowout area with a lithic concentration. It is situated adjacent to (west) Feature 1 and incorporates Feature 12. The blowout is 11.62 m N/S by 18 m E/W.

Feature 12. A possible hearth, comprising a cluster of 22 rocks, many of which are fire cracked. A few of the rocks are mano fragments.

Feature 13. A blowout area, 4 m N/S by 6.5 m E/W with small scatter of basalt flakes.

Feature 14. A small blowout area, 4 m N/S by 6.5 m E/W with small scatter of flakes and broken rocks.

Feature 15. A blowout area, 17.5 m N/S by 12.5 m E.W with a few small lithic concentrations consisting of chert flakes, basalt flakes, and ground stone fragments. One area is a concentration of 20 small decortication flakes.

Feature 16. A blowout area, 10 m N/S by 11.5 m E/W containing lithic concentrations of basalt and chert cores and flakes and ground stone fragments.

Feature 17. A small erosional channel occurs between Features 16 and 17; thus lithics are continuous between the features, but each feature is a separate blowout area. Feature 17 blowout is 8 m N/S by 7.5 m E/W. Lithics within the feature consist of chert and basalt flakes, ground stone fragments, and many pieces of broken basaltic rocks.

Feature 18. A slab metate in the northernmost portion of a large area 50 to 60 m in diameter which contains several small blowouts and hillocks, with a very light scatter of lithics occurring in the blowouts. The metate measures 29 cm long (fragmentary), 32 cm wide, and 3 cm thick.

Feature 19. A stone circle containing a broken rock concentration in an area 1.6 m N/S by 1.5 m E/W. The circle is constructed of 12 stones, the largest of which is 13 by 13 cm. No chipped stone was found in association.

Feature 20. A concentration of artifacts 1.27 m N/S by 0.69 m E/W situated within a large blowout area. The concentration contains fractured rocks and chert and rhyolite thinning flakes.

Feature 21. A concentration of six slab metate fragments all probably from one original metate. Fragments occur in an area 79 cm E/W by 46 cm N/S.

Feature 22. A partially buried isolated slab metate 21 cm long (fragmentary), 20 cm wide, and 3 cm thick made from andesite or quartzite. A few lithic flakes are in association.

Feature 23. An isolated basin metate fragment, 23 cm long (fragmentary), 15 cm wide, and 12 cm thick found in association with basalt shatter.

Feature 24. An isolated slab metate fragment, 24 cm long (fragmentary), 17 cm wide, and 6 cm thick found without associated artifacts.

Feature 25. An artifact concentration located in a blowout area. It includes one hammerstone, chert and basalt flakes, and broken rocks and covers an area 42 cm N/S by 30 cm E/W.

Feature 26. An isolated mano eroding out from a sandy hillock. Mano measures 9 cm long, 8 cm wide, and 3 cm thick.

Feature 27. A blowout area 8 m N/S by 10 m E/W with an artifact concentration consisting of ground stone fragments, basalt and chert flakes, fractured rocks, and one hammerstone.

Stratum 5: Sulphur Spring Basin

AZ CC:13:14

Elevation: 1266 m
Site Size: 60 m N/S by 70 m E/W
Field Designation: AEPCO 225

Environmentally this site is characterized by the predominance of dense, mounded stands of alkalai-sacaton grass interspersed with lower, barren, open hardpan areas (Figure 60). A few shrubby mesquites grow in the vicinity of the site. Soil is Crot sandy loam, a fine alkaline soil with a low erosion hazard. As with other sites in this stratum, it is hard to determine whether soil is forming and vegetation is becoming established, or the opposite is occurring. At AZ CC:13:15, a nearby site, the lessee stated that to his recollection grass was definitely on the increase. Regardless of historic trends, undoubtedly both wind and water erosion and deposition have occurred in the past and have affected vegetation composition and coverage.

Figure 60. AZ CC:13:14, general environment of site, view northeast. Willcox Playa and Dos Cabezas Mountains are in the background.

Willcox Playa is located 1.4 km to the west; low dunes along old shorelines are visible from the site. In fact, pluvial Lake Cochise once inundated the site location and Pleistocene beach ridges still exist to the east. The site's ground slope is only 2 to 3 percent, similar to that of the greater surrounding area. Due to geomorphologic processes which have created the existing Sulphur Spring Valley topography, there are no drainages in the site vicinity. Several small runnels drain periodic sheetwash erosion northwesterly through the site to a low marshy swale nearby.

There is no naturally occurring lithic raw material on or around the site. This assessment was made after only a cursory examination of the site vicinity, but due to the high visibility of surface material in this micro-environment and the nature of topography and vegetation distribution, it is made with a high degree of confidence.

The AEPCO R-O-W crosses the western half of the site. The major human disturbance to these archaeological remains is attributed to motorized traffic along a jeep trail (Figure 61). Proposed tower A-41 is situated just outside the site boundary to the south. Due to the surficial nature of the cultural resources, cattle grazing and natural erosion have affected the artifact condition and distribution.

With the exception of one bullet cartridge, the site consists entirely of lithic artifacts in an easily defined space. A grid system was used for surface collection. After reconnoitering the site area and marking boundaries, artifacts were collected and a map drawn (Figure 61). One dense concentration of lithics, ground stone, and cracked rock was designated Feature 1 and investigated as a unit. Artifact frequencies for each collected grid unit are illustrated in Figure 62.

Three 1 m^2 units were excavated with shovel and trowel in order to test for cultural depth. All fill was passed through 1/4 inch mesh screen. The first of these test units was at 15N 10E, at the edge of a grassy mound near Feature 1. Two arbitrary 5 cm levels were excavated, and one lithic artifact was recovered from the uppermost level. The loose sand and organic detritus topsoil gave way to a hard-packed sandy loam at 5 cm below present ground surface. There was no evidence of cultural deposition below the aeolian topsoil. Excavation in 35 N 10E was similarily tested and no artifacts were recovered, although the stratigraphy was virtually identical. The third unit, 25N 25E,was dug to a total depth of 30 cm. Removal of the topsoil in a 5 cm level was followed by the excavation of a 10 cm level. Neither level produced evidence of cultural deposition. Next, a 15 cm level was removed to better define the stratigraphy; this fill was not screened. This last level consisted of a moister, harder-parked sandy clay loam. All areas were backfilled to approximate the original surface contour. The excavation results confirmed the suspicion that cultural deposition was only surficial.

Feature 1. The 5 m^2 unit, 25N 15E, was designated as Feature 1 (Figures 63 and 64). Although artifacts were present in all surrounding grids, the total number and density of artifacts within this grid unit was more than four times that of any other grid (Figure 65). In addition, this area contained the greatest number of ground stone and cracked rock, suggesting a task-specific activity area. Although the 5 m^2 grid unit is an artificial boundary, the use of this size recovery space allowed isolating Feature 1 material in analysis as well as integrating it with the general site collection for comparative purposes.

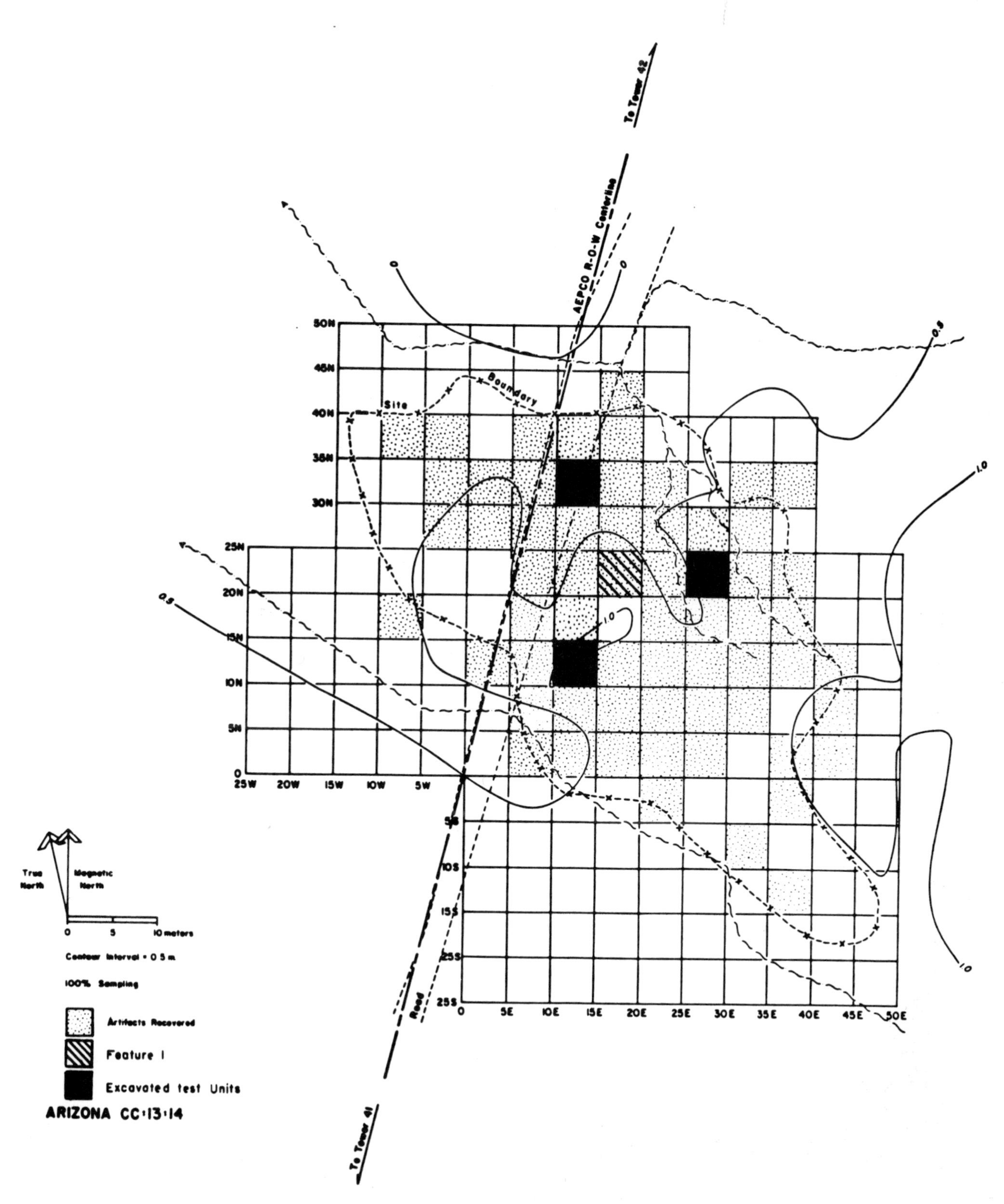

Figure 61. AZ CC:13:14, site map.

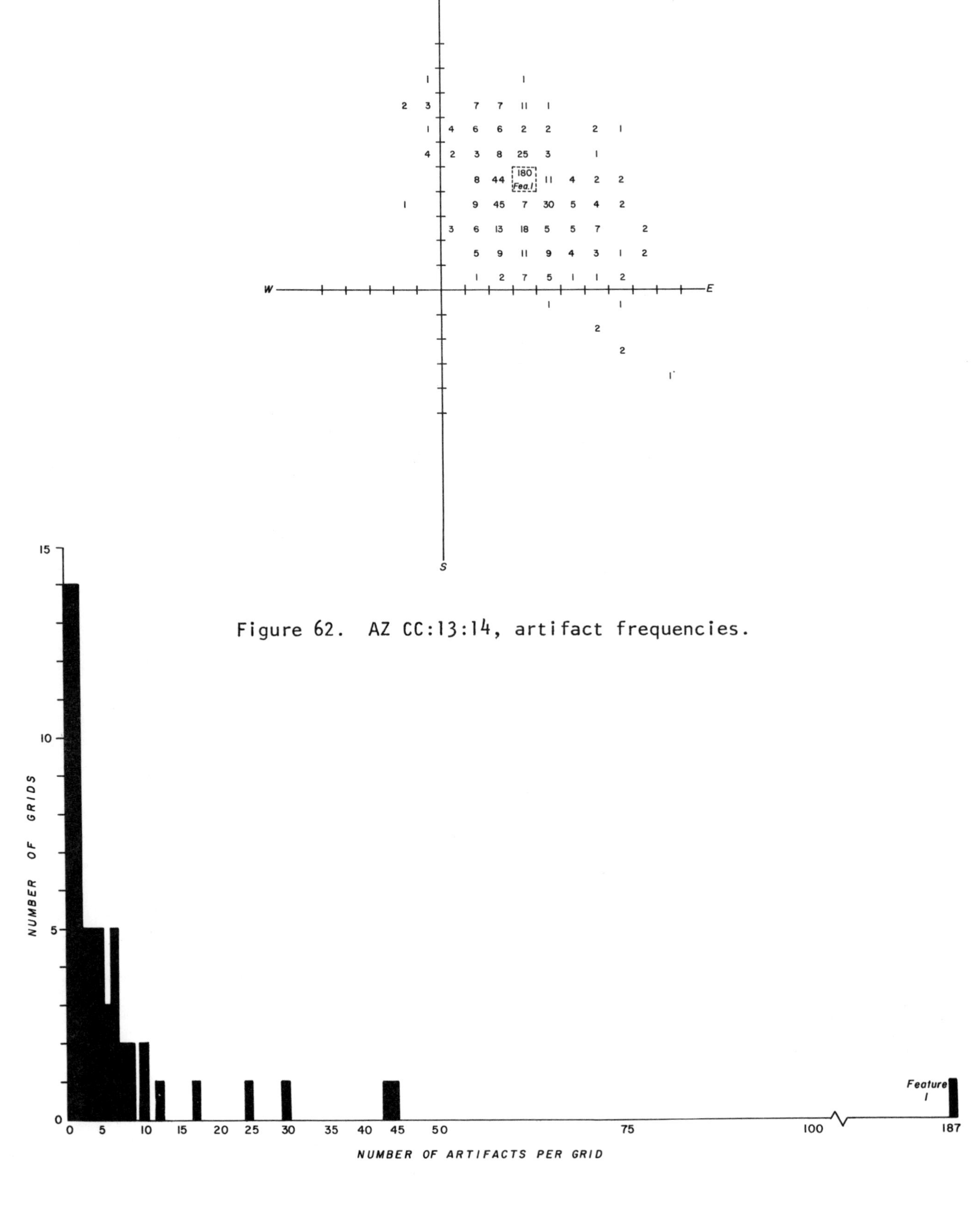

Figure 62. AZ CC:13:14, artifact frequencies.

Figure 65. AZ CC:13:14, artifact quantity per grid.

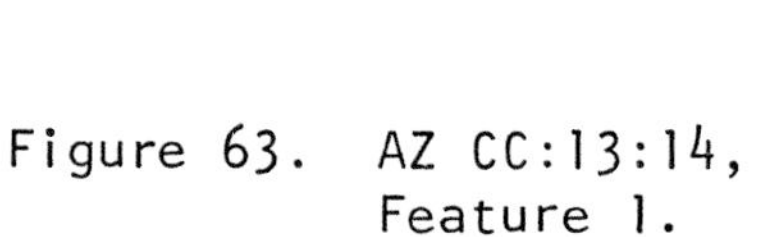

Figure 63. AZ CC:13:14, Feature 1.

Figure 64. AZ CC:13:14, Feature 1, closeup.

Feature 1 was mapped by point provenience methods and collected (Figure 66). The profiles illustrate the gentle easterly slope of this feature. No subsurface testing was conducted due to the negative results of previous site testing. Four ground stone fragments and their corresponding contact soils were collected for pollen analysis, as was one general site surface pollen sample.

The absence of charcoal and fired earth precluded gathering data for dating purposes. Six soil samples from surface and substrate proveniences were collected for identification and correlation.

AZ CC:13:15

Elevation: 1281 m
Site Size: 240 m N/S by 95 m E/W
Field Designation: AEPCO 227

This site is located in the Sulphur Spring Basin. The immediate site environment is a markedly level area on which alkali-sacaton grass is predominant, with sparse population of saltbush and cane cholla. Although the edge of Willcox Playa is now 1.3 km to the west-northwest, the site location

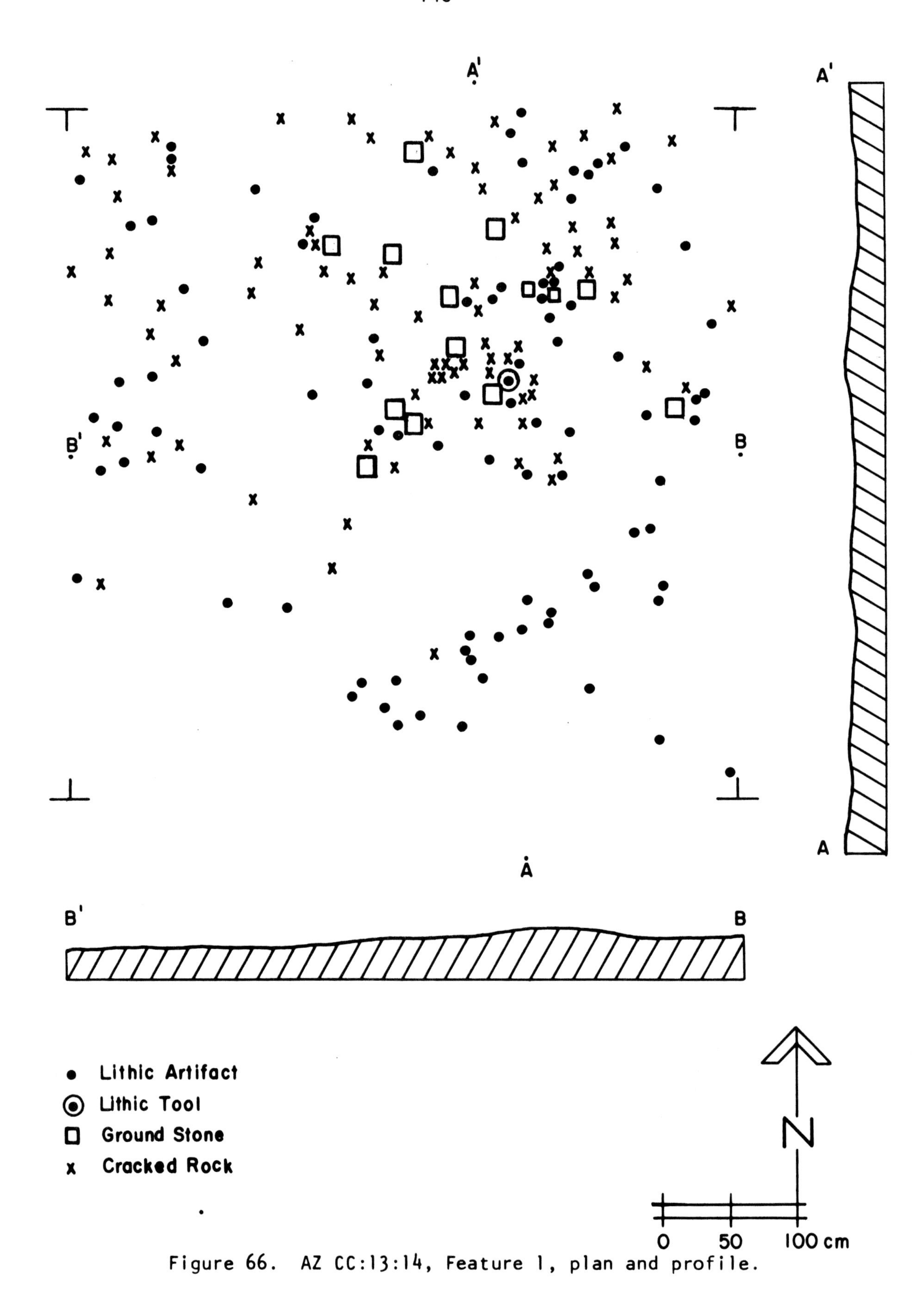

Figure 66. AZ CC:13:14, Feature 1, plan and profile.

was once inundated by pluvial Lake Cochise. The Crot series soil, a deep, strongly alkaline sandy loam, reflects this past environment. There is a complete absence of lithic raw material in site vicinity, attributed to the area's geologic history.

Much of the site and surrounding areas are devoid of vegetation. Ground cover is approximately 40 percent, and that which is present forms distinct low hummocks. Open areas are eroded by multidirectional sheetwash and shallowly dissected by runnels draining to the west. These features give a deflated appearance to the area, although the lessee, W.D. Wear, Jr. of Willcox, stated that grass cover has greatly increased over the past 40 years (Figure 67).

In addition to site disturbance caused by natural factors such as wind and water erosion and the possible covering of artifacts by encroaching soil and vegetation, cattle grazing is evidenced by deep hoof impressions in the dried soil. Additionally, a two track ranch road bisects the site on its eastern margin. Proposed tower A-37 is in the northeast corner of the site.

Figure 67. AZ CC:13:15, general environment of site, showing dense grass and barren areas.

The survey crew described the site as a moderately dense pottery sherd scatter with one sherd concentration. Research recommendations included surface collecting, mapping, and subsurface testing. Although the data recovery crew discovered at least one additional sherd and ground stone concentration not previously noted by the survey, it was decided that collecting by point provenience methods would be more rapid than using a grid system. After site boundaries and all artifacts were flagged it was discovered that the alidade was inoperable, thus precluding point provenience collection and requiring the use of a grid system. As a result of this delay, less than 100 percent collection was achieved (Figure 68).

After collecting the entire R-O-W by 5 m^2 grids, a buffer strip approximately 35 m wide was examined on both sides of the transmission line corridor. Thus, the entire site area east of 50W was fully investigated. Time constraints ruled out gridding and collecting the remaining area, so a section west of 50W was sampled. A nonprobabilistic sampling plan was used, which enlarged the basic 5 m^2 recovery space to a 25 m^2 for sampling purposes. Artifact density in each of these units was subjectively ranked and several were selected to fulfill the goal of collecting a large artifact population in a limited amount of time which would best reflect the nature of artifact distribution. Within each 25 m^2 sample unit actual collection was conducted by the basic 5 m^2 grid. Though not quantifiable, the 32 percent areal sample resulted in an approximate 70 percent artifact sample.

Virtually all artifacts were recovered in open areas. Pottery accounted for 98.9 percent of all artifacts, with lithics, ground stone, and historic cartridges constituting 0.4 percent each. The quantity of sherds (1,200) is probably artificially inflated due to their extremely fragmentary state. This condition may be a result of breakage by grazing animals.

The sherds occurred across the entire site surface. Lithics were concentrated in one area along the centerline near 25N, and the ground stone was divided between the two main concentrations near 25W and 125W. Spent .50 caliber ammunition was scattered within the site. The overall distribution of surface artifacts is illustrated in Figure 69.

Of 840 grid units, 520 (62 percent) were examined. Only 116 (22 percent) of these contained artifacts. No subsurface testing was conducted, but the excavation results at two other Stratum 5 sites, AZ CC:13:14 and 16, which have extremely similar environmental features, suggest that cultural deposition is only surficial.

AZ CC:13:16

Elevation: 1279 m
Site Size: 55 m N/S by 195 m E/W
Field Designation: AEPCO 226

AZ CC:13:16 is situated in the Sulphur Spring Basin. On-site vegetation is dominated by alkalai-sacaton grass; yucca and cane cholla are present, but rare. This vegetation occurs in intermittent, hummocky patches

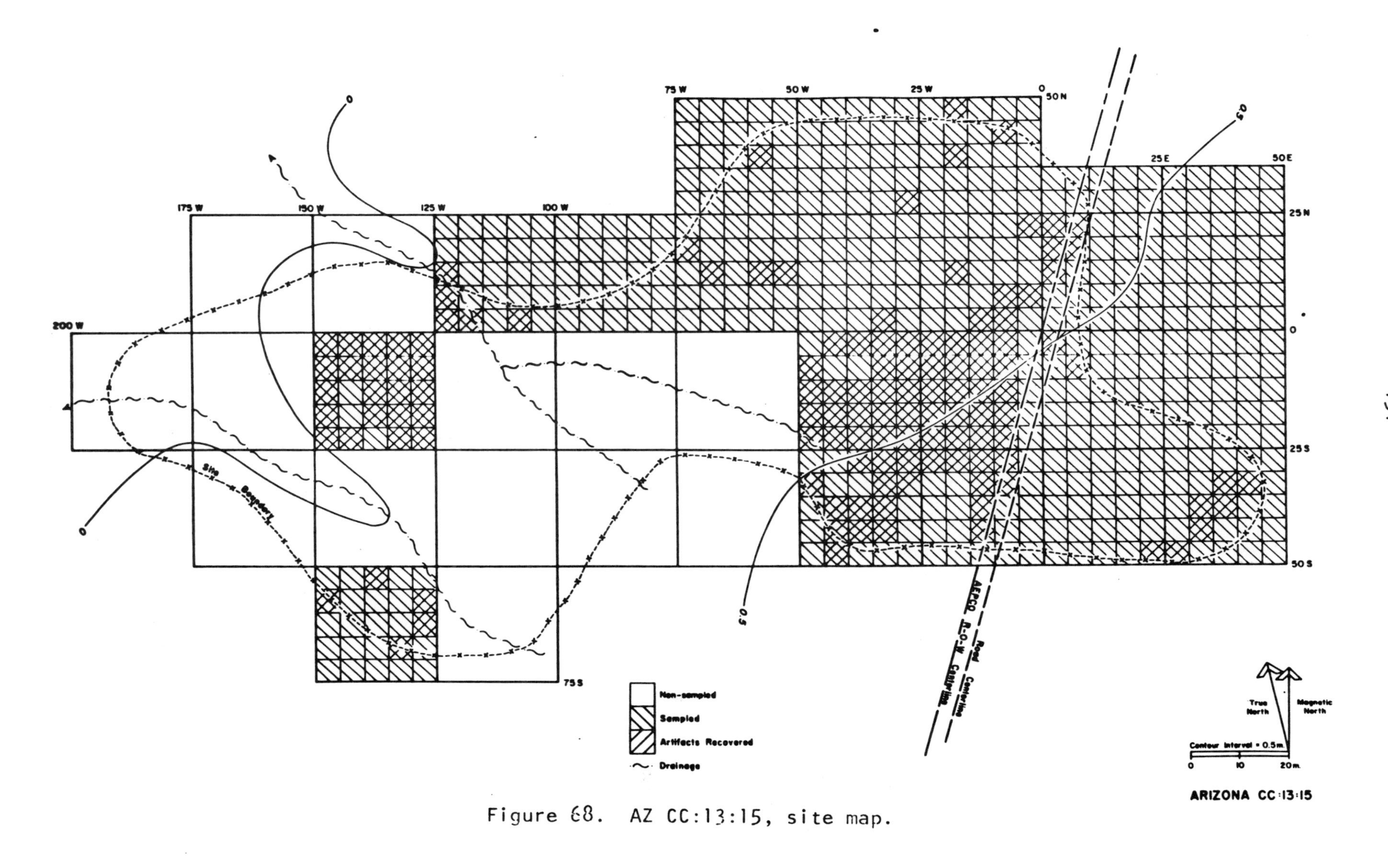

Figure 68. AZ CC:13:15, site map.

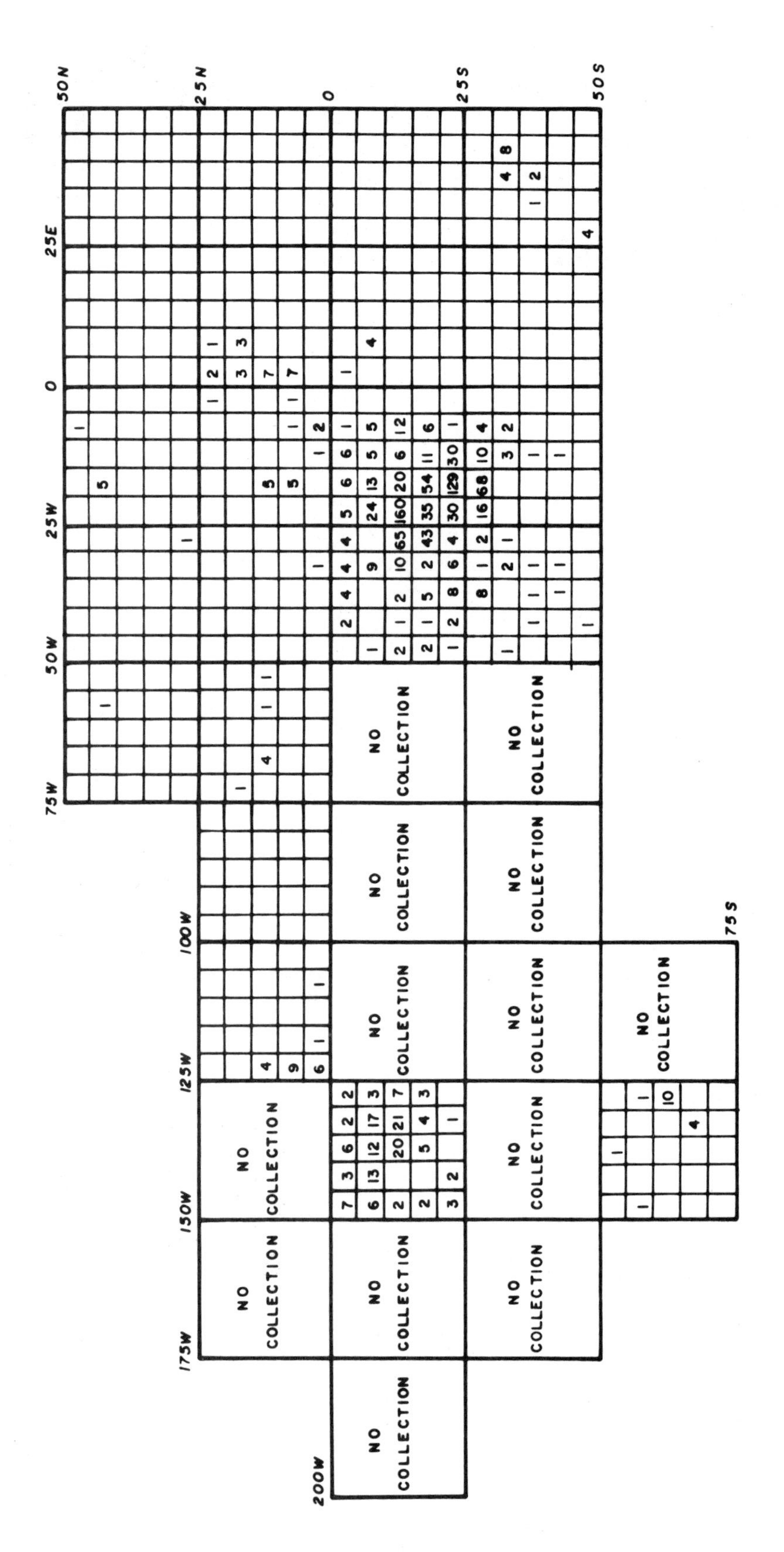

Figure 69. AZ CC:13:15, artifact frequencies.

surrounded by large barren areas. Soil is Crot series sandy loam, a fine, deep deposit on which a hardpan surface has formed. Aeolian sand covers this soil in vegetated areas. Besides the microrelief of the hummocks on hardpan, the rolling site topography generally slopes to the west and north. Several rivulets carry water off the site in these directions. The topographic situation is that of a beach dune along an extinct lake margin. Larger, sandy dunes surround the site at various distances, and Willcox Playa is 0.8 km west (Figure 70).

Figure 70. AZ CC:13:16, general environment of site, looking west. In the background are Willcox Playa, the Apache Electric Station, and Dragoon Mountains.

A brief visual reconnaissance of the site vicinity identified similar vegetation and topographic features in the surrounding area. From a high point on the eastern site edge a 360 degree view is available while in lower site elevations further west the view is restricted. Overall site relief is approximately 2 m.

The AEPCO R-O-W crosses the south side of AZ CC:13:16, and existing tower 27 and proposed tower A-28 are located near the center of this section. A majority of both the site area and artifacts occur outside the AEPCO R-O-W to the north. Besides the limited human disturbance to this site associated with the original transmission line construction, the remains of a barbed wire fence, presumably along a section line, indicate additional human disturbance and probably signify that the area has been grazed historically. Natural degradation, primarily in the form of sheetwash erosion, has undoubtedly been a major form of site disturbance.

Mapping, surface collecting, and subsurface testing were recommended by the survey. Due to the dispersed nature of the artifacts, each artifact was mapped by point provenience methods and bagged separately (Figure 71). An exception was made for artifacts clustered within a 10 cm diameter area, which were considered as one unit for ease in mapping and collection. In this dispersed distribution three concentrations of 12 to 15 artifacts each are evident.

A substantial portion of the collection was lithics of dubious human modification. Because no lithic raw material is available on the site or in nearby areas, it was considered worthwhile to collect this material for further study. The collection of 122 artifacts was dominated by tiny, fragmented sherds (53.3 percent), lithics in lesser numbers (30.3 percent), and a little ground stone (4.1 percent). Cracked rock comprised 10.6 percent. Two gun shells were also collected.

Two heavy metates were found, presumably as de facto refuse (Figures 72 and 73). Since their respective grinding facets were face down, a pollen sample was taken from under each and they were bagged separately for pollen wash. In addition to these activities, subsurface testing was conducted in a 1 m by 2 m unit at the edge of a grassy mound near an artifact concentration. One arbitrary 5 cm level following the existing ground slope was excavated. Fill was passed through 1/8 inch mesh screen. As no artifacts were recovered, and since the substrate was extremely similar to that at AZ CC:13:14 where there was no subsurface cultural deposition, testing was halted and the unit was backfilled.

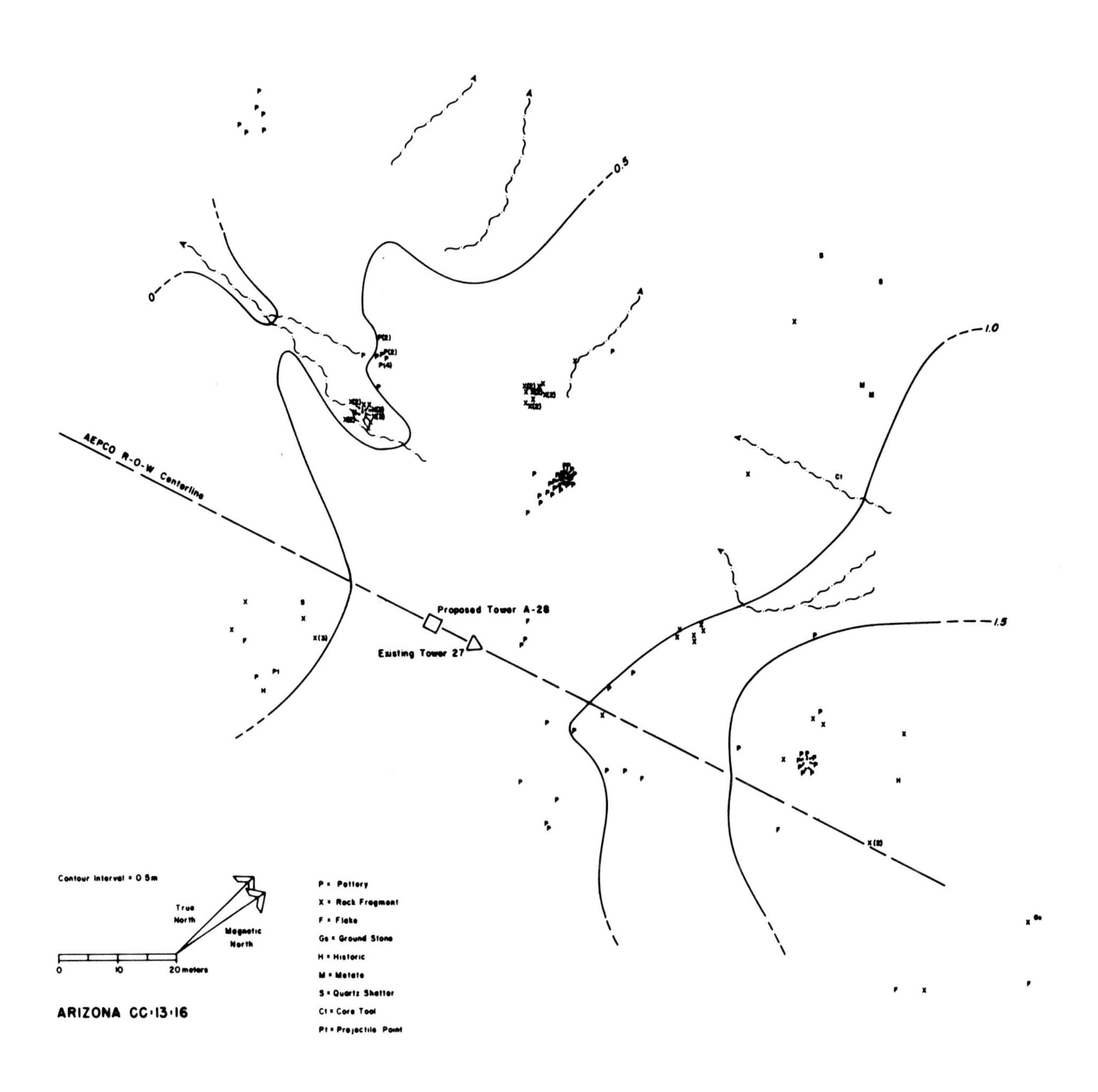

Figure 71. AZ CC:13:16, site map.

Figure 72. AZ CC:13:16, general view of site, looking west with beach ridge in background. The two metates are in the center.

Figure 73. AZ CC:13:16, close-up of two metates in situ.

CHAPTER 5

CERAMIC ANALYSIS

by Howard M. Davidson

Introduction

The ceramic analysis was designed to obtain as much information as possible from the AEPCO II collection with consideration for the condition of the pottery, time, funding, and analytic skills. As can be seen in Table 17 plainware ceramics predominate. Most of the plainware sherds are small and many are in poor condition. Seventy-five percent are eroded on more than half of their surface. The decorated sherds are small and many lack clearly discernible designs. Furthermore, there are only 71 rim sherds and no whole or reconstructible vessels. Obviously, variables such as vessel size and shape, surface finish, and decoration are not the appropriate focal point for this study.

A broad range of study variables was selected which would characterize the entire collection and yet be manageable in terms of available time and skills (Table 18). The emphasis of this research is on paste and temper variability in plainwares, and is presented first. Included are the descriptive results and an analysis of the technological-functional relationships. Following this, a report on the few recovered decorated sherds is presented.

Table 17. Sherd frequencies by site

Site	Plainware	Redwares and Decorated	Total
AZ CC:6:3	-	1	1
AZ CC:6:7	152	3	155
AZ CC:10:11	1	-	1
AZ CC:9:2	2	1	3
AZ CC:9:3	1	-	1
AZ CC:13:6	2	-	2
AZ CC:13:11	893	109	1002
AZ CC:13:15	1270	-	1270
AZ CC:13:16	62	7	69
	2383(95.2%)	121(4.8%)	2504

Table 18. Ceramic analysis code

Field	Columns	Variable	Code Value	Attribute
1	1	Analysis type	2	Ceramics
2	5- 7	Site number	taken from artifact	Provenience
3	8-11	North-south grid		
4	12-15	East-west grid		
5	16	Quad		
6	17	Level		
7	18	Feature number		
8	19-23	General artifact number		
9	24-25	Specific artifact number		
10	26-27	Thickness		Actual measurement
11	28-30	Grid sherd weight		Actual measurement
12	31-33	Grid sherd number		Actual count
13	37	Surface condition exterior	1	Noneroded
			2	Eroded, 50%-
			3	Eroded, 50%+
14	38	Surface,condition, interior	1	Noneroded
			2	Eroded, 50%-
			3	Eroded, 50%+
			4	Indeterminate
15	39	Construction	1	Coil/Scrape
			2	Paddle/Anvil
			3	Combination
			4	Other
			5	Indeterminate
16	40	Apparent Porosity	1	None
			2	1%
			3	3%
			4	5%+
			5	Indeterminate
17	41	Filler Modal Size	1	Very Fine
			2	Fine
			3	Medium
			4	Coarse
			5	Very Coarse
			6	Granular
18	42-43	Filler Sorting	1	Very Fine-fine
			2	Very Fine-medium
			3	Very Fine-coarse
			4	Very Fine-very coarse
			5	Very Fine-granular
			6	Fine-medium
			7	Fine-coarse
			8	Fine-very coarse
			9	Fine-granular
			10	Medium-coarse
			11	Medium-very coarse
			12	Medium-granular
			13	Coarse-very coarse
			14	Coarse-granular
			15	Very Coarse-granular

Table 18. Ceramic analysis code (continued)

Field	Columns	Variable	Code Value	Attribute
19	44	Filler Density	1	5%
			2	10%
			3	20%
			4	30%
			5	40%
			6	60%
			7	80%
20	45	Filler Modal Shape	1	Very Angular
			2	Angular
			3	Subangular-Subrounded
			4	Rounded
			5	Very Rounded
21	46-47	Filler Material, dominant	1	Quartz
			2	Feldspar
			3	Calcite
			4	Other Mineral
			5	Miscellaneous Minerals
			6	Rock Fragments
			7	Sherd
			8	Organic
			9	Indeterminate
			10	Mica
22	48-49	Filler Material, subdominant	1	Quartz
			2	Feldspar
			3	Calcite
			4	Other Mineral
			5	Miscellaneous Minerals
			6	Rock Fragments
			7	Sherd
			8	Organic
			9	Indeterminate
			10	Mica
23	50	Surface Color Irregular	1	None
			2	Exterior only
			3	Interior only
			4	Exterior and Interior
			5	Exterior; interior indeterminate
			6	Interior; exterior indeterminate
			7	None exterior; interior indeterminate
			8	Exterior indeterminate; none interior
			9	Indeterminate; indeterminate

Table 18. Ceramic analysis code (continued)

Field	Columns	Variable	Code Value	Attribute
24	51	Core/Streak	* 0/1	Absent/Present
25		Surface Finish, exterior		
	52		0/1	Crazing
	53		0/1	Pitting
	54		0/1	Scraping Marks
	55		0/1	Polishing
	56		0/1	Temper
	57		0/1	Fire Blackening
26		Surface Finish, interior		
	58		0/1	Crazing
	59		0/1	Pitting
	60		0/1	Scraping Marks
	61		0/1	Polishing
	62		0/1	Temper
	63		0/1	Fire Blackening
27	64	Sherd Position	1	Rim
			2	Neck
			3	Base
			4	Body
			5	Other
			6	Indeterminate
28	65	Vessel Form	1	Open
			2	Closed
			3	Other
			4	Indeterminate
29	66	Rim/Neck Form (wall)	1	Straight
			2	Expanding
			3	Contracting
			4	Shoulder
			5	Other
			6	Indeterminate
30	67-68	Rim/Neck Form (lip)	1	
			2	
			3	
			4	
		Note: Lip form after	5	
		Colton (1953:44,fig. 10).	6	
			7	
			8	

* 0 = present
1 = absent

Plainware Ceramics: General Considerations

In the Southwest, plainware pottery is one of the most common cultural items found at sites. In spite of this predominance, plainware sherds have usually been given secondary attention in favor of decorated wares. In some areas, such as the AEPCO II project region, certain plainware types have not even been fully described. The AEPCO ceramic analysis has attempted to rectify this situation. The goals were (1) to describe technological and functional variability in plainware sherds, (2) to compare the AEPCO II materials to other collections from the project region, and (3) to serve as a pilot study to assess the value of the approach used over that of more conventional analysis.

Background to the Study

In developing a research design for this aspect of the analysis, the plainwares were compared to the AEPCO I and San Simon Village materials in storage at the Arizona State Museum. In 1945 Sayles classified the San Simon sherds as Alma Plain, after the original type description presented by Haury (1936a). Westfall (1978), analyzing a much smaller AEPCO I collection, discerned enough differences from Alma Plain to label the AEPCO I sherds "Brown plainware" and wrote a working description of them. The AEPCO II plainware sherds are similar to those of both collections, but also have identifiable differences. The variability of plainwares from this region, then, is the subject of this study.

It was hoped that previous research might help to orient the present study, and thus ceramic analyses in the Southwestern archaeological literature were examined. Few presented a refined analysis of plainware sherds (see Leone 1968; Plog 1976; Windes 1977 for exceptions). Several aspects of this problem serve to illustrate why plainware studies are needed.

First is the assumption that plainwares are made locally and thus have little cultural significance. But it is not clear whether "local" refers to site, region, or cultural group and whether raw materials are also local or imported. For example, Fulton and Tuthill (1940) explicitly assume local origin for the plainwares at the Gleeson Site, as does Haury (1936b) for the Harris Site. DiPeso (1951) defined Babocomari Plain as a village-specific plainware, and later adopted the appellation "Indigenous utilitarian ware" for the plainware at Reeve Ruin (DiPeso 1958). Few researchers, however, have tested assumptions of local origin; those who have, relied primarily on petrographic temper analysis, a method of limited usefulness due to the variable sensitivity of the test (Shepard 1956). [See Brown 1973, Plog (1976), and Loose (1977) for successful applications.]

Ethnographic and ethnoarchaeological accounts illustrate a variety of practices which result in different ceramic spatial distribution. Dobyns (1956:121) reports that for the Pai, clay sources were not private domain and individual bands used the same raw materials to produce similar products which crosscut cultural group boundaries, with a resulting wide distribution. The Yuma use a sherd temper, which, according to Rogers (1936:31) normally must be imported from outside their usual range. Studies outside the Southwest also have provided data on this topic. William Longacre of the Department of Anthropology, University of Arizona, has said that through research in the Philippines, he has found ceramic raw material homogeneity within villages and recognizable differences between them. Thompson (1958), investigating Yucatec Maya potters, and David and Hennig (1972), researching African groups, both report intervillage technological variability due to trade. Rye and Evans (1976) petrographically determined some village-specific tempering practices but found a high degree of overall similarity. In sum, pottery of any one provenience may or may not represent products locally manufactured from locally available materials. This problem deserves more attention in future research, with concepts defined and employed more precisely.

A second problem, and one common to most descriptions in the type-variety taxonomic system, is a lack of a standard terminology. Few researchers have defined either the scales or terms they have used. A good example of this is the use of terms for temper size. Table 19 shows some of the scales which have been used that employ overlapping size classes and terms.

A third problem is that plainware variables often are not interpreted culturally, so that variability due to idiosyncratic behavior may be used in determining types and compared to features which have widespread technological, functional, and stylistic significance.

Finally, investigators have neglected plainwares in favor of decorated ceramics because the latter offer more attributes to study and greater temporal variability.

In spite of stylistic limitations, taxonomic vagueness, ambiguities in terminology, and unwarranted assumptions about technology and behavior, there are arguments for doing plainware research. One of the most important is that as an artifact class plainwares have been neglected relative to their frequency of occurrence. Plainware is often the largest single class of material culture recovered. In southeastern Arizona and southwestern New Mexico, over 50 percent of the potsherds belong to this class (Nesbitt 1938; Haury 1936b; Sayles 1945; DiPeso 1958). Also, if style is considered in light of Sackett's (1977) definition, then plainwares may be highly stylized.

If it is accepted that ceramic technology is a good indicator of cultural variability, as proposed by Nicklin (1971), and that material culture is related to patterned behavior (Schiffer 1976), then pottery provides a valid object for study whether it is decorated or not.

Research Topics

Because of project limitations and the nature of the collections, it was decided to concentrate on one aspect of plainwares—paste and its qualities. This conforms to Rice's view (1976:541-2) that paste composition analyses should follow a formal procedure and be applied to a series of specific problems. One of the important elements of paste is filler (or temper). As it is used in this analysis, the term follows Shepard (1956:25) and applies to nonplastic temper materials found in the paste, whether purposely added or occurring naturally in the clay.

Table 19. Temper size scales

	Ceramics				Geology and Soils		
mm	Gifford (1953)	Colton (1953)	Shepard (1956)	Bennett (1974)	Wentworth (1922)	Udden (1914)	mm
0 .1 .2 .3 .4	very fine fine	very fine fine medium	fine	very fine fine	silt very fine fine medium		0.0 .177 .354
.5 .6 .7 .8 .9	medium	coarse	medium	medium	coarse		.5 .707
1.0 1.1 1.2 1.3 1.4 1.5 1.6 1.7 1.8 1.9	coarse	very coarse	coarse	coarse very coarse	very coarse		1.0 1.44
2.0 2.1 2.2 2.3 2.4 2.5 2.6 2.7 2.8 2.9	very coarse	gravel			granite		2.0 2.83
3.0 3.1 3.2 3.3 3.4 3.5 3.6 3.7 3.8 3.9 4.0							3.0 4.0

The importance of paste filler technology is highlighted in many studies. For example, filler composition has been used to distinguish pottery types (Hargrave 1932; Colton 1958; Schroeder 1958). Investigators have also studied temper size (DiPeso 1958:87; Fontana and others 1962:135) and amount (Thompson 1958; Rye and Evans 1976:130). Windes (1977) and Shepard (1956) posit that filler shape is important as it can affect vessel strength. Ethnographic studies show that temper is consciously varied by potters to achieve desired functional effects. Some groups temper cooking vessels differently than other vessels (Rogers 1936; Thompson 1958; Rye and Evans 1976). In at least one instance, a Papago woman constructed water coolers (ollas) to be more porous than water storage jars through different tempering practices (Fontana and others 1962). Raab (1973) and James (1974) argue that archaeological data support use of different tempers for different functions.

For this study it was assumed that prehistoric behavior was similar to that of the ethnographic examples above and that patterning of filler attributes would occur. The central hypothesis for the AEPCO plainware study was that technological variations exist and would be shown by quantitative and qualitative attribute measurement. This and other hypotheses relating technology to function would be tested by analysis of variables such as thickness, porosity, filler modal size, sorting, density, and shape, and dominant and subdominant filler material. These concepts will be explored below.

Research Methodology

The 2,378 plainware sherds recovered from four AEPCO sites (AZ CC:6:7, AZ CC:13:11, CC:13:15, and AZ CC:13:16) comprise the bulk of data for the plainware analysis. Thirty-seven sherds from five AEPCO I sites and 48 from the San Simon Village were used for comparison.

Once the variables were selected it was necessary to design measurement techniques which would be accurate, efficient, and easily duplicated. The approach chosen was based on that recommended by Pettijohn, Potter, and Seiver (1972) for sedimentary petrographers. In this approach, the sherd is conceived of as a comglomeration of clay, or cement, nonplastic filler, and open spaces or interstices, and it is measured as if it were a sedimentary structure. A freshly broken cross section of each sherd was cleaned with a dilute hydrocholoric acid solution. This enhanced filler recognition and interstice visibility. The sherd was then examined with a 10X hand lens, and then under a Bausch and Lomb zoom (.7-3X) binocular microscope. Size and sorting measurements were made at 10X with a double scale ocular reader calibrated to 0.1 mm. All other paste variables (porosity, density, shape and filler material) were examined at 20X.

Porosity and density were measured using a comparison chart for visual percentage estimation such as those developed by Folk (1951) and Bennett (1974). After a specimen was examined microscopically the sherd was compared to a chart (without magnification) to find the value corresponding to that of the sherd. These charts are illustrated in Figure 74.

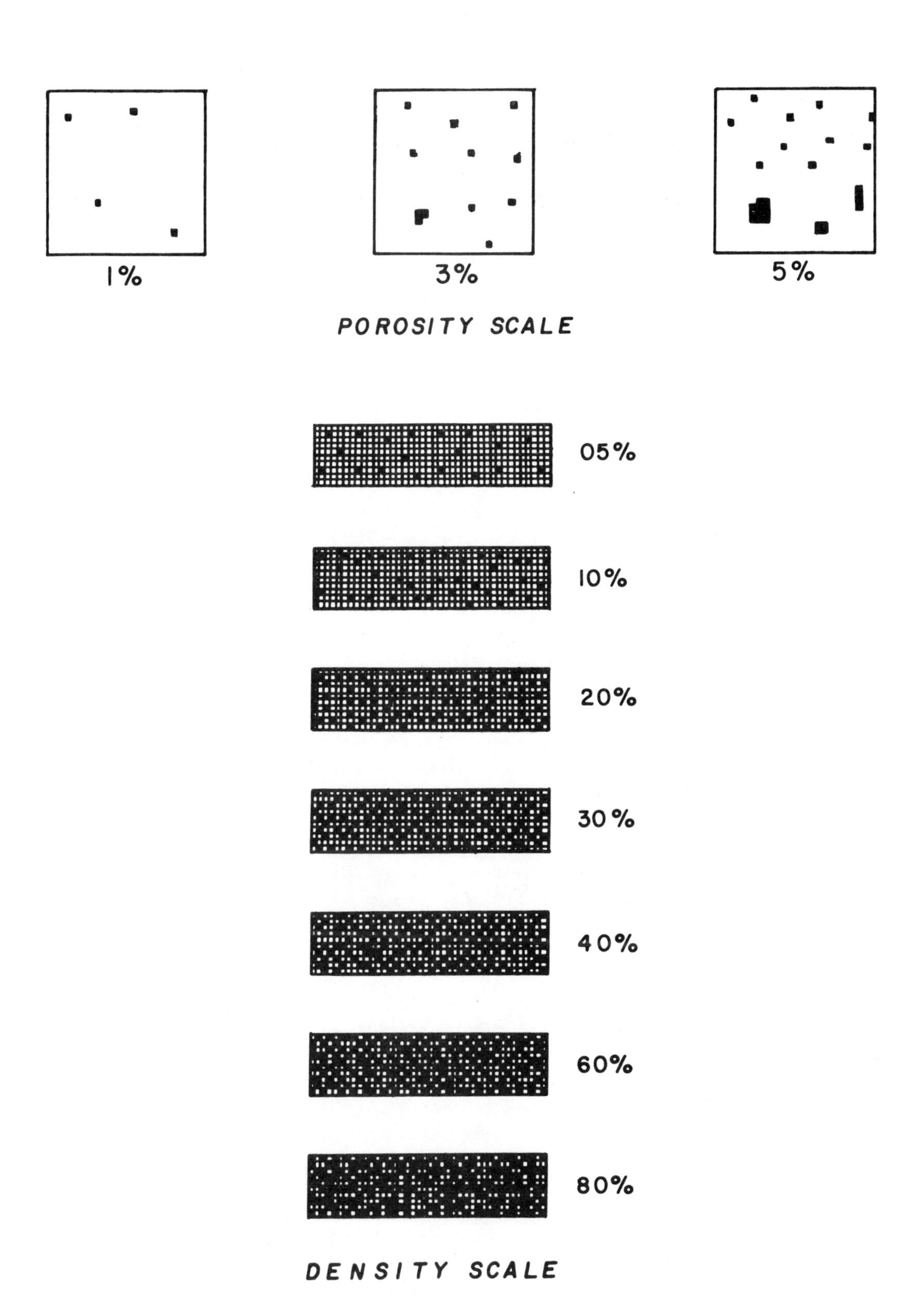

Figure 74. Visual percentage estimation of porosity and density.

Size was measured using the Wentworth (1922) scale, which is accepted by the National Research Council, and is based on the natural relation between sediment size and transport. Size terms used here are from this scale. Shape, or roundness, was measured according to Pettijohn (1957); the reader is referred to that work for descriptions and illustrations. It should be noted that after discussion with Robert O'Haire (Arizona Bureau of Mines and Mineral Technology), it was decided to lump subangular and subrounded into one class, as in practice this distinction is difficult to make.

The "sorting" of the filler was not measured in the geologic sense of the term, where it represents a dispersion of particles by size. This kind of measurement requires that frequent distributions for all size classes be determined, which was impractical for this analysis. Instead, sorting here refers to a measure of simple filler size range, calculated by identifying the smallest and largest size class represented. Both dominant and subdominant filler was limited to easily identifiable attributes such as common single (or groups of) minerals or other materials. This was done for two reasons. First, a preliminary sample showed that alluvial sand was the primary constituent in all sherds. Also, a refined mineral identification was beyond the abilities of the researcher.

Collection biases and project constraints demanded that not all the sherds be subjected to every measurement. Sherd condition and time limited the number of measurements made on any one specimen. For example, thickness was measured only when both surfaces of the sherd were present. On some very eroded sherds, surface finish could not be determined. An arbitrary minimum length of 1 cm was required for each cross section examined for filler attributes, and many sherds were thus eliminated due to their size. This sample was further reduced by eliminating sherds with labeled catalog numbers which would have been destroyed in breaking the sherd. A total of 484, or 20 percent of all plainware sherds, were subjected to filler analysis. Later, it became evident that some variables would have to be abandoned. Preliminary assessment indicated that the least desirable (or feasible) information was surface color and finish, vessel form, and sherd position; these were eliminated.

The AEPCO I and San Simon Village collections are represented by 37 and 48 sherds, respectively; within these samples there are inherent biases. First, 76 percent of the AEPCO I sherds are from one vandalized site, and are probably rejects from pot-hunting activities which selected for whole pots or decorated sherds. The San Simon village sample represents the entire phase sequence as defined by Sayles (1945), with sherds from 24 different pithouses. Almost all (96 percent) are rim sherds.

It has been assumed that both the AEPCO II and comparative samples are representative of the total populations and are thus valid for statistical comparisons. All data were recorded on Fortran coding sheets and subsequently punched onto computer cards. Data were analyzed using FREQUENCIES, CROSSTABS, and ONEWAY subprograms from the Statistical Package for the Social Sciences (Nie and others 1975). The primary statistic used was the chi-square, which tests for the existence of an association between variables. If variables are independent, a low significance level is obtained, and when variables show a nonrandom relationship, a high significance level is reached. The accepted level of significance is $p \leq .05$. To interpret the nature of associations, cell frequencies were compared.

Numerical Analysis and Results

The plainware attribute frequencies for all sites are listed in Table 20. Once tabulated, the distribution of several variables was not fully statistically tested. For these variables, either the percentages achieved were so disparate that no further tests were necessary, or the variables were not considered important to the hypotheses. Two filler variables were given this treatment: filler shape and material type. The description of these precedes the presentation of examples with more substantial variation.

It is known that angular filler helps to create a potentially stronger vessel (Shepard 1956:27). It was hypothesized that if this quality were known and desired, then a high percentage of angular to very angular filler would be discovered in the sherds. Among the AEPCO II sites, over 90 percent of the sherds exhibited subangular to subrounded temper. The exception was AZ CC:13:11, where about 80 percent of the sherds are subangular-subrounded and the remaining have angular temper. The AEPCO I materials are similar to those of this latter site, with 81 percent of the sherds having subangular-subrounded filler and 19 percent having angular filler. Also, 94 percent of the San Simon Village sherds have subangular-subrounded filler. These percentages indicate a high degree of similarity between sites, except for the two anomalous cases (AZ CC:13:11, AEPCO I) which, when grouped, are significantly different from the majority ($X^2=58.61$, 1 df, $p < .001$). Yet even here the angular filler represents only a minor percentage of the total. The results are interpreted as showing that increased vessel strength due to angular filler was either an unknown or undesired quality. Two sites are possible exceptions but it is unclear what this difference means.

For all sites, both filler material variables are represented by nearly 100 percent of one attribute. The dominant filler material is overwhelmingly miscellaneous minerals and the subdominant filler is crushed rock. The term subdominant may be misleading, however, as crushed rock is actually rare as filler in the collection. In fact, the identification of a subdominant type was not meaningful at the level of this analysis. Within the filler, quartz and feldspar commonly account for more than 50 percent in any sherd, usually in a 1:1 ratio. Mica is the next most common mineral, with muscovite more plentiful than biotite. Other minerals occurring, but rarely, are hematite, limonite, sanadine, and amphibole. Refined mineralogical and petrographic analyses were beyond the scope of this project. Neither the filler type measurement nor the mineral identification suggested a place of origin or any specialized tempering practices for the plainware. The other variables exhibited differing degrees of variation.

Table 20. Plainware sherd attribute frequencies

Variable	Column	Attribute	AZ CC:6:7	AZ CC:13:11	AZ CC:13:15	AZ CC:13:16	AEPCO I	San Simon Village
Thickness	3 mm		2	5	7			
	4 mm		17	101	112	2	1	
	5 mm		44	256	257	6		5
	6 mm		23	202	146	13	11	22
	7 mm		4	82	35	9	9	11
	8 mm		4	17	9	4	5	4
	9 mm		6	6		2	3	3
	10 mm		1		1		4	3
	11 mm			3				
	12 mm						2	
Surface condition, exterior	1	Noneroded				2		
	2	Eroded, 50%-	42	110	148	20		
	3	Eroded, 50%+	30	18	586	29		
	4	Indeterminate	79	360	536	15		
Surface condition, interior	1	Noneroded						
	2	Eroded, 50%-	42	79	83	8		
	3	Eroded, 50%+	46	104	725	46		
	4	Indeterminate	93	311	462	12		
Construction	1	Coil/Scrape						
	2	Paddle/Anvil	3	4	3	3		
	3	Combination						
	4	Other						
	5	Indeterminate	148	490	1267	63		
Apparent porosity	1	None				14		
	2	1%	7	5	58	18	1	
	3	3%	44	70	96	9	13	16
	4	5%	24	83	21	4	23	32
	5	Indeterminate						
Filler modal size	1	Very fine	8					
	2	Fine	36	36	74		4	13
	3	Medium	29	101	67	41	25	27
	4	Coarse	2	19	25	4	6	8
	5	Very coarse		2	7		2	
	6	Granular						

Table 20. Plainware sherd attribute frequencies (continued)

Variable	Column	Attribute	AZ CC:6:7	AZ CC:13:11	AZ CC:13:15	AZ CC:13:16	AEPCO I	San Simon Village
Filler sorting	1	Very fine-fine						
	2	Very fine-medium						
	3	Very fine-coarse	12	6	27			2
	4	Very fine-very coarse	34	114	49	9	11	23
	5	Very fine-granular	11	37	75	9	26	23
	6	Fine-medium						
	7	Fine-coarse	1					
	8	Fine-very coarse	8		5	19		
	9	Fine-granular	9	1	14	8		
	10	Medium-coarse						
	11	Medium-very coarse						
	12	Medium-granular			3			
	13	Coarse-very coarse						
	14	Coarse-granular						
	15	Very coarse-granular						
Filler density	1	5%						
	2	10%						
	3	20%		2	3			
	4	30%	2	1	23			1
	5	40%	19	10	30	37	4	9
	6	60%	29	91	71	8	27	24
	7	80%	25	54	46		6	14
Filler modal shape	1	Very Angular						
	2	Angular	1	29			7	3
	3	Subangular-subrounded	73	126	171	46	30	45
	4	Rounded	1	3	2			
	5	Very rounded						

Table 20. Plainware sherd attribute frequencies (continued)

Variable	Column	Attribute	AZ CC:6:7	AZ CC:13:11	AZ CC:13:15	AZ CC:13:16	AEPCO I	San Simon Village
Filler material, dominant	1	Quartz						
	2	Feldspar						
	3	Calcite						
	4	Other mineral						
	5	Miscellaneous minerals	72	156	173	46	37	48
	6	Rock fragments	3	2				
	7	Sherd						
	8	Organic						
	9	Indeterminate						
	10	Mica						
Filler material, subdominant	1	Quartz						
	2	Feldspar						
	3	Calcite						
	4	Other mineral						
	5	Miscellaneous minerals	4	2				
	6	Rock fragments	64	148	165	46	37	48
	7	Sherd						
	8	Organic	2					
	9	Indeterminate	5	2	9			
	10	Mica						
Surface color, irregular	1	None	8	11	59	26		
	2	Exterior only	2	6	25	4		
	3	Interior only	1	4	79			
	4	Exterior and interior	1	7	42			
	5	Exterior; interior indeterminate	14	11	38	7		
	6	Interior; exterior indeterminate		16	20	1		
	7	None/indeterminate	22	9	62	4		
	8	Indeterminate/none	4	49	29			
	9	Indeterminate/indeterminate	25	135	916	22		

Table 20. Plainware sherd attribute frequencies (continued)

Variable	Column	Attribute	AZ CC:6:7	AZ CC:13:11	AZ CC:13:15	AZ CC:13:16	AEPCO I	San Simon Village
Core/streak	* 0/1	Core/streak **	9/66	65/84	60/821	5/61	5/32	20/27
Surface finish, exterior	0/1	Crazing	52/2	41/13	69/92	15/10		
	0/1	Pitting	5/49	1/53	0/161	1/24		
	0/1	Scraping Marks	22/32	29/25	119/42	22/3		
	0/1	Polishing	6/48	1/53	2/159	8/19		
	0/1	Temper	3/51	0/54	1/160	0/25		
	0/1	Fire blackening	51/3	53/1	161/0	25/0		
Surface finish, interior	0/1	Crazing	33/3	53/4	31/103	13/2		
	0/1	Pitting	2/34	0/57	0/134	0/15		
	0/1	Scraping marks	11/285	34/23	63/71	5/10		
	0/1	Polishing	3/33	1/56	0/134	7/8		
	0/1	Temper	2/34	0/57	0/134	0/15		
	0/1	Fire blackening	36/0	57/0	129/5	10/5		
Sherd form	1	Rim	5	18	28			
	2	Neck	5	3	1	1		
	3	Base						
	4	Body						
	5	Other						
	6	Indeterminate	141	480	1441	65		
Vessel form	1	Open	3	11	27			
	2	Closed	6	8				
	3	Other						
	4	Indeterminate	142	482	1243	66		
Rim/neck form (wall)	1	Straight	2	8	20			
	2	Expanding		7	2			
	3	Contracting	3	2	2			
	4	Shoulder		1				
	5	Other						
	6	Indeterminate			1			

* 0 = absent
1 = present
** first number = absent
second number = present

Table 20. Plainware sherd attribute frequencies (continued)

Variable	Column	Attribute	AZ CC:6:7	AZ CC:13:11	AZ CC:13:15	AZ CC:13:16	AEPCO I	San Simon Village
Rim/neck form	1							
(lip)	2							
Note: Lip forms	3		1	6	11			
after Colton	4		3	2	15			
(1953:44, fig.10).	5							
	6			1				
	7							
	8			1				
	9							
	10				1			
	11				1			
	12			7				

Note: Totals in the text are correct; discrepancies with this table are due to secondary analysis.

Sorting exhibited some intersite variability. Ethnographically, filler is sorted in several ways to remove large particles and obtain more homogeneous material (Brugge 1964; Gifford 1932; Dobyns 1956). It was hoped that by measuring the range of filler sizes within individual sherds an index of sorting would be determined which could be related to the care with which clay is prepared. Extremely well-sorted materials are defined as those limited to one size class; on the other end extremely poorly sorted filler cross cut the six size classes. The materials examined were very heterogeneous with respect to sorting. Over 99 percent of the sherds included four size classes and 34 percent cross cut the entire size range. Thus, the materials are poorly sorted. In addition, approximately 40 percent of the sherds have some granular filler. However, some variability between sites with respect to filler sorting is evident. AZ CC:13:15 has the widest range of sortings, and when grouped with AEPCO I and San Simon Village data, these sites show consistently more heterogeneity than the others, especially AZ CC:6:7 and AZ CC:13:16. The degree to which this is culturally meaningful is difficult to determine due to the sorting definitions used. The ranges of individual attributes may be mutually exclusive or may overlap. More information might have been gained by using a refined scale of sorting based on the percentage of each size class per sherd.

The results indicate that apparently, careful sorting was either unknown or not culturally desirable, as it certainly would have been possible to obtain more homogeneous and finer-grained filler. The common sorting ranges in the sample are characteristic of alluvial sands, such as those found in washes throughout the Sulphur Spring and San Simon valleys. When filler sorting information is combined with filler shape and material type data, there is strong evidence for the use of alluvial sands as filler material. This patterning indicates that the prehistoric pottery makers employed easily available filler materials which required a minimum of preparation. This hypothesis could be tested in future research by collecting natural material and subjecting it to more refined analysis along with archaeological specimens.

Variability among sites relative to thickness was also demonstrated. The overall range is 3 to 12 mm; at AEPCO II sites the range is 3 to 11 mm with a mean of 5.4 mm. A one-way analysis of variance for thickness for all sites shows that there is wide variation among sites ($F=47.7$, 5 df, $p \leq .001$). The mean and 95 percent confidence intervals at each site are illustrated in Figure 75. It is obvious from this that dramatic differences are present among sites. Low sample numbers correspond to large confidence intervals, which might indicate a need for better samples from these sites. However, the differences might be valid indicators of vessel forms or sizes, with thicker sherds representing large vessels or jars and small pots or bowls indicated by thinner sherds. In our data, the ratio of jar to bowl rims at AZ CC:6:7 is 0.67:1 and at San Simon Village, 2.3:1. However, based on the paucity of rims in the sample and the lack of restorable vessels, the results are inconclusive and only suggest a hypothesis which could be tested on existing whole vessel collections. If this relationship is valid, then cultural variation may have been identified and could be applied to site interpretation.

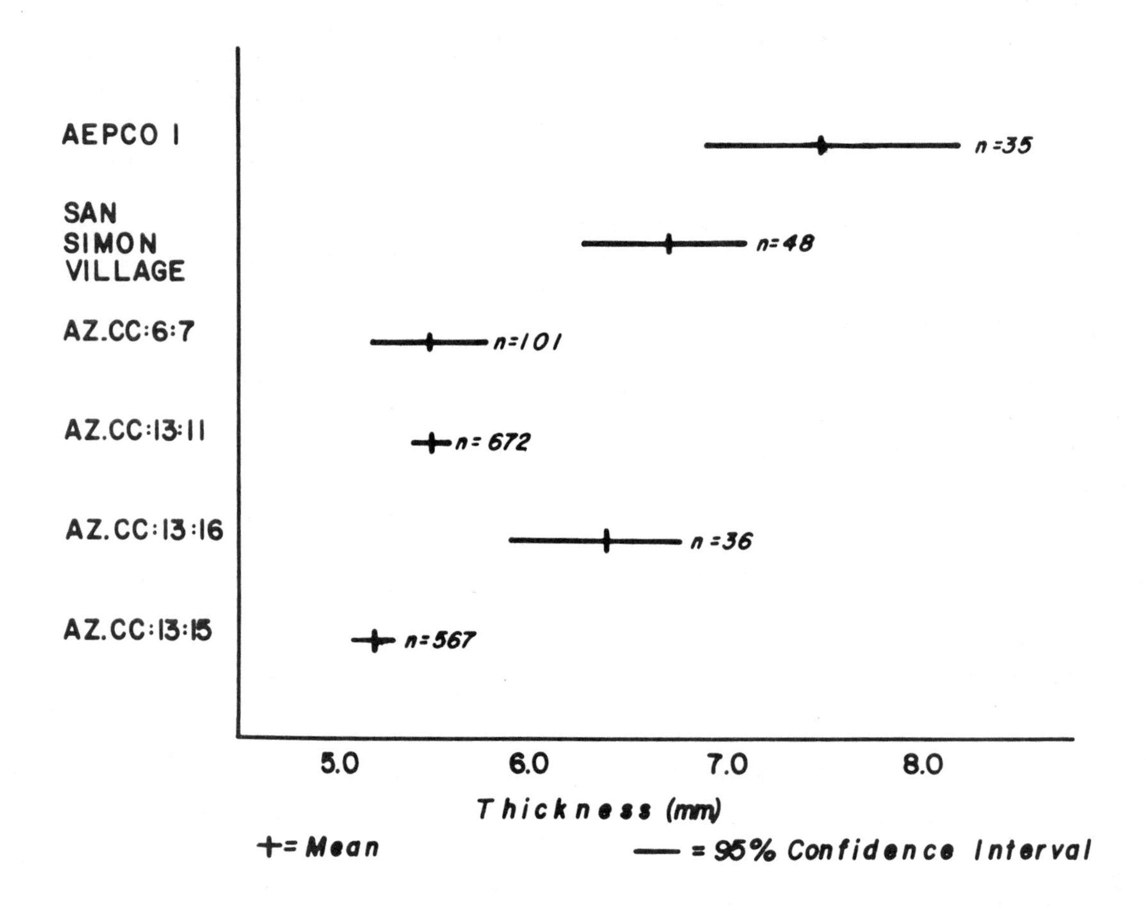

Figure 75. Sherd thickness expressed in 95 percent confidence intervals.

Measurable variation also exists relative to site filler modal size (Figure 76). The greatest divergences from the overall modal size (medium) are at (1) AEPCO I sites, where the filler is much larger than the norm, (2) AZ CC:6:7, where it is much finer than the norm, and (3) AZ CC:13:15, where a bimodal distribution occurs. These variations could relate to functional differences and will be explored in more detail below.

Filler density values were not only variable among sites but also were much higher than predicted. While ethnographers record variation in amount of filler added to clay, that amount is generally between 30 to 50 percent (Brugge 1964; Rogers 1936; Thompson 1958; Rye and Evans 1976). The modal class of the collection being analyzed was 60 percent density, with 40 and 80 percent roughly equal as the next most common amounts. In only 6 percent of the cases was the density less than or equal to 30 percent.

This discrepancy may be due to several factors. First, as ethnographically reported, many potters only estimate the amount of filler added. Some of these measurements are made in terms of weight, and others in terms of volume. It is also questionable whether density as measured on a sherd cross section is a valid indicator of the amount of filler used. However, if density is relatively homogeneous throughout a sherd, then the value obtained could be phrased in terms of an index, rather than a relative frequency. This still could be culturally meaningful.

The variability represented by the collections is most evident at three sites (Figure 77). San Simon Village, AZ CC:6:7 and AZ CC:13:11 have a relatively large percentage of high-density (heavily tempered) sherds when compared to the expected values. AZ CC:13:15 exhibits a larger amount of lower density pottery. This variability will also be examined below.

The last major variable, porosity, is found to vary greatly among sites (Figure 78). The AEPCO I group, San Simon Village, and AZ CC:13:11 exhibit a larger value than average for the highest porosity category (5 percent). Conversely, AZ CC:13:16 and AZ CC:13:15 have lower than average porosity values. This variable was tested to determine if it is related to actual porosity.

Thirty sherds selected from AZ CC:6:7 representing the 3 percent and 5 percent porosity classes were subjected to a test similar to that described by Shepard (1956). Instead of boiling all sherds, one-half of each class was merely soaked for comparison, and the time was reduced from the recommended 2 hours to 30 minutes. Thus, the values obtained are not true porosities, but rather index values. While the porosities obtained for individual sherds in each group overlapped, the mean class values are distinctly different, with a proper correlation between observed and experimentally derived values. That is, when grouped, the 3 percent class has a porosity index of 13.6 percent (N=20) and the 5 percent class has a porosity index of 21.5 percent (N=10). These results validate the estimation procedure and further indicate that true apparent porosity is between four to five times the value observed here. This relationship could easily be quantified with more thorough testing.

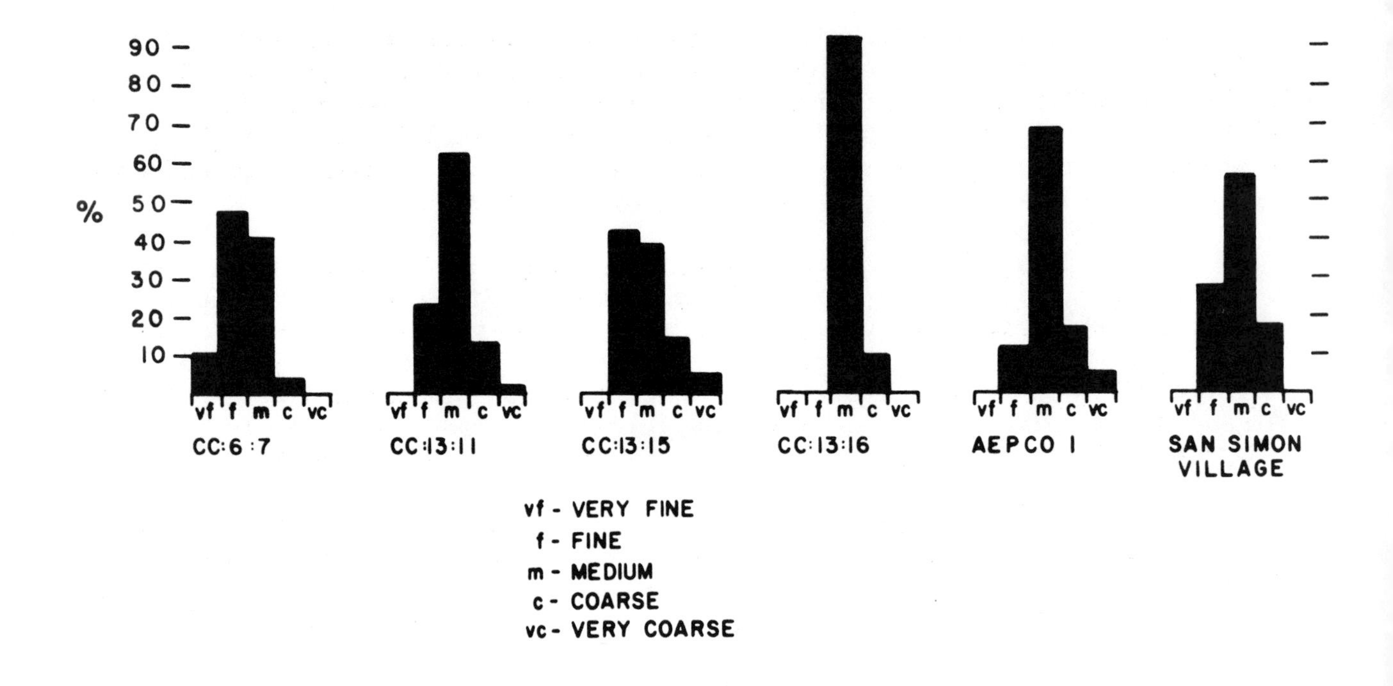

Figure 76. Sherd filler size by site.

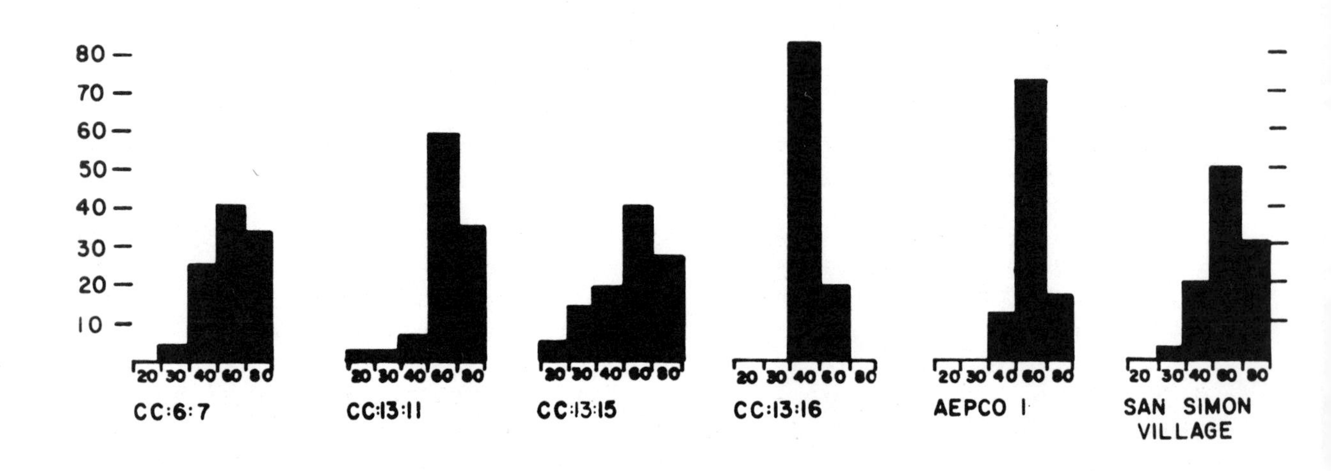

Figure 77. Sherd filler density by site.

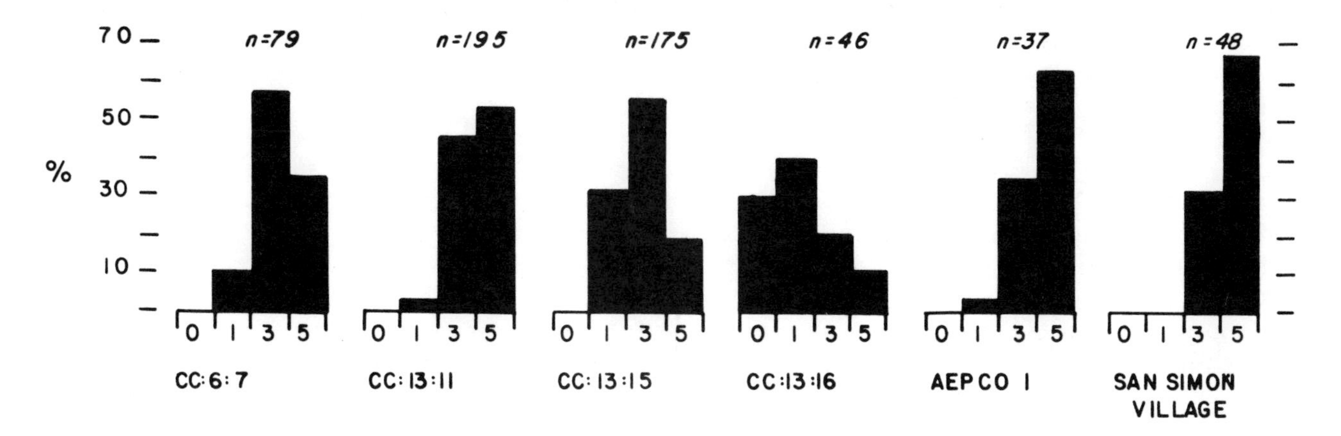

Figure 78. Sherd porosity by site.

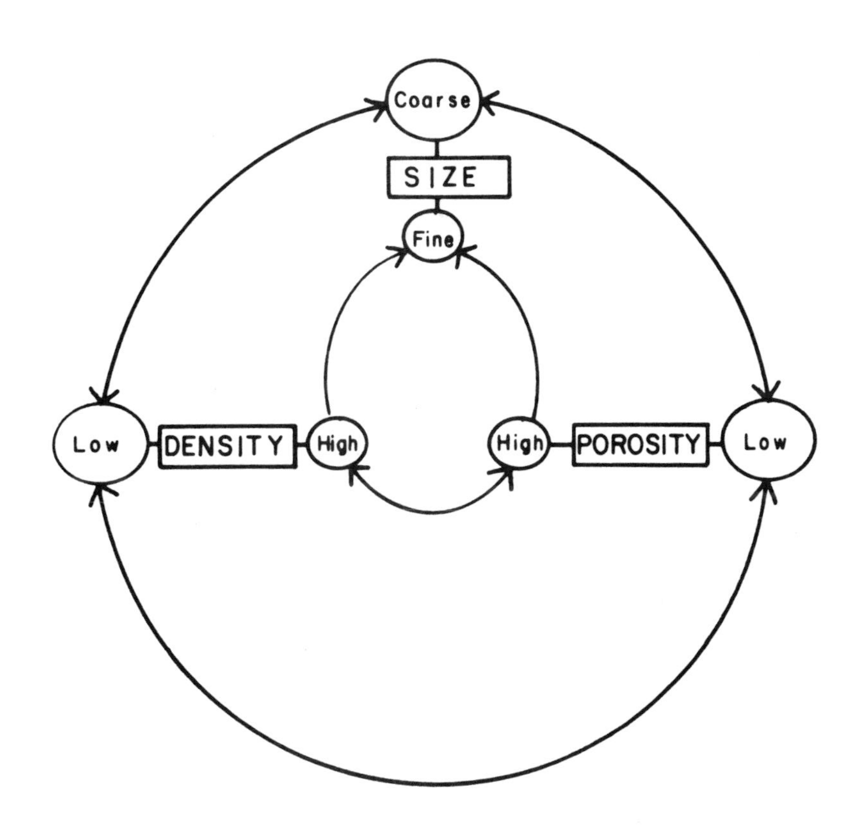

Figure 80. Ceramic filler model: Relationships between density, porosity, and size.

Several other technological variables were measured for the AEPCO II collection alone. Analysis of sherd smoothing and polishing showed that both bowl and jar fragments were present. This was confirmed by rim analysis, where a 2:1 ratio of jar to bowl sherds was found. In comparison, San Simon Village rim sherds show a 2.3:2 ratio. The range of variation in plainware rim form is illustrated in Figure 79.

In firing, some sherds were fully oxidized and bear no surface discolorations. Eighty-eight percent of the specimens measured have some degree of core streaking and about 40 percent show irregular surface colors. While this latter variable is primarily due to firing, some color variation may be due to postdepositional changes. It was difficult to identify construction methods, but both paddle-and-anvil and coil-and-scrape techniques are present in the sample. The former was identified in more instances although it may not actually have been the more common practice. Postconstruction variables such as surface crazing and pitting were also measured on some of the sherds, but as time was short, these variables were not thoroughly analyzed. The data gathered do indicate that the AEPCO II collections include a wide range of attributes, and we recommend that future research should consider these features more fully.

In sum, these general, descriptive results indicate a high degree of variation in the pottery of southeastern Arizona. Variation at the technological (pot-making) level has been measured and identified for plainwares from four AEPCO II sites, the AEPCO I group, and San Simon Village. To achieve a better understanding of this variation and its relation to functional and other cultural relationships, additional tests were made.

Technological-Functional Relationships

Many tests of association were carried out to answer specific questions about technological-functional variability in the plainware ceramics. The most important of these relate to porosity, filler size, and filler density.

First, one problem encountered during analysis needs to be mentioned. In some tests, all sherds were grouped in one unit to test the significance of associations between several pairs of variables. The results of these tests indicate that most associations are statistically significant. This was very interesting, yet it was hard to understand how so many of the tests which were not significant at the individual site level could become significant when the data were lumped. A possible source of error was that at one site, AZ CC:13:15, virtually all tests indicated significant associations. On closer inspection of this site collection, it was apparent that the large sherd number might actually represent only a small number of vessels. If this was the case, and if there was a relatively high degree of homogeneity from sherds fo the same vessel, then the misleading conclusions might result. The other collections were examined and are considered to be free of this potential bias. When the same tests were rerun without the data from AZ CC:13:15, the results were similar. Clearly, some other phenomenon is at work here. One possibility is that in the chi-square tests, the number of attribute

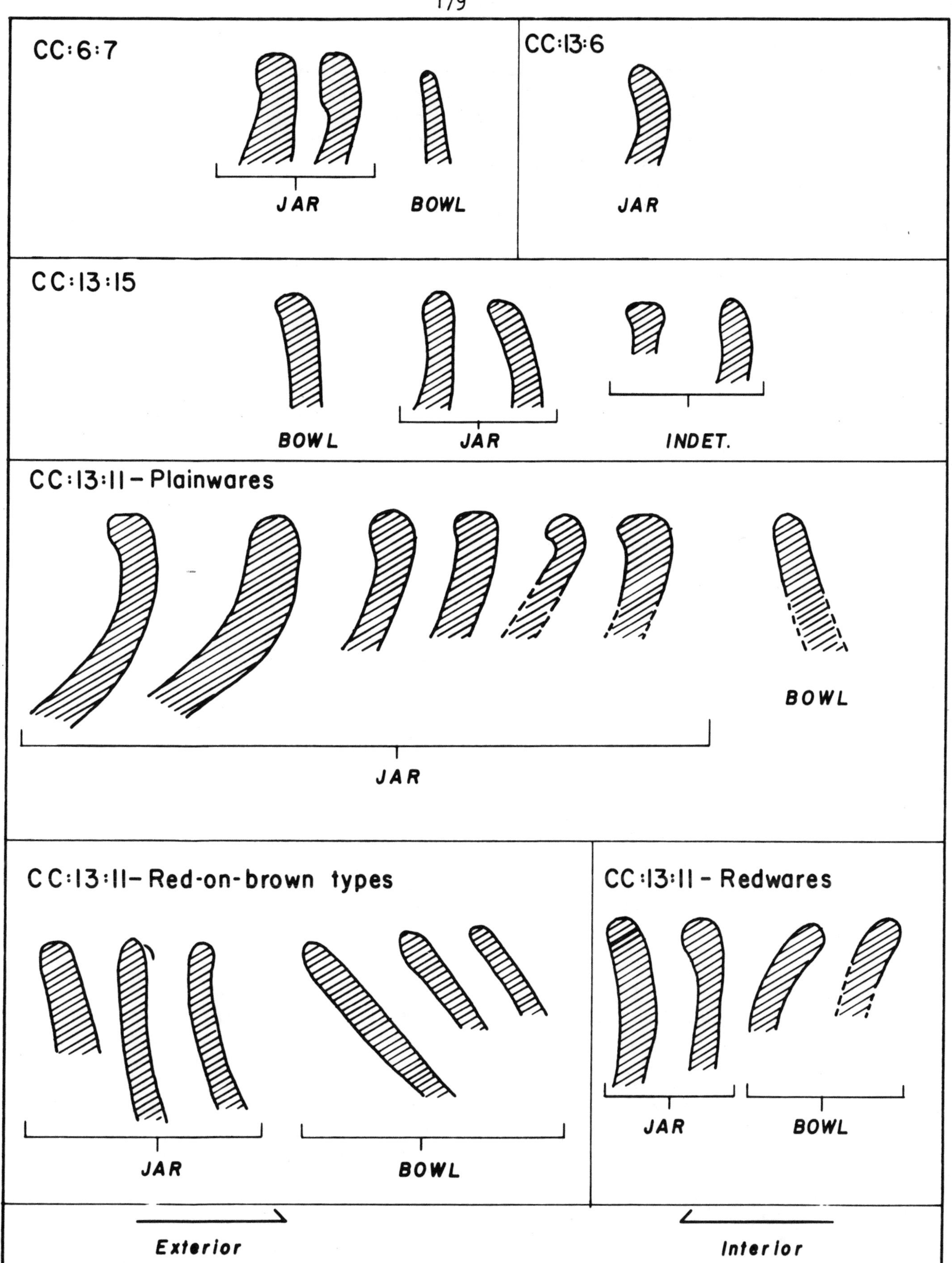

Figure 79. Plainware rim sherd forms.

equal to or near zero is near the maximum allowed for valid comparisons; but this applies only to a few tests. Another possibility is that as the number of cases increases, it is easier to obtain a higher chi-square value and thus a higher level of significance. One final possibility is that the lumped data reveal trends not apparent at individual sites. Any or all of these could be affecting the test results. All chi-square table frequencies were examined to provide valid interpretations of the hypothesis testing.

The functional variable of greatest interest here is porosity. Therefore, its association with technological variables was tested to see if patterning existed. Geologically, porosity of sedimentary structures is a function of five main factors: grain size, sorting, shape, packing, and compaction (Pettijohn 1957). The research collections were considered homogenous with respect to shape, and since cultural sorting of temper was not apparent, this variable was also eliminated. Density was used instead of packing and compaction, since it was impossible to measure these two properties directly. In the end, therefore, only two technological variables were considered: filler modal size and filler density. Hypotheses on the relationship between porosity and temper size were generated from geologic and ethnographic models. In geological theory, porosity should not vary with size, but experiments show that finer-grained particles have higher porosities than coarser filler (Pettijohn 1957:86). Thus liquid storage and cooking vessels would be expected to contain coarse filler, while fine temper would be used in dry storage vessels and in ollas where the greater porosity would increase evaporative cooling.

Ethnographically, fine-grained filler is functionally related to liquid storage vessels, and coarse-grained temper to cooking vessels (Thompson 1958; Rogers 1936; Rye and Evans 1976). This latter function is expected, given the natural properties of filler, but the former practice runs counter to what geologic theory suggests. If the vessels are functioning as storage containers and not as water coolers, then this natural property of fillers is being ignored. One ethnographic account of olla manufacture states that the potter uses coarse-grained filler to create a more effective cooling vessel (Fontana and others 1962). This is also in opposition to what is expected theoretically. However, it is known that angular filler is more porous than rounded particles (Pettijohn 1957:86); in this case the increased angularity of the crushed rock filler is probably responsible for the greater porosity.

The relationship between porosity and filler modal size was then tested. Two sites, AZ CC:6:7 and AZ CC:13:15, independently exhibited significant associations between filler modal size and porosity (X^2=14.3, p=.026; X^2=20.2, 6 df, p=.003). Both indicated associations between finer temper and higher porosity, and coarser temper and lower porosity. (At the remaining sites this association is present but not significant). This is in line with the natural properties of filler. The relationship was explored further by combining size and porosity attributes into two classes—very fine to fine filler versus medium to granule filler, and less than 5 percent porosity versus 5 percent porosity. Again, the association was significant at these two sites (X^2=5.3, 1 df, p=.002; X^2=16.1, 1 df, p=.001). (The remaining sites show the same trend at levels which are not significant statistically).

When all data from AEPCO II sites were combined and tested with the collapsed variable classes, the chi-square test showed that high porosity was related to fine temper and low porosity was associated with coarse temper (X^2=5.2, 1 df, p=.023). Thus, the ethnographically modeled hypothesis that fine temper is related to liquid storage and coarse temper to ollas is rejected and the geologic-ethnographic hypothesis that coarse temper may have been used in cooking vessels and fine temper in dry storage vessels is accepted. This admittedly simple explanation is made without supporting evidence such as vessel shape, fire blackening, or food remains which are not available for this sample. At least on the technological level, the associations have been demonstrated. Cultural interpretations of these phenomena can be based on the pattern discovered but must be made with the knowledge of the limitations of the hypothesis.

Another relationship that inspired interest was that of filler density to porosity. Geologically, there is no factor directly equivalent to density as measured in this experiment. It is similar to packing (the arrangement of particles), and compaction. In nature, the tightest packing with the minimum of voids tends to prevail, so that this variable is usually not considered by geologists. As the porosity of the average sandstone, for example, varies little with respect to packing and compaction, the natural model suggests that the porosity of sherds also would vary little in relation to density.

Many, but not all of the tests at the individual site level and with the grouped data bore out this hypothesis by relating porosity and density at statistically significant values (for example the data from AEPCO II sites as a group yielded the following results: X^2=92.7, 12 df, $p \leq .001$). Consistently, lower porosity is associated with lower filler density and higher porosity with higher filler density. It would thus appear that with respect to porosity there exists technological patterning. This implies a functional relationship which should be tested more fully before definite interpretations are made.

The final functional relationship examined is that of filler modal size and density. Because both of these variables are nonrandomly patterned with porosity at statistically significant levels, it was hypothesized that an association between filler size and density exists. Most of the individual sites exhibited statistically significant associations between these two variables, and some of the grouped tests also substantiated this hypothetical relationship. (For example, the test between size at the 1a and 2a classes and density at a less than 50 percent and greater than 50 percent class yielded a X^2=24.9, df=1, $p \leq .001$). The results indicate that finer filler modal size is associated with high filler density, and that coarser filler is associated with lower density. It is apparent from the grouped data frequency distributions that a more meaningful division might have been made, such as that between the 60 percent and 80 percent classes. Time was not available to check this latter prediction but the information gained was sufficient to indicate the nature of the association. As this test is not a measure of directional significance, it has not been established that these two variables, filler modal size and filler density, are in fact the independent values which determine the porosity. However, the results are suggestive of this functional relationship and are interpreted that either variable is a valid index of relative porosity values.

One further test should be mentioned. As alluded to before, Westfall (1978) felt that the AEPCO I "Brown plainware" differed from Alma Plain, and she provided a working description of the former for analysis purposes. It was not considered a new "type;" rather, a tentative identification was made pending further data collection. Chi-square tests run on the data from AEPCO I and San Simon Village indicate that the only difference between the samples is with respect to paste or core/streak attributes (Table 21). While there are biases in the samples, and limitations to these tests, it appears there is a high degree of similarity between plainwares at these sites with respect to filler attributes. The distinction that Westfall made may still be valid, however. One of the differences she observed was surface finish, and although this was not measured in the study, a definitely higher polish was noted for the plainwares from the AEPCO I sites and San Simon village.

Ceramics from three of the four AEPCO II sites (AZ CC:6:7, AZ CC:13:11, and 15) also were compared to both of the AEPCO I and San Simon Village collections. The tests indicate that all of these AEPCO II materials are statistically different from both the AEPCO I and San Simon Village plainwares (Table 22). Two sites, AZ CC:6:7 and AZ CC:13:15, are very different from the comparative materials. For each of these, similarities exist only between one or two of the six variables compared in each collection. The other site, AZ CC:13:11, is substantially more similar to the comparative data, differing only in two or three of the variables examined. Most of this similarity is with the interrelated techno-functional variables: porosity, filler size, and density. The conclusion drawn from these results is that these materials may reflect a range of functions similar to those of the AEPCO I and San Simon Village materials.

Table 21. Intersite comparisons of plainwares:

AEPCO I and San Simon Village

Thickness	*
Porosity	+
Size	+
Sorting	+
Sorting	+
Density	+
Core/Streak	-
Shape	-

- = statistically different ($p \leq .05$)
+ = statistically similar
* = unsufficient data

Table 22. Results of statistical comparison of plainwares

	AEPCO I with AEPCO II			San Simon Village with AEPCO II		
	AZ CC:6:7	AZ CC:13:11	AZ CC:13:15	AZ CC:6:7	AZ CC:13:11	AZ CC:13:15
Thickness	-	-	+	-	-	+
Porosity	-	+	-	-	+	-
Size	-	+	-	-	+	-
Sorting	-	-	-	-	-	-
Density	-	+	-	+	+	-
Core/Streak	+	-	+	-	+	-
Shape	-	+	-	+	-	+

- = Statistically different ($p \leq .05$)
+ = Statistically similar
* = unsufficient data

Summary and Conclusions

Variation in plainware pottery from southeastern Arizona has been studied and some of the differences and similarities which exist in the AEPCO II and comparative collections have been identified. This research has focused on nine ceramic variables, eight of which deal with paste. Each provided some information on the ceramic technology.

Filler material was predominantly a heterogeneous mixture of miscellaneous minerals and rock fragments in varying proportions. These inclusions are primarily subrounded to subangular in shape and are poorly sorted. The analysis of these three variables suggests that filler probably consists of immediately available materials which were subjected to a minimum of preparation. It easily falls within the composition of the alluvial sands commonly found throughout the region. Thus, no idiosyncratic tempering practices are suggested and no specific locality of origin is identified.

The modal filler size is medium grained, but three sites vary significantly from this value. AZ CC:13:15 has a bimodal distribution, and the AEPCO I collection has much coarser filler. Filler density values were much higher than those reported ethnographically, with the average value being 60 percent. AZ CC:6:7, AZ CC:13:11, and San Simon Village have higher values, and AZ CC:13:15 and 16 have lower than average values. The modal porosity class is 3 percent, and AZ CC:6:7, AZ CC:13:11, San Simon Village, and AEPCO I collections exhibit higher than average values while AZ CC:13:15 and 16 have lower values (Table 23). For this analysis, density and porosity attributes are interpreted as indices rather than actual values.

Table 23. Technological-functional relationships of plainware filler

Size		Density		Porosity	
Finer	AZ CC:6:7	Higher	AZ CC:6:7	Higher	AZ CC:6:7
	AZ CC:13:15		-		-
	-		AZ CC:13:11		AZ CC:13:11
	-		San Simon V.		San Simon V.
	-		-		AEPCO I
Coarser	AEPCO I	Lower	-	Lower	-
	AZ CC:13:15		AZ CC:13:15		AZ CC:13:15
	-		AZ CC:13:16		AZ CC:13:16

The relationship between density and porosity and function (as indicated by fillersize) was examined. A tripartite relation between dichotomized variables was demonstrated (Figure 80). Lower density is related to coarser filler and both are related to lower porosity. Conversely, higher density is associated with finer filler and both of these are associated with higher porosity. With respect to both filler size and density, porosity follows the natural geologic models. Only one large exception to this rule exists. As illustrated in Table 23 above, the AEPCO I coarser filler is associated with higher porosity values. There is an explanation for this phenomenon, however. It was noted earlier that the filler of this collection is significantly more angular than most examples. It was also noted that both geologic and ethnographic evidence suggests that angular filler is more porous than rounded material.

Thickness was analyzed, and the results indicate that there is a wide range represented from the collections. There appears to be greater variation between sites than within them, but it is uncertain if this is indicative of cultural or functional differences.

Other variables provided less information. Various degrees of surface finish were noted, both paddle-and-anvil and coil-and-scrape construction techniques are in evidence, and varying levels of oxidation were realized in firing.

Intersite comparisons were designed to analyze the variability between sites with respect to six filler categories. Results indicate that the AEPCO II materials are dissimilar to the AEPCO I and San Simon Village collections and that these comparative data are essentially similar to each other. However, the plainware from one AEPCO II site, AZ CC:13:11, is similar to both comparative collections. This may be due to functional similarities. All three collections have high porosity values and both the San Simon Village and AZ CC:13:11 groups have a relatively higher jar-bowl ratio.

Several problems were encountered during the analysis. One of these is the amount of time that was required to conduct detailed studies. More time was consumed than had been anticipated, and some variables had to be eliminated from the study. Anyone considering this type of ceramic research should carefully identify the specific scope of questions answerable with limited time and funds.

This pilot study was designed to cover a large amount of territory which had never been systematically examined. A goal was to discover what types of information could be obtained from plainware pottery. Many areas were overlooked by this research, and when these are identified and combined with the results presented herein, a systematic approach to the analysis of plainwares will have been established.

This type of study is not recommended for all future research, but it was well suited to this project's collection, in which the plainwares made up 95 percent of the sherds. As used here, analysis of plainware ceramics provided technological and functional information, and established that plainware sherds are useful reflections of human behavior.

A topic which deserves additional study is the relationship between technology and function. Both of these aspects should be pursued to achieve a fuller understanding of plainwares as measures of site activities and cultural relationships.

Using well-dated deposits to more accurately place plainwares in a temporal sequence might allow for the discovery of changes in technology and function through time. With further research, a more appropriate method for distinguishing different "types" of plainwares could be discovered. It is hoped that the reader has gained a sense of what is possible from the research presented in this pilot study.

Decorated Ceramics

As stated in the introduction to this chapter, little information could be obtained from this artifact class. Only 121 decorated sherds (4.8 percent of the total) were recovered (Table 17), and many sherds were so small and eroded that only speculations regarding identification were possible. Further, little detailed information is available and only a few comparative studies on the decorated pottery of the San Simon and Sulphur Spring valleys have been made. Two studies (Brown 1973; Mills and Mills 1969) discuss sites with polychrome wares, but the sites are probably later than the AEPCO II sites.

One study (Sayles 1945) concerns the red-on-brown ceramic series of this region. This is the San Simon series of the Mogollon Brownware tradition (Colton 1955:6). However, variability in the types defined by Sayles is based on a single excavation at San Simon Village. Other studies of sites west of the project area (Tuthill 1950) discuss the Dragoon series red-on-brown pottery found in sites in the San Pedro River Valley. However, the AEPCO ceramics could not be matched to this series.

Despite these problems, sherds were typed as specifically as possible. For many of the sherd identifications several opinions were solicited. While there is often disagreement among individuals in classifying even well-known Southwestern types (Fish 1978), the use of several opinions expanded the potential range of identifications for any one sherd. Sherd identifications, dates, and frequencies of occurrence are tabulated in Table 24 and discussed on a site-by-site basis.

Table 24. Decorated ceramic types from the AEPCO II sites

Type	Number	Dates
AZ CC:6:3		
Cord-marked Rim	1	A.D. 1100-1300 (Breternitz 1966)
AZ CC:6:7		
Unidentified Corrugated	2	
Unidentified Red Ware	1	
AZ CC:9:2		
Reserve Plain Corrugated	1	A.D. 1050-1200 (Rinaldo and Bluhm 1956)
AZ CC:13:16		
Sacaton Red-on-buff	2	A.D. 950-1100 (Haury 1976)
Unidentified Red-on-buff	5	
AZ CC:13:11		
Galiuro Red-on-brown	8	A.D. 650-950 (Wheat 1955)
Encinas Red-on-brown	32	A.D. 950-1100 (Wheat 1955)
Unidentified San Simon branch Red-on-brown sherds	10	
Rillito Red-on-brown	3	A.D. 700-900 (Kelly 1978)
Rincon Red-on-brown	1	A.D. 900-1100 (Kelly 1978)
Unidentified Santa Cruz series Red-on-brown sherds	1	
Mimbres Bold Face Black-on-white	5	A.D. 950-1100 (Haury 1936a)
Unidentified Red Ware	27	
Unidentified White Ware	8	
Unidentified Red Ware or Red-on-brown	14	

AZ CC:6:3. One isolated sherd was collected from this site, and is classified as "Cord-marked Rim." This is an undescribed type found at Point of Pines, Arizona, northeast of the project area. It is comparable to Tularosa Fillet Rim (Wendorf 1950), except that the decoration consists of cord impressions.

AZ CC:6:7. The one redware and two corrugated sherds recovered from this site could not be identified as to type. The redware sherd, however, could indicate early Mogollon presence at the site.

AZ CC:9:2. A single sherd of Reserve Plain Corrugated was recovered from the loose topsoil of a test pit at this site. On the basis of a lone sherd, it is not clear whether the site was once occupied by Mogollon groups or if the sherd represents a trade item.

AZ CC:13:16. The seven sherds recovered from this site are probably from the same vessel, but only two retain any decoration. They resemble Sacaton Red-on-buff: Safford Variety (Gifford 1957) but contain mica, which that variety does not normally have. They may be Rincon Red-on-brown (Kelly 1978), which is typical for the Tucson Basin, but have more characteristics of the Gila Basin variety of Sacaton Red-on-buff (Haury 1976). Not enough of the vessel is present to positively identify the variety. Regardless, all the possible types discussed above are roughly contemporaneous. The significance of the sherds as intrusive types cannot be ascertained.

AZ CC:13:11. This site contributed 109 sherds, or 91 percent of the total AEPCO II decorated sherds. As can be seen in Table 24, most of the sherds cannot be assigned to a specific type, but some comments can be made. Most of the redwares are similar to San Francisco Red at San Simon Village. Sayles (1945) considered the San Simon redwares to fall within this type as defined by Haury (1936a). However, they could be Reserve Red, a later type (Nesbitt 1938), or some other redware. In any case, they are a recognized Mogollon ware, but of limited use for dating purposes.

The San Simon series red-on-brown types at the AEPCO II sites are representative of those defined by Sayles for San Simon Village. The Santa Cruz series red-on-brown types are typical for the Tucson Basin west of the project region. Many of these Santa Cruz series sherds closely resemble the Gila-Salt Basin types, and also are similar to Safford variety red-on buff. The unidentified red-on-buff sherds could belong to any one of these variants. Despite problems with identification, the dates are relatively secure.

Mimbres Bold Face Black-on-white is common in this region, although it is considered a trade type by Sayles (1945).

The last group of decorated sherds from this site is whiteware, but the sherds are too eroded to be identified.

Summary

The decorated sherds are mostly small and eroded, and therefore difficult to classify. The pottery does indicate that the AEPCO II sites containing pottery were probably used some time during the period A.D. 700 to 1300. Most sherds date from A.D. 900 to 1100, and thus correspond to the Encinas phase of the San Simon branch (Sayles 1945) and may indicate occupation by this cultural group. They also suggest contact with Mimbres groups to the northeast and with the Hohokam to the west and northwest. The usefulness of applying identifiable, time-sensitive pottery types to analysis of cultural context will be explored in the final chapter of this report.

CHAPTER 6

GROUND STONE ANALYSIS

by Deborah A. Westfall

Introduction and Analysis Methodology

Ground and pecked stone artifacts were recovered from nine of the 11 sites investigated in the AEPCO Dos Condado-Apache R-O-W corridor. While the percentage of sites containing ground stone is high, the actual number of pieces per site is low, and the majority are extremely fragmentary. Recognizable tools constitute 94 (70 percent) of the 134 pieces collected from all sites.

Initial sorting into basic morphological types followed the system used for the Ventana Cave ground stone (Haury 1950). Although the AEPCO sites occur in the Cochise culture area defined by Sayles (1949), Sayles' generalized artifact descriptions limit the usefulness of comparing Cochise culture material with the AEPCO ground stone. With consideration given to the similarities between the Ventana and Cochise ground stone tool kits, as pointed out by Haury (1950:319), the use of the Ventana classification system allows for flexibility in determining possible temporal and cultural affinities for the AEPCO material.

The analysis focused on first obtaining basic attribute information on the ground stone, which was recorded on ASM analysis forms. The attributes included: rock type, shape, cross section, metric dimensions, number and position of grinding facets, wear stage, and weight. These data are on file at the Arizona State Museum, Cultural Resource Management Section.

Concerning descriptive terminology, Sayles (1949) preferred the inclusive term "milling stone" to designate the stationary nether grinding stone, stating that the term "metate" sould be reserved for the substantially modified trough metate type typical of Hohokam and Mogollon. Similarily, he applied the term "handstone" to the hand-held abrading stone, which corresponds to Haury's "one-hand mano." Sayles viewed the mano as the typical loaf-shaped subrectangular grinding stone generally used with trough metates. The AEPCO analysis uses Haury's terminology, since it is applicable to wider range of morphological types and allows for more detailed observations. Pieces that were extremely fragmentary and unclassifiable have been subsumed under "miscellaneous ground pieces."

Initial perusal of the AEPCO ground stone revealed differences when compared to the typical Cochise culture artifacts described by Sayles (1949). These were: (1) ground stone accounted for only a small percentage of the total artifact assemblage, contrasted to high frequencies reported by Sayles for Cochise culture sites, and (2) manos were on the whole smaller and less modified than those described for Cochise. In general, the AEPCO artifacts resembled the early Ventana Cave material.

It was thought that an intensive functional analysis of the ground stone would provide a more complete description of site activities. Complete specimens were so few, however, and surface context often disturbed by erosion and relic collecting, that a functional or spatial analysis using complicated statistical methods was not warranted. Therefore, the discussion that follows will be limited to a description and comparison of the form and frequency of ground stone tools recovered. Site function as related to ground stone use and the cultural implications thereof are discussed in the conclusions to this chapter.

Description of the Collections

AZ CC:6:3

The single ground stone artifact collected from the site is a bifacially ground one-hand mano fragment of coarse-grained red granite. It is a naturally rounded cobble and no pecking to shape is evident. The primary use surface is pitted from pecking and ground smooth; the secondary use surface reveals only light usage. In lateral cross section, the two ground facets form a wedge shape. The artifact's dimensions are 9.5 cm long (incomplete), 5.6 cm wide (incomplete), and 3.5 cm thick.

AZ CC:10:6

Three ground stone artifacts were collected from within the grid column. A bifacial basin metate fragment of rhyolite tuff was recovered from grid unit 65N 15W. It is only a side portion of the metate, slightly modified to shape. Both use surfaces exhibit dense pitting from pecking with the lowermost surfaces ground very smooth. The dimensions are as follows:

Overall:	Length	15.6 cm (incomplete)	
	Width	15.4 cm (incomplete)	
	Thickness	9.0 cm (maximum)	
Grinding Facets:		Ventral	Dorsal
	Length	13.0 cm (incomplete)	9.6 cm (incomplete)
	Width	7.0 cm (incomplete)	8.2 cm (incomplete)
	Thickness	3.0 cm	2.5 cm

Grid unit 25N 5W yielded what is probably the side portion of a rhyolite slab metate that exhibits evidence of only light grinding. It is too fragmentary for dimensions to be useful for comparative purposes.

Table 25. AZ CC:9:2, mano attributes

Provenience	Material	Morphological type: 1-hand	Morphological type: 2-hand	Morphological type: Indeterminate	Body Shape	Transverse cross-section	Dimensions: Length	Dimensions: Width	Dimensions: Thickness	Grinding Surfaces
10N 5W	Quartzite	X			Globular	Biplanar	5.7*	5.6*	5.1	BF
10N 5W	Granite	X			Globular?	Biplanar	8.0*	7.4*	5.6	BF
30S10W	Vesicular Basalt		? X		Subrectangular	Biconvex	3.3*	3.4*	3.0	BF
65S10E	Quartzite	X			Globular	Wedge	7.0*	7.0*	5.5	BF
70S10E	Schist		X		Subrectangular	Biconvex	7.9	9.5	4.8	Blank
80S10E,L-3	Quartzite			X	Indeterminate	Indeterminate	4.6*	5.5*	3.0*	UF?
80S10E,L-4	Basalt			X	Indeterminate	Plano-irregular	6.2*	2.3*	4.0*	?
85S 5W	Granite	X			Indeterminate	Plano-irregular	7.4*	5.6*	4.7*	UF?
85S10W	Rhyolite	X			Ovoid	Planoconvex	9.9	7.7	4.2	UF
85S15W	Diorite	X			Subrectangular	Planoconvex	9.7	8.9	5.2	UF
90S15W	Granite	X			Ovoid	Convex-irregular	10.0	8.1	4.7	UF
95S10E	Quartzite			X	Indeterminate	Convex-irregular	3.0*	3.7*	3.2*	UF?
100S10W	Quartzite	X			Ovoid	Plano-irregular	9.2	6.9	5.0	UF
100S10W	Granite	X			Ovoid	Planoconvex	8.6	5.8*	5.0	UF
100S15W,L-1	Basalt	X			Indeterminate	Biplanar	4.7*	4.6*	3.0	BF
105S10E	Granite	X			Ovoid	Convex-concave	9.2	7.7	3.6	UF
105S10E	Granite	X			Ovoid	Planoconvex	9.3	7.4	4.0	UF
110S10E	Granite			X	Indeterminate	Planoconvex	3.9*	4.2*	5.2	BF
110S15W	Basalt	X			Ovoid	Planoconvex	7.6	4.4*	4.1	BF
IA 6(60S25E)	Basalt	X			Indeterminate	Biconvex	5.2*	4.9*	3.0	BF
IA10(60S25E)	Quartzite	X			Indeterminate	Plano-irregular	7.0	4.5*	3.1	UF
IA26(80S20E)	Basalt	X			Indeterminate	Plano-irregular	4.8*	4.0*	5.7*	BF
IA29(85S15E)	Meta-Sedimentary	X			Indeterminate	Indeterminate	8.9	6.2*	4.0*	UF?
IA30(85S20E)	Granite	X			Ovoid	Biplanar	8.8*	7.4	3.5	BF
IA32(85S20E)	Diorite	X			Ovoid	Wedge	7.0*	7.5	4.7	UF
IA43(100S10E)	Quartz	X			Indeterminate	Biconvex	5.6*	4.0*	4.0	BF
IA59(100S15E)	Granite	X			Subrectangular	Wedge	7.2*	8.5*	5.3	BF
Unknown	Granite	X			Discoidal	Wedge	5.3*	8.5	5.2	BF

* = Incomplete (fragmentary); UF = Unifacially ground; BF = Bifacially ground; IA = Isolated artifact

The third artifact is an end or side fragment of a bifacial granite one-hand mano. The edge has been moderately pecked to a convex shape, and only a small portion of both grinding facets are present. The artifact measures 5.0 cm long (incomplete), 2.3 cm wide (incomplete), and 3.5 cm thick.

AZ CC:10:11

An isolated, small slab metate or lapstone was found on the surface of Locus 1, unit 20S 15W. It is a natural tabular rhyolite slab without edge modification (for shaping) or pecking (for roughening). It measures 26.0 cm long, 24.2 cm wide, and 4.0 cm thick. One surface exhibits moderate grinding over an oval area 19cm long and 18 cm wide. The opposite surface exhibits no evidence of grinding.

AZ CC:9:2

This site yielded the largest number of ground stone artifacts: 7 complete and 22 fragmentary manos, 20 metate fragments, 1 complete metate, 4 pestles, and 61 miscellaneous ground pieces. Attributes of the manos and metates are presented in Tables 25 and 26.

Nearly all the manos collected and those observed elsewhere on the site are hand-sized water-rounded cobbles with minimal intentional shaping other than that resulting from use. Granite was most commonly used, with quartzite, basalt, and other materials used in lesser amounts (Table 27). As would be expected, durable igneous materials seem to be the preferred material for ground stone tools. The dominant shape represented in the collection is the flattened ovoid mano. Six of the seven whole manos exhibit this shape, and a majority of the fragmentary pieces may be from manos originally ovoid in outline (Figure 81). Only two could be tentatively identified as typical subrectangular, loaf-shaped manos. One is a mano blank, the second an end fragment of a well-made mano. It is not known if this could be a two-hand mano, but it closely resembles a single-hand rectangular mano found at Ventana Cave (Haury 1950: Figure 70c).

Bifacial manos constitute 46.4 percent of the total unifacial manos 32.1 percent, and 21.4 percent are too fragmentary to determine the number of original grinding surfaces. No faceted use surfaces were observed on any of the manos although four are slightly wedge shaped in profile. Size is variable, but none of the recovered manos exceeds 10 cm in length. The mean dimensions, taken from the whole manos are: length 9.6 cm, width 7.6 cm, and thickness 4.4 cm. Determination of wear stage on grinding surfaces is subjective and was ranked as beginning, intermediate, and advanced. This attribute was recorded on the analysis form, but is not included in the tables because such a judgement is arbitrary. For purposes of discussion, however, many showed intermediate to advanced use. It was noted that while many manos were broken the useful life of the artifact had not been exhausted. The small number of whole manos recovered in contrast to the high frequency of mano fragments may be explained in several ways: (1) collectors have

Table 26. AZ CC:9:2, metate attributes

Provenience	Material	Morphological Type: Slab	Morphological Type: Shallow basin	Morphological Type: Indeterminate	Number of grinding surfaces present	
5S10E	Basalt			X	2	
25S25E	Phyllite	X			2	
70S10E	Granite	X			2	
75S15E	Granite	X			1	
85S10W	Basalt	X			1	
90S15W	Meta-sedimentary	X			2	
100S10E	Phyllite	X			2	
100S10E	Meta-sedimentary	X			1	
105S15W, L-2	Basalt	X			1	
110S 5W	Basalt	X			1	
120S 5W	Rhyolite			X	1	
120S 5W	Quartzite	X			1	
IA 12(70S25E)	Phyllite		X		2	
IA 22(80S20E)	Meta-sedimentary	X			1	(complete metate)
IA 25(80S20E)	Phyllite		X		2	
IA 39(95S25E)	Basalt	X			1	
IA 44(100S15E)	Phyllite	X			1	
IA 47(95S25E)	Phyllite		X		2	
IA 54(60S20E)	Basalt	X			1	
IA 63(105S10E)	Schist	X			1	
Unknown	Basalt	X			1	

Table 27. AZ CC:9:2, ground stone raw material frequencies

Material Type	Manos: Number	Manos: Percent	Metates: Number	Metates: Percent
Quartzite	6	21.4	1	4.8
Basalt	6	21.4	7	33.3
Granite	10	35.7	2	9.5
Schist	1	3.6	1	4.8
Rhyolite	1	3.6	1	4.8
Diorite	2	7.1	0	0
Quartz	1	3.6	0	0
Phyllite	0	0	6	28.6
Meta-sedimentary	1	3.6	3	14.3
Total	28		21	

removed whole manos from the site, (2) the R-O-W transects a trash area, (3) surface erosion has displaced artifacts, (4) manos were salvaged by the prehistoric inhabitants. The first three can be amply demonstrated, but the fourth can only be verified by investigation into undisturbed portions of the site.

Despite the high number of manos recovered and observed at the site, only one whole metate was recovered and none was observed in the immediate area outside the R-O-W. The lessee of the land stated that collectors commonly remove large visible artifacts such as metates and manos from this site and others in the vicinity. This may explain the scarcity of whole metates. The recovered specimen is a flat slab metate of gneiss-like material. It measures 34.0 cm long, 19.0 cm wide and 7.2 cm thick. No shape packing is evident and use is minimal. The metate fragments found during grid collection and testing are for the most part small irregular chunks ranging in size from 4 to 14 cm. The majority are made from abrasive igneous rocks such as granite, basalt, rhyolite, and a low-grade metasedimentary rock closely resembling schist. Based on general morphological attributes,

Figure 81. AZ CC:9:2, typical manos.
a, diorite, 9.7 cm long;
b, quartzite, 9.2 cm long;
c, granite, 8.8 cm long;
d, rhyolite, 9.9 cm long.

16 pieces (76.2 percent) may be fragments of flat slab metates, 3 (14.3 percent) are shallow basin metate fragments, and 2 (9.5 percent) are of indeterminate shape. Eight pieces were bifacially ground, 13 showed only unifacial grinding. It is impossible to extrapolate original metate dimensions and shapes from these pieces, but they probably represent typical examples of slab metates of the Chiricahua stage Cochise, as illustrated by Sayles (1949) and Haury (1950). Six metate pieces made from phyllite are thin and well worn and retain a fair portion of their original sides. These may represent lapstones, rather than the larger bulky grinding slab.

Three, possibly four, pestles were found, of which three are illustrated in Figure 82. As such, they represent three distinct morphological types, but the chronological and cultural significance cannot be ascertained since all were found on the surface. The first (Figure 82a) is shaped from a narrow piece of coarse schist, carefully pecked to an elongated cylindrical shape. One end is a rough and irregular chisel-like bit but does not exhibit battering or crushing. The opposite end is rounded and displays light use-polish. It measures 37.6 cm long, 7.1 cm wide and 5.0 cm thick. The second (Figure 82b) is shaped from a flat tabular piece of schist. One end is absent, while the bit end is blunt, rounded, and slightly crushed from use. It measures 25.6 cm long (incomplete), 6.1 cm wide, and 4.2 cm long. The third pestle is a short piece of schist-like metamorphic rock pecked into a cylindrical shape 7.6 cm long, 5.1 cm wide, and 4.4 cm thick. Both rounded ends are blunt and irregular. The fourth artifact (not illustrated) appears to be a basalt pestle preform that broke during manufacture. Dense pecking marks occur along one edge and apparently reflect attempts to shape the piece. Some light battering is present on the convex end. None of the pestles displays heavy battering marks, as would be expected from use in a stone mortar or prolonged use. It is possible these were used in wooden mortars or simply were not heavily used.

Sixteen miscellaneous ground pieces constitute the remainder of the collection. These are small pieces ranging from 3 to 8 cm in size. Many of these could be exfoliated pieces of either metates or manos, but their original morphology remains unknown.

During field investigations it was noted that ground stone artifacts were most numerous within the R-O-W between units 50S and 125S. The occurrence of individual artifacts has been plotted in Figure 83, which indicates two general clusters. It was thought that if there were differences between cluster assemblages, they might be attributed to different processing activities or different activity orientations. Tabulation of discrete artifact attributes revealed that bifacial manos were more frequent than unifacial manos in the eastern cluster and the reverse was true for the western cluster. The significance of this cannot be fully deduced because the total number is so small, consisting of eight manos and mano fragments in the western area and 15 in the eastern section. Metate distribution only indicates that unifacially ground slab metate fragments were more numerous in both areas. In summary, intensive food processing activity in the eastern cluster (Loci 1 and 3) is suggested; the western cluster (Locus 2) most likely is a trash area.

Figure 82. AZ CC:9:2, pestles.
Length of (a) is 37.6 cm.

Figure 84. AZ CC:13:16, metates.
a, granite unifacial slab metate;
b, quartzite bifacial shallow basin metate.

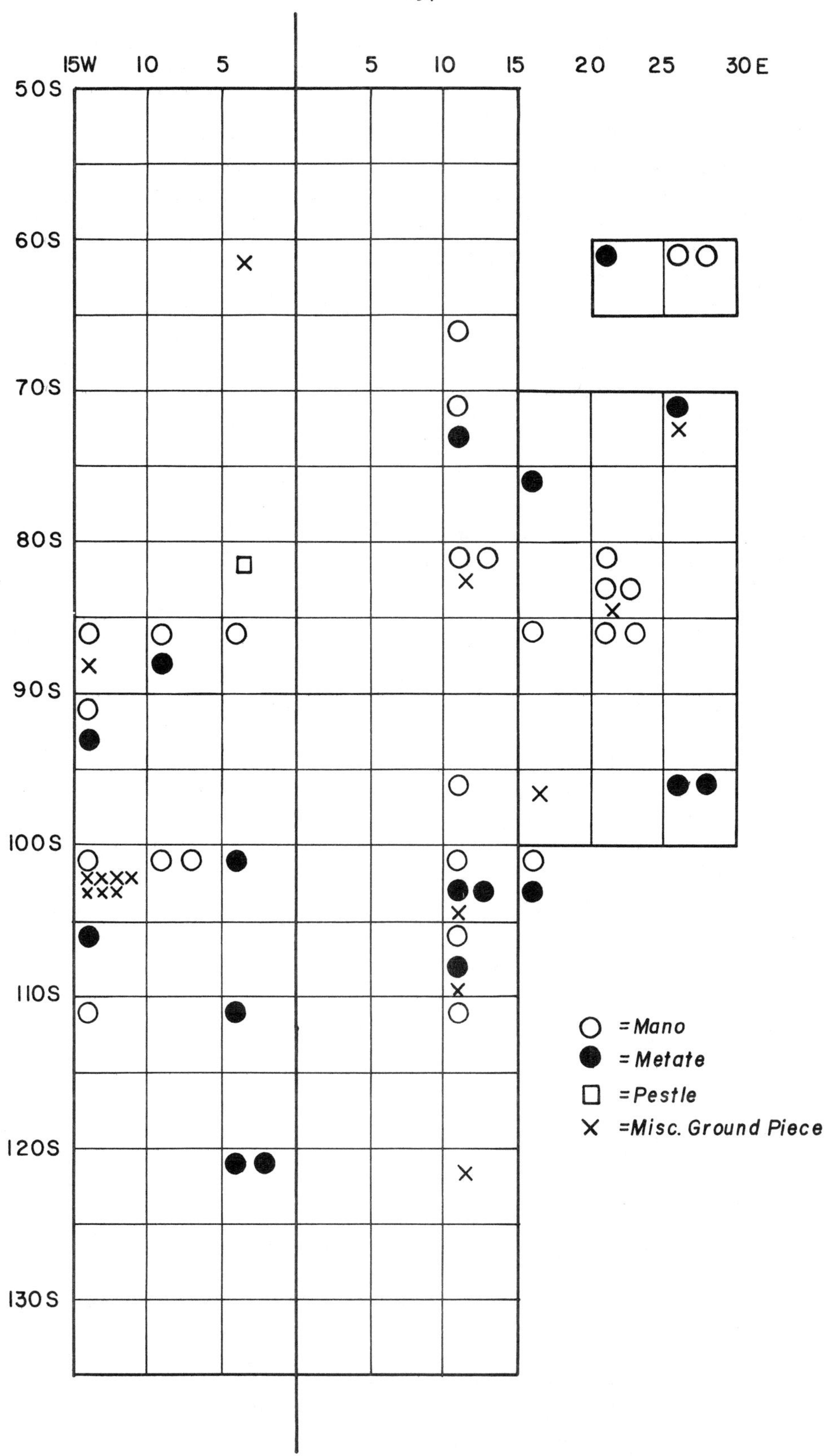

Figure 83. AZ CC:9:2, distribution of ground stone artifacts in central portion of R-O-W.

AZ CC:13:11

A small quantity of ground stone in identifiable form was recovered from this site: two whole and three fragmentary one-hand manos, three metate fragments and twelve small miscellaneous pieces of ground schist. The mano attributes are listed in Table 28. The metate pieces are so fragmentary that their original form can only be postulated. One is a fragment, perhaps of a basalt slab metate; the second is possibly a shallow basin metate fragment of metamorphosed sedimentary rock; the third is a piece of metamophosed sedimentary rock with a ground and polished concave surface. All appear to be in an intermediate to advanced stage of use. The 12 miscellaneous fragments are exfoliated pieces probably from a schist metate or mano. Their tiny size reveals nothing beyond that they are a component of a ground stone tool kit once in use at the site.

Table 28. AZ CC:13:11, mano attributes

Provenience	Material	Morphological Type	Body Shape	Transverse cross section	Length	Width	Thickness	Grinding surface(s)
Features 1 - 3	Quartzite	One-hand mano	Ovoid	Biconvex	9.8	7.7	3.6	BF
Features 1 -33	Rhyolite	Indeterminate	Spheroid	Biplanar	4.5*	3.9*	4.8	BF
5N20W,8EQ, L-4	Quartzite	One-hand mano	Ovoid	Plano-convex	6.4*	4.7*	2.2	BF
15N15W	Granite	One-hand mano	Ovoid	Biconvex	6.9*	6.6*	2.5	BF
50N 5E	Quartzite	One-hand mano	Triangular	Biconvex	10.5	8.7	4.0	BF

* = Incomplete (fragmentary)

It is not clear why so few metate pieces were found considering the number of metates represented at the site. No restorable pieces are present. Pieces of broken metates may have been salvaged for use elsewhere, or the reverse may be the case, where those fragments found were brought in from elsewhere. None of the pieces shows reuse or post breakage modification. If they were used as cooking stones, all traces of thermal alteration have since eroded. But assuming that the fragments represent a ground stone tool kit once in use at the site, at least five manos and three metates are represented.

AZ CC:13:6

Ground stone collected from within the R-0-W primarily consists of irregular fragments of 10 metates and 10 manos. Igneous materials constitute the majority of the manos, whereas the metate fragments are nearly evenly divided in composition between igneous and abrasive metamorphic rocks. Since only one complete mano was found, little can be said about the ground stone tool types within the R-0-W corridor except to support the opinion that vegetal processing was a major activity at the site, as is evident from the great number of grinding tools on the dune top. Pertinent attribute information on mano and metate fragments is provided in Tables 29 and 30. The pattern of distribution of the ground stone within the R-0-W appears random and no task-specific activity areas can be recognized, although ground stone is more frequent in the southernmost section of the R-0-W. It is likely that the fragments are trash items discarded from activity areas on the southern dune crest. Several recovered pieces indicate that despite their fragmentary condition the useful life of the implement had not been exhausted.

On the dune top, mano and metate fragments are found clustered with broken unmodified rock and with broken and burned rock, suggesting secondary use of ground stone fragments for heating in food preparation.

In addition to the 20 mano and metate fragments, eight miscellaneous small pieces exhibiting one ground facet each were recovered. Their original tool morphology cannot be determined.

A possible pestle or crusher was recovered from unit 85S 0E. It is an irregular, hefty, elongated quartzite cobble measuring 19.1 cm long (incomplete), 11.4 cm wide, and 7.2 cm thick. The narrow distal end is crushed and rounded from heavy battering and the stone shows sooting from burning after fragmentation. Although no mortars or deep basin metates were seen within the R-0-W, the morphological attributes of this tool suggests its use for pounding or crushing.

Generally speaking, the artifacts collected from this site share attributes with those found at AZ CC:13:11; that is they are manufactured from similar materials, the majority are extremely fragmented, and the basic flat ovoid one-hand mano is the most common type. Again, flat slab or shallow basin metates are the typical metate form. The material from CC:13:6 was especially useful for the analysis because many artifacts were heavily encrusted with caliche. This allowed preservation of thermally altered features on stone, such as fire-blackening, that was not observed on "clean" pieces at other sites. The burned artifacts from AZ CC:13:6 indicate that mano and metate fragments were reused either as hearth stones or for cooking stones. This is one function of "trash" items not immediately apparent at first glance, since prolonged surface exposure may have eradicated all traces of fire blackening and associated charcoal pieces.

Table 29. AZ CC:13:6, mano attributes

Provenience	Material	Morphological Type	Body Shape	Transverse Cross section	Length	Width	Thickness	Grinding Facets
5S 0E	Quartzite	Indeterminate	Indeterminate	Convex-irregular	3.6*	3.4*	2.4*	UF?
5S 0E	Basalt	One-hand	Ovoid	Planoconvex	6.5*	4.6*	7.1*	BF
10S 0E	Basalt	Indeterminate	Indeterminate	Plano-irregular	2.7*	1.7*	3.2*	UF?
30S15W	Basalt	Indeterminate	Ovoid	Biconvex	3.2*	3.7*	5.0	BF
40S15W	Basalt	Indeterminate	Indeterminate	Planoconvex	2.8*	2.7*	3.8	BF
70S 0E	Basalt	Indeterminate	Indeterminate	Convex-irregular	4.3*	3.6*	2.3*	UF?
85S15W	Quartzite	Indeterminate	Indeterminate	Convex-irregular	3.8*	3.0*	3.5*	UF?
40N15W	Granite	One-hand	Ovoid	Biconvex	11.4	7.4	4.8	BF
210N10E	Basalt	One-hand	Subrectangular	Biconvex	9.4	5.8*	6.9	UF
215N5W	Diorite	Indeterminate	Indeterminate	Wedge	6.6*	1.4*	4.5	BF

* = Incomplete

Table 30. AZ CC:13:6, metate attributes

Provenience	Material	Morphological Type			Number of grinding surfaces
		Slab	Shallow Basin	Indeterminate	
5S 5W	Basalt	X			1
60S 5W	Schist	X			1
65S 5E	Basalt			X	1
70S 5W	Basalt	X			1
85S10E	Quartzite	X			1
15N 5W	Granite	X			2
25N 0E	Meta-sedimentary	X			1
100N25W	Rhyolite		X		1
150N 0E	Granite	X			1
200N 5W	Quartzite			X	1

AZ CC:13:14

Three metates and a possible fourth metate or mano are represented in 21 fragments collected from this site. Although discrete metate forms are suggested by basic morphological attributes, in no case is it possible to determine the original size of the artifacts. No manos could be definitely identified.

The first specimen consists of two large side portions of a rhyolite bifacially ground shallow basin metate. The sides of the thick slab are only minimally pecked to shape. Both use surfaces are heavily pecked, the roughening extending to the edges of both surfaces. The wear pattern does not demonstrate an exclusively bidirectional or rotary grinding motion, but a combination of both. The surfaces are well worn in the basin centers, with smoothness decreasing outward to the sides.

The second artifact is represented by 11 pieces of a unifacially ground slab or shallow basin metate. The pieces are composed of a course-textured gray rhyolite similar to the first metate. The use surface on all pieces is pitted from pecking and is ground very smooth. Three of the pieces are slightly concave, while the remaining six are slightly convex to flat. One characteristic of the pieces that suggests they may be parts of a basin metate is the difference in range of thickness. The largest piece is 6.1 cm thick, the thinnest 3.1 cm thick. This range in thickness may indicate a deep basin, from a thick outer wall to a thinner, well-worn basal surface. However, thickness difference also may be a function of overall stone morphology, that is, the metate slab could be thick at one end, thinning toward the opposite end.

The third artifact is a restored side piece of a bifacially ground, burned quartzite slab metate. The side exhibits pecking to shape, and both surfaces are pitted from pecking and ground smooth. Both use surfaces are slightly concave, dipping toward the former center of the metate.

The fourth artifact is a small fragment of quartzite with one well-ground surface, too small to determine its original morphological type.

Typical of sites in the southernmost portion of the R-O-W, the metates are not completely restorable because several pieces are missing. The one burned fragment indicates reuse of ground stone pieces for either hearth stones or heating rocks. Again, if the prehistoric people were salvaging certain portions of broken metates, the reasons are not clear. It is possible such pieces were reused as small abrading surfaces. If the fragments do represent whole metates once present at the site, use of two shallow basin metates and one slab metate in processing wild plant foods is suggested as one activity.

AZ CC:13:15

Only two pieces of ground stone and a possible mano blank were collected from this site. One piece is a mano fragment of coarse-textured gray rhyolite, plano-convex in cross section. The second is a quartzite mano fragment that exhibits battering on two edges; apparently the fragment was reused as a hammerstone or pestle. The third piece is an irregularly fragmented coarse-textured purple rhyolite cobble. The only evidence of modification is a side that has been extensively pecked to a convex shape. The high incidence of ceramics and low ground stone count suggests that gathering was a dominant activity and only minimal, perhaps initial, food processing was done.

AZ CC:13:16

The two metates at this site, while basically similar, reflect two morphologically distinct types: a unifacial slab metate and a bifacial shallow basin metate (Figure 84). The first is a thick, blocky granite slab with unmodified rounded edges. The use surface is pitted and roughened from pecking, and is ground over nearly the entire surface. It measures 33.8 cm long, 24.7 cm wide, and 10.1 cm thick. The second metate is made from a natural block of quartzite. The block has not been altered to shape, although the back and one side exhibit uniform, regular pecking. This could have been done to blunt the edges. Both surfaces are heavily pitted and roughened from pecking, and grinding extends from end to end, with the heaviest usage in the central basin portions. The basin dimensions are:

	Ventral	Dorsal
Length	16.5 cm	15.0 cm
Width	10.5 cm	9.6 cm
Depth	1.0 cm	0.7 cm

A third piece of ground stone is a small miscellaneous fragment of granite of unknown morphology. It could represent either a third metate or a mano. No whole manos were found; it is likely they were retained for future use.

Discussion

The collection of metates, manos, and pestles from the AEPCO II sites constitutes a limited data base for making conclusive statements about activities. The extreme fragmentation of the majority of specimens and disturbed surface context argue for a conservative interpretation. These sites can be contrasted to those investigated on the northern segment which had little or no ground stone. Further, they contribute additional information to a body of data accrued during recent years of research.

It is not known if the single mano fragment at AZ CC:6:3 was actually used at the site since no metate was found. The red granite is not local to the site area and may have been obtained from the San Simon or Gila valleys. As such it may have been originally associated with a riverine site, in which ground stone tools are commonly found.

The isolated small slab metate at AZ CC:10:11 suggests food preparation connected either with lithic knapping activities or wild plant gathering and processing. As with many sites containing surface artifacts determining functional relationships is sometimes hazardous. An alternative hypothesis is that the slab was used in some way to aid in lithic reduction. Either interpretation is equally likely. But, assuming the slab was used in food preparation, the proximity of AZ CC:10:11 to the larger, more diversified sites AZ CC:6:6, AZ CC:10:6 and 7, with their numerous ground stone tools, would suggest some correlation between AZ CC:10:11 and these other sites. Assuming a mixed foraging subsistence base the occurrence of ground stone tools in isolated context is to be expected.

Although only three ground stone artifacts were collected from AZ CC:10:6, these were at the periphery of the site transected by the R-O-W. Observations outside the R-O-W indicated that much more ground stone is present, and thus the items collected from the R-O-W represent only a small fraction of the total range of ground stone. The deep basin metate fragment is suggestive of those typical for the San Pedro stage Cochise (Sayles and Antevs 1941:24). This is the only deep basin metate found in any of the investigated sites, and would support the opinion that the site could be dated to the San Pedro stage. However, AZ CC:10:6 is also situated in an environmental area much different from the AEPCO sites where flat slab and shallow basin metates are the norm. That is, more diversified and different plant species occur in the site vicinity. Sites with slab and shallow basin metates occur in the desert grassland environment of the Sulphur Spring Basin and Willcox Playa. More research at AZ CC:10:6 is needed to explore the problem of whether environmental factors, temporal change, cultural peculiarities, or some combination of these are responsible for differences in the ground stone tool kit.

The ground stone tools found at sites in the Sulphur Spring Basin (AZ CC:13:14, 15, and 16) reflect a special situation, occurring as they do where raw material in the form of stream cobbles for manos and large slabs suitable for metates is rare and must be brought in from some distance. This is also true for chipped stone tools occurring at these sites. These factors suggest specialized activity related to desert grassland resources. Further interpretation of site activities in the Sulphur Spring Basin will be deferred to the concluding chapter of this report.

Ground stone tools at the two sites in the Willcox Playa dunes (AZ CC:13:6 and 11) do not differ significantly from those found in the Sulphur Spring Basin. This, however, is so only because the material collected is too fragmentary to be adequate for good comparative studies. What may be significant is that no marked differences can be observed between the ground stone assemblages of the two zones (other than the greater quantity of material at AZ CC:13:6). This suggests some cultural continuity between the sites and therefore aids in determining some aspect of subsistence-settlement patterns.

The ground stone tools at AZ CC:9:2 while more numerous do not exhibit significant typological variation when compared to each other or to tools at other sites. The AZ CC:9:2 tools are similar to those at AZ CC:13:6 in the following respects: (1) much of the material is trash, indicating an occupation of some duration, (2) raw material types are similar (basalt, granite, and quartzite, in particular), (3) mano forms are identical, and (4) slab metates are the dominant form, followed by shallow basin metates; no deep basin metates are represented. AZ CC:9:2 is unique in that well-made pestles were found, whereas only one was tentatively identified for AZ CC:13:6. This may be due, however, to the nature of the sample; a much larger portion of AZ CC:9:2 was sampled than was the case for AZ CC:13:6. The pestles could indicate that mortars made of stone or wood were in use at AZ CC:9:2 at one time. No permanent bedrock or boulder mortars could be located at the site. Thus it is possible that plant processing activities involving a mortar and pestle were carried out elsewhere (for example, bedrock mortars were found at AZ CC:6:6 and 7, and AZ CC:10:7 to the north), and pestles were saved in much the same way as hammerstones and manos. Haury, noting that a pestle was found at a Sulphur Spring stage site at Double Adobe, states that mortars and pestles appear in the Southwest at an early date and also were widely used by later groups, especially those dependent on natural plants (Haury 1950:324). The pestles at AZ CC:9:2 do bear resemblance to forms found at Ventana Cave, yet no good description is available for those found in Cochise culture sites. Sayles states that while pestles do occur in the Chiricahua stage, only in the San Pedro stage are the mortar and pestle first found as fully developed implements. The largest pestle at AZ CC:9:2 resembles one illustrated by Sayles for the San Simon branch (Sayles 1945:Plate 34). In summary, the pestles at AZ CC:9:2 find their counterparts in sites of other ages and cultures. Because of this commonality, the pestles are not useful for drawing conclusions about cultural affiliation.

Comparison of the AEPCO material with that recovered from sites investigated elsewhere in southeastern Arizona aids in reconstructing site activities, as well as in determining the role of sites in the general prehistoric settlement subsistence pattern in this region. Two sites in particular are cited below as examples of basic site types represented in the AEPCO Project sample. An extended discussion of comparable site activities is not the intent here but will be reserved for the concluding chapter of this report.

One important site is the Gold Gulch Site (AZ CC:10:2) on the northern bajada of the Dos Cabezas (Huckell 1973:128). This site is a temporary camp tentatively assigned to the San Pedro stage Cochise on the basis of stylistic artifact attributes. Chipped stone tools and debitage comprised the majority of cultural material, while ground stone included two slab metates and two whole and one fragmentary one-hand manos. The site is believed to be a specialized activity site oriented primarily to hunting pursuits (Huckell 1973:128).

The second example is the Fairchild Site (AZ FF:10:2) located on Whitewater Draw in the southern Sulphur Spring Valley (Windmiller 1973). The Cochise culture component of this site includes both the Chiricahua and San Pedro stages. The ground stone recovered from the site includes 10 complete metates, 79 manos, 2,674 metate fragments and 1,791 mano fragments. Chipped stone tools and debris were also plentiful, and several hearths and caches were found. The site as a whole reflects diversified subsistence pursuits, perhaps on a seasonal basis (Windmiller 1973:161). This is in contrast to the short-term specialized activities represented at the Gold Gulch Site, yet both sites are recognized as representative of Cochise culture and are significant in demonstrating site variability within this cultural tradition.

In comparing ground stone artifacts of the AEPCO sites with those of the Gold Gulch and Fairchild sites several noteworthy similarities are apparent. The most obvious is that morphologically, manos and metates from the AEPCO sites are identical to those from the Gold Gulch and Fairchild sites, and these, in tern, can be related to the Cochise culture ground stone types. The AEPCO material can perhaps be more precisely assigned to the Chiricahua stage on the basis of metate and mano forms; AZ CC:10:6 exhibits aspects of the San Pedro stage in addition to Chiricahua stage characteristics. It must be noted that the slab metate and one-hand mano have a long history, and certain forms may persist into a later phase.

As has been pointed out previously, the majority of ground stone artifacts are extremely fragmentary. Windmiller found a similar occurrence at the Fairchild Site; however, unlike the AEPCO material, many fragments showed evidence of burning, and also were frequently found associated with hearths. Windmiller suggested that fragments often were heated for stone boiling in the preparation of food as has been demonstrated ethnographically:

> Stones...and worn grinding implements were heated in the fire, then transferred to baskets filled with gruel or water that was eventually boiled through repetition of this process. As each fire hearth was abandoned, stones were left scattered around the feature (Windmiller 1973:157).

This sort of activity could explain the burned and fractured ground stone fragments at AZ CC:13:6, as well as the numerous pieces of fire-cracked rock at this site and at AZ CC:13:11 and 16. Although no hearths were observed, it is suggested they may have once been present, and all traces have been subsequently eradicated. It is worth nothing that deposition at the Fairchild Site prevented postdeposition artifact alteration, a convenience not enjoyed by the AEPCO artifacts. Windmiller also recorded four caches of ground stone fragments. Since these appeared intentionally clustered and were unburned, he postulated a magico-religious purpose (Windmiller 1973:158). It may be more likely, however, that these fragments were simply conveniently piled in preparation for heating. Only at AZ CC:13:11 and 6 was this type of clustering apparent. Since naturally occurring rock is scarce in the vicinity of these sites, it may be a factor of conservatism that ground stone fragments were retained and reused for activities other than grinding.

Summary

Investigations along the entire AEPCO R-O-W have allowed exmaination of a regional sample of cultural resources. This has permitted an examination of the reasons for variability (or lack of it) among artifact assemblages in different microenvironments. Analysis of the ground stone has focused not only on reconstructing subsistence activities at sites where milling equipment occurs, but also considers the question of why ground stone artifacts are not found at other sites.

One point discussed in Chapter 2 was the importance of ground stone in establishing cultural "hallmarks" for the Cochise culture. Cochise development was determined by stylistic change and changing ratios of ground stone tools to chipped stone tools. Sayles' "Cochise Basic Pattern" (1949:27-8) is based on relative frequencies of ground vs. chipped stone. He maintains that the earlier stages, Sulphur Spring and Chiricahua, emphasized gathering over hunting, and that hunting became important only in the San Pedro stage, based on the predominance of flaked tools. But higher frequencies of one tool type over another do not presuppose dominance of the inferred activity for a cultural stage or even for a cultural tradition. Rather, sites are viewed as loci of specialized activity which are components of a larger system of diversified subsistence pursuits of various groups over a period of time. This is the approach advocated by Jennings (1973), Hayden (1970), Rogers (1958), and Irwin-Williams (n.d.). This is not to negate the work of Sayles, but to emphasize the necessity for flexibility in site interpretation, in order that a wider range of sites, particularly those without diagnostic artifacts, be considered as components of a single subsistence system. Jennings (1973:3), citing Irwin-Williams (1967), appraises the problem of cultural determination based on artifact style and inferred function:

> ...in all the formulations of the Desert Culture concept the lower level analytical data (artifact inventories) were fuzzily and improperly incorporated with the higher level synthetic statement being sought. Thus, at one point the slab milling stone and basketry are identified as "hallmarks" of the Desert Culture as defined. The student whose early artifact complex lacks the millstone can correctly deny that he is dealing with the Desert Culture as defined. The absence of the millstone does not, however, invalidate the major concept of an Archaic exploitative substratum.

The AEPCO ground stone assemblages conform to some of the basic Cochise characteristics as defined by Sayles, but at the same time their greater value lies in support of the hypothesis that a broad based aboriginal subsistence system existed in the region, and that special artifact classes represent local adaptation to available resources. The assumption that the presence or absence of ground stone relates to specific subsistence pursuits is in turn related to availability of resources in certain microenvironments. Absence of ground stone does not correspondingly mean that Archaic (Cochise) people were not at a particular site, but quite possibly, a lithic scatter site could be a locus of different resource use by the same people that used ground stone elsewhere. Except for two sites in the San Simon Basin, ground stone was not found at any limited activity (nonhabitation) site in the R-O-W corridor until the transect reached the desert grassland zone.

The data clearly indicate that plant gathering and processing were important activitues at the sites in the Sulphur Spring Valley and immediate environs, and it is only in this area that ground stone is found in any appreciable quantity. The lack of features such as hearths and pits at these sites indicates only specialized, short-term use. They appear to be focal points for specific plant gathering activities, as well as for food preparation. It is likely that AZ CC:13:14, 15 and 16 represent areas of initial procurement and processing of grassland resources, and that partially prepared plant products were returned to larger base camps (such as, for example, AZ CC:13:6 and AZ CC:9:2) or village sites elsewhere.

CHAPTER 7

LITHIC ANALYSIS AND INTERPRETATION

by Kenneth Rozen

Introduction

Approximately 9,000 lithic artifacts were collected from the 11 AEPCO II sites selected for data recovery. The analysis of this material was undertaken assuming that differences among the lithic assemblages from each of the sites, both in terms of the frequencies with which different classes of reduction products occur and the range of form present within any given class could have been produced by the interaction of several factors, briefly outlined below.

Probably of greatest interest to the archaeologist is variation which reflects different activities and behavior. For instance, artifacts produced by quarrying will differ from those produced by tool manufacture; tools used to perform one groups of tasks may differ from those used to do something else; and tools made by one group of people may differ stylistically from those made by another group.

Collections may also differ for reasons which are essentially unrelated to human behavior. Differences in the characteristics and availability of lithic raw materials may, for example, contribute strongly to intersample variation. Natural processes such as sheetwash erosion and soil deposition may be responsible for intersample variation where the effects of these processes on the surface distribution of artifacts have been unequal at different sites.

Different collection methods used by the AEPCO field crews at various sites, and differences in the extent to which sites have been selectively collected by amateurs have also contributed to variation among lithic collections.

Since all of the above-mentioned factors have no doubt caused variation, a wide range of research problems could have been formulated. However, a number of inherent limitations of the data had to be considered in selecting a research focus for the AEPCO II lithic analysis. One of the most obvious concerns data recovery methods. In some cases sites were small enough to permit either a 100 percent artifact collection, or at least an extension of the grid system to encompass the major portion of the artifact distributions. In other cases, hwoever, sites were so large that collection was confined to the R-O-W and its immediate vicinity. Therefore, research objectives which require that the artifacts collected from all of the sites are representative of the entire range of artifact variability present on each site could not be accomplished.

Because the vast majority of artifacts were collected from the surfaces of the AEPCO sites, the temporal relationships among sites, and in most cases among individual artifacts on the same site, cannot be verified. The problem of site contemporaneity is further complicated by the scarcity of temporally or culturally diagnostic artifacts. Consequently, explaining intersite variability in terms of traditional or temporal factors was not appropriate as the major focus of analysis.

Another problem arising from the surface context of most of the artifacts concerns the kind and extent of postdepositional destructive forces which have acted on the site surfaces. These forces include previous transmission line construction, cattle grazing, sheetwash erosion, road construction, and in one instance, the construction of a stock tank. In vew of the likelihood that these disturbances have caused considerable damage to artifact edges, explaining intersite variation primarily through use-wear analysis was also deemed inappropriate.

Research Objectives

A group of research problems largely unaffected by the limitations discussed above concern intersite variation as it relates to different kinds of lithic reduction and associated behaviors. For example, raw material procurement, primary reduction, tool manufacture, tool use and discard, or combinations of these activities may have left qualitatively and quantitatively different remains. A related group of questions which might be successfully answered deals with the ways in which differences in the nature and availability of raw materials have contributed to intersite variation. The primary research objective of the AEPCO II lithic analysis, then, was to assess the ways different reduction activities and associated behavior and differences in the nature and availability of raw materials have interacted to produce the intersite variation.

The secondary objective was to typologically describe the range of tool form present in the collections and to identify differences among the collections in terms of the frequencies with which certain tool types occur. Since this analysis was not designed to provide a basis for making inferences about the functional and stylistic significance of various tool types, explanations for intersite variation with respect to tool form and frequency must remain hypothetical. The principal value of this aspect of the study is as a descriptive system for future research.

Chapter Structure

The following section "Theoretical Considerations", presents major assumptions about the ways in which different reduction activities and differences in the nature and availability of raw materials contribute to intersite variation. The framework used to interpret the results are also established. Since formal variation in the attributes analyzed may also have been caused by factors unrelated to reduction activities and raw materials, the role of these other factors in contributing to the characteristics of collections is discussed. Also included is a discussion of some theoretical considerations relevant to the identification of tools for typological study.

The next section, "Methodology and Data Presentation," provides definitions of the terms used and of the collections analyzed, attributes recorded, attribute observation methods, and the resultant data. Included is a discussion of the method by which the tool typology was developed and descriptions of the individual tool types.

In "Comparative Observations," univariate descriptive statistics are used to compare the collections. Significant intersite variation is identified with respect to each of the variables recorded.

More general patterns of variation involving all the attributes are discussed in "Patterns of Variation."

Following this, in "Site Interpretations", explanations for intersite variation are given within the framework of the theoretical orientation. Since the nature and availability of raw material is important to the interpretations, the raw material setting of each site is briefly reviewed at the beginning of each discussion. Where applicable, information not directly incorporated into the analysis, such as the spatial distribution of artifacts, will be used to strengthen inferences about site activities.

Theoretical and practical problems encountered during the analysis are then examined in "Problems and Discussion" and their implications for the preceding interpretations are discussed.

Finally, in "Synthesis", more general statements regarding the significance of intersite variation are formulated from the individual site interpretations.

Theoretical Considerations

Reduction Activities and Associated Behaviors

A major assumption of this study is that different reduction activities produce qualitatively and quantitatively different remains. One means of showing how various stages of reduction contribute to differences among collections of artifact is through use of a model showing the relationship between reduction stages and their respective products. Collins (1975) presented such a model in the form of a flow diagram tracing the process of manufacture and use from raw material procurement to tool discard, including seven reduction stages each of which corresponds to a distinctive product group. After explaining the model, Collins then applied it to the analysis of artifacts recovered from two stratified sites in order to demonstrate interstratum variability in terms of the extent to which the various product groups were represented.

During the initial stages of the AEPCO II lithic analysis, a model similar to, but more complex than that proposed by Collins was developed. The purpose of this model was to identify all the possible reduction sequences which could result from a single episode of tool manufacture and use. Although it was hoped that this model would be useful in explaining intersite variation in terms of different reduction activities, it became obvious during the course of research that its applicability as an analytical tool was limited.

The most serious problem with theoretical constructs of this nature is that individual artifacts cannot in many cases be confidently assigned to their respective product groups on the basis of morphology alone. For example, a flake struck from a core which should be assigned to Collins' core preparation and initial reduction product group (Group II), may be practically indistinguishable from a flake which was itself struck from another flake, and which belongs either to Collins' "primary trimming" or "secondary trimming and shaping" product group. As Collins points out (1975:15-16), inferences about reduction activities based on single specimens are not reliable. This is because the range of formal variability of the artifacts of one product group may overlap with that of another product group. Therefore, models like Collins' may produce misleading results when they are used as frameworks for the classification of individual artifacts, solely on the basis of their formal characteristics. While an application of such a model in this fashion may produce a grouping of artifact according to patterned associations of formal attributes, the significance of the groups with respect to postulated reduction activities is uncertain. How, then, can manufacturing sequence models be of use in explaining artifact variability in terms of different reduction activities? Collins suggests (1975:17) that inferences about reduction activities are strongest when artifacts treated as populations show consistent patterns of variability which can be compared to experimentally determined correlates between behavior and artifact attributes. Yet, in the application of the model, Collins does not make explicit the attributes used to distinguish artifacts produced by different activity sets or their correlation with experimental evidence. Thus, the method used to separate artifacts produced by different activities is not clear. For example, Collins reported (1975:26) that Stratum 5 of the Arenosa Shelter in Texas yielded a total of 5,811 flakes. Of these, 3,803 were identified as the products of core preparation and initial reduction, 1,560 "conform to GROUP III [optional primary trimming] expectations", and 448 were classified as waste from secondary trimming. Collins further states that direct hard hammer percussion is the prevalent technique represented by the artifacts of all three product groups. Assuming that flakes produced by hard hammer direct percussion tend to be relatively thicker and show more pronounced bulbs of percussion than soft hammer flakes, one might suspect that these attributes were used to infer the techniques by which Stratum 5 flakes were made. However, one can only guess which attributes were examined to determine whether a hard hammer flake was produced as a result of initial primary reduction, primary trimming, or secondary trimming. Since the criteria by which the flakes were sorted into the three groups are not stated, one might suspect that Collins has identified more theoretical product groups than he can realistically distinguish in an archaeological context.

Because of the problems encountered in placing artifacts into a large number of groups, the reduction sequence model developed for the AEPCO II lithic analysis was simplified to more realistically account for intersite variation. With this model it is assumed that the reduction sequence by which a particular artifact was produced need not be known in order to make more general statements about the activities reflected in a collection of artifacts. Rather, such inferences can be made by examining the frequency of artifacts of different classes and by assessing formal variability wihtin these classes. Jelinek (1976:21) states that:

> We can recognize three kinds of sites with respect to the stone tool manufacture and use; those primarily devoted to manufacture, those showing only selected products of manufacture, and those including both evidence of manufacturing and evidence of the use of tools...manufacturing sites yield quantities of exhausted and suitable partially worked cores, broken or misshapen flakes and preforms, and great quantities of debris resulting from reduction of cores and/or preforms. In contrast, sites on which little or no manufacturing debris is present yield primarily exhausted or broken tools or larger flakes. The presence of exhausted and broken tools on sites, along with strong evidence of lithic manufacture, is generally taken to indicate a wider range of activities than a simple manufacturing station.

Although this idealized, tripartite scheme is essentially that which is used in this analysis, it may be expanded and presented in the form of a flow diagram (Figure 85). It should be emphasized that the flow diagram is not intended to be a framework into which individual artifacts can be pigeonholed. Its purpose is to show how groups of artifacts produced by different activities may be distinguished on the basis of their general characteristics, frequencies, and form. The model identifies three kinds of reduction activities. They are primary reduction, secondary reduction, and modification reduction. Primary reduction is defined as the reduction of a piece of lithic raw material which has not previously been artificially detached from another piece. Secondary reduction is defined as the reduction of a piece of material which was struck from another piece as the result of primary reduction. Modification reduction could, strictly speaking, be any of the above reductions, but can be viewed as a special case in that it always follows use.

For the following brief descriptions of reduction products it should be noted that the terms "primary" and "secondary", in reference to flakes, are devoid of implications concerning the amount of cortex which is present. Rather, these terms refer to the reduction sequence by which flakes are produced.

Primary reduction, as Collins (1975:21) points out, may be done to produce a quantity of usable flakes or to shape a core tool, or perhaps both. Whichever, primary reduction produces cores or core tools, flakes, flake fragments, and quantities of irregular, angular fragments of various sizes (chunks and shatter). The selected products of primary reduction may be core tools destined for immediate use, or flakes and suitable fragments selected either for use or further reduction.

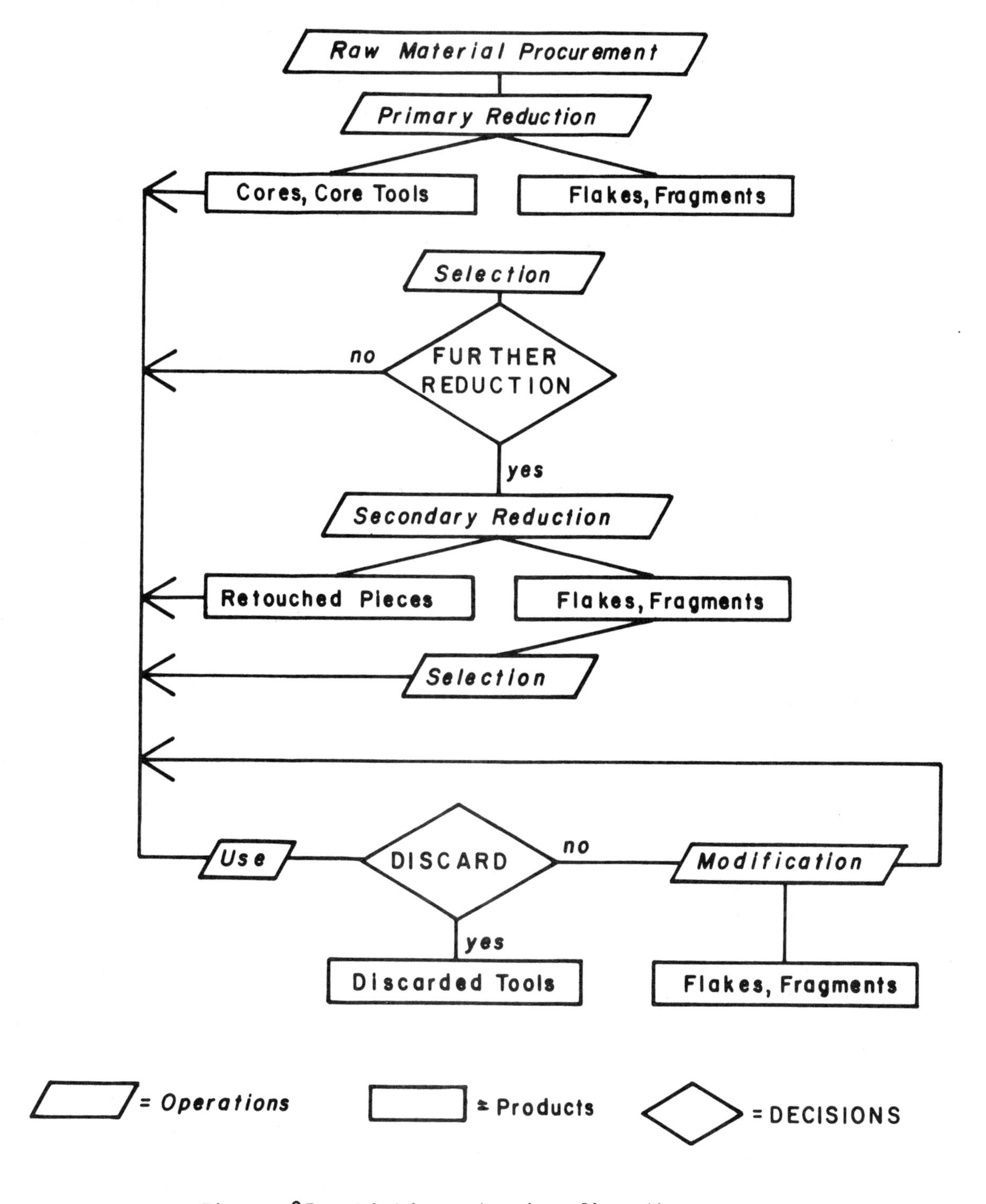

Figure 85. Lithic reduction flow diagram.

Secondary reduction may have been done to achieve two objectives. Most often, the reduction of primary flakes was done to shape a tool. This results in various kinds of retouched flake implements as the selected products and great quantities of small flakes and fragments as the debris. Other artifacts which result from this kind of secondary reduction, but which may not be selected for immediate use or further reduction, are those which were rejected because of accidental breakage or some other manufacturing problem such as a flaw in the stone, or the development of a platform angle from which a flake cannot be struck. The reduction of primary flakes may also have been done to obtain more conveniently sized flakes from a single, large primary flake. The selected products of reduction would be the secondary flakes, and the resultant fragments and secondary core (flake core) would be rejected.

Theoretically the selection of the products of reduction for still further reduction could go on endlessly. Thus the reduction of a secondary flake would be tertiary reduction, and the reduction of a tertiary flake would be quaternary reduction. But obviously, the number of reduction stages is limited by the decreasing size of the objects through successive stages of reduction. It is assumed, therefore, that the number of artifacts that have been produced through tertiary reduction is very low in most samples, and pieces resulting from quaternary reduction are probably nonexistent. These kinds of reductions are not shown in the flow diagram.

Finally, the flow diagram indicates that items selected for use may either be discarded after use, or subjected to further reduction (modification reduction) in order to maintain their usefulness. In the event that no modification reduction is done, the last group of material to be deposited in the archaeological record consists of used, unwanted, selected products of primary and secondary reduction. Should modification proceed, quantities of small flakes ("resharpening" and "scraper renewal" flakes) and fragments are produced in addition to the discarded tools.

One aspect of the model not made explicit by the flow diagram is that physical transportation of reduction objects and products can occur at any point along the sequence from raw material procurement to tool discard. Thus, the entire sequence could occur at a single locus or at many loci.

In comparing this model to Jelinek's generalized scheme, it can be seen that his manufacturing sites yield material which is produced by both primary and secondary reductions. Those sites which he identifies as yielding the selected products of manufacture (tool use sites) are represented in the AEPCO model by the use, modification, and discard loop of the diagram. His third kind of site, those yielding evidence for both tool manufacture and use, correspond to sites at which the material produced by primary reduction and/or secondary reduction is found in association with material produced by the use, modification, discard loop of the flow diagram.

The essential difference between Jelinek's scheme and the AEPCO model is that in the latter, manufacture is treated as two separate kinds of reduction; primary and secondary. In addition, the number of different kinds of sites which can be distinguished on the basis of the co-occurrence of different activities can be expanded from Jelinek's three, to considerably more. For example, several types or combinations of activities could be: primary reduction only, secondary reduction only, use only, primary and secondary reduction only, secondary reduction and use only, and primary reduction, secondary reduction, and tool use.

Having described the basic features of the model, the problem of distinguishing the different activities in an archaeological context can be addressed. Undoubtedly differences between groups of artifacts resulting from different reduction activities will be most pronounced when two samples, each representing a single kind of reduction, are compared. For example, differences will be more pronounced between a sample representing only primary reduction and one reflecting only secondary reduction, than between primary reduction and a combination of both primary and secondary reduction. The following describes ways that different activities, occurring by themselves may be identified. Characteristics of groups of artifacts reflecting more than one activity will also be examined.

As was mentioned earlier, primary reduction is expected to produce cores, flakes, flake fragments, and irregular, angular fragments of various sizes (chunks and shatter). Secondary reduction produces retouched pieces rather than cores, secondary flakes, flake fragments, and shatter. Thus, one way of distinguishing the two activities in terms of artifact frequency is that the former produces cores, while the latter does not. While the retouched pieces resulting from secondary reduction may often be removed to the locus of tool use, rejected unfinished tools may be present in samples which are representative of secondary reduction. Such artifacts should not be found where only primary reduction has occurred. Both kinds of reduction produce quantities of flakes and fragments. The ratio of flakes to flake fragments and shatter characteristic of the two kinds of reduction may be variable and may be affected by the properties of the raw materials, the specific technique of reduction, and the desired product of the reduction. While some primary reductions may produce a lower ratio of flakes to fragments than some kinds of secondary reduction, in certain situations, the opposite may be true. In view of the assumed variability of this ratio, and in the absence of quantitative experiments controlling for the abovementioned factors, the usefulness of the ratio of flakes to fragments for distinguishing primary and secondary reduction is limited. Nevertheless, this study assumes that the flakes and fragments produced through primary reduction, when treated as a population, are <u>qualitatively</u> different from the same kinds of products resulting from secondary reduction. For example, in considering flakes, those produced by primary reduction will tend to be larger and will exhibit a greater range of size. In contrast, those produced through secondary reduction will tend to be smaller and exhibit, as a population, a more restricted range of size.

Another important difference between flakes produced by primary and secondary reduction is the quantity of cortex present. Cortex is expected to occur more frequently and in greater amounts on primary flakes than on secondary flakes. Thus, the amount of cortex characteristic of a flake population may indicate the kind of reduction represented in the sample.

The fragments resulting from the two kinds of reduction may also differ in terms of size and cortex. Those produced by primary reduction will be larger, exhibit a greater size range, and have more cortex than those resulting from secondary reduction.

Assuming that tool discard and modification occurred more often at the locus of tool use, groups of artifacts which exhibit a high frequency of retouched pieces and larger flakes, and a low frequency of smaller flakes, fragments, and nontool cores, can be interpreted as evidence of tool use.

While primary reduction, secondary reduction, and tool use and modification may have occurred separately, these activities may also have occurred at the same locus. Therefore, it is important to identify the characteristics of an assemblage that reflects more than one of these activities.

A group of artifacts representing both primary and secondary reduction, should contain both cores and unfinished, rejected tools. The combination of both primary and secondary flakes should result in a population of flakes whose size range may be similar to that of primary flakes alone, but whose size frequency distribution will be more strongly skewed towards the smaller flake sizes, reflecting the presence of the smaller secondary flakes. The amount of cortex present on flakes of the composite population should be less than that characteristic of only primary flakes, and yet, should be greater than that found in populations of only secondary flakes. The size and amount of cortex on various kinds of fragments will also be intermediate between the two kinds of reduction performed separately.

Groups of artifacts which reflect primary and secondary reduction and tool use may be similar to those representing only tool manufacture in terms of the presence of cores and in the characteristics of the flakes and fragments. But, they should also exhibit higher frequencies of retouched pieces. This is expected at such a site because, in addition to rejected, unfinished tools, broken and/or exhausted tools would also be available for retouching.

The following list summarizes basic assumptions about the ways different reduction activities and their associated behaviors directly contribute to the characteristics of groups of artifacts:

1. Primary reduction produces cores and/or core tools, flakes, flake fragments, and irregular, angular fragments of various sizes.

2. Secondary reduction produces retouched pieces including preforms, flakes, flake fragments, and shatter.

3. Assuming that tool discard and/or modification occurred at the locus of tool use, tool use produces broken and/or exhausted tools.

4. In relation to secondary reduction, primary reduction produces flakes and fragments which are larger, exhibit a greater range in size, and have more cortex.

5. The physical transportation of the selected products of reduction can occur at any point along the sequence from raw material procurement to tool discard.

6. Where different activities have occurred at the same locus, the resultant assemblage will exhibit a mixture of the characteristics of the material produced by the separate activities.

7. This is an important assumption which, up to present, has only been implicit "...most materials on lithic sites [barring the occasional loss of a functioning artifact] probably represent what was no longer wanted by the inhabitants of the site when they left the locality" (Jelinek 1976:21).

Raw Materials

Differences in the characteristics of raw materials may also contribute to intersite variation, regardless of the reduction activities that occurred. Where pieces of material available for reduction are large, it is expected that flakes will be larger than those found in regions were only small pieces of raw material were available. In addition to affecting the sizes of flakes that can be produced, the size of the raw material can be related to the amount of cortex found on flakes. For large pieces of material, the ratio of the surface area to volume will be small in comparison to the ratio of the surface area of a smaller piece of material to its volume. Therefore, more cortex should be found on flakes produced from small pieces of raw material than on flakes produced from larger pieces. Indirectly, raw material size may have an effect on tool form. In regions where only very small pieces of material are available, the small size of the flakes produced may impose a limit on the kinds of flake tools that can be manufactured. While lightweight flake implements could have been produced, heavier implements, such as large scrapers, planes, and choppers could not have been made. These heavier implements may have been made on small cobbles or larger pebbles. If this were the case, the assemblage would more strongly reflect primary reduction as the dominant activity. Where larger sizes of raw material permit production of larger flakes, a greater variety of flake tool forms will be found, and secondary reduction will be more strongly represented.

Raw material variability also contributes to differences between groups of artifacts with respect to the flaking characteristics of different rocks. While grain size, elasticity, the presence or absence of structural flaws and a number of other factors related to raw material flaking properties can be identified, it is beyond the scope of this presentation to discuss in detail how these factors affect raw material predictability. It is assumed, however, that when raw materials are predictable, flakes will be more regularly shaped. Conversely, when the flaking properties of the material are less predictable, irregular fragments and chunks are likely to be more prevalent. Indirectly, differences in the flaking properties of various raw materials may contribute to differences among groups of artifacts in that materials with certain properties may have only been suitable for certain kinds of reduction or particular techniques of reduction. For example, where fine-grained, brittle, homogeneous rocks were available, techniques of secondary reduction by pressure and direct soft hammer percussion may have been used more frequently than in areas where only more elastic, coarser-grained materials were available. Different reduction techniques may be apparent in the two resulting groups of artifacts.

The availability of raw material may contribute indirectly, but strongly, to the characteristics of a collection. Where raw materials were scarce, the available resources probably were used to their fullest potential. Cores were fully reduced, the products of reduction were continually subjected to reworking, and tools were maintained for longer periods before being discarded.

It is expected in such situations that cores will tend to be smaller, show more flake removal, have less cortex, and possibly more frequently multi-directional than cores recovered from regions of more abundant lithic resources. Characteristics reflecting tool exhaustion should also be present in areas poor in raw material. Such characteristics may be smaller tool size, more extensive retouch, steeper edge angles, and a more fragmentary general condition. In contrast, tools found in areas rich in raw materials may have been subjected to fewer formal modifications, and therefore would tend to be larger, less extensively retouched, less fragmentary, and in general, more closely resemble fully functional artifacts. If a scarcity of raw material stimulated more intensive use of lithic resources, the flakes and fragments found in areas poor in raw materials may be smaller and have less cortex than those from areas of abundant materials. Extensive reduction of cores may produce more smaller primary flakes than with less complete primary reduction. Also, the continual reworking of tools will result in the production of many small flakes and contribute to a stronger representation of secondary reduction.

Another factor expected to indirectly contribute to the characteristics of assemblages, and which could be related to raw material availability, is the nature of site occupancies. On sites occupied for long periods of time, the accumulated by-products of past reduction may have served as the "raw material" for subsequent reduction. Even if raw materials were locally available, the products of previous reductions could be reworked to the point where it became necessary to begin primary reduction on fresh materials. Thus, materials collected from sites occuped for long periods of time, or intensively occupied for a shorter period of time, or both, can be expected to have certain characteristics in common with groups of artifacts recovered from areas scarce in raw materials. Cores from long term habitation sites may show more intensive reduction than those from short occupation-limited activity sites, even though both sites may be located in close proximity to lithic resources. It may also be expected that long term habitation sites should yield material which more strongly reflects secondary reduction activities as a result of the reworking of the products of past reductions. In contrast, sites occupied for only a matter of hours, such as those reflecting limited tool manufacture and/or use, should yield artifacts which do not show evidence of continual reworking. Thus, raw material availability can be thought of in absolute terms (the volume of material per unit area) or in relative terms (the amount available in relationship to the demand).

The final group of factors contributing to differences among collections are related either to natural or artificial processes which have had their effect long after sites were abandoned. Where sites occur on a sloping surface one may expect that artifacts of different sizes were transported downslope at different rates as the result of sheetwash erosion. In comparing groups of material recovered from nearly horizontal surfaces to those collected from ridgetops or slopes, the frequency of small artifacts may be less in the latter situation, even though the two groups may have been the same in this respect at the time of artifact deposition.

Differences in the ways sites were collected may also be a factor contributing to intersample variation. Samples from sites collected by an intensive examination of the surface by individuals on their hands and knees can be expected to show higher frequencies of smaller artifacts such as shatter. In contrast, sites collected by walking systematic transects to locate artifacts should have higher frequencies of larger artifacts because smaller ones may not have been seen.

The last consideration is the extent to which sites have been collected by amateurs. Where this has happened frequently, sites will probably yield artifact samples which may have few "desirable" artifacts. In relation to lithics, this probably means that some retouched pieces, especially whole projectile points, may be underrepresented.

In conclusion, intersite variation with respect to artifact assemblages is assumed to be a result of the interaction of all of the factors described above and probably others as well. Realistically, any study which attempts to define the role of any one factor in contributing to intersite variability must also account for variation which could have been contributed by other factors.

Tool Manufacture and Use

Tool manufacture and use produces three basic categories of implements: unretouched flake tools, retouched pieces, and core tools.

Unretouched Flake Tools

It is assumed that suitable flakes and fragments were selected for their sharp edges, used without modification, and then discarded. Such behavior will be reflected in the archaeological record by the presence of unretouched utilized flakes and fragments.

Retouched Pieces

Retouched pieces represent an attempt to alter the form of a flake in accordance with functional and/or stylistic criteria. When this attempt was sucessful, it is assumed that the resulting implement was used and perhaps subjected to further modification, until it was no longer needed or useful, at which time it was discarded. Such implements should be visible in the archaeological record as utilized, retouched, and discarded tools. If the implement was accidentally broken during manufacture, or some other manufacturing problem encountered, then unused, broken, retouched pieces and preforms should be found in association with manufacturing debris. In some instances, retouched pieces may have been produced when an unretouched flake was used, then subsequently modified to enhance its usefulness, used again, and then discarded.

Core Tools

As previously indicated, primary reduction may have been done to produce quantities of usable flakes or to fashion a tool from the core itself. In the latter case, the resulting artifact may show attributes which reflect its intended use or stylistic preferences of its maker. Such characteristics could be regularity of the edges or a distinctive geometric shape. Although cores, whose primary function was to provide usable flakes, may lack regularly shaped edges, there is no reason to assume that they could not have subsequently been used as tools.

In summary, almost any piece of stone with a sharp edge could have been used. Therefore, the first step in comparing samples of artifacts in terms of tool form and frequency is to separate the tools from the other artifacts. Perhaps the most easily recognized tools are retouched flakes. But, cores which exhibit recurring combinations of certain attributes that strongly suggest intentional shaping to conform to functional and/or stylistic criteria may also be tools (core tools). An exception to this assumption must be made when elaborate core preparation techniques were used to produce flakes of particular sizes and shapes.

Small flaked pebbles, which might technically be classified as cores, could have been used as tools. Because the formal distinction between small cores and pebble tools may not be obvious, the classification of small flaked pebbles as pebble tools rather than small cores depends more on interpretation than on form. However, some flaked pebbles may have forms which cannot reasonably be associated with an intention to produce flakes for use. For example, small, thin, naturally discoidal pebbles exhibiting marginal flake removal are more reasonably interpreted as retouched pieces rather than cores whose purpose was to produce flakes.

Unretouched flakes and fragments and cores whose form indicates no obvious intentional shaping for use may be identified as having been used if there is use-wear on the artifacts' edges. The degree of confidence with which use can be inferred depends largely on the ability to distinguish use-related edge alteration from that which may have been caused by other factors. The most obvious sources of nonuse edge alteration on the AEPCO II artifacts (trampling by livestock, vehicle disturbance, and sheetwash erosion) were identified in the introduction to this chapter as related to the surface context of most of the artifacts. Other, perhaps less obvious sources of edge alteration have to do with the treatment of artifacts during and after their recovery. In many instances, material from excavated units was thrown into screens and then vigorously shaken to separate artifacts and small gravels from the soil. Edge alteration may also have occurred when paper bags containing large numbers of artiracts were subjected to repeated jostling during transportation from the field and during artifact washing.

Tringham and others (1974) have suggested, on the basis of experiments, that artifacts having edge alteration resulting from use can be distinguished from artifacts with edge alteration from trampling and rolling by comparing the resultant minute flake scars, as those of the former are more uniform in size and tend to occur in close proximity to one another. Microflaking caused by trampling and rolling tends to be more sporadically distributed around the artifacts' edges, and the flake scars are less uniform in size. But, while criteria such as regularity of microflake size and localization of microflaking may be of some use in determining if the edge alteration characteristic of a sample of artifacts is the result of use or other factors, the use of these criteria to infer the origin of microflaking on a single artifact is questionable for the purpose of this study.

While in some cases, use may have caused localized, regularly spaced, or overlapping microflake scars, in other instances it could have resulted in more sporadic microflaking, or none at all. Although sporadic distribution of microflake scars of varying sizes may be characteristic of nonuse edge alteration, some destructive forces, such as cattle trampling, can easily produce localized, overlapping, microflake scars as the result of crushing. Therefore, sorting artifacts into different categories on the basis of differences in the location, number, and size of flake scars, and labeling these categories with terms like "utilized," "intensively utilized," or "lightly utilized," is unrealistic. The valid interpretation of microflake scar variation as it relates to use depends on the degree to which variation contributed by other factors can be controlled. This is true for the interpretation of variation in other formal attributes as well. The criteria suggested by Tringham and others (1974) for distinguishing use from nonuse edge alteration cannot be directly applied to the AEPCO materials for two reasons. First, they are based on experimental studies in which flint was the only material used. The AEPCO II artifacts are made from a variety of materials, at least some of which may have flaking properties which differ considerably from those of flint and which may make them more or less sensitive to forces of edge alteration. Second, the destructive forces to which the AEPCO II artifacts have been subjected include others beyond the trampling by human feet and rolling mentioned by Tringham.

The extent to which different destructive forces have caused edge alteration on AEPCO II lithic artifacts is largely unknown. The characteristics of edge alteration resulting from various forces on different raw materials are also unclear. Because this study cannot answer these questions, description of variation among the collections in terms of tool form and frequency focuses on retouched pieces and cores which exhibit obvious indications of intentional shaping for use. It does not deal with artifacts which can be identified as tools solely on the basis of edge alteration attributes.

Methodology and Data Presentation

This analysis consists of three stages; description of the collections in terms of a number of variables, comparison of the resulting data in order to identify intersample variation, and explanation of the identified variation within the theoretical framework.

Briefly, the material from each site was described in terms of the frequencies with which four different kinds of reduction products occur. The four basic categories that are distinguished are (1) cores and core tools, (2) unretouched complete flakes, (3) retouched pieces, and (4) unretouched fragments.

Formal variation within the retouched piece category is dealt with typologically and will be described and discussed at the end of this section. Variation within the remaining three categories is described with respect to a number of formal attributes listed by artifact category in Table 31.

Table 31. Formal lithic attributes recorded by artifact category

Category	Attributes Recorded
Cores and core tools	weight cortex direction of flaking number of flake scars
Unretouched complete flakes	length width thickness cortex
Unretouched fragments	weight cortex

In addition to those attributes listed above, raw material type and texture were recorded on artifacts of all categories, including retouched pieces.

In order that the data could be manipulated with the aid of a computer, attribute observations were recorded in a numeric code on IBM Fortran coding sheets, then punched on Hollerith cards. A reproduction of the numeric attribute code used is given in Table 32.

In order to identify significant intersample variation, and to examine the relationships between variables, a number of univariate and bivariate statistical techniques were applied to the data. This was done through the use of SPSS subprograms: FREQUENCY, CROSSTABS, ONEWAY, and CONDESCRIPTIVE (Nie and others 1975).

Table 32. Lithic attribute code.

Field	Columns	Variable	Value	Condition
1	1	Analysis type	1	Lithic
2	2-7	ASM Site Number		
3	8	Locus		
4	9-12	North-south grid		
5	13-16	East-west grid		
6	17	Sample number		
7	18	Quad		
8	19	Level		
9	20	Feature		
10	21-25	General artifact number		
11	26	Specific artifact number		
12	29-30	Raw material type	1	Rhyolite
			2	Chert
			3	Chalcedony
			4	Jasper
			5	Obsidian
			6	Quartzite
			7	Quartz
			8	Andesite
			9	Basalt
			10	Vesicular Basalt
			11	Schist
			12	Shale
			13	Gneiss
			14	Hematite
			15	Unknown metamorphic
			16	Unknown sedimentary
			17	Unknown igneous
			18	Limestone
			19	Granite
13	38	Texture	1	Very fine
			2	Fine
			3	Medium
			4	Coarse
			5	Very coarse
14	40-41	Stage of manufacture	11	Core/core tool
			12	Unretouched complete flake
			13	Fragment
			14	Retouched piece
			15	Retouched natural fragment
			16	Shaped schist
			17	Hammer stone

Table 32. Lithic attribute code (continued).

Field	Columns	Variable	Value	Condition
15	43-45	Length	Observed value to nearest mm	
16	46-48	Width	Observed value to nearest mm	
17	49-50	Thickness	Observed value to nearest mm	
18	52	Cortex	0	0%
			1	0-10%
			2	10-50%
			3	50-90%
			4	90-100%
			5	100%
19	54	Direction of flaking	1	Unidirectional
			2	Bidirectional
			3	Multidirectional
20	56-57	Number of flake scars	Observed value	
21	59-62	Weight	to the nearest gm	

Definition of the Collections

AZ CC:6:3

Of the 152 lithic items collected, 133 artifacts were analyzed. Nineteen were judged nonartifactual because they lacked any clear evidence of human modification. For the most part, these items were small angular pebbles and chalcedony fragments.

AZ CC:10:6

Four hundred and sixty-nine artifacts were analyzed from this site. This total includes artifacts collected during both the testing and data recovery phases. Attributes were recorded on 368 artifacts from the surface and on 101 artifacts from subsurface units. Surface and subsurface materials were treated as a single collection. One hundred and eleven pieces of cracked rock and natural fragments were collected but not analyzed.

AZ CC:10:11

Approximately 4,000 lithic items were collected from this site. Artifacts collected from Locus 1, Locus 2, and Sample 2 were analyzed. The material from Sample 1 could not be examined because of time limitations (Refer to Chapter 4, Figure 29 for the locations of the areas collected). Locus 1, Locus 2, and Sample 2 were treated as separate collections, so that possible differences between these areas could be identified.

A total of 1,574 items was recovered from Locus 1. As mentioned in Chapter 4, the lack of structural homogeneity in the raw material from Locus 1 made it difficult to distinguish intentional flaking from natural fracturing along planes of weakness. Items on which no clear evidence of an impact could be seen were not analyzed, although some of these 517 pieces may be artifactural. In order to save time, the remaining 1,057 artifacts were sampled. This was done by first sorting the artifacts into the basic reduction categories and tabulating the number within each. Categories which contained more than 100 items were then sampled to reduce the number of artifacts to be analyzed. Sampling within categories was accomplished by numbering each artifact consecutively and selecting 100 artifacts by using a table of random numbers.

Materials from Locus 2 that were analyzed include all artifacts from within the grid system except those collected as "isolated artifacts." These were excluded because they would have biased the frequency data in favor of retouched pieces and cores. A large quantity of small angular fragments, which showed no evidence of being either the result of chipping activity or retouching, were not analyzed. The significance of Feature 4, a discrete concentration of these items, will be discussed later. Artifacts from Features 2 and 3, located outside of the grid system, were not analyzed because of time limitations. Examination of these materials has yielded some information which will be presented in the interpretation section. A total of 250 artifacts from Locus 2 was analyzed.

Approximately 1,300 pieces were collected from Sample 2. Because the outcrop which served as the source of the raw material is so close to the collection area, distinguishing artifacts from natural fragments was a problem. The major criterion used to separate artifactual from nonartifactual materials was the presence or absence of hertzian features. It should be noted, however, that the separation of artifacts from nonartifacts in this situation was by no means an exact process. A certain percentage of the 1,165 pieces treated as artifacts may not be man made, and some items treated as nonartifacts may be the result of intentional reduction. Because of the collection, the material was sampled by the same method as that used to sample material from Locus 1.

AZ CC:10:13

Of the approximately 433 items collected from AZ CC:10:13, 340 were analyzed. Those collected but not analyzed were flake-like fragments presumed to be thermal spalls. Cobbles resembling cores but which are also probably the result of thermal spalling were also excluded from the analysis. A small number of items were not analyzed because they were apparently produced by the action of heavy tracked equipment. Artifacts from all the features and the general grid system were treated as a single collection.

AZ CC:10:14

One hundred and fifty of the 199 pieces collected from this site were analyzed. The remaining 49 pieces were excluded because they were either thermal spalls or flakes made by heavy equipment impact.

AZ CC:9:2

A total of approximately 3,248 lithic artifacts was recovered from the surface collection and test excavations of AZ CC:9:3; the large size of this collection required that a sample be taken. The surface material from each grid square was first tabulated. Then, grid squares located between 55 m and 110 m south of the datum were selected at random in order to obtain an approximately 30 percent sample of the 2,127 surface artifacts. The selection of the following 28 grids yielded 650 artifacts for analysis:

55S SW	75S 15E	90S 5W	100S 10W
55S 5E	80S 5E	90S 15E	100S 5W
60S 0E	80S 20E	90S 25E	105S 15W
60S 10E	80S 25E	95S 5W	105S 10W
70 0E	85S 10W	95S 0E	105S 0E
70S 25E	85S 5W	95S 5E	105S 15E
75S 10E	85S 15E	95S 10E	105S 25E

A total of 1,141 artifacts was recovered from the subsurface levels of the three excavcated grid squares (80S 10E, 85S 15W, and 100S 15W). This material was treated as a separate collection for the purposes of sampling and analysis. Sampling was done for each square as follows: the number of artifacts from all levels was tabulated, each artifact was assigned a consecutive integer, and 30 percent of the artifacts were selected by using a table of random numbers. The samples from each of the three squares were made to identify differences between materials with respect to the excavated units or to individual 5 cm levels.

AZ CC:13:11

Approximately 980 chipped stone artifacts were collected from AZ CC:13:11 of which 614 were analyzed. Among those not analyzed were a large number of small fragments of phyllite and schist which had no hertzian features. Examination of this material with a 10x hand lens showed that a few of these items exhibited ground surfaces. It was therefore assumed that the bulk of this material may have been the result of the natural exfoliation of larger pieces of ground stone implements, and were given over to ground stone analysis. Other items not analyzed were some irregular, large chunks of coarse-grained cracked rock that exhibited no evidence of hertzian features. Attributes were recorded on the remaining 614 artifacts, including 121 from the surface and 493 from all subsurface levels. Surface and subsurface materials were treated as a single collection, with no attempt to identify variation among materials from different levels or horizontal proveniences.

AZ CC:13:6

Approximately 148 lithic items were collected from the surface of AZ CC:13:6. This material was combined with 52 pieces collected from the surface collection during testing at this site. Of these 200 artifacts,

68 were analyzed; those excluded were approximately 50 pieces of cracked rock and a number of schist and phyllite fragments of various sizes. There was no evidence that they had been made by deliberate reduction.

AZ CC:13:14

Five hundred and seventy-four lithic items (excluding ground stone) were collected from AZ CC:13:14. Of these, 417 were analyzed. Those excluded from the analysis were 85 pieces of cracked rock identified as such in the field, and an additional 72 pieces of rock excluded because closer examination revealed no evidence that they were produced by intentional flaking. They are probably smaller fragments of thermally cracked cobbles or fragments of ground stone on which no ground surface is present. Artifacts collected from the general grid system and Feature 1 were analyzed as a single collection.

AZ CC:13:15

Only five lithic artifacts, including three small fragments of basalt, a ryholite fragment, and one basalt flake fragment, were recovered from AZ CC:13:15. Because of the extremely small size of this collection, AZ CC:13:15 was excluded from any formal lithic analysis. The possible significance of these artifacts will be briefly discussed in the interpretation section.

AZ CC:13:16

Of the 59 nonground lithic items recovered, only nine showed intentional reduction. These materials include a projectile point, a basal fragment, a thick, scraper-like core tool, two basalt flakes, and five pieces of shatter, all made of basalt except for one of crystalline quartz. The remaining items include 29 angular fragments of pink limestone and 21 small pieces of various coarse-grained rocks, none of which appear to be the product of intentional lithic reduction. Because of the small number of lithic artifacts, AZ CC:13:16 was excluded from that portion of the analysis which deals with reduction activities and raw materials. The significance of these materials will be briefly discussed in the interpretation section.

In summary, the 12 collections compared in the analysis include all artifacts from AZ CC:6:3, AZ CC:10:6, AZ CC:10:11 Locus 2 (except those collected as "isolated artifacts" and those from Features 2 and 3), AZ CC::10:13 and 14, AZ CC:13:6 and 11 and 14 and samples taken from AZ CC:10:11 Sample 2, AZ CC:9:2 (surface artifacts), and AZ CC:9:2 (subsurface artifacts).

Category and Attribute Definitions and Procedures

Artifacts were sorted into the following four basic reduction stage categories. The artifacts in each category were then measured and various attributes recorded.

Cores

Any artifact which exhibited one or more negative bulbs of percussion and which could be identified as not having been artificially detached from another piece of raw material was classified as a core. Cores and core tools were not distinguished during this stage of the analysis.

Complete Flakes

Flakes whose proximal and distal ends and both lateral edges were intact and which exhibited no retouch were classified as unretouched complete flakes.

Fragments

Artifacts assigned to this category include flake fragments of various sizes, small, angular fragments (shatter), and large irregular fragments (chunks). None of the artifacts classified as fragments show evidence of being modified, although some of the larger chunks exhibit negative bulbs of percussion and are probably core fragments.

Retouched Pieces

A piece of stone struck from another piece of stone and subsequently further reduced was classified as a retouched piece. Only artifacts with retouch flake scars 3 mm or more in length were classified as retouched pieces; those exhibiting flake scars less than 3 mm in length were classified as unretouched. Both complete and fragmentary retouched artifacts were included in this category. Artifacts such as projectile points and other bifaces were also classified under this category, even though they exhibit retouch which is so extensive that it could not be determined if they were made on flakes or from raw material.

In addition to the above four categories, a relatively small number of artifacts were retouched tabular natural fragments and thermal spalls. Although these artifacts were distinguished from the above category during attribute recording, they were later combined with retouched pieces. Also, a very small number of hammerstones, and two examples of shaped schist artifacts were encountered. Although separate categories were established for these items during the attribute recording these artifacts were later combined into a single group called "other." The absolute and relative (percentage) frequencies of the artifacts with respect to the stage of manufacture are given in tabular form for each collection in Appendix III, Table 36.

Measurement of Attributes

Measurements of length, width, and thickness were made on all artifacts in the complete unretouched flake category. These measurements were also taken on those artifacts in the retouched piece category if they were flakes on which the retouch did not remove features critical to measurement. All measurements were taken with vernier calipers to the nearest millimeter; the dimensions measured are as follows:

Length was measured as the distance from the point of percussion to the most distant point on the interior surface of the flake. When the distal end on the flake terminated in a hinge fracture, as was frequently the case, length was measured to the center of the distal edge.

Width was measured as the distance between opposite lateral edges at right angles to the length, at the approximate midpoint of the length.

Thickness was measured as the distance between the internal and external surfaces, in the same plane as (but perpendicular to) the width, at the approximate midpoint of the length.

The lengths and widths of each of the approximately 900 flakes that were measured will not be included in this presentation. These data are in length-width scatter diagrams in the section on comparative observations (see Figure 97). The absolute and relative frequencies of flakes with respect to thickness are given in tabular form for each collection in Appendix III, Tables 37 and 38.

Estimations of the amount of cortex were made on all complete flakes including retouched flakes. This was done by placing each flake in one of six arbitrarily defined classes on the basis of the percentage of the exterior cortical surface. The definitions of the cortex classes are as follows: Class 0 (0%), Class 1 (0-10%), Class 2 (10-50%), Class 3 (50-90%), Class 4 (90-100%). The absolute and relative frequencies of flakes with respect to these cortex classes for each collection are given in tabular form in Appendix III, Table 39.

Attributes recorded on cores include weight, cortex, direction of flaking, and number of flake scars. Each core was weighed on an Ohaus triple beam balance (capacity = 2610 g). Values were recorded to the nearest gram.

The method of cortex estimation on cores is essentially the same as that used to estimate cortex on flakes. Each core was placed in one of five classes arbitrarily defined on the basis of the percentage of the estimated cortical surface. Class definitions are the same as those given for cortex on flakes, with the exception that the 100 percent cortical class (Class 5) is omitted for obvious reasons.

Observations on core flaking direction were made on the basis of the origins of flake scars with respect to three imaginary, perpendicular axes intersecting at a single point. Cores were assigned to one of the three classes defined as follows:

Unidirectional. Flake scars running parallel to only one axis, and in the same direction (all flake scars originate from the same platform).

Bidirectional. Flake scars running (1) parallel to only two axes, or (2) parallel to only one axis but originating from two platforms, one at either end of the imaginary axis of flaking.

Multidirectional. Cores showing flake scars parallel to three axes or parallel to only two axes but originating from both ends of at least one flaking axis.

Cores showing a single, large flake scar that was used as a platform for the removal of other flakes were classified as unidirectional, even though they are technically bidirectional. Estimations of the number of flake scars on cores were recorded by counting the number of flake scars present which are 1 cm or more in maximum dimension.

The core weight data will be presented in the following section on comparative observations of the data. The absolute and relative frequencies of cores with respect to cortex, direction of flaking and number of flake scars are given in Appendix III, Tables 40 and 41. It should be noted that for some sites, core samples with data on cortex, direction of flaking, and number of flake scars may be less than the actual number of cores for each collection. This is because observations of these attributes, particularly direction of flaking and number of flake scars, were sometimes not recorded if it was felt that they could not be reliably determined because of the coarseness of the raw material.

Weight and cortex were recorded for artifacts assigned to the unretouched fragment category. Fragments were individually weighed to the nearest gram on the triple beam balance, and those weighing less than 0.5 g were recorded as zero values on the coding sheets. For the purposes of computer manipulation of the data, the zero values were later converted to 0.5 g. Cortex on fragments was recorded as being either present or absent. For each collection, the minimum, maximum, and mean fragment weight, and the absolute and relative frequencies of fragments by cortex are given in Appendix III, Table 42.

It is assumed in this study that the most important criteria for the selection of particular rocks for specific manufacturing purposes were their individual flaking properties. These criteria are not necessarily the same as those used to define petrologic material types. Undoubtedly, broad correlations can be drawn between some gross petrologic material types and particular flaking properties. For instance, basalt is less amenable to pressure flaking than are various kinds of siliceous chemical precipitates such as chert, jasper, and chalcedony. However, in many raw material types, particularly igneous rocks, a wide range of variation in characteristics can exist which affect flaking properties. A good example can be seen in the rhyolites from AZ CC:6:3. Here the term "rhyolite" can be correctly applied to a number of materials which appear to have very different flaking qualities. At one end of the scale there is an extremely fine-grained, homogenous, white rhyolite; at the other end, there are coarse-textured gray and pink rhyolites of comparatively heterogeneous structure. Because flaking qualities vary considerably in materials which can be classified as "basalt," "rhyolite," "quartzite," "andesite," and so forth, these terms are of only limited use in explaining artifact variability as it may relate to different kinds of raw material. Accordingly, correlations between petrologically defined material types and other kinds of artifact variability were not made. Nonetheless, observations of raw material types were recorded since such information would be useful in determining raw material sources and the extent to which the raw material of the artifacts reflects the kinds of materials available. Raw material texture is an important characteristic related to the flaking qualities of rocks, and was recorded so that its relationship to other variables, primarily flake size, could be defined.

Both raw material texture and raw material type were recorded for artifacts of all categories. This was done by placing each artifact in one of the following five arbitrarily defined texture classes: very fine, fine, medium, coarse, very coarse. These classes were represented by five selected pieces of rock with textures at approximately equal intervals along a continuum from fine to coarse. A piece of obsidian represented the finest class, and a piece of rhyolite showing macroscopically visible mineral crystals of about 1 to 2 mm in size represented the coarsest texture class.

Each artifact was visually compared to each of the five rock specimens and matched to the texture class which most closely resembled the texture of the artifact. In addition to the five texture classes mentioned above, a sixth class was established for a number of artifacts which had two or more distinctly different textures. This was done only if material of the two textures was present in a ratio of approximately 1:2 (by volume) or greater. The absolute and relative frequencies of the artifacts by texture class is given in Appendix III, Table 43.

Raw material type was recorded on all artifacts. Raw material was identified by macroscopically visible characteristics, following the guidelines provided in Classification of Rocks (Travis 1955). The absolute and relative frequencies of artifacts by raw material type are given in Appendix III, Table 44. Such data for the material analyzed from AZ CC:10:11 Sample 2 are not presented because all artifacts from this locality are assumed to be made of materials derived from the same raw material outcrop.

Methodology of Tool Typology Construction

After a collection had been sorted into the reduction product categories, all artifacts identified as retouched pieces and core tools were set aside. In addition, a comparatively small number of artifacts assumed to be hammerstones and some small flaked pebbles possibly representing tools were also separated from the rest of the artifacts. With the completion of the observation and recording of attributes for all collections, all artifacts to be subjected to typological manipulation had been isolated. Rather than defining types as they were encountered in the collection from each site, the typology was developed by treating the tools from all sites as a single collection. This enabled the entire range of tool form present in the materials to be viewed at once, and helped to ensure that the criteria used to define types were applied equally to artifacts from different sites.

Since the primary purpose of the typology was to provide a framework for formal description, and thus a means by which differences among collections could be identified in terms of the frequencies with which different types of tools occur, the typology had to satisfy two seemingly contradictory requirements in order to be useful. First, for the purposes of description, it was important that the level of specificity used to distinguish types be fine enough that a group of artifacts showing different combinations of recurring attributes were not lumped by imposing a classification which was too broad. For example, distinguishing artifacts solely on the basis of whether they are unifacial or bifacial is not justified when, within these groups, patterned associations of other attributes can be observed. In such a case, typological splitting could be done in order to identify more specific patterns or variability.

Second, for the purposes of making comparisons among sites with respect to tool frequencies, the types could not be so numerous and finely split that similarities and differences between sites in terms of more general patterns of variability would be obscured.

In effect, an attempt to identify patterns of variation among collections in terms of tool form and frequency is thwarted when too few types are established (types contain too little formal information), and is also unsuccessful when types are too numerous (contain too much formal information). Ideally, the extent to which a typology "splits" as opposed to "lumps" should reflect the ways attributes co-occur rather than the individual archaeologist's training or preference.

In practice, the typology for the AEPCO II tools was developed by physically grouping the artifacts according to similarities and differences with respect to a number of formal attributes. Since the artifacts could be regrouped in different ways depending on the level of specificity used to distinguish types and the relative importance ascribed to different attributes, this "trial and error" approach yielded several different typologies. Of these alternatives, the typology described below was chosen as best satisfying the objectives of the study. The outline below shows the basic features of the classification system used to describe AEPCO II tools.

Before proceeding with the explanation of tool typology and the description of individual types, a few comments concerning nomenclature should be made. The names used for the types are a mixture of both functional and purely formal terms. Whenever possible, names which describe artifact form were used in order to avoid functional implications. However, in some cases where no convenient formal term could be applied, functional terms (such as "scraper") were used because they are understood by most archaeologists as referring to a particular morphology. The use of these terms should not be taken to mean that specific functions are assumed for artifacts having functional names.

I. Light Retouched Pieces

A. Unifacial
1. Notches
2. Scrapers
   a. end scrapers
   b. side scrapers
   c. multiside scrapers
3. Denticulate Tools
4. Irregularly Retouched Flakes (large)
5. Irregularly Retouched Flakes (small)
6. Gravers/Perforators
7. Burins
8. Miscellaneous Flaked Chunks
9. Miscellaneous Uniface Fragments

B. Bifacial
1. Small Percussion Flaked Bifaces
2. Projectile Points

II. Heavy Tools

A. Unifacial
1. Planes
2. Choppers

B. Bifacial

III. Pebble Tools

IV. Hammerstones

- -

Type Descriptions

Light Retouched Pieces

By far the largest category, light retouched pieces include flakes, chunks, and natural fragments which show some sort of retouch. Also included are artifacts such as small bifaces and projectile points whose technological origin cannot be determined because the retouch is so extensive. In almost all cases, artifacts of the light retouched piece category are less than 10 cm in maximum dimension. While these artifacts generally correspond to what are frequently referred to as "flake tools" (as opposed to "core tools") this terminology is avoided because not all of the artifacts were obviously made on flakes. Light retouched pieces are further distinguished on the basis of whether the retouch is predominantely unifacial or bifacial.

Light Retouched Pieces: Unifacial

Notches. Artifacts classified as notches are those which were dealt a single blow that resulted in the removal of a flake whose scar created a concavity in the edge of the artifact. Although most notches are between 30 and 60 mm in maximum dimension, some are as small as 25 mm and others as large as 100 mm. The width and depth of the concavities themselves are also highly variable between examples. No tendency was noted for the concavity to occur in a particular location, either with respect to the artifact's long axes or interior vs. exterior flake surfaces. Some typical notches are illustrated in Figure 86.

Scrapers. Following Haury (1950:212) scrapers are defined as artifacts having one flat or nearly flat face, not modified by chipping, and one convex face, low or high, modified by retouching to produce the working edge. Although artifacts conforming to these criteria which have denticulated edges are treated as "serrated" scrapers by Haury, such implements are discussed as "denticulates" in the AEPCO II typology.

Three types of scrapers were distinguished in the AEPCO materials on the basis of differences in the location of the retouched edge: end scrapers, and multisided scrapers. The location of the retouched edge was defined in relationship to the artifacts maximum dimension, and not to flake features such as the point of impact of the detaching blow, proximal and distal ends, or left and right lateral edges.

End Scrapers. Ranging in size from 33 to 71 mm, most end scrapers are between 50 and 60 mm in length. Although retouching is usually confined to the artifact's end, in a few instances the retouch extends for a short distance along one or both of the sides. In terms of edge shape, most end scrapers exhibit some degree of convexity, frequently with jagged or irregular edges. At least one example has a distinctly concave retouched edge, and four reveal retouching which produced a short, blunt projection on the end. The morphology of the retouch flake scars suggests that retouch was done by direct, probably hard hammer, percussion. The flake scars seldom extend inward from the edge for a distance greater than about one-quarter of the artifact's total length. In a few cases, a high ridge runs roughly parallel to the long axis on the face opposite that which served as the platform for the removal of the retouch flakes. In this respect, these scrapers are reminiscent of the "keeled" forms described by Haury (1950:227). However, since in no case was the "keel" produced by the removal of retouch flakes, but was a feature existing on the artifact before retouching, the term "keeled" cannot be applied. Some typical end scrapers are illustrated in Figure 87.

Side Scrapers. Ranging in size from 35 to 102 mm in length, side scrapers are essentially very similar to end scrapers, but different in that retouch occurs continuously along one of the artifact's sides. For the most part, the retouch appears to have been by means of direct hard hammer percussion and frequently resulted in somewhat jagged or irregular edges. Despite this irregularity of the edges, in most examples convex, shallowly concave, and approximately straight edge shapes can be distinguished. Some typical side scrapers are shown in Figure 88.

Multiside Scrapers. A comparatively small number of scrapers, varying in size from 41 to 76 mm in length, showed retouch on more than one edge, and were thus classified as multiside scrapers. Included in this type are scrapers which were retouched around the greater portion of their perimeters and which tend to be oval or discoidal in shape. Also included are scrapers retouched on two ends, two sides, one side and one end, and two sides and one end. Generally speaking, these forms tend to be rectangular or subrectangular in outline. Some multiside scrapers are illustrated in Figure 89.

Denticulate Tools. Artifacts showing unifacial retouch along one or more edges consisting of a series of concavities separated from each other by projections, and which creates a serrated edge were classified as denticulate tools. In most examples, the individual concavities between the "teeth" are simple notches produced by a single blow. In a very few cases, the concavities were produced by the removal of more than one flake. The width, depth, and regularity in spacing of the concavities varies considerably among examples. Although most denticulate tools appear to have been retouched by direct percussion, a few showing the finest serration with the most regularly spaced concavities might have been retouched by means of pressure flaking. Ranging in size from 24 to 95 mm in length, most of these implements are retouched along only one side. However, a few double side and end denticulates occur. Some typical denticulate tools are illustrated in Figure 90.

Irregularly Retouched Flakes (large). These artifacts are flakes, ranging in size from 42 to 93 mm in maximum dimension, which show discontinuous, predominately unifacial retouch. Typically, from three to six, seldom overlapping, retouch flake scars are present, producing an irregularly shaped edge. Generally, the retouch flake scars extend inward from the edge for only a very short distance and tend to be localized along one of the sides. While irregularly retouched flakes resemble denticulate tools in that they have irregular edges produced by unifacial retouch, they are distinguished in that the retouch creates a much less pronouncedly serrated edge. The term "subdenticulate" might well be applied to these artifacts.

Irregularly Retouched Flakes (small). These are essentially very similar to the above described type but are distinguished arbitrarily on the basis of size (22 to 36 mm).

Gravers/Perforators. Artifacts exhibiting unifacial retouch which isolates a single projection were classified under this type. While "gravers" can be distinguished from "perforators" on the basis of differences in the morphology of the bit of the projection (gravers having chisel-like bits and perforators having more sharply pointed bits), real variation in their form was such that drawing a distinction between gravers and perforators could not be justified. Although several kinds of gravers/perforators are present, the most common form is a flake having sides which converge at the distal end to form a point, and which exhibits steep, unifacial retouch on the exterior surface of the flake, on one side, in close proximity to the distal end, forming a projection. Much less frequent are graver/perforators whose projections are isolated from the flake's edge by retouch on both sides of the bit. Graver/perforators range in size from 22 to 76 mm.

Figure 86. Notched pieces. a, CC:10:13, rhyolite; b, CC:6:3, rhyolite; c, CC:10:11 Sample 2, felsite; d, CC:9:2, quartzite; e, CC:10:14, rhyolite; f, CC:10:6, rhyolite; g, CC:6:3, chalcedony.

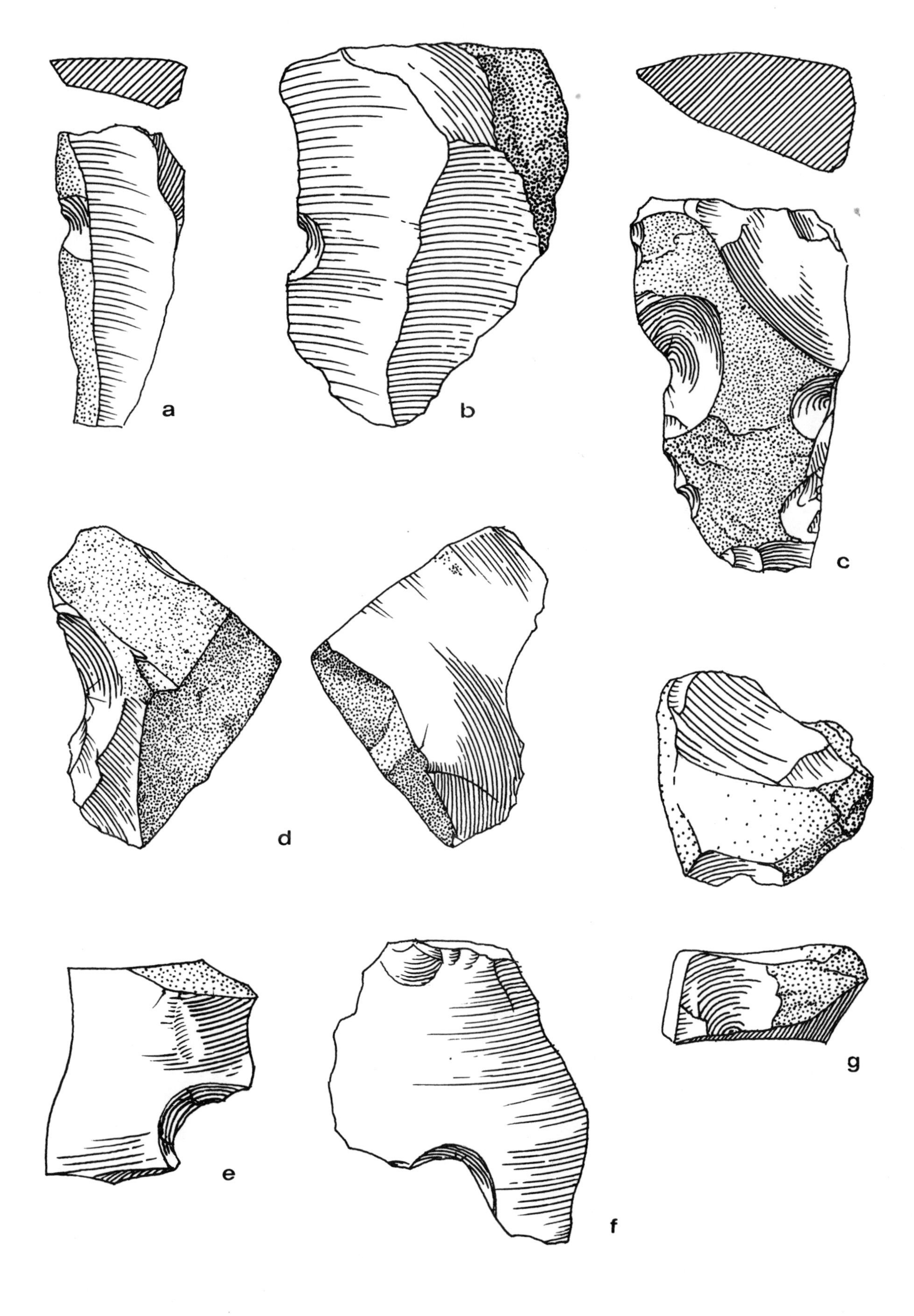
a
b
c
d
e
f
g

Figure 87. End scrapers. a,e, CC:10:13, rhyolite; b, CC:9:2, quartzite; c, CC:9:2, basalt; d, CC:13:14, igneous; f, CC:10:11 Locus 2, felsite.

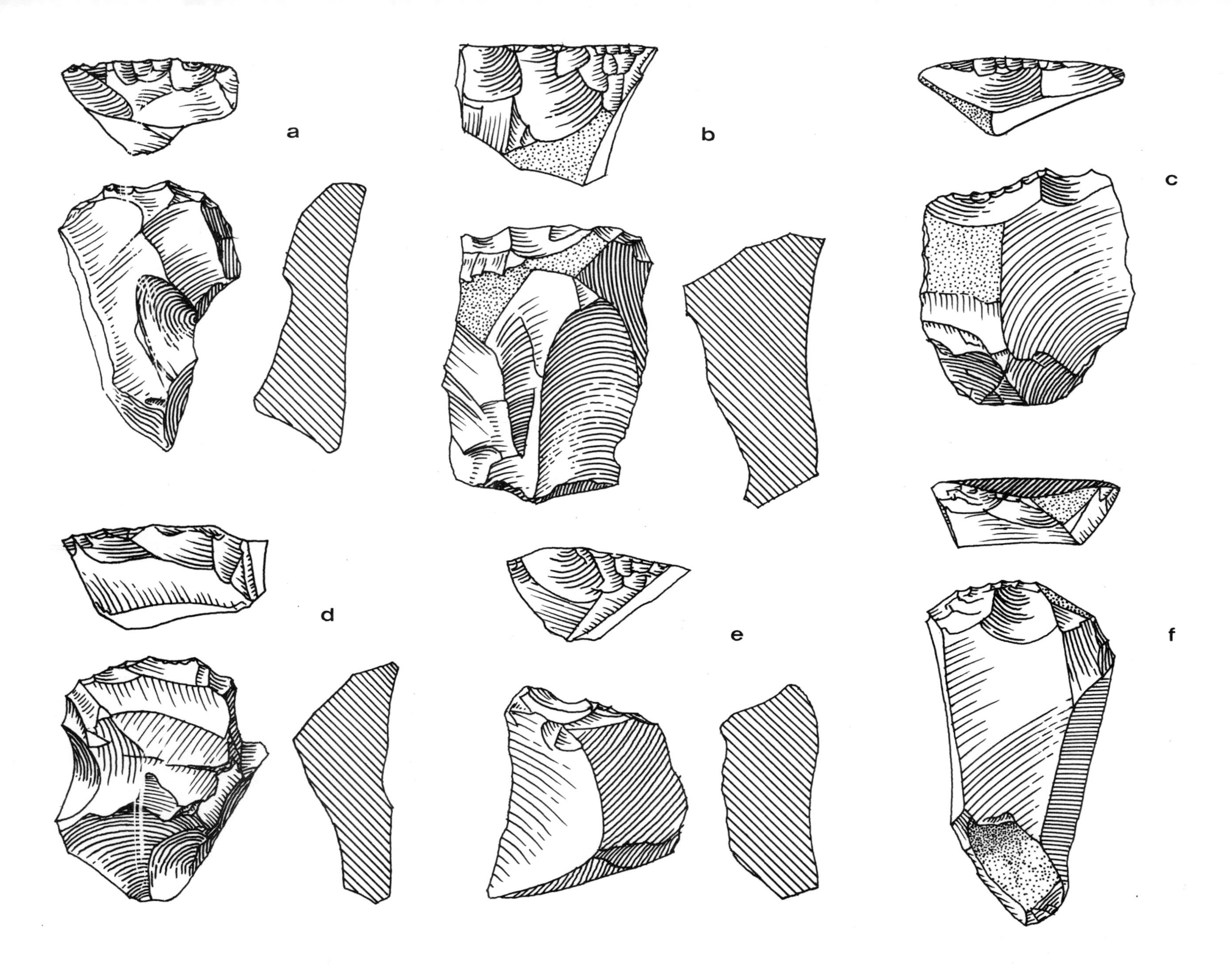
a
b
c
d
e
f

Figure 88. Side scrapers. a, CC:10:14, rhyolite; b, CC:10:11 Locus 2, rhyolite; c, CC:10:6, rhyolite; d, CC:10:6, chert; e, CC:9:2, basalt; f, CC:10:13, rhyolite.

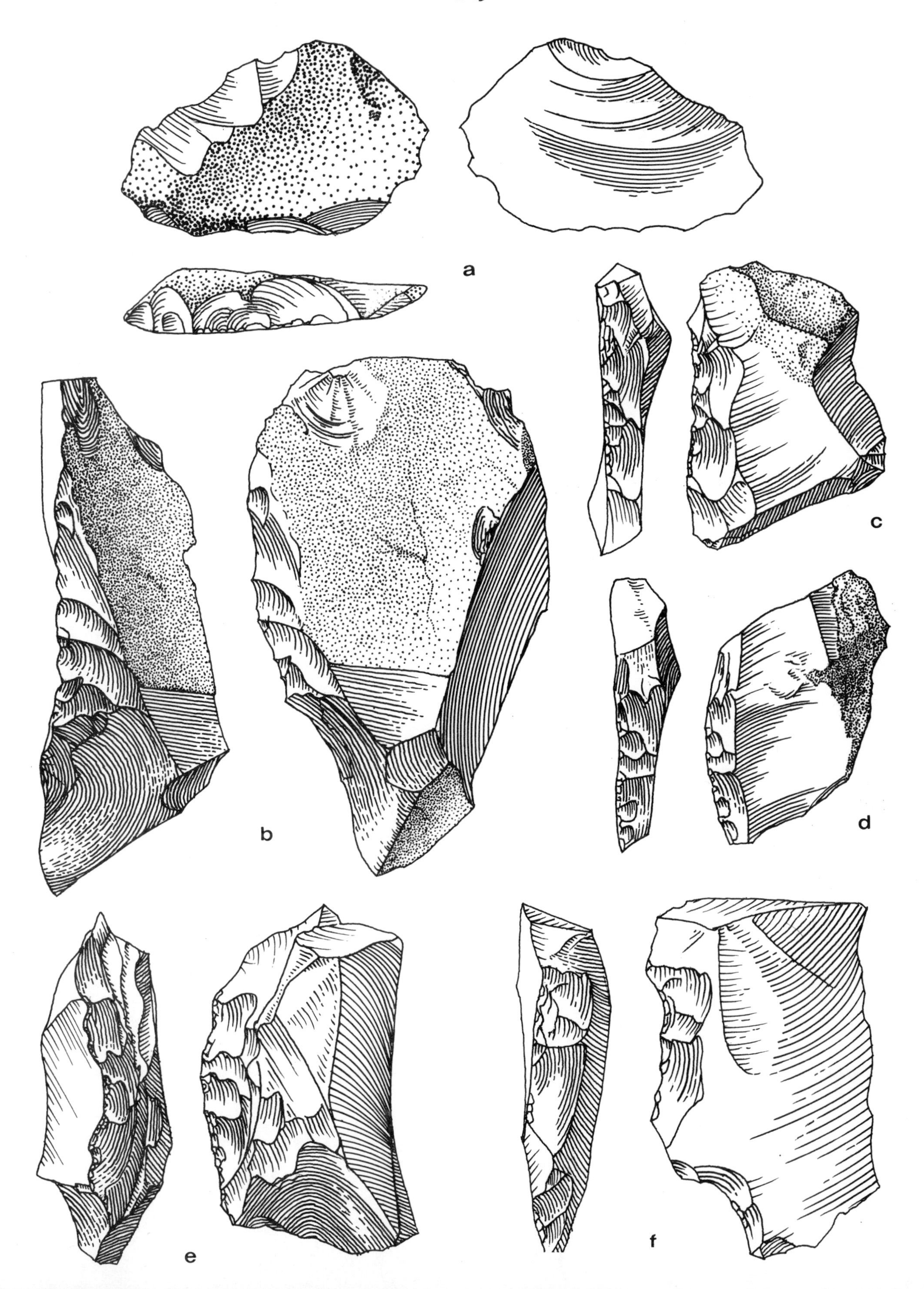
a
b
c
d
e
f

Figure 89. Multiside scrapers. a, CC:9:2, basalt; b, CC:10:11, Locus 1, felsite; c, CC:10:14, rhyolite; d, CC:10:13, rhyolite.

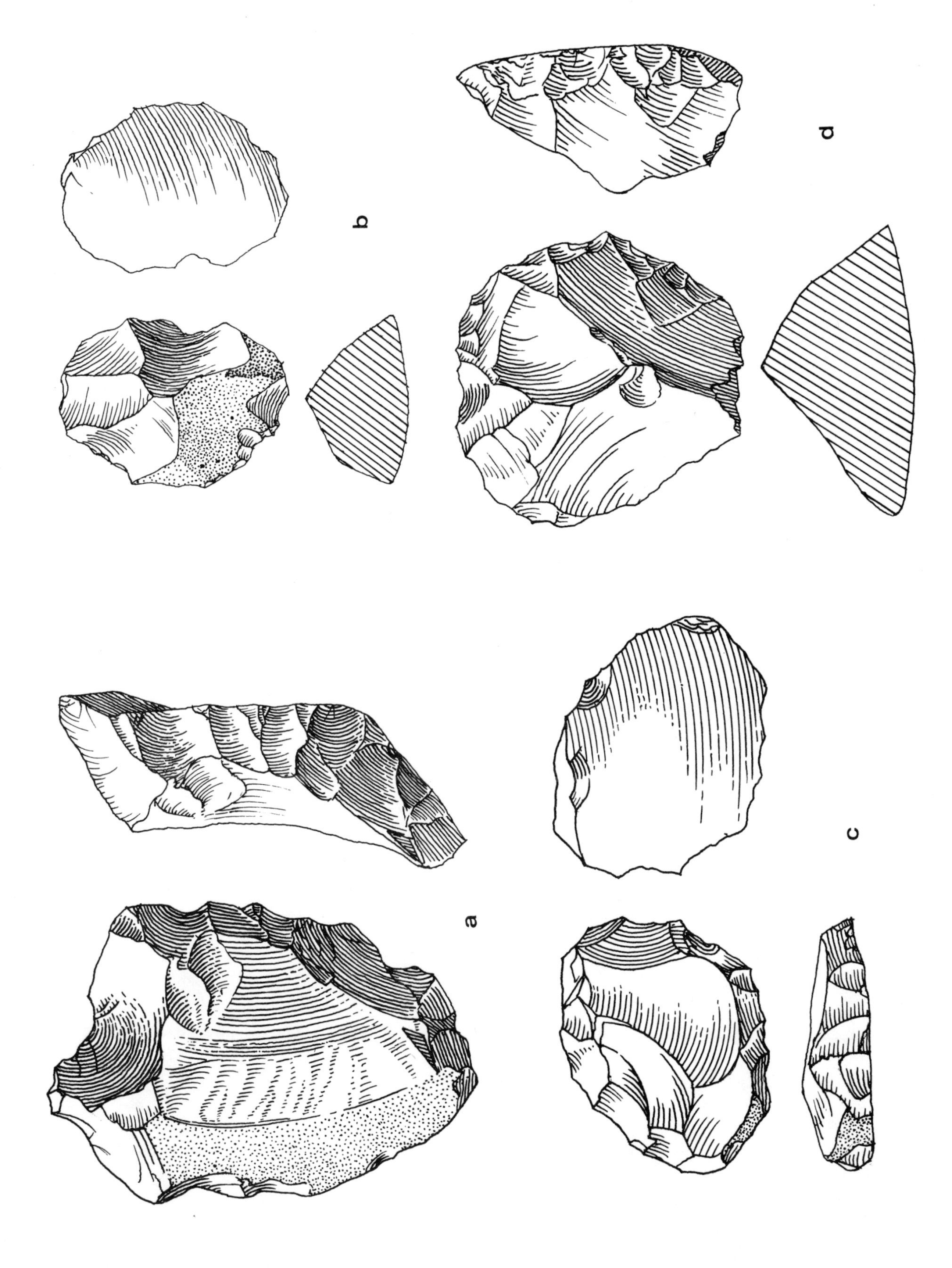

b
d
a
c

Figure 90. Denticulates. a, CC:10:13, rhyolite; b, CC:9:2, rhyolite; c, CC:10:14, rhyolite; d, CC:13:14, basalt; e, CC:10:11 Locus 2, chalcedony.

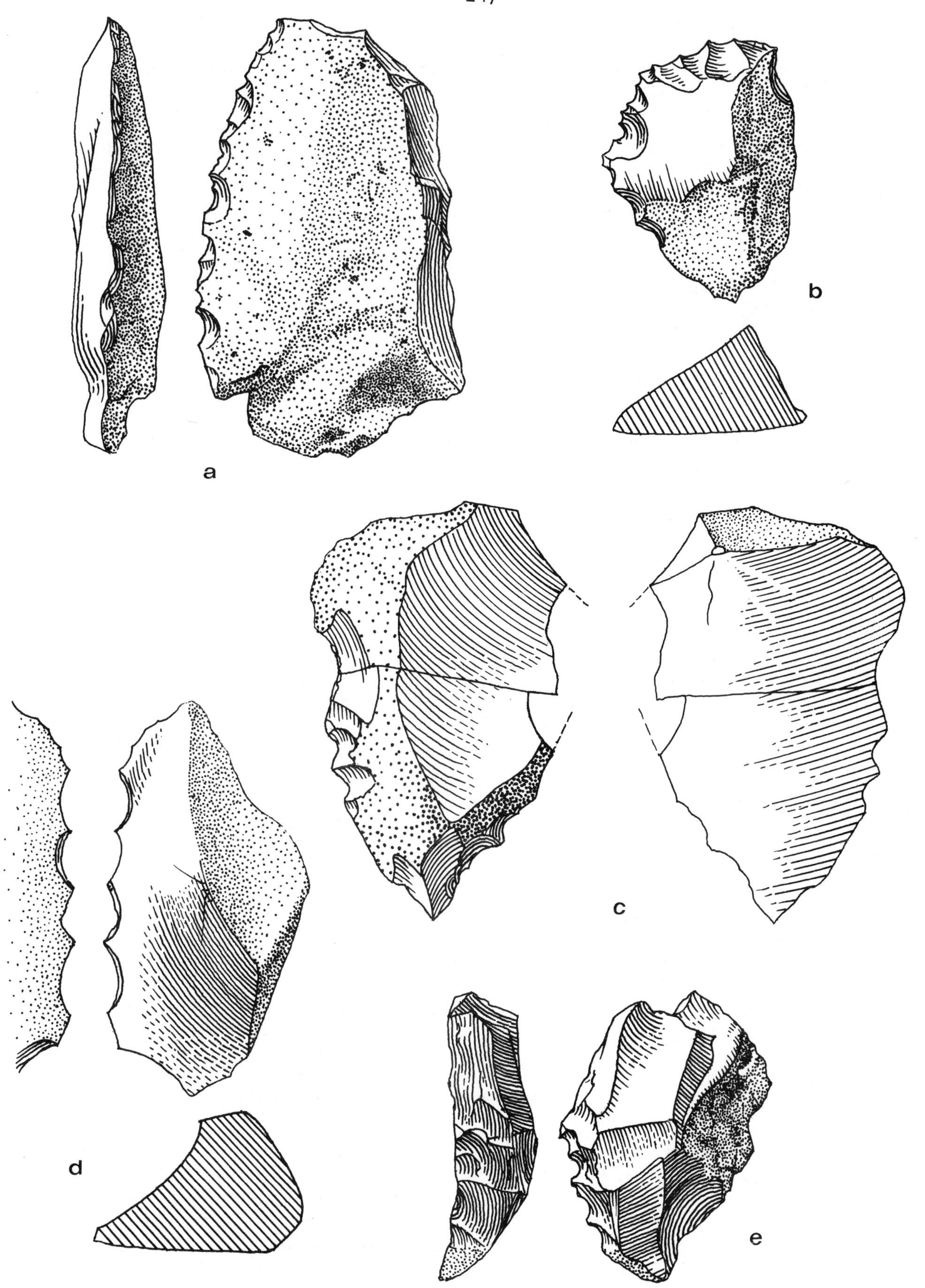
a
b
c
d
e

Burins. Four artifacts were classified as burins. Two of these collected from AZ CC:10:11 Sample 2 are naturally tabular fragments which were dealt blows in such a way as to remove long, thin flakes ("burin spalls") from at least one of the edges. This produced a chisel-like edge at the intersection of the platform to which the retouching blow was delivered and the negative bulb of the burin spall scar. The other two burins collected from AZ CC:9:2 (surface) show the kind of retouch but are made on flakes rather than natural fragments. Burins range in size from 42 to 71 mm.

Miscellaneous Flaked Chunks. This category was established in order to account for a relatively large number of irregularly shaped, angular fragments of stone which usually exhibit between two and four flake scars resulting from the removal of flakes after the fragment itself had been detatched from another piece of stone. Usually polyhedral in form, and ranging in size from 25 to 93 mm, the location of the retouch flake scars on most examples suggests that little or no attempt was made to produce a regular working edge. While one might call these artifacts "amorphous scrapers," it seems more likely that they are secondary cores rather than tools.

Miscellaneous Uniface Fragments. Broken artifacts showing unifacial retouch, but of such fragmentary condition they could not be assigned with confidence to any of the types identified thus far, were called uniface fragments. Included are artifacts which appear to have been broken during manufacture. Also included are artifacts which show less weathering on the surface of the snap or break than is found on the rest of the artifact, suggesting that they may have been broken some time after they had been discarded by their users. Although uniface fragments range in size from 16 to 83 mm, most are about 30 to 40 mm.

Light Retouched Pieces: Bifacial

Small Bifaces (complete and broken). Complete artifacts of this type are characteristically biconvex in cross section, usually irregularly oval, discoidal, or lanceolate in outline, exhibit flake scars resulting from the removal of flakes from both faces, and range in size from 32 to 96 mm in length. Continuous bifacial retouch is usually present along 50 to 100 percent of the perimeter, and the retouch flake scars frequently extend inward from the edge for a distance equal to about one-quarter to one-half of the artifact's width. In some instances, almost the entire surface of both of the faces is covered by retouch flake scars, while in other examples the retouch is less extensive and it is possible to identify the interior surfaces of the flake from which the biface was made. While there is considerable variation among examples with respect to relative thickness and edge regularity, most small bifaces tend to be thick in relation to their length and width, tend to have irregular, wavy edges, and were probably produced by direct percussion. On some examples, pronounced step fracturing is present along one portion of the perimeter, and suggests that many blows were delivered to the edge in an unsuccessful attempt to remove a flake. Incomplete small bifaces, about as numerous as complete examples, appear to be the remains of artifacts which snapped perpendicular to their long axes, possibly during manufacture. All of the fragments appear to be pieces of different artifacts. Because most of the small bifaces have irregular edges, and because many are broken and/or appear to represent unsuccessful attempts at bifacial thinning, it is likely that many of the artifacts are unfinished tools or "preforms." Some typical small bifaces are shown in Figure 91.

Projectile Points (complete and broken). Artifacts classified as projectile points are similar to the above-described type in that they exhibit bifacial retouch around most of their perimeter, have a biconvex cross section, and are usually triangular, lanceolate, or oval in outline. However, projectile points are distinguished from small bifaces on the basis of three criteria. First, the morphology and spacing of the retouch flake scars on projectile points strongly suggests that at least the final step in the manufacture of these tools was accomplished by pressure flaking rather than by direct percussion. In comparison tothe flake scars on small bifaces, those of projectile points tend to be smaller and more numerous, tend to be more regularly spaced, and are usually longer in relation to their width, often extending inward from the edge for a distance equal to one-half or more of the artifact's width. In general, the retouch on projectile points produced more regular edges than that characteristic of small bifaces.

Second, projectile points tend to be smaller than small bifaces. Whereas most of the latter are about 60 mm in length, complete examples of projectile points range in size from 19 to 50 mm, with most being about 30 mm in length.

Finally, projectile points are distinguished from small bifaces in that most of the former exhibit some aspect of form which indicates that the artifacts were hafted. Although it was beyond the scope of this study to develop a detailed projectile point typology, a brief description of the major variants in the collections will be presented.

Of those projectile points which show obvious specializations of form to facilitate hafting, two general categories can be distinguished on the basis of the form of the base (that portion of the implement that is assumed to have been hafted). First, there are those points which possess one or more basal notches, and second, there are those whose sides are constricted at the base to form a stem. Projectile points that are notched can be further classified on the basis of the number and location of the notches. For example, some of the points have only a single, usually shallow, notch on one end that produces a concave base, while others have two notches, one on each of the sides near the base. Some projectile points of the side-notched variety are also notched at their bases. Stemmed projectile points can be divided into two major groups—those whose stems converge at the hafted end of the artifact to form a point, and those in which the sides of the stem are parallel or only slightly converging.

In addition to those types which are either notched or stemmed, a comparatively small number of small, pressure-flaked bifaces which show no obvious specializaiton of form to facilitate hafting were also classified as projectile points. In general, these artifacts tend to be lanceolate or elongated oval

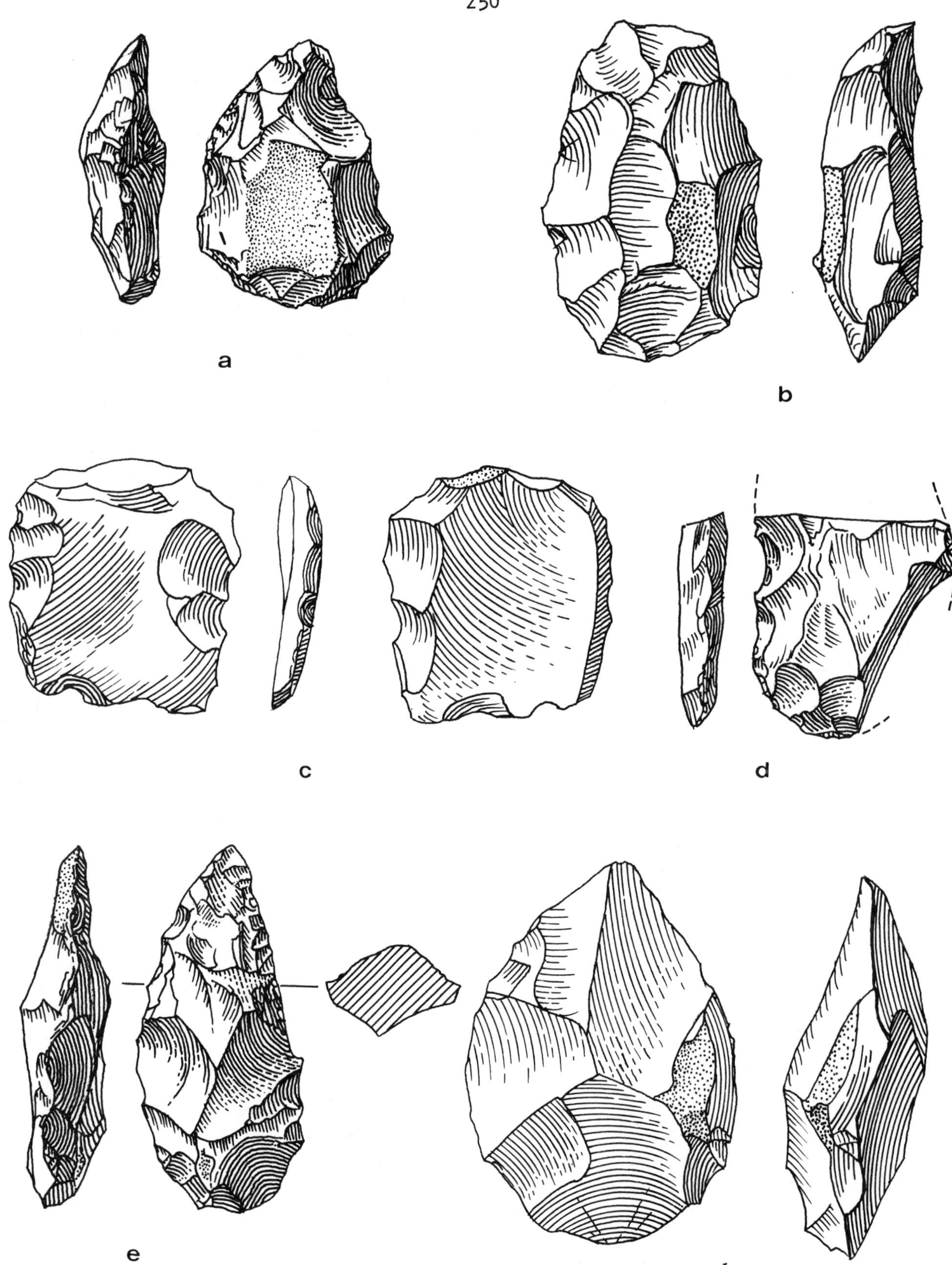

Figure 91. Small bifaces. a, CC:9:2, quartzite; b, CC:6:3, rhyolite; c,f, CC:10:14, rhyolite; d, CC:10:6, chert; e, CC:10:11 Locus 2, rhyolite.

in outline, and may have been hafted even though they are neither notched nor stemmed. The artifacts shown in Figures 92 and 93 were chosen to illustrate the range of formal variation in the projectile points of the AEPCO II collection.

Heavy Tools

Heavy tools are distinguished from light retouched pieces primarily on the basis of size, and are generally over 100 mm in maximum dimension. Most heavy tools are made on cobbles and are therefore core tools, although a small number of heavy tools consist of very large retouched flakes. Like light retouched pieces, heavy tools are separated into two major categories on the basis of whether the working edge was shaped by unifacial or bifacial flake removal.

Heavy Tools: Unifacial

Planes. In many aspects of form, these implements are similar to scrapers. All appear to have been made on cobbles, and have one flat surface which extends for much of the artifact's entire length, and which served as the platform for the unidirectional removal of flakes to form the working edge. Planes are irregularly circular or oval in outline, and are stongly planoconvex in cross section. In some examples, the thickness of the artifact, measured as the distance from the planar surface to the highest point on the opposite (convex) face, is as great as any dimension measured in the plane of the flat surface. The percentage of the artifact perimeter that shows flake scars from shaping the working edge is variable, but seldom exceeds 50 percent. In general, planes tend to have a very steep, angled working edge which in some cases approaches 90 degrees. Although planes resemble scrapers in shape, they differ in size. Planes are much larger than scrapers, ranging from 80 to 120 mm in length.

Unifacial Choppers. This is a diverse group of implements, some of which are made on cobbles and others which are made on large, thick flakes. All exhibit unifacial flake removal to produce a working edge on what is usually less than half of the artifact's perimeter. Choppers show less consistency in form than do planes, both with respect to shape and to character of the working edge. In general, however, choppers tend to be irregularly rectangular or oval in outline, and usually have a subrectangular cross section. The angle of the working edge tends to be less than that characteristic of planes, those with the lowest edge angles being cleaver-like. Unifacial choppers range in size from about 95 to 140 mm, and most are about 100 mm.

Heavy Tools: Bifacial

With but one exception, all of these artifacts are large, thick flakes which exhibit continuous bifacial retouch along one edge. In most examples, the retouch tends to be localized at one end, in relation to the long axis

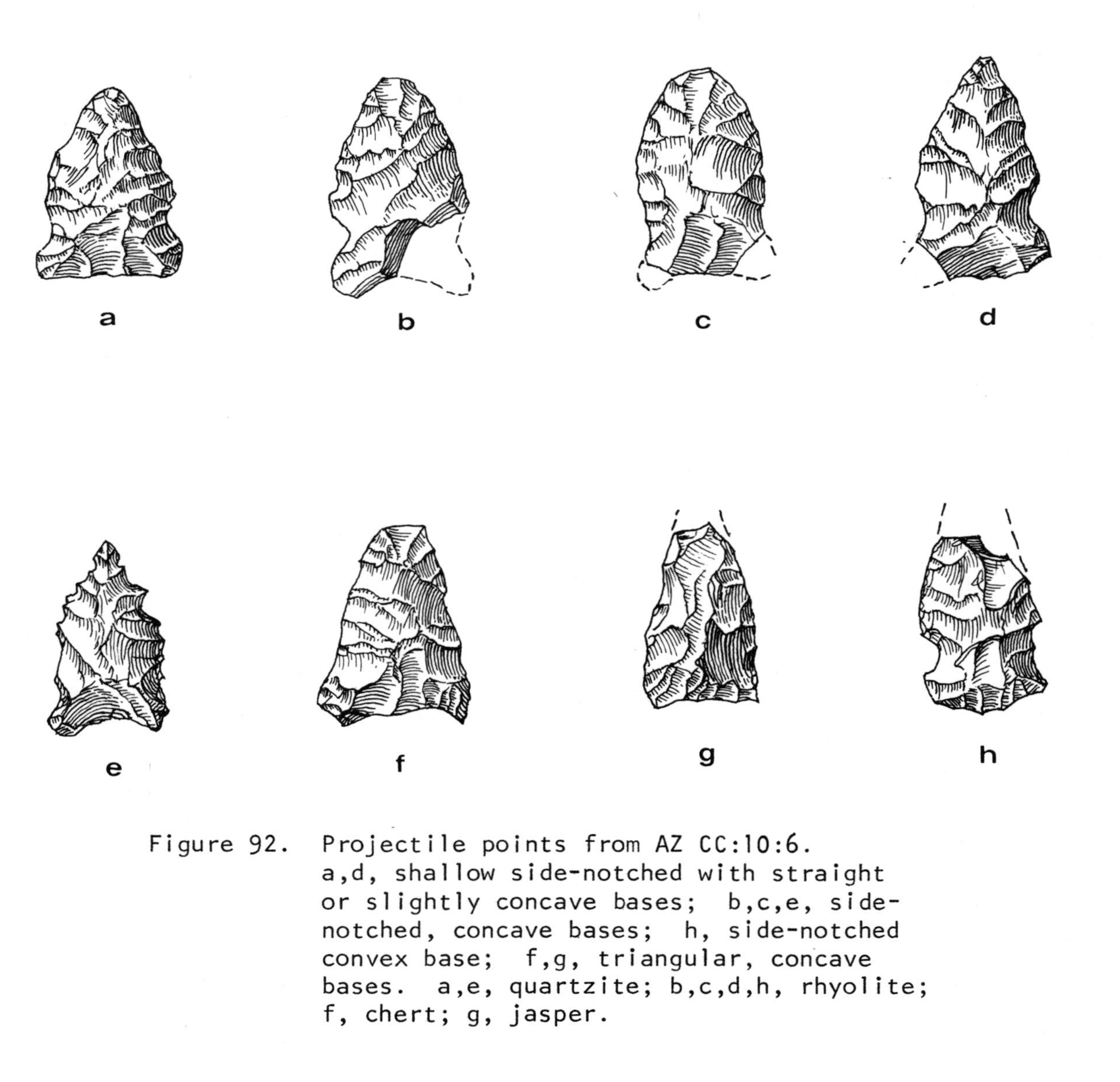

Figure 92. Projectile points from AZ CC:10:6. a,d, shallow side-notched with straight or slightly concave bases; b,c,e, side-notched, concave bases; h, side-notched convex base; f,g, triangular, concave bases. a,e, quartzite; b,c,d,h, rhyolite; f, chert; g, jasper.

of the artifact, and creates an irregularly shaped edge. Whether these artifacts represent finished tools (bifacial choppers) or the initial stages of bifacial reduction to shape a tool is not clear. The only heavy biface that is not made on a large flake was collected from AZ CC:13:6, and is made on a cobble. Heavy bifaces range in size from 106 to 120 mm in length.

Pebble Tools

A comparatively small number of artifacts, most of which were collected from AZ CC:6:3, consist of flaked pebbles which have forms suggesting that they were intended to be used as tools, rather than to serve as a source of flakes. Ranging in size from about 30 to 80 mm, these artifacts are highly variable in shape, and include both unifacial and bifacial forms. Some of the pebble tools bear a strong resemblance to various types of light retouched pieces, especially the scrapers and denticulate tools, and differ principally in that they are made on pebbles rather than flakes. Some typical pebble tools are shown in Figure 94.

Hammerstones

Most of these artifacts are spheriods or subspheriods, measuring between 55 to 79 mm in diameter, which show battering over 50 to 100 percent of their surfaces. Most examples are polyhedral cores and are rounded from battering.

Comparative Observations

Reduction Product Frequencies

Histograms of the relative frequencies of artifacts by reduction product categories are given for each of the collections in Figure 95. These histograms show that, with but one exception (AZ CC:6:3), the collections are all similar to each other in that reduction product frequencies are of the same relative magnitudes. In descending order of frequency, the artifact classes are unretouched fragments, unretouched complete flakes, retouched pieces, and cores. AZ CC:6:3 represents a dramatic departure from this pattern, with cores making up almost 50 percent of the collection. In descending order of frequency, the remainder of artifacts from AZ CC:6:3 are unretouched complete flakes, unretouched fragments, and retouched pieces.

Although the remaining 11 collections show the same relative magnitudes of reduction product frequencies, variation among these collections can be seen by comparing the frequencies of any one artifact type. For example, retouched pieces are more abundant at AZ CC:10:15 than they are at AZ CC:13:14, and the frequency of cores at AZ CC:10:13 is higher than it is at AZ CC:13:11. In order that the collection could be more easily compared with respect to reduction product frequencies, a single cumulative graph was constructed

Figure 93. Projectile points from AZ CC:9:2. a-e, contracting stemmed; f-i, small, parallel stemmed; j,k, shallowly side-notched, concave bases; l,m, ovate forms with no modifications to facilitate hafting; n,o, side-notched, convex bases; p, a typical form. a,b,d,g,m,n, rhyolite; c,l, chert; e,f,p, obsidian; h, basalt; i, igneous; j, chalcedony; k,o, jasper.

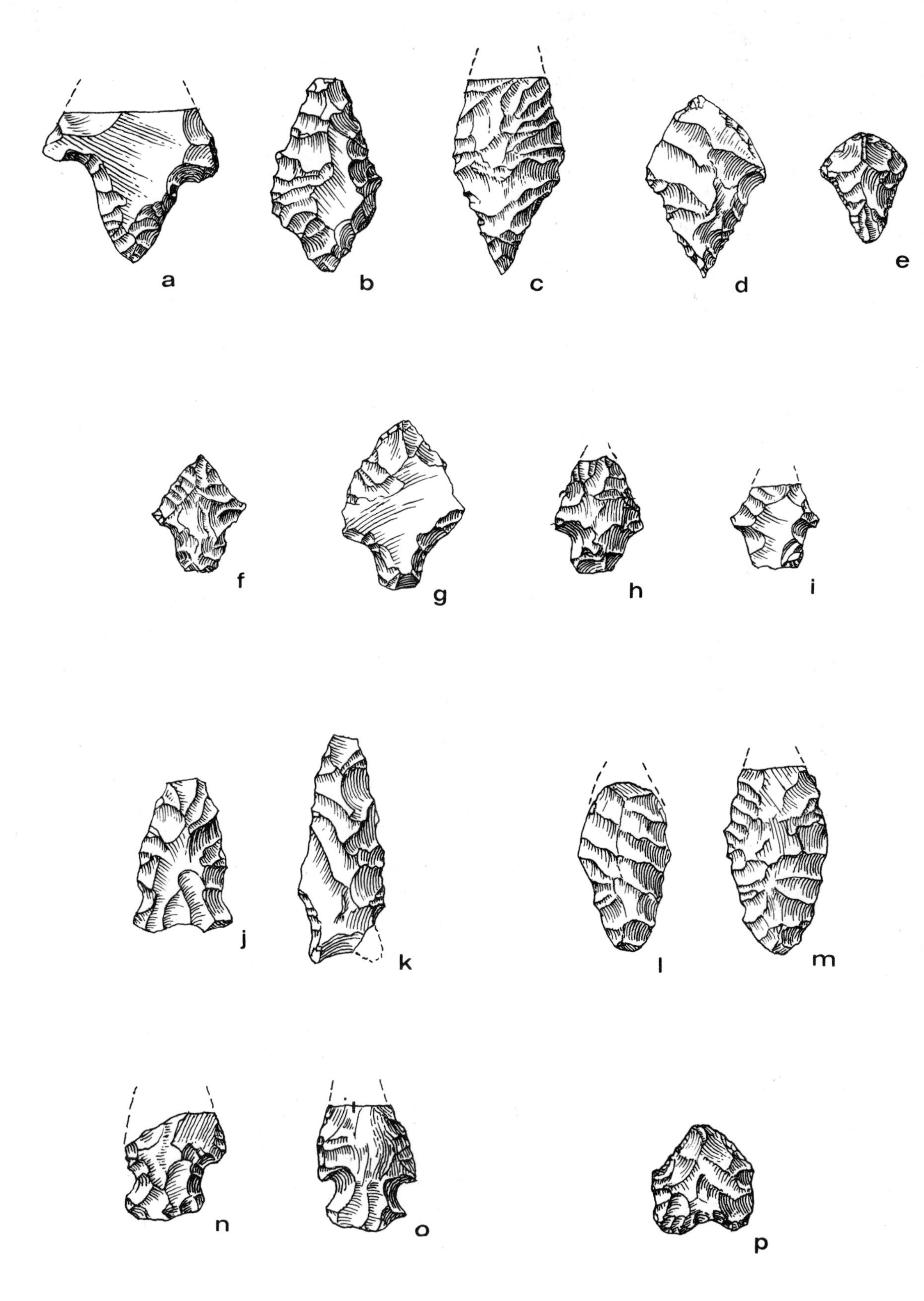
a
b
c
d
e
f
g
h
i
j
k
l
m
n
o
p

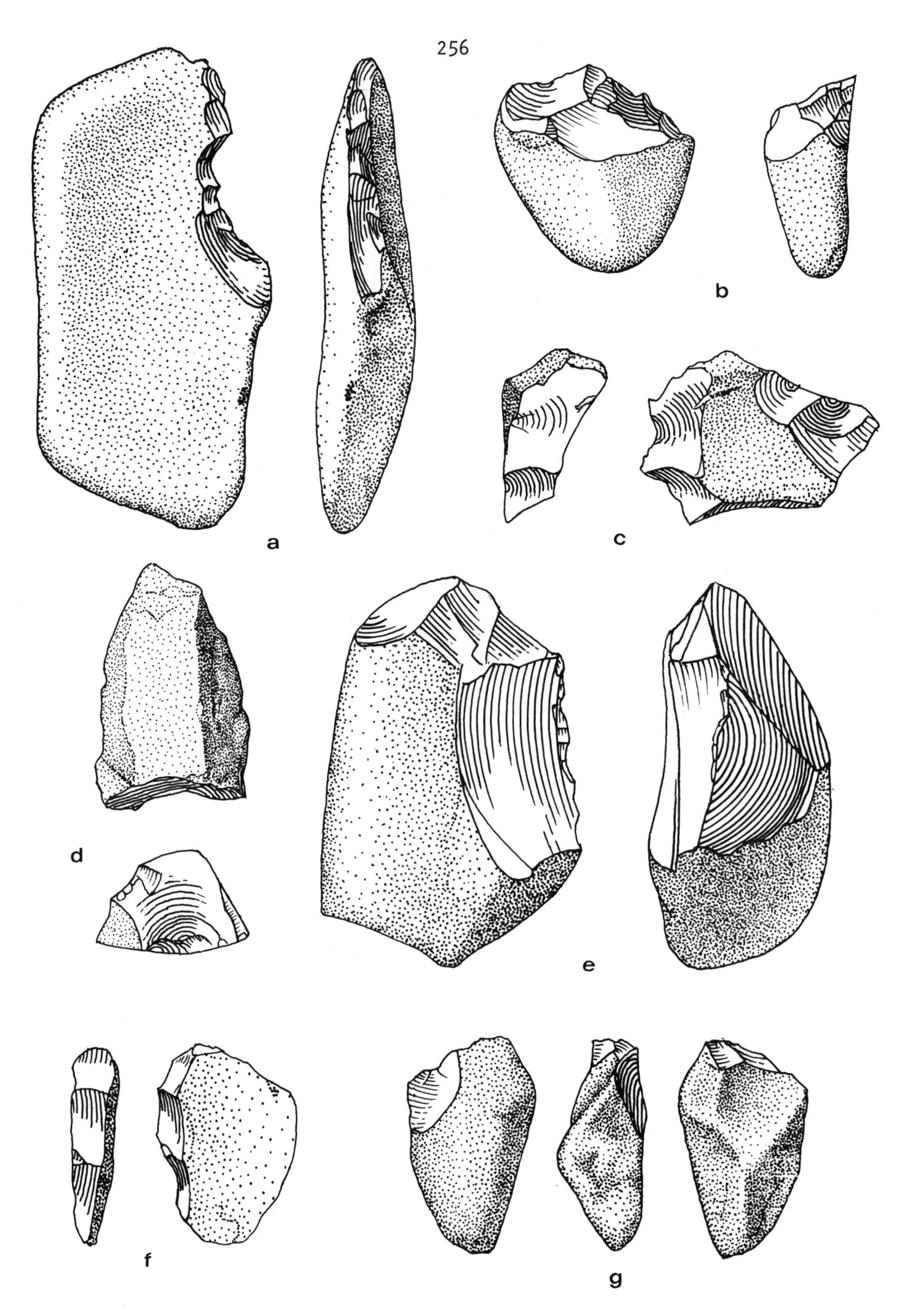

Figure 94. Pebble tools from AZ CC:6:3. a, basalt; b, metamorphic; c,d,g, rhyolite; e, gneiss; f, chalcedony.

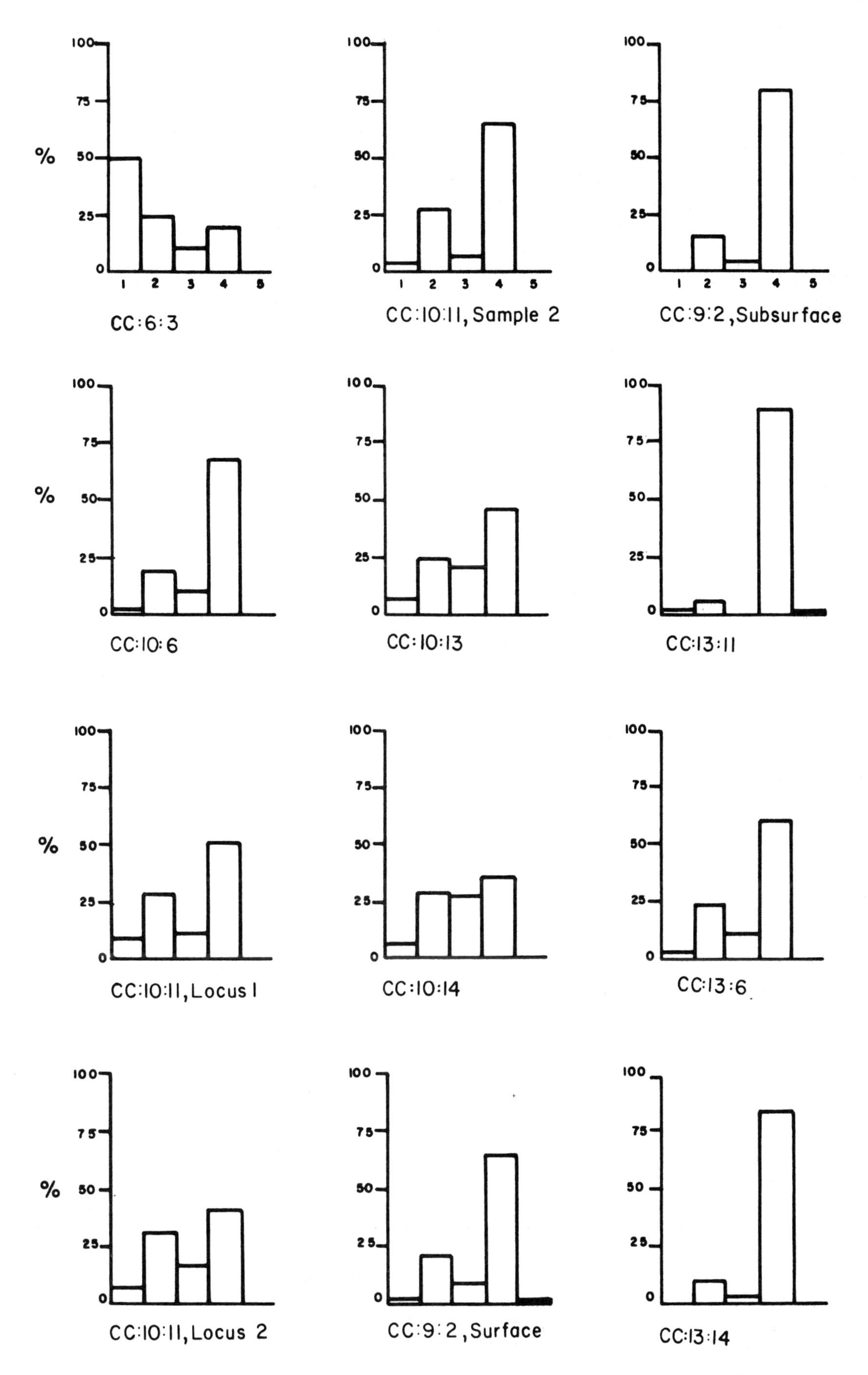

Figure 95. Reduction product frequency histograms

(Figure 96). On the basis of this graph, three general groups of collections can be distinguished. AZ CC:13:14, AZ CC:13:11, and AZ CC:9:2 (subsurface) are distinguished from all other collections in that they show the highest frequencies of unretouched fragments and the lowest frequencies of cores, unretouched complete flakes, and retouched pieces. AZ CC:10:11 Sample 2, AZ CC:10:6, AZ CC:9:2 (surface), and AZ CC:13:6 are slightly higher in cores, unretouched complete flakes, and retouched pieces, and lower in unretouched fragments. AZ CC:10:13, AZ CC:10:14, AZ CC:10:11 Locus 1 and 2 are grouped together because they show the highest core frequencies and lowest unretouched fragment frequencies of any of the collections, with the exception of AZ CC:6:3. The four collections contained in this last group can be divided into two subgroups on the basis of the frequency of retouched pieces. The collections from AZ CC:10:13 and 14 are higher in retouched pieces than those from AZ CC:10:11 Locus 1 and 2.

Complete Flakes

Length, Width, and Thickness of Complete Flakes. In order that differences among the collections in terms of the frequencies with which flakes of various shapes and sizes occur could be identified, length-versus-width scatter diagrams were constructed (Figure 97a-l). This was done by plotting the length and width of each flake as a single point in relation to a vertical axis representing length and a horizontal axis representing width in one millimeter increments.

The scatter diagrams indicate that differences exist in terms of the range of flake sizes and shapes, the degree to which flakes tend to be concentrated or dispersed around certain dimensions, and the lengths and widths which show the greatest concentration of flakes. It is important to note that one source of variation in the scatter diagrams is the different sample sizes. For example, AZ CC:9:2 (surface) in comparison to AZ CC:13:6 shows a much denser concentration of flakes in the region defined by 10 to 20 mm length and 10 to 20 mm width (Figure 97f, k). This observation cannot be used to infer variation between the collections because the sample size of flakes from AZ CC:13:6 is very small. The problem of small sample size can also be seen when comparing the diagrams from AZ CC:9:2 (subsurface), AZ CC:13:11, AZ CC:13:6, and AZ CC:13:14. Minor differences might be identified, but because of the small sample sizes, these collections are considered indistinguishable in terms of flake length and width.

When the sample sizes are larger, differences can be identified with more confidence. It is clear, for example, that the flakes from AZ CC:9:2 (surface) tend to be smaller than those from AZ CC:10:13 (Figure 97f, g). It is also evident that flakes from AZ CC:9:2 (subsurface) tend to cluster more tightly along the length-equals-width line. In contrast, flakes at AZ CC:10:13 are more dispersed and exhibit a greater range of size and shape (Figure 97i,g).

In some cases differences in the diagrams of two collections are so great that there may be some basis for inferring variation, event through the sample sizes are small. For example, AZ CC:10:14 and AZ CC:13:14 both have only approximately 50 flakes. It is obvious, however, that flakes at AZ CC:10:14 tend to be larger and exhibit a greater range of size and shape,

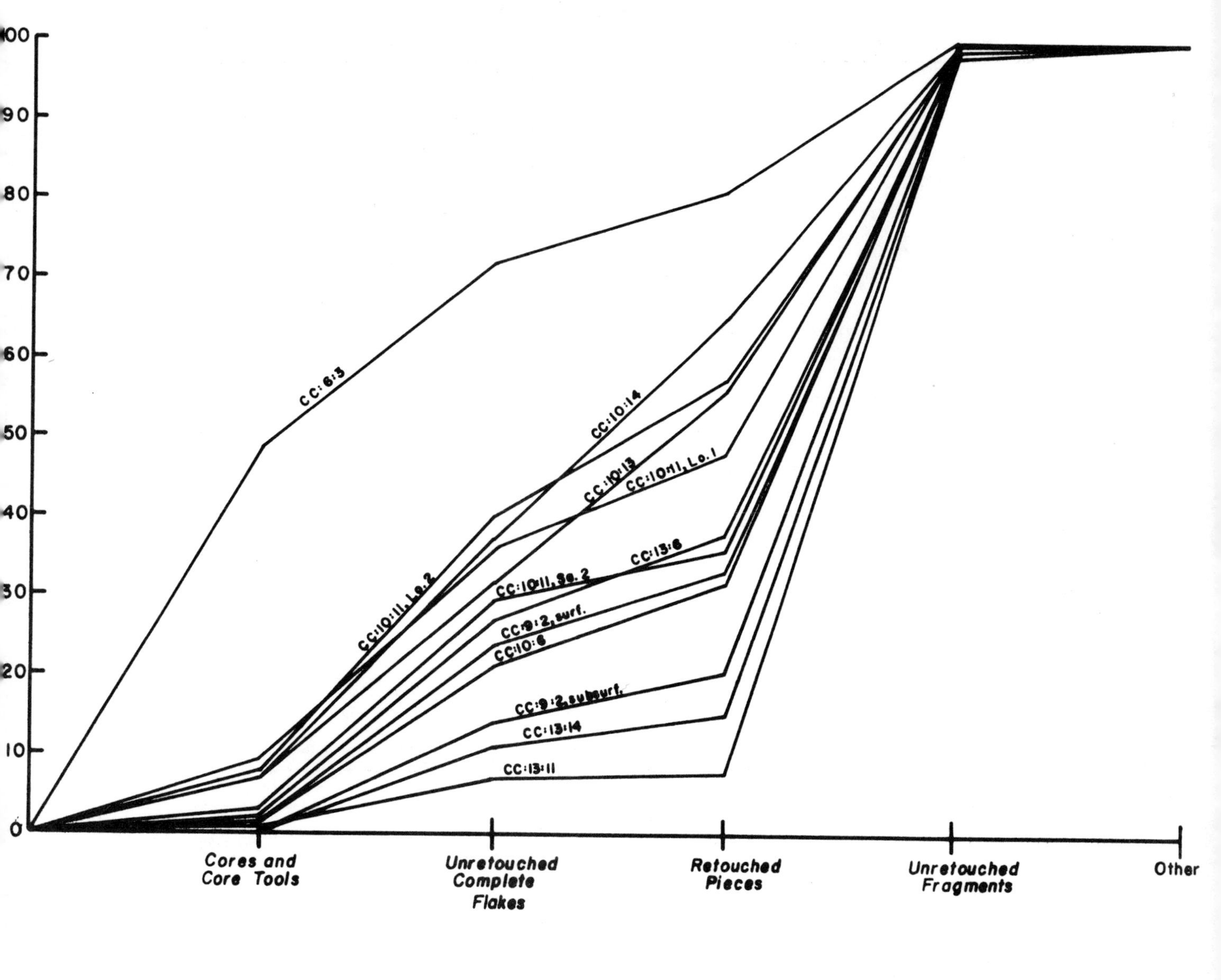

Figure 96. Cumulative graph of lithic artifact frequencies by category and site.

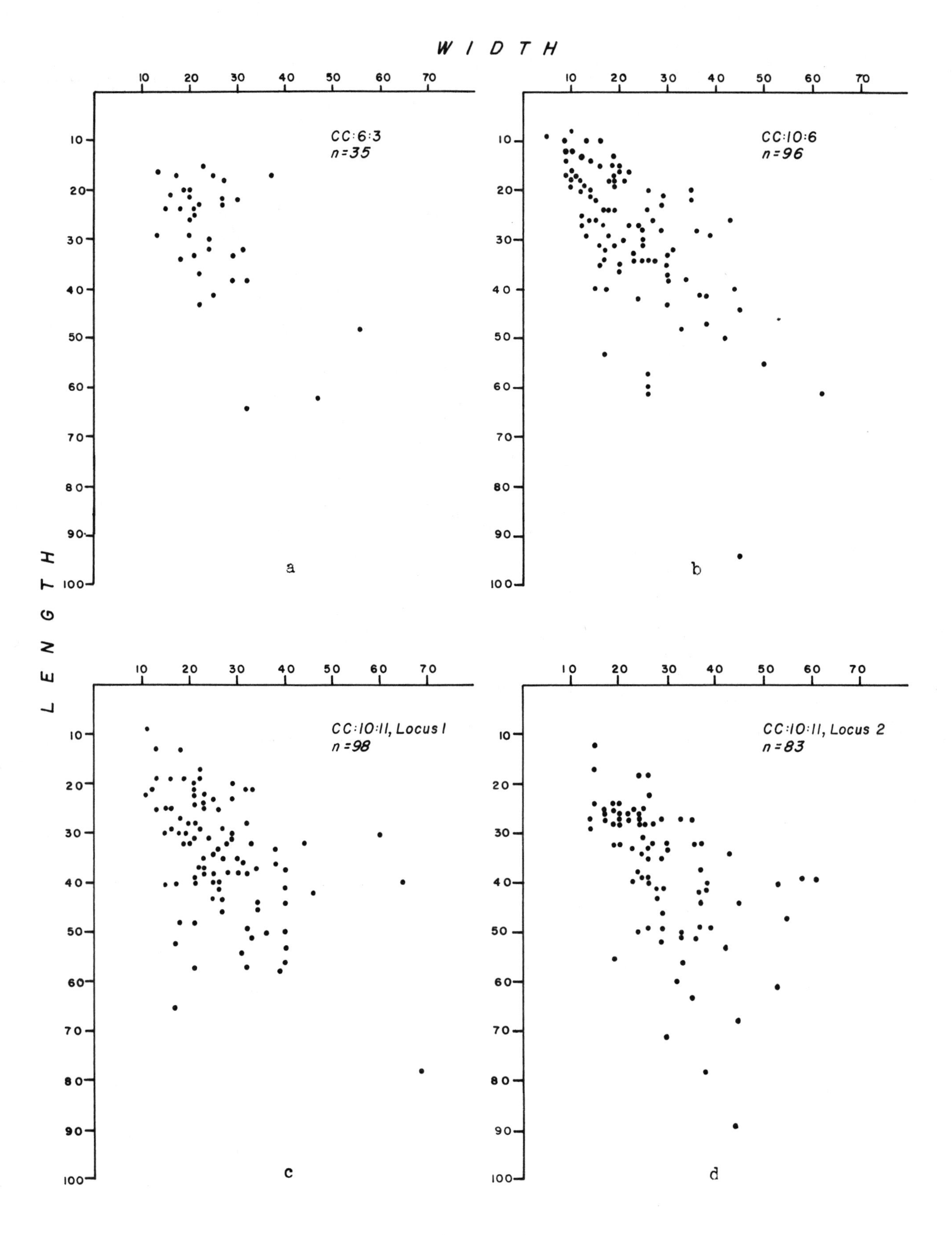

Figure 97. Flake length and width scatter diagrams.

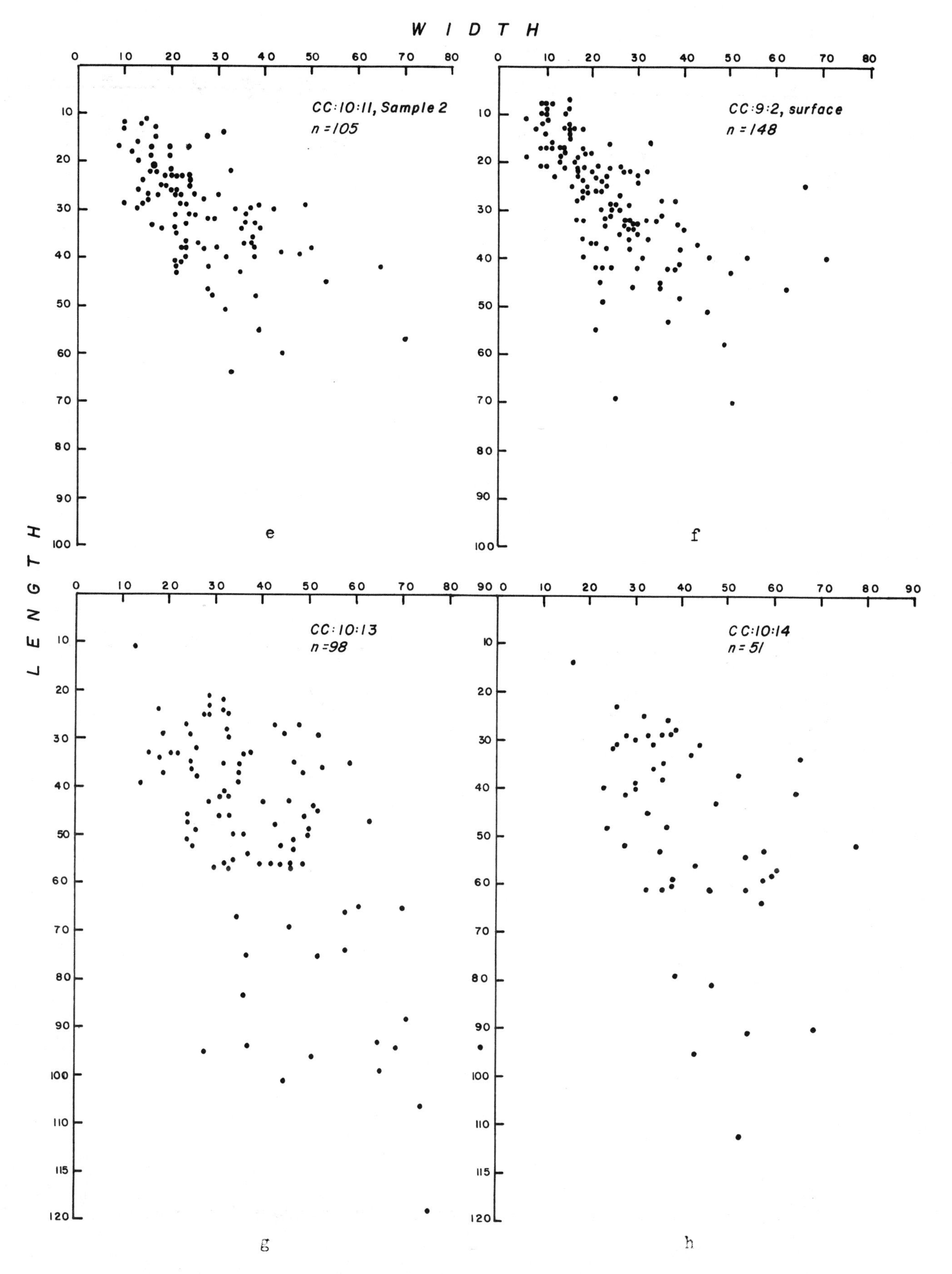

Figure 97. Flake length and width scatter diagrams (continued).

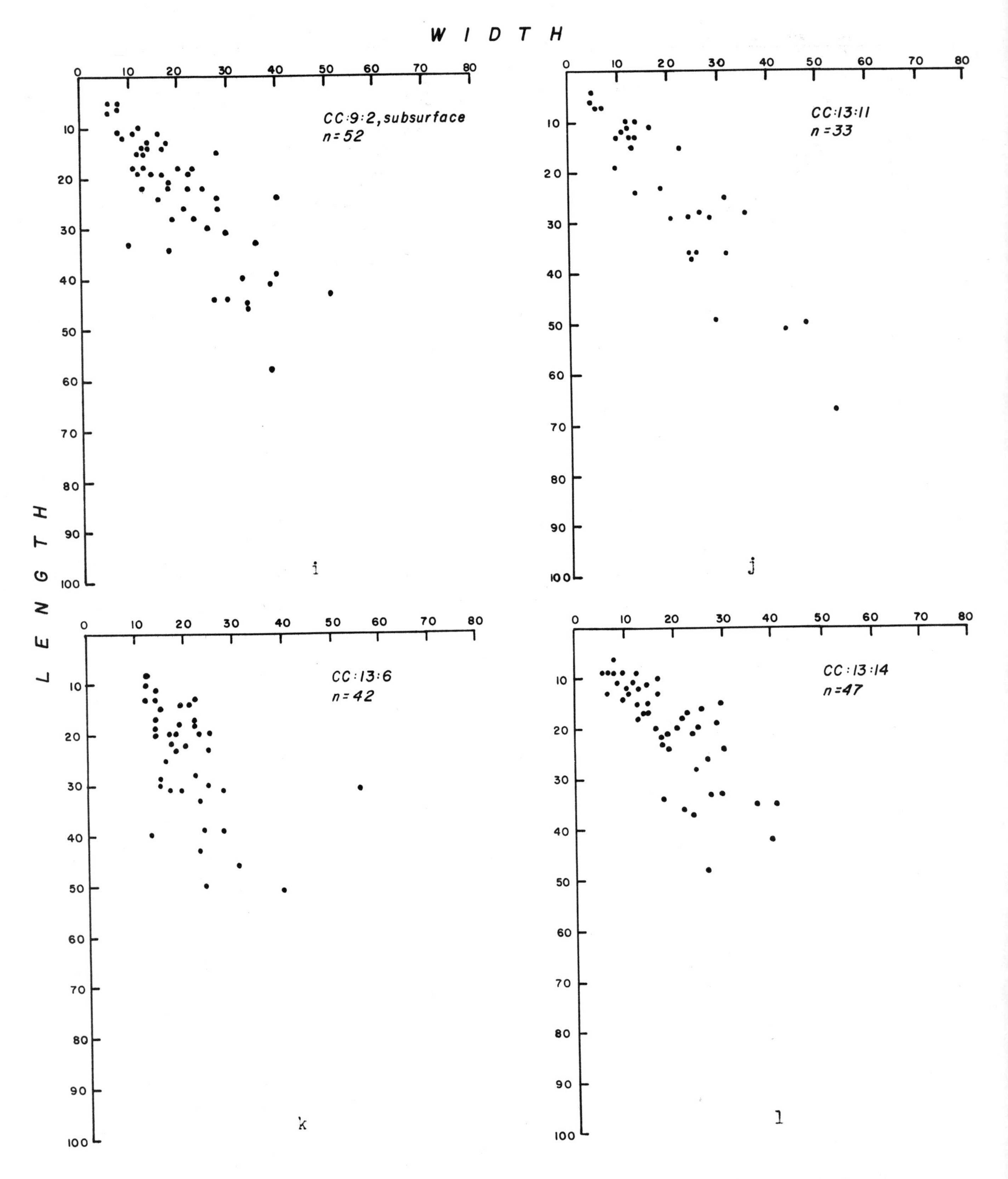

Figure 97. Flake length and width scatter diagrams (continued).

and in general, look very similar to those from AZ CC:10:13 (Figure 97g,h). The diagram for AZ CC:13:14 shows a much more restricted distribution, with flakes tending to be smaller than those at AZ CC:10:14 (Figure 97h, l).

In order that the basic characteristics of the flake samples be more easily assessed, the mean lengths and widths of flakes for each collection were plotted on a single scatter diagram (Figure 98). This figure indicates that in all cases, flakes tend to be slightly longer than they are wide, and that there is a continuum of mean flake length and width with respect to size. Flakes from both AZ CC:10:13 and 14 are larger than flakes from any other collection. AZ CC:10:11 Locus 1 and Locus 2 have the next largest mean lengths and widths, with Locus 2 being about 2 mm greater in mean length and about 1 mm greater in mean width. Because the mean lengths and widths for the rest of the collections are close together (within a range of 10 mm length and 7 mm width), and because the sample sizes for some of these collections are very small, differences cannot be identified as easily. For example, the similarity of AZ CC:13:6, 11, 14, and AZ CC:9:2 (subsurface) evident in the scatter diagrams (Figure 97) is also apparent in Figure 98. AZ CC:13:6, 11 and AZ CC:9:2 have nearly identical mean widths, and differ from each other in terms of mean length by only 2 mm or less. The collection showing the smallest flake length and width, AZ CC:13:14, can probably not be distinguished from AZ CC:13:6, 11, or AZ CC:9:2 (subsurface).

AZ CC:9:2 (surface), AZ CC:6:3, AZ CC:10:6, and 11 Sample 2 are all very similar with respect to mean length and width, with AZ CC:9:2 (surface) and AZ CC:10:6 being almost identical (Figure 98).

In the hope that differences among the collections with respect to flake length and width could be statistically demonstrated, the SPSS program "ONEWAY" was used to perform an analysis of variance on the length and width data, including the calculation of the 95 percent confidence intervals for the mean length and width for each collection. The results of this analysis indicate that for almost all collections the 95 percent confidence interval of any one collection overlaps, with both the intervals for the collections having the next largest and smallest mean length and width. While the overlapping of the length and width confidence intervals may in some cases be attributed to small sample sizes, it is also the product of the standard deviations calculated for length and width which tend to be very large in comparison to those for thickness. This suggests that thickness may be a more useful variable for the purposes of distinguishing samples of flakes. Further, if it is assumed that length, width, and thickness are correlated by mere virtue of the fact that they are nonindependent variables, then differences among samples in terms of thickness may be used to infer variation in length, width, and general flake size, as well.

Making this assumption, attempts at demonstrating differences in terms of flake size were focused on thickness. Figure 99 shows flake thickness frequency histograms for each of the collections as constructed from the data given in Appendix III, Table 38. These frequency distributions are similar to each other in that they are skewed to the left. However, differences can be identified in terms of range, mode, and the degree to which they are

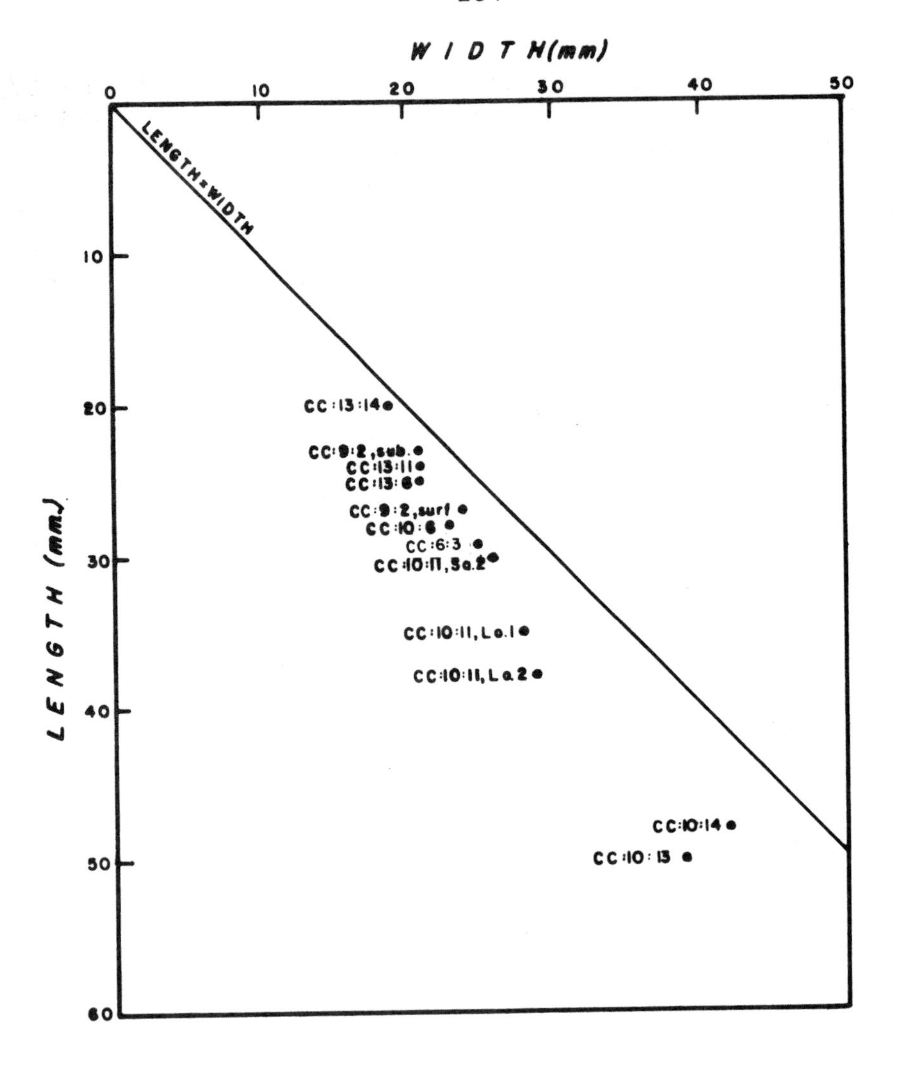

	Mean Length	Mean Width
CC:6:3	29.1	24.7
CC:10:6	28.3	22.5
CC:10:11, Locus 1	34.8	28.2
CC:10:11, Locus 2	37.5	29.2
CC:10:11, Sample 2	30.5	25.8
CC:10:13.	49.8	39.2
CC:10:14	48.1	41.7
CC: 9:2, Surface	27.2	23.6
CC:9:2, Subsurface	23.2	20.9
CC:13:11	24.0	21.0
CC:13:6	24.6	20.6
CC:13:14	19.9	19.3

Figute 98. Mean flake length and width scatter diagram for all lithic collections.

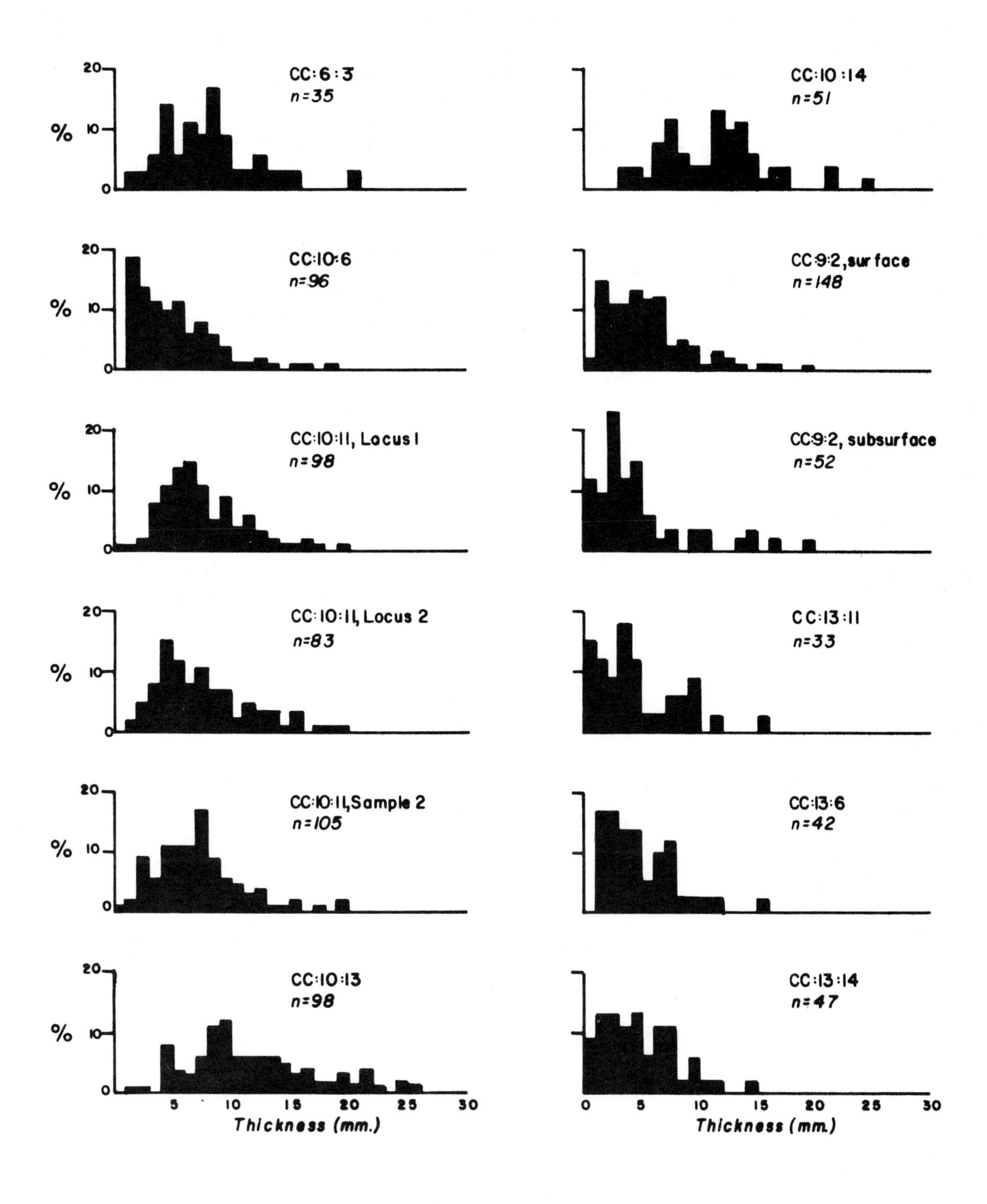

Figure 99. Flake thickness frequency histograms for all lithic collections.

skewed. It will be noted, for example, that in comparison to the other distributions, those for AZ CC:10:13 and 14 exhibit the greatest ranges, have high modes, and are not as strongly skewed. In contrast the distributions from AZ CC:9:2(surface and subsurface), AZ CC:10:6, AZ CC:13:6, 11, and 14 exhibit smaller ranges, the lowest modes, and are the most strongly skewed in comparison to the other collections. The distribution for AZ CC:6:3, AZ CC:10:11 Locus 1 and 2, and AZ CC:10:11 Sample 2 are similar to the above in that they have about the same range, but they differ in that they are less strongly skewed and have higher modes.

An analysis of variance of the flake thickness data was done using the SPSS subprogram 'ONEWAY', which among other values, calculated the mean, standard deviation and 95 percent confidence interval for the frequency distribution for each sample of flakes. These values are given in Appendix III, Table 45. Figure 100 shows the 95 percent confidence intervals for the mean thicknesses for each collection plotted against a single thickness scale.

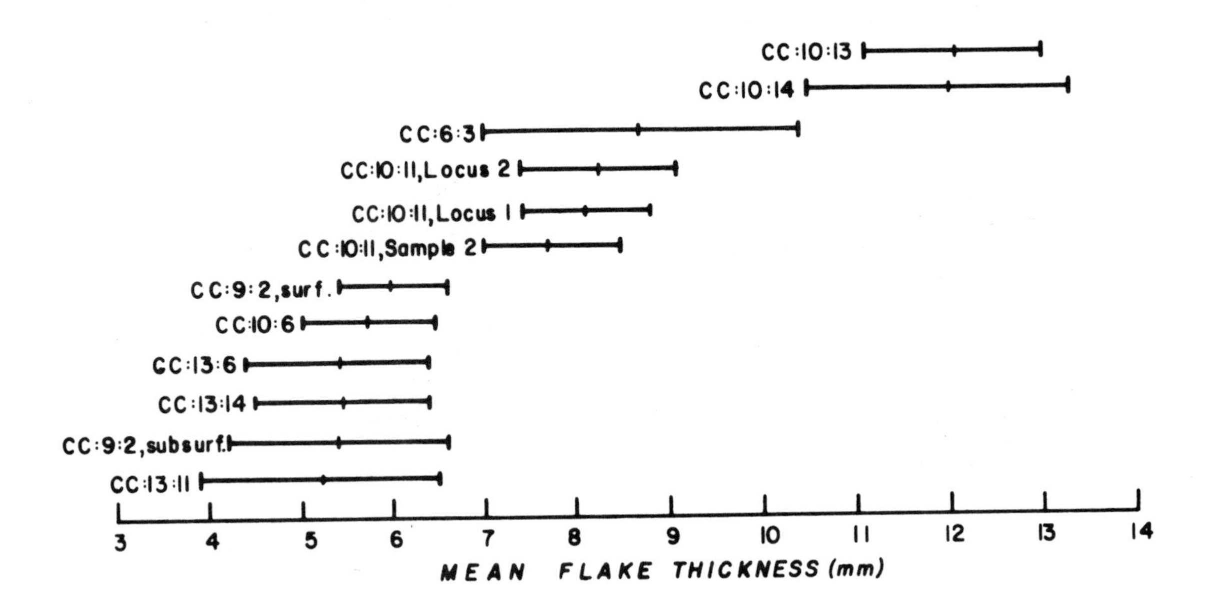

Figure 100. Ninety-five percent confidence intervals for the mean thickness for flakes in each collection.

This figure suggests that three groups of collections can be distinguished on the basis of flake thickness; those having mean flake thicknesses between 5 and 6 mm (AZ CC:13:6, 11, 14, and AZ CC:10:6, and AZ CC:9:2 surface and subsurface), those having mean thicknesses between 7 and 9 mm (AZ CC:10:11 all collections, and AZ CC:6:3), and those having mean thickness of about 12 mm (AZ CC:10:13 and 14). That only three groups of collections can be statistically distinguished out of a total of twelve samples is not surprising considering that the small size of some of the samples causes the confidence intervals to be wide. Therefore the chances of intervals overlapping are increased.

If it is assumed that thickness is correlated with length and width, then, it can be said that three groups of collections can be distinguished on the basis of flake size—small, medium, and large. In fact, when the collections are arranged in order of mean thickness, the sequence is not exactly the same as that obtained when the collections are arranged in order of width or thickness. The most obvious descrepancy between the relative magnitudes of thickness and length can be seen in the data from AZ CC:6:3. While this collection has the third largest mean thickness, its mean length is only the sixth largest. This indicates that flakes from AZ CC:6:3 tend to be unusually chunky in shape in comparison to flakes from the other collections.

Although the sequence of the samples when ordered by increasing mean flake thickness is not the same as that obtained when the samples are arranged by mean flake length or width, in no case do descrepencies in the order cross cut the three groups of samples as defined by the thickness confidence intervals. Therefore, the assumption that length, width, and thickness are correlated would seem to be valid, although variation in flake shape between the samples is suggested.

In summarizing variability in terms of flake size and shape, it is clear that the small size of some of the samples has placed a limit on the level of specificity which can be used in distinguishing the samples. However, it is reasonable to assume that the collections can be confidently assigned to one of the three flake size categories as defined by difference in thickness. As populations, flakes from AZ CC:10:6, AZ CC:9:2 (surface and subsurface), AZ CC:13:6, 11, and 14 tend to be small. Medium sized flakes are characteristic at AZ CC:10:11 Locus 1, Locus 2, and Sample 2, and at AZ CC:6:3. Samples of flakes which fall into the large category are those from AZ CC:10:13 and 14. Variation among the samples in terms of flake shape is suggested by differences in mean thicknesses in relation to length and width, but the significance of these differences is unclear when comparing collections which only have small samples of flakes.

Cortex on Complete Flakes. As originally recorded, flakes were placed in one of six classes on the basis of the percentage of the exterior surface that was observed to be cortical. For the purposes of the analysis, the two classes representing the least percentage of cortex, (Class 0 and 1) were combined. Also combined were the two classes representing the greatest percentages of cortex (Classes 4 and 5). This was done because it was felt that the distinctions between 0 percent and 0 to 10 percent cortex, and between 90 to 100 percent and 100 percent cortex were neither useful nor necessary in view of the distributions obtained. Therefore, histograms showing the frequency distribution of flakes with respect to only four cortex classes (Figure 101) are presented for each collection. The cortex classes are as follows: Class 1 (0 - 10 percent), Class 2 (10 - 50 percent), Class 3 (50 - 90 percent), and Class 4 (90 - 100 percent).

Inspection of these figures indicates that the collection can be placed into three arbitrarily defined groups on the basis of the histogram shapes. First, there are those samples in which approximately 50 percent or more of the flakes fall in the 0 - 10 percent cortex class, with the remainder composed of progressively lower percentages distributed across the higher cortex classes. Collections assigned to this group are from AZ CC:10:6, AZ CC:10:11 Locus 2 and Sample 2, AZ CC:9:2 (surface and subsurface), AZ CC:13:6, 11, and 14. These collections are said to have low levels of cortex on flakes.

Second, there are those collections in which flakes are more or less evenly distributed with respect to the cortex classes, such as those from AZ CC:10:11 Locus 1 and AZ CC:10:13. These two collections have samples of flakes which show moderate cortex levels.

Third, there are those collections which have high levels of cortex on flakes, such as those from AZ CC:6:3 and AZ CC:10:14. In the case of the former, the 50 to 90 percent class is the most strongly represented, while in the latter, flakes having 10 to 50 percent cortex are most frequent.

It should be emphasized that the categorization of the collections into these three groups is largely a matter of convenience for the purposes of comparative discussion, and that in fact, a continuum exists in terms of the frequency with which flakes having various amounts of cortex occur. It will be noted, for example, that, that within the collections designated as having low levels of cortex on flakes, AZ CC:9:2 (subsurface) has a frequency of over 80 percent for the 0 to 10 percent class while for the same class, AZ CC:10:11 Locus 2 shows a frequency of only about 48 percent.

Cores

Only three samples had enough cores to permit intersample, statistical comparison. Samples from AZ CC:6:3, AZ CC:10:11 Locus 1, and AZ CC:10:11 Sample 2 yielded 64, 92, and 38 cores, respectively. In addition to these samples, the data collected on cores from AZ CC:10:13 and 14 were combined to produce a fourth sample of 35 cores.

Frequency histograms for cores with respect to cortex, number of flake scars, direction of flaking for each of the four samples, and the mean, maximum, and minimum core weights are listed in Figure 102.

The data from AZ CC:6:3 reveal several basic characteristics of cores from this site. First, they tend to be small. Both the mean weight and the range are less than those for any of the other samples. Second, they have a

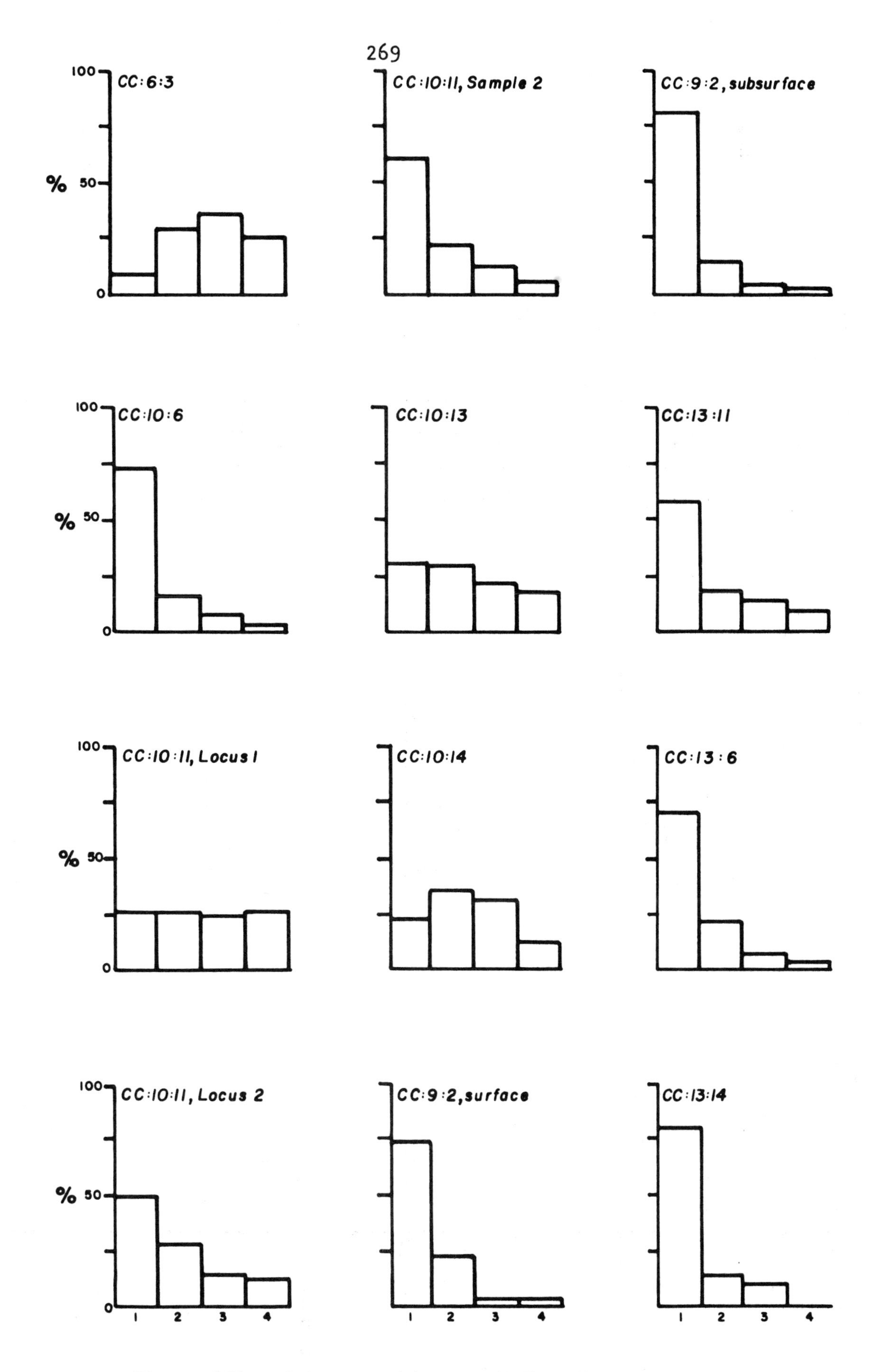

Figure 101. Frequency histograms for flakes by cortex classes for each collection.

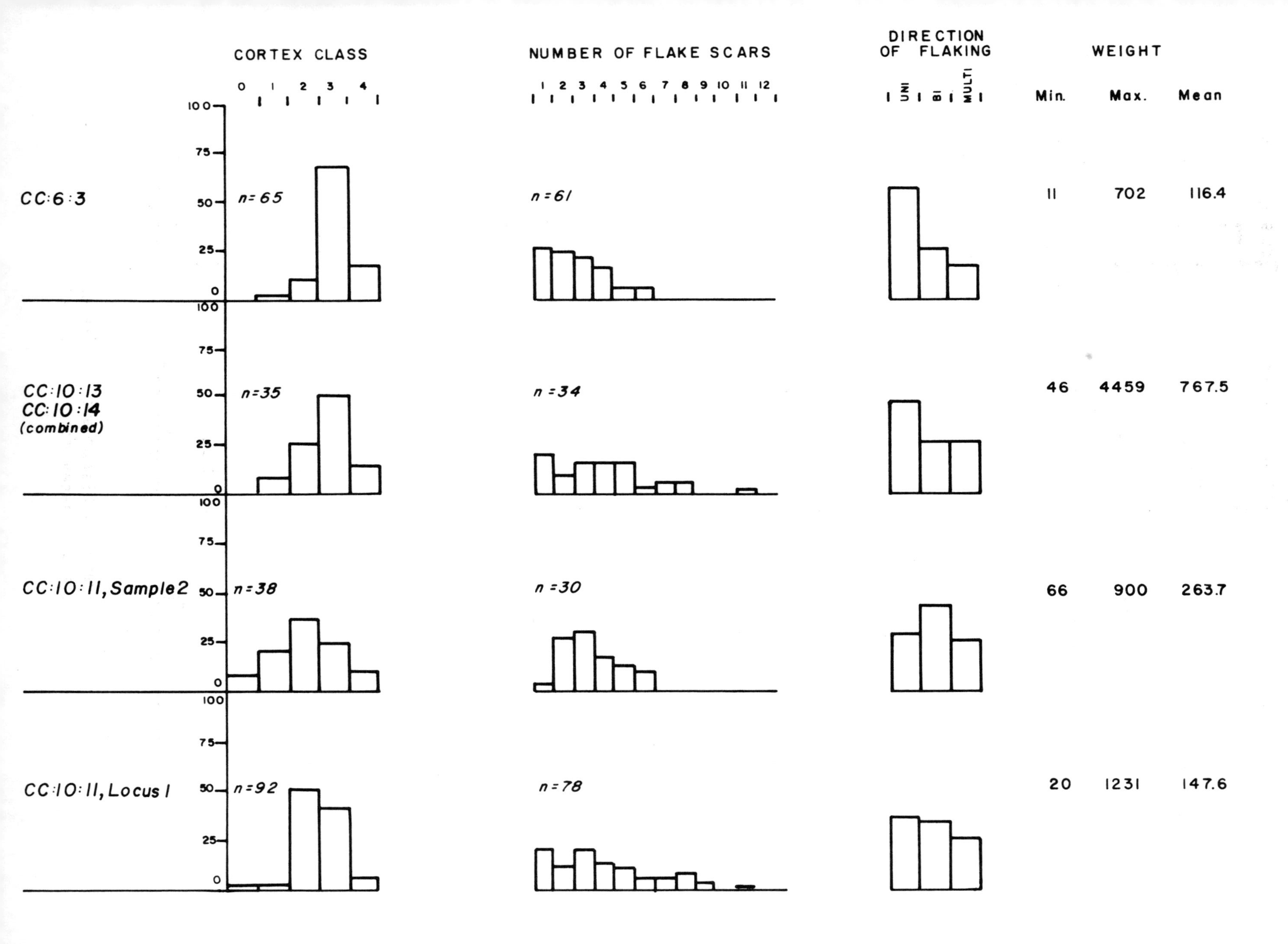

Figure 102. Core data frequency histograms.

lot of cortex, with almost 60 percent having 50 to 90 percent of their surfaces cortical. Third, over 50 percent of them are unidirectional, with bidirectional cores being the second most and multidirectional cores the least abundant. Finally, approximately 50 percent of the cores from AZ CC:6:3 show only one or two flake scars, those having one flake scar being more frequent. The remainder is made up of cores having three, four, five, and six flake scars in decreasing order of frequency.

The histograms obtained for cores from AZ CC:10:13 and 14 are similar to those from AZ CC:6:3 in that the modal cortex class, number of flake scars, and direction of flaking are the same. Nonetheless, differences can be identified. While cores having over 50 percent cortex are the most frequent in both samples, they are less strongly represented in the sample from AZ CC:10:13 and 14, than they are at AZ CC:6:3. Cores assigned to the 0 percent and 0 to 10 percent cortex classes are more numerous at AZ CC:10:13, and 14 than they are at AZ CC:6:3. Unidirectional and multidirectional cores are less common at AZ CC:10:13 and more common at AZ CC:10:14 than they are at AZ CC:6:3. In addition, cores from AZ CC:10:13 and 14 are more evenly distributed with respect to number of flake scars than they are at AZ CC:6:3. Generally cores with low numbers of flake scars are less frequent, and those with high numbers are more frequent at these two sites than at AZ CC:6:3.

The most striking difference between cores from the two samples is seen in the weight data. The sample from AZ CC:6:3 shows the smallest mean weight and range, while cores from AZ CC:10:13 and 14 have the largest.

The cortex histograms for AZ CC:10:11 Locus 1 and Sample 2 differ from those described above in that the modal cortex class is in the 10 to 50 percent category in both cases. At AZ CC:10:11 Locus 1, approximately 50 percent of the cores have cortex on 10 to 50 percent of their surfaces; the majority of the remainder consists of cores in the 50 to 90 percent class. For Sample 2, the distribution is different in that cores are more evenly distributed around the mode. The 50 to 90 percent class is not as strongly represented as it is at Locus 1, and the 0 and 0 to 10 percent classes are more strongly represented. The distribution of cores with respect to number of flake scars at Locus 1 is very similar to that obtained for AZ CC:10:13 and 14. Cores having one scar are most frequent. As the number of scars increases (up to 11), the percentage contributed to the total sample decreases. In contrast, the histogram from Sample 2 shows the mode to be at three scars rather than one, with approximately 30 percent of the cores attributable to this category.

Sample 2 differs from all the others in that bidirectional rather than unidirectional cores are the most frequent. Although unidirectional cores are the most numerous at Locus 1, this sample differs from those of AZ CC:6:3 and AZ CC:10:13 and 14 in that bidirectional cores are only slightly less common than unidirectional cores. Cores at Locus 1 tend to be smaller than those from Sample 2, but are larger than those from AZ CC:6:3.

Fragments

Appendix III, Table 42 gives the absolute and relative frequencies of fragments from each collection with respect to presence or absence of cortex.

Also listed are the mean, maximum, and minimum weights. Data for fragments from AZ CC:6:3 are not given because the sample size was insufficient for comparative purposes.

The collections can be arbitrarily separated into two groups on the basis of cortex frequencies. First, there are samples in which over 50 percent of the fragments exhibit cortex. Samples having high frequencies are those from AZ CC:10:13, 14, AZ CC:10:11 Locus 1, and AZ CC:10:11 Locus 2. Of these, AZ CC:10:11 Locus 1 has the highest frequency (77 percent) and AZ CC:10:11 Locus 2 the lowest (56 percent).

The remaining samples show comparatively low frequencies of cortical fragments, ranging from 34.7 percent at AZ CC:10:6 to 17.7 percent at AZ CC:13:11.

The weight data for fragments from AZ CC:13:11, AZ CC:9:2 (surface and subsurface), AZ CC:13:14, and AZ CC:10:6 indicate that fragments in these samples tend to be very small, with the modal weight being either one gram or less than half of one gram. The mean fragment weights from the remaining collections range from 1.9 g (AZ CC:13:11) to 4.7 g (AZ CC:9:2). Collections tending to have somewhat larger fragments are those from AZ CC:10:11 (all samples) and AZ CC:13:6, with mean weights ranging from 7.7 g at AZ CC:13:6 to 11.4 g at AZ CC:10:11 Sample 2. Artifacts assigned to the fragment category at AZ CC:10:13 and 14 are much larger than those in any other sample, having mean weights of 20.6 and 34.9 g respectively.

Raw Material Texture

The data given in Appendix III, Table 43 were used to construct a histogram showing the relative frequencies of all artifacts with respect to the texture classes for each collection (Figure 103).

The histograms for AZ CC:6:3 and AZ CC:10:11 Sample 2 show that these collections are unlike any of the others, in that more artifacts are assigned to the very fine texture class than to any other class. Both AZ CC:6:3 and AZ CC:10:11 Sample 2 show gradually decreasing frequencies of artifacts with increasing texture classes. This pattern is also apparent at AZ CC:10:11 Sample 2, but here approximately 20 percent of the artifacts were assigned to the mixed category.

Samples from AZ CC:10:6, AZ CC:10:11 Locus 1 and Locus 2, AZ CC:13:6, and AZ CC:13:14 are similar in that artifacts assigned to the fine texture class are the most frequent in each case. Within these samples, AZ CC:13:6 and 14 show a stronger representation of the medium texture class than do samples from AZ CC:10:11 Locus 1 and 2, both of which have distributions which are more skewed towards the finer texture classes. AZ CC:10:6 shows the most even distribution of artifacts with respect to the classes.

The histograms obtained for samples from AZ CC:10:13, 14, AZ CC:9:2 (surface), and AZ CC:13:11 indicate that these samples are similar to each other, and different from the others in that artifacts of the medium texture

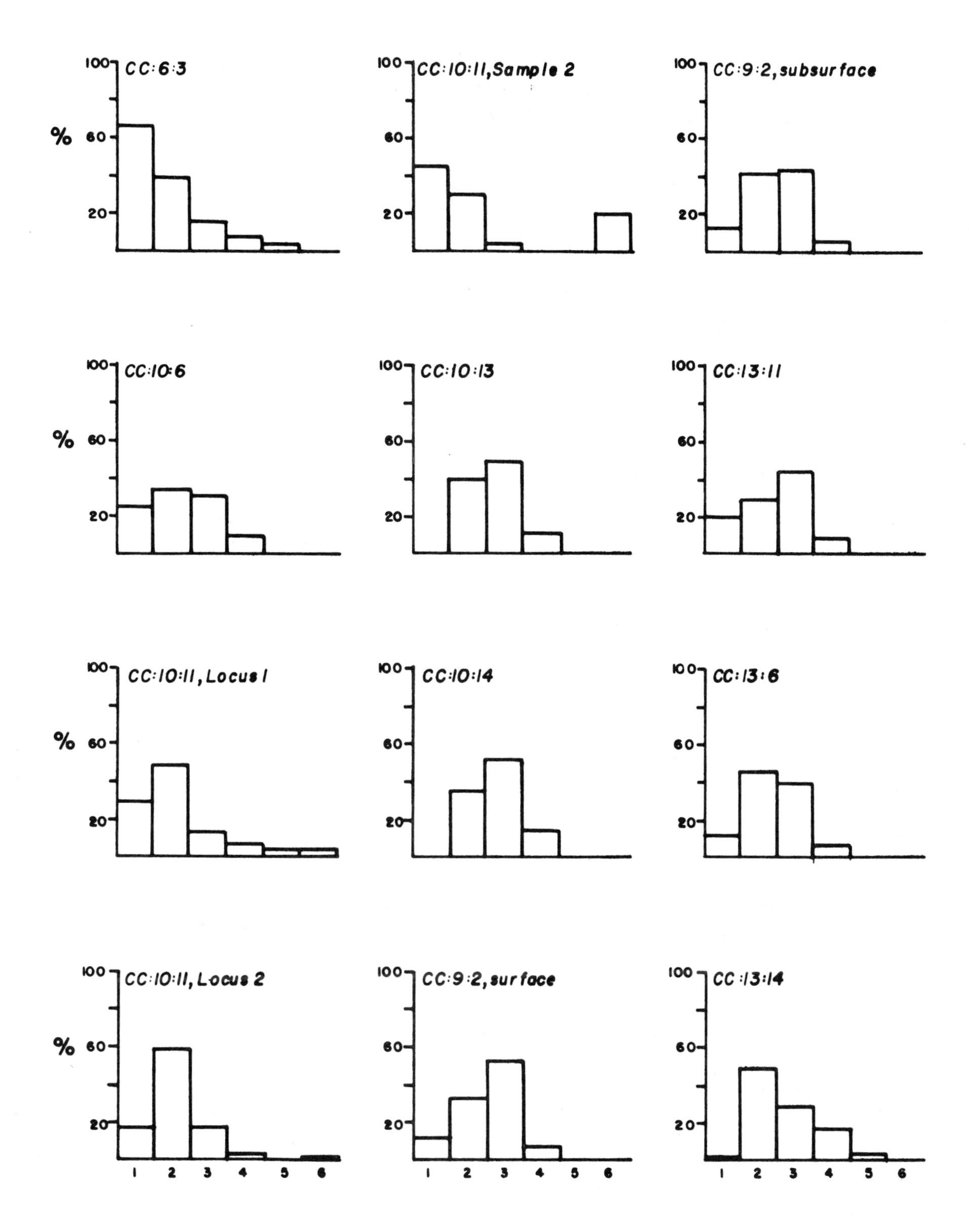

Figure 103. Artifact frequency by raw material texture class for each site.

class outnumber artifacts of any of the other classes. AZ CC:10:13 and 14 are similar in that artifacts of the fine and coarse classes are the second and third most frequent, respectively.

Samples from AZ CC:9:2 (surface) and AZ CC:13:11 follow this pattern to the extent that fine-textured artifacts are the second most frequent in both instances, but different from AZ CC:10:13 and 14 in that the very fine texture class is more strongly represented.

The histogram obtained for AZ CC:9:2 (subsurface) is similar to those for AZ CC:9:2 (surface) and AZ CC:13:11, but differs in that the fine and medium textures are about equally represented.

Raw Material Type

Examination of Appendix III, Table 44 indicates that two groups of collections can be distinguished on the basis of raw material composition. First, there are those samples which are chiefly composed of only one or two raw material types. Collections having relatively homogeneous compositions are those from AZ CC:10:13, 14, and AZ CC:10:11 (all collections). Second, there are those collections which are composed of a greater variety of materials. Collections having relatively heterogeneous compositions are those from AZ CC:6:3, AZ CC:10:6, AZ CC:9:2 (both surface and subsurface), AZ CC:13:11, AZ CC:13:6, and AZ CC:13:14.

Rhyolitic materials constitute the greater portions of the homogeneous collections, contributing from about 63 percent at AZ CC:10:11 Locus 2 to close to 100 percent at AZ CC:10:11 Locus 1. Another characteristic which the homogeneous collections have in common is that the nonrhyolitic remainder consists almost exclusively of chalecedony, ranging in opacity from translucent to completely opaque white.

Of those collections having more heterogeneous compositions, those from AZ CC:6:3 and AZ CC:10:6 can be distinguished from the others in that rhyolitic materials, and silicates (cherts, and chalcedonies) are first and second most frequent, respectively. Lesser percentages are contributed by quartzite, quartz, andesite, basalt, jasper, and obsidian (only at AZ CC:10:6). Collections from the surface and subsurface of AZ CC:9:2 are very similar to each other, being mainly composed of, in decreasing order of frequency, basalt, quartzite, and rhyolite. Jasper, chalcedony, andesite, quartz, and obsidian contribute lesser percentages. Quartzite is the most frequent material (about 45 percent), in the collection from AZ CC:13:11, with basalt and jasper, in that order, comprising the greater part of the remainder. Lesser percentages are contributed by an unidentified, dark greenish igneous material, quartz, and rhyolite. The composition of the sample from AZ CC:13:6 is essentially very similar to that of AZ CC:13:11 but shows a lower percentage of quartzite as the most frequent type (about 37 percent), a slightly higher frequency of basalt, a lower frequency of jasper, and a higher frequency of rhyolite. The most common material at AZ CC:13:14 is the same unidentified igneous material present at AZ CC:13:11 and 6. Rhyolite is the second most abundant, with quartzite, basalt, chalcedony, andesite, obsidian, and jasper making up the remainder.

Comparative Observations of Tool Frequency

The absolute frequencies of tools are given by type for each of the collections in Appendix III, Table 46. These data indicate that, with the exception of AZ CC:10:11 Locus 1, all of the collections contain less than 100 tools. AZ CC:10:11 Locus 1 yielded 117, but 30 of these are miscellaneous flaked chunks. Because of the likelihood that these artifacts are secondary cores rather than tools, and should thus be excluded from comparative observations of tool frequencies, the sample size from AZ CC:10:11 Locus 1 is reduced to 87.

Comparison of the individual collections to identify variation in tool frequency could be made, and such variation might reflect different activities, traditions, or other subjects of archaeological interest. However, differences among the collections could also be the product of chance circumstances of sampling. Because the role of chance is contributing to the observed frequencies increases with decreasing sample size, and because of the small sample sizes in the AEPCO collection, the significance of variation in tool frequencies as it may relate to different activities or traditions is uncertain. Accordingly, detailed comparisons of all collections in terms of tool frequencies will not be made. With respect to several particular tool types, however, more general patterns of variation can be seen when the collections from the Sulphur Spring Valley are grouped and compared to collections from north of the valley. Tool frequencies given in the following discussion were calculated, including all types except flaked chunks, hammerstones, and pebble tools.

As was previously mentioned, uniface fragments are unifacially retouched pieces which are too fragmentary to be classified under any of the more formal specified types, and may represent tools broken during manufacture or possibly during modification after use. Approximately 24.6 percent of the tools from the Sulphur Spring Valley sites are uniface fragments. In contrast, uniface fragments make up only about 7.5 percent of the tools from sites north of the Sulphur Spring Valley. These data suggest that tools are not only relatively less abundant in the Sulphur Spring Valley, but they also tend to be more frequently broken.

An exception to this pattern is AZ CC:10:6. In comparison with other sites located north of the valley, uniface fragments are relatively more abundant at AZ CC:10:6. While uniface fragments make up 7.5 percent of the tools from AZ CC:10:11 (all collections, n=161), 5.1 percent at AZ CC:10:13 (n=59), and 5.8 percent at AZ CC:10:14 (n=39), the frequency of the artifacts at AZ CC:10:6 is 15.4 percent (n=52). In this respect, AZ CC:10:6 is more similar to sites within the Sulphur Spring Valley like AZ CC:9:2 where uniface fragments make up 18.3 percent of the tools (both collections, n=71).

Another casual observation is that notches and irregularly retouched pieces seem to be relatively more abundant in most of the sites outside the Sulphur Spring Valley than at sites within the valley.

Summary of Observations and Patterns of Variation

Table 33 summarizes the basic characteristics of each collection as identified thus far. The terms used to describe reduction product frequencies are the same as those defined earlier. It should be noted that these terms do not refer to comparisons of frequencies of different artifact categories. Rather, they compare the frequency of a particular reduction product at a given site to the range of frequency for that same artifact category as defined by all collections (except AZ CC:6:3).

The terms "large," "medium," and "small" describing flake size refer to samples of flakes having mean thicknesses of approximately 5 to 6 mm, 7 to 9 mm, and 12 mm respectively.

The terms "high," "moderate," and "low," in reference to cortex on flakes, indicate that flakes having either 10 to 50 or 50 to 90 percent cortex are the most frequent, that flakes are evenly distributed by cortex class, and that flakes having 0 to 10 percent cortex are the most frequent, respectively. Flakes from AZ CC:10:11 Locus 2 are identified as having "moderate to low" cortex levels, indicating that the 0 to 10 percent class is the most frequent, but is not as strongly represented as it is in collections having "low" levels of cortex on flakes.

The terms "small," "medium," and "large" used to describe fragment size refer to collections having mean fragment weights of approximately 2 to 5 g, 8 to 11 g, and greater than 20 g, respectively. Collections in which over 50 percent show cortex are said to be high in cortex on fragments, and those in which less than 50 percent of the fragments are cortical are termed low.

Collections having heterogeneous raw material compositions are those in which no more than approximately 50 percent of the artifacts are of the same material. Collections in which 60 percent or more of the artifacts are of the same material are termed homogeneous.

A quick glance at Table 33 will show that no two collections are exactly the same with respect to all variables. In order to identify all the similarities and differences in terms of all variables, the collections could be compared two at a time. While this approach would have the advantage of being detailed and thorough, it would be extremely time consuming, and necessitate making hundreds of comparative statements. Further, it would do little to elucidate patterned associations between variables and collections. Therefore, it will be more useful for the purposes of comparative discussion to group the collections on the basis of shared characteristics.

The first group of collections which will be considered ocnsists of the materials from AZ CC:10:6, AZ CC:9:2 (both collections), AZ CC:13:6, 11, and 14. Characteristics common to these collections are that both flakes and fragments tend to be small and noncortical, and the raw material composition is heterogeneous. Generally speaking, these collections also show a tendency

Table 33. Summary of lithic collection characteristics.

	Reduction Product* Frequency				Unretouched Flakes		Unretouched Fragments		Cores				Raw Materials		
	Cores	Unret. flakes	Ret. pieces	Unret. frags.	Size	Cortex	Size	Cortex	Size (mean wt.)	Cortex (modal)	No. of flake scars (modal)	Direction (modal)	Texture (modal)	Composition	Dominant raw material
AZ CC:6:3	65/48.9	31/23.3	12/9.0	25/18.8	med.	high	insufficient sample		small (116 g)	50-90%	1	uni.	very fine	heterogeneous	rhyolite
AZ CC:10:6	7/1.5	91/19.4	51/10.8	320/68.2	small	low	small	low	insufficient sample size				fine	heterogeneous	rhyolite
AZ CC:10:11 Locus 1	92/8.7	292/27.6	122/11.6	55.1/52.1	med.	mod.	med.	high	small (148 g)	10-50%	1	uni.	fine	homogeneous	rhyolite
AZ CC:10:11 Locus 2	20/8.0	81/32.4	41/16.4	107/42.8	med.	mod.-low	med.	high	insufficient sample size				fine	homogeneous	rhyolite
AZ CC:10:11 Sample 2	38/3.3	305/26.2	70/6.0	751/64.5	med.	low	med.	low	med. (264 g)	10-50%	3	bi.	very fine	homogeneous	rhyolite
AZ CC:10:13	24/7.1	85/25.0	73/21.4	158/46.5	large	mod.	large	high	large (768 g)	50-90%	1	uni.	medium	homogeneous	rhyolite
AZ CC:10:14	11/7.3	44/29.3	42/28.0	53/35.3	large	high	large	high					medium	homogeneous	rhyolite
AZ CC:9:2	9/1.4	148/22.8	59/9.1	428/65.8	small	low	small	low	insufficient sample size				medium	heterogeneous	basalt
AZ CC:9:2 subsurface	0/0.0	50/15.8	14/4.4	253/79.8	small	low	small	low					medium-fine	heterogeneous	basalt
AZ CC:13:11	8/1.3	33/5.4	5/0.8	559/91.0	small	low	small	low					medium	heterogeneous	quartzite
AZ CC:13:6	4/2.4	41/24.4	18/10.7	105/62.5	small	low	med.	low					fine	heterogeneous	quartzite
AZ CC:13:14	0/0.0	45/10.8	16/3.8	356/85.4	small	low	small	low					fine	heterogeneous	unidentified igneous

* = The category "other" is excluded from this table

towards relatively low frequencies of cores and high frequencies of unretouched fragments in comparison to most of the other collections. Within this group, two subgroups can be distinguished on the basis of reduction product frequencies. AZ CC:9:2 (subsurface), AZ CC:13:11 and 14 are similar to each other in that they show very low frequencies of cores (0 percent at AZ CC:9:2 and AZ CC:13:14, to 1.3 percent at AZ CC:13:11), very low frequencies of unretouched complete flakes (5.4 percent at AZ CC:13:11 to 15.8 percent at AZ CC:9:2 subsurface), low frequencies of retouched pieces (0.8 percent at AZ CC:13:11 to 4.4 percent at AZ CC:9:2 subsurface), and very high frequencies of unretouched fragments (79.8 percent at AZ CC:9:2 subsurface to 91.0 percent at AZ CC:13:11). In contrast, the second subgroup consisting of the collections from AZ CC:10:6, AZ CC:9:2 (surface), and AZ CC:13:6 tend to show slightly higher frequencies of cores (1.4 percent at AZ CC:9:2 surface to 2.4 percent at AZ CC:13:6), higher frequencies of unretouched complete flakes (19.4 percent at AZ CC:10:6 to 24.4 percent at AZ CC:13:6), higher frequencies of retouched pieces (9.1 percent at AZ CC:9:2 surface to 10.8 percent at AZ CC:10:6), and lower frequencies of unretouched fragments (62.5 percent at AZ CC:13:6 to 68.2 at AZ CC:10:6).

The second major group of collections to be considered consists of the material from AZ CC:10:11 Locus 1 and Locus 2, AZ CC:10:13, and 14. Characteristics which these collections have in common are, in comparison to the six sites mentioned above, higher frequencies of cores, unretouched complete flakes, and retouched pieces; lower frequencies of unretouched fragments; larger flakes and fragments both having more cortex; and homogeneous raw material compositions. Within this second group, two subgroups can be distinguished primarily on the basis of differences in flake and fragment size. Although flakes and fragments from AZ CC:10:11 Locus 1 and Locus 2 tend to be larger and have more cortex than flakes of any of the collections of the first group, they tend to be smaller than those from AZ CC:10:13 or 14. Cores from AZ CC:10:13 and 14 are also larger than those from either AZ CC:10:11 Locus 1 or Locus 2.

One collection which cannot be easily placed in either of the two basic groups identified is from AZ CC:10:11 Sample 2. In terms of flake and fragment size, AZ CC:10:11 Sample 2 more closely resembles collections of the second group, AZ CC:10:11 Locus 1 and Locus 2 in particular. Yet the amount of cortex on these artifacts is more similar to cortex levels characteristic of collections of the first group and is low in comparison to AZ CC:10:11 Locus 1 and Locus 2, AZ CC:10:13, and 14. The reduction product frequencies for AZ CC:10:11 Sample 2 are intermediate between those characteristics of the two groups.

Finally, the collection from AZ CC:6:3 can be put in a class all by itself on the basis of reduction product frequencies. All of the other collections are similar to each other in that the reduction products frequencies are, in descending order of magnitude, unretouched fragments, unretouched complete flakes, retouched pieces, and cores. The collection from AZ CC:6:3 is unique in that cores make up almost half of the sample.

Turning to relationships between specific variables, a comparison of the flake size data with that for cortex on flakes for all the collections, suggests that smaller flakes tend to show little cortex, and conversely,

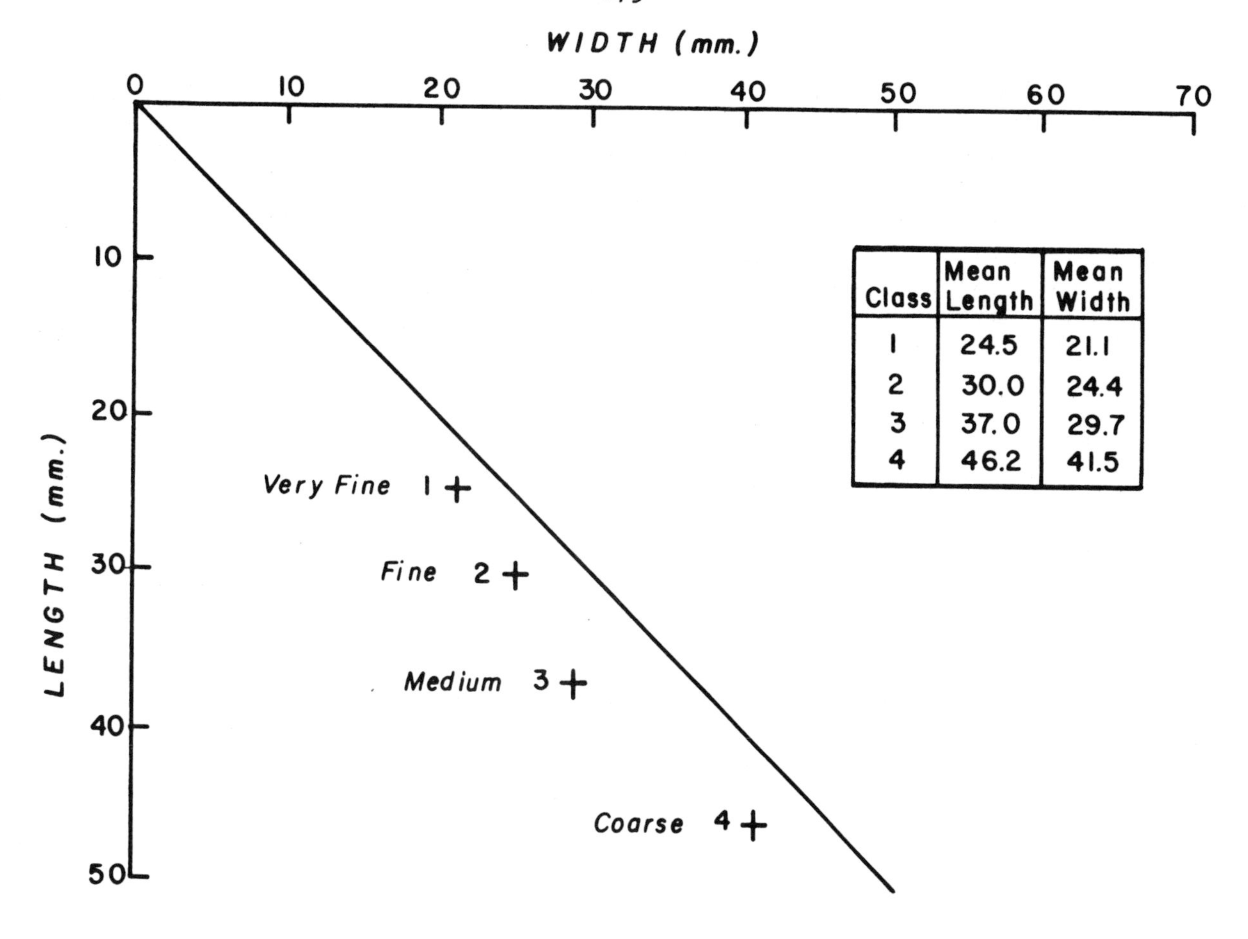

Class	Mean Length	Mean Width
1	24.5	21.1
2	30.0	24.4
3	37.0	29.7
4	46.2	41.5

Figure 104. Mean flake length and width by raw material texture class for all sites.

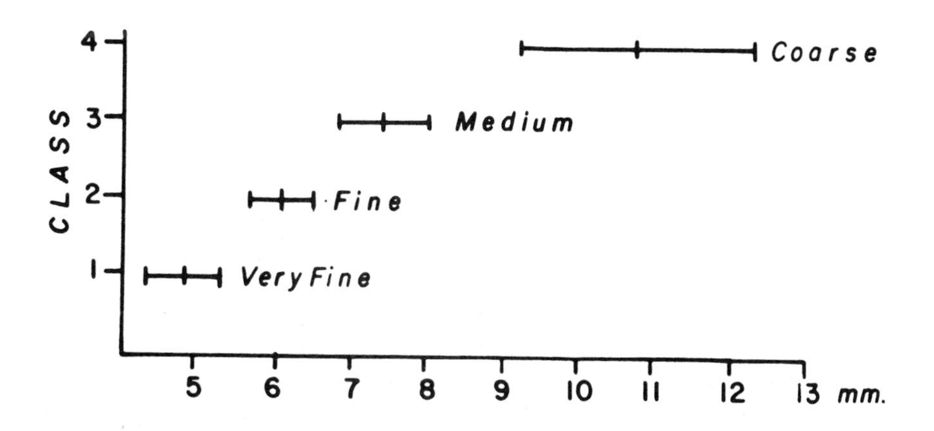

Figure 105. Ninety-five percent confidence intervals for mean flake thickness by raw material texture class.

larger flakes tend to have more cortex. In order to statistically demonstrate this relationship, a Chi square test was applied to determine if a nonrandom association exists between flake thickness and the cortex classes. This test was performed on all complete flakes treated as a single sample, and was accomplished through the use of the SPSS program CROSSTABS. The results of the test confirmed that flakes of different sizes are not randomly distributed with respect to the cortex classes, and that smaller flakes tend to have smaller percentages of cortical exterior surfaces, with percentages increasing with increased flake size.

Another relationship that was examined is between raw material texture and flake size. Figure 104 is a scatter diagram showing the mean length and width of complete flakes by texture classes 1 to 4 (very fine to coarse), for all sites combined. Data for texture classes 5 and 6 (very coarse and mixed) are not shown because of insufficient sample sizes. This figure suggests that flakes of the finer textures tend to be smaller than those of the coarser textures. The SPSS program ONEWAY was used to perform an analysis of variance of flake thickness by raw material texture. The resultant data, given in Appendix III, Table 47 were used to construct the 95 percent confidence interval for the mean flake thickness of each texture class (Figure 105). That the confidence intervals do not overlap further strengthens the inference that raw material texture decreases with decreasing flake size.

In conclusion, some observations can be made concerning site location and characteristics of the respective chipped stone assemblages. Sites located along the southern portion of the transmission line in the Sulphur Spring Basin, Willcox Playa dunes, and Dos Cabezas lower bajadas (AZ CC:9:2, AZ CC:13:6, 11, and 16) have collections with the following characteristics: high frequencies of unretouched fragments; low frequencies of cores, retouched pieces, and complete flakes; and heterogeneous raw material composition. The chipped stone at AZ CC:10:6 also shares these characteristics, but the site is located on the Pinaleño Mountains upper bajada.

In contrast, the collections from most of the sites located north of this region (Pinaleño Mountains bajadas) tend to show higher frequencies of cores, retouched pieces, and complete flakes, and lower frequencies of unretouched fragments. Generally speaking, the flakes and fragments are larger and show more cortex than those from sites in the vicinity of Willcox Playa.

Homogeneous raw material compositions of chiefly rhyolite materials are characteristic of these collections from sites in the Pinaleño bajadas zone. In contrast, the collections from the areas surrounding the Willcox Playa all tend to have heterogeneous raw material compositions in which rhyolite is not the most frequent type.

Finally, the very general observation can be made that the collections from around the Willcox Playa are similar to each other with respect to most of the variables examined, and that the collections from outside this area, exhibit greater diversity among themselves with respect to most variables. Some of these latter collections such as AZ CC:10:13, show high frequencies of cores while others such as AZ CC:10:6, show low frequencies. Some have smaller flakes and fragments with less cortex and some have much larger flakes and fragments with more cortex. While most have homogeneous raw material composition, others such as AZ CC:6:3 and AZ CC:10:6 do not. Some, such as AZ CC:10:13 and 14 have very large cores while others, AZ CC:6:3 for example, tend to have very small cores. It is apparent that this kind of diversity is not characteristic of the collections from the areas surrounding the Willcox Playa.

Site Interpretations

AZ CC:6:3

AZ CC:6:3 is situated on the west terrace of the San Simon River, an alluvial deposit in which gravels of a wide variety of rock types are abundant. Basalt, rhyolite, gneiss, quartzite, jasper, chalcedony, agate, and chert occurring in the form of cobbles and pebbles are common on near the site. In the central portion of the site (see Figure 21), these materials are particularly plentiful, and occur in such concentration as to create a semipavement. While raw materials having flaking properties conducive to lithic manufacture appear to be abundant in the semipavement, most occur in small pieces rarely exceeding 10 cm in length.

The collection of artifacts form AZ CC:6:3 is unlike that of any of the other AEPCO II collections in its extremely high frequency of cores. In fact, cores are almost as numerous as all other reduction products combined. Many of the flakes and fragments struck from the cores were not recovered. A number of explanations can be offered to account for this. One possibility is that primary reduction was done on the site, and the resulting flakes removed from the site for use elsewhere. Another possibility is that many of the cores were reduced elsewhere and brought to the site to be used as tools. Both these explanations, however, seem unlikely in view of the fact that workable raw materials occur not only on the site itself, but throughout the surrounding region as well. The transportation of materials, either from the site in the form of flakes or to the site in the form of cores, was probably not necessary. The most plausible explanation for the extremely high frequency of cores and very low frequency of flakes is that the artifacts from AZ CC:6:3 represent primary reduction of immediately available small cobbles and pebbles for use on the site, and that artifact recovery by the AEPCO field crew was biased in favor of cores. Due to the wide extent of the site and the apparent low artifact density, collections were made by walking systematic transects to locate artifacts, rather than establishing a grid and intensively examining each unit. Consequently, larger artifacts such as cores were probably seen and collected more frequently than the smaller flakes and fragments.

That the major reduction activity at AZ CC:6:3 was primary reduction of small cobbles and pebbles is supported not only by the high frequency of cores, but also by the form of the cores and flakes. Although in some instances, small core size could indicate that primary reduction was carried out intensively and stopped only when cores were almost exhausted, the data (cortex, direction of flaking, number of flake scars) clearly demonstrate this is not the case. The small size of the cores is a reflection of the small size of the raw materials available. Almost 70 percent of the cores show cortex on 50 to 90 percent of their surfaces, and the majority of cores are unidirectional and exhibit only one to three flake scars. This indicates that primary reduction was usually not intensive. A number of explanations can be offered for why primary reduction was not done beyond the removal of a small number of flakes. First, the cores from AZ CC:6:3 may be mostly pieces which were tested then rejected for further reduction because of poor flaking properties. This interpretation seems reasonable for some of the larger, coarser-grained cores of rhyolite and quartzite, but seems inadequate to explain why so many of the smaller, finer-grained homogeneous cores of jasper, chalcedony, and rhyolite were not more fully reduced. A more reasonable explanation concerns the intensity of the occupation of the site and the availability and size of the raw materials. Specifically, the general absence of ceramics and ground stone implements, the low artifact density in most portions of the site, and the apparent lack of subsurface archaeological remains all tend to suggest that AZ CC:6:3 represents a nonintensive, short-term occupation. If this assumption is correct, it is likely that the demand for raw material never approached the limits of the supply, and intensive reduction to minimize the number of flakes obtained from each core would not have been necessary. Further, intensive primary reduction might well have been inconvenient for the knapper because of the generally small size of the raw material.

If primary reduction of small cobbles and pebbles immediately at hand was the principal reduction activity, then one would expect the flakes to be small and to exhibit large amounts of cortex. This is precisely what the metric and cortex data for the flakes indicate.

Although primary reduction seems to have been the dominant reduction activity, the presence of 12 retouched pieces suggests that a limited amount of secondary reduction to shape tools was also carried out, assuming that these artifacts were not manufactured elsewhere and brought to the site.

In addition to inferences about reduction activities drawn from the frequency and form of the artifacts, more direct evidence is provided by reconstructable reduction episodes. During the analysis, some of the flakes were fitted to flake scars on the cores from which the flakes were detached A deliberate attempt to locate artifacts which articulated with one another produced seven reconstructable reduction episodes, including both partial and complete sequences. All of the artifacts contained in the reconstructions were collected from the central portion of the site (see Figure 22). Generally, each reconstruction includes one core and a small number of flakes. Two of the reconstructions are of particular interest because they provide evidence for secondary reduction. One of these consists of a small, multidirectional core and three flakes of a very fine-grained white igneous rock. When the artifacts are reassembled, they produce a small pebble about 35 mm in length, which is complete except for one small flake. One of the flakes in the reconstruction was retouched and is classified as a small denticulate tool. The other less complete reconstruction contains a small core and three flakes of a fine-grained, gray igneous stone. One of the flakes is retouched and is classified as a graver/perforator. If it is assumed that these retouched pieces are finished tools, and that tool discard occurred at the locus of tool use, then these reconstructions provide strong evidence that in at least two cases raw material procurement, primary reduction, tool manufacture (secondary reduction), tool use, and tool discard all took place within a very small area, perhaps only a matter of meters. The other reconstructions, and indeed many of the other artifacts, might well represent the same sort of behavior, except that secondary reduction does not seem to have been a common product.

A number of reasons can be offered for why secondary reduction (retouching) is not strongly represented in the collection from AZ CC:6:3. To some extent, data recovery emphasized the larger primary flakes more than the smaller, less cortical secondary flakes. However, the evidence for primary reduction is so overwhelming that it is probably safe to assume that collection biases have not contributed significantly to the absence of evidence for secondary reduction. An alternative explanation is that the tasks which were performed on the site could be satisfactorily accomplished through the use of the sharp edges on unretouched flakes and cores. Secondary reduction to shape a tool may simply not have been necessary in most instances. Retouch to sharpen flake edges would probably have been inconvenient because of the small size of most flakes, and was probably unnecessary because of the abundance of raw material from which fresh flakes could be struck.

Another possibility is that larger tools may have been made more frequently on pebbles, rather than on flakes. A number of flaked pebbles from AZ CC:6:3 have forms which suggest that they were intended to be used as tools and not simply a source of flakes. It is interesting to note that several of them bear a strong resemblance in terms of edge morphology to some of the retouched pieces. It is possible that the pebble tools represent an adaptive response to a situation in which large pieces of raw material were scarce.

In summary, AZ CC:6:3 appears to represent a nonintensive occupation of uncertain temporal and cultural affiliation. Primary reduction of raw materials available on the site was the most frequent reduction activity. Although raw material was abundant, its small size limited flake size. Little secondary reduction was done, and it is likely that some tools were made on pebbles in the absence of larger flakes. Reconstructable reduction sequences provide some evidence to suggest that raw material procurement, tool manufacture including both primary and secondary reduction, tool use, and tool discard were all done within a short distance of each other. Further study of the collection would be necessary to help clarify the tasks which were preformed.

AZ CC:10:6, AZ CC:9:2 (surface), and AZ CC:13:6

The collections from these sites are so similar to one another with respect to most of the variables that they are grouped for the purposes of interpretation and discussion.

AZ CC:10:6 is located on an east sloping ridge on the eastern bajada of the Pinaleño Mountains. Cobbles of igneous and metamorphic rocks, though scarce on the site itself, are common along the edges of the ridge and in Willow Springs Wash, about 30 m south of the site. AZ CC:9:2 is located on the lower western bajada of the Dos Cabezas Mountains, about 8 km northeast of the Willcox Playa. Raw material for lithic manufacture is scarce on and in the vicinity of the site. The only naturally occurring rocks on the site are small igneous and metamorphic gravels seldom exceeding 30 cm in diameter, and possibly some larger cobbles of phyllite and schist. AZ CC:13:6 is situated on the sand dunes about 4.5 km northeast of the Willcox Playa. The substrate at and surrounding the site is devoid of naturally occurring rocks. The analysis indicates that primary reduction, secondary reduction (tool manufacture), and tool use and discard occurred at all three sites. Evidence of primary reduction is limited and is far outweighed by that of secondary reduction.

The strongest evidence for primary reduction at these sites is the presence of cores, albeit a relatively small number making up but 1.4 to 2.4 percent of the artifacts from each collection. At AZ CC:9:2, cores make up 1.4 percent of the artifacts and may be slightly underrepresented because some of the artifacts classifed as hammerstones are probably made on cores. However, even if all the hammerstones are assumed to be cores and the two categories combined, the frequency of cores would still be only 2.3 percent.

While the larger, more cortical flakes from these sites are probably primary flakes, most of the flakes are small and show little or no cortex. One explanation for the small flake size is that it may be related to small raw material size. If the initial stages of primary reduction did not occur elsewhere, however, then this explanation must be rejected because of the absence of cortex on the flakes.

There are three explanations that can account for both the small flake size and the lack of cortex. First, most of the flakes may have been produced by secondary reduction. Second, small cores, which underwent decortication elsewhere, may have been brought to the site and further reduced. Third, primary flakes struck from small, noncortical cores could have been brought to the site. This would account for the low frequency of cores as well as the characteristics of the flakes.

While the small size of and lack of cortex on flakes may be a result of all three circumstances, some of the retouched pieces and the frequency and form of the fragments suggest that many of the flakes were produced by secondary reduction (tool manufacture or modification). Many of the small bifaces from these sites are broken or show evidence of a problem encountered during manufacture, suggesting that they are unfinished tools. The uniface fragments may also represent tools that broke during manufacture. Assuming that many of the small bifaces and uniface fragments are unfinished tools, the presence of these artifacts at AZ CC:9:2 and AZ CC:13:6 indicates that tool manufacture occurred and probably produced sizeable quantities of small, noncortical flakes and fragments. Providing further evidence that secondary reduction occurred on these sites, about 63 to 68 percent of the artifacts are mostly small, noncortical fragments, many of which are pieces of shattered flakes. At AZ CC:9:2, many of the fragments are pieces of very small, thin flakes with parallel sides, suggesting that they were produced by pressure flaking.

The presence of retouched pieces other than unfinished tools indicates that tool use, as well as manufacture, also occurred at the sites.

The only direct evidence for modification reduction at the three sites comes from AZ CC:9:2. One uniface fragment which has a decidedly rounded and polished edge shows flake scars from the removal of flakes from the rounded edge that probably occurred after use.

Because of the complete absence of naturally occurring rock at AZ CC:13:6, one can assume that all material for lithic reduction was imported to this site. At AZ CC:9:2 adn AZ CC:10:6, thescarcity of sizeable pieces of material in the substrate suggest that much of the lithic material at these sites was also imported. One characteristic common to all three collections is heterogeneous raw material composition. At AZ CC:9:2 and AZ CC:13:6, the compositions probably reflect the procurement of raw materials from a number of different sources. The predominant types in these collections are basalt and quartzite, possibly obtained from the upper bajadas and foothills of the Dos Cabezas Mountains. At AZ CC:9:2 basalt is more prevalent than quartzite, and at AZ CC:13:6 the reverse is true. This difference may reflect the site's proximity to different sources in the higher elevations surrounding the Sulphur Spring Valley or may simply be the result of chance sampling of portions of the sites. While jasper, chert, chalcedony, fine-textured rhyolite, and (at AZ CC:9:2) obsidian may have been obtained from natural sources in the region around the valley, it is also possible that some of these materials were obtained through trade.

The heterogeneity of the raw material composition at AZ CC:10:6 may be a result of the procurement of material from Willow Springs Wash, where a number of predominantly coarse-textured igneous rocks are available. However, it is likely that most of the finer-textured materials from which many of the artifacts were made were obtained from sources located further away. Possibly, much of the finer-textured rhyolite and chalcedony was acquired from sources located higher up on the bajada of the Pinaleño Mountains to the west of AZ CC:10:6, perhaps at sites similar to AZ CC:10:11 or 13. The origin of the obsidian and jasper is unknown, but it seems likely that it came from sources located some distance from the site.

The question of why evidence for secondary reduction ismore pronounced than that for primary reduction deserves further discussion. The most obvious explanation is that AZ CC:10:6, AZ CC:9:2, and AZ CC:13:6 are sites where tool manufacture, use, and possibly modification were the most frequent activities involving lithic artifacts. Although it is certain that some cores were brought to the sites and reduced, it is also likely that primary flakes produced elsewhere were brought to the sites and reduced in the process of tool manufacture. It is also possible that tools manufactured elsewhere were brought to the sites, used, and then modified before being discarded. If more primary flakes and finished tools rather than cores were brought to the sites and reduced, one would expect that evidence of secondary reduction would predominate over that of primary reduction. Thus, the collections from these three sites could be interpreted as being largely composed of the debris produced by the reduction of selected products of primary reductions which occurred elsewhere.

However, in evaluating the significance of evidence of primary and secondary reduction, where both were done at the same place, and where most of the material for reduction was imported, other factors beside the form in which the material was brought to the sites must be considered.

One such factor is the possibility that the number of artifacts produced by a single episode of each kind of reduction may be different. For example, the reduction of a flake into a biface or projectile point could produce more artifacts than a single episode of core reduction. If this were the case, the AEPCO analysis would indicate a stronger representation of secondary reduction simply because it contributed more artifacts to the archaeological record per episode than did primary reduction.

Perhaps one of the most important factors to be considered is that the artifacts probably represent the end products of reduction sequences more often than they represent items produced by the complete range of lithic manufacture. Where the manufacturing sequence involved both kinds of reduction at the same locus, one can expect to recover more secondary reduction products than primary reduciton products. One can also expect that the degree to which evidence of primary reduction has been obscured or destroyed by subsequent secondary reductions will depend largely on the intensity or thoroughness of the reduction of lithic materials at the site.

Assuming that the scarcity of raw material at AZ CC:9:2 and AZ CC:13:6 created a need to use the available materials to their fullest potential, it is likely that most primary flakes produced on these sites were reduced, either to shape a tool or modified after use. If many primary flakes were reduced to such an extent that they could not be measured as complete flakes, the metric and cortex data may be biased in favor of secondary flakes, assuming that primary flakes were selected for reduction more frequently than secondary flakes. Because of the scarcity of raw material in the areas surrounding AZ CC:13:6 and AZ CC:9:2, it is also possible that products of primary flakes and cores may have been removed from the sites to be used elsewhere.

Another possible reason for the apparent lack of evidence of primary reduction is that, because of the scarcity of raw material, primary reduction may have been done intensively to obtain the maximum number of flakes from each core, producing more smaller flakes and fragments than if primary reduction had stopped sooner.

Thus, it is likely that the small flakes and fragments from AZ CC:9:2 and AZ CC:13:6 consist of a mixture of artifacts produced by secondary reduction and those items produced by primary reduction which were to small for further reduction.

The scarcity of raw material at AZ CC:9:2 and AZ CC:13:6 and the likelihood that lithic resources were used to their fullest potential can also be related to the nature of the occupations of these sites. The large size of AZ CC:9:2, the high artifact density in most portions of the site, and the presence of significant quantities of ground stone implements and subsurface artifacts suggest that the site represents a relatively long, perhaps seasonal, semipermanent occupation. AZ CC:13:6, first recorded as a habitation site by Haury in 1956, also probably represents a comparatively long, semipermanent occupation. Assuming that both sites represent either long or intense occupations, it is likely that the raw material shortage was particularly acute in relation to the demand. As a result, larger pieces of material produced by past reductions may have been continually recycled, further contributing to evidence of secondary reduction. Larger pieces of material may also have been continually recycled, further contributing to evidence of secondary reduction. Larger pieces of material may also have been scavenged from the sites by people passing through the area after the sites were abandoned.

Considering the scarcity of raw material and the nature of the occupations at AZ CC:9:2 and AZ CC:13:6, one cannot conclude on the basis of the relative lack of evidence of primary reduction, that lithic material was brought to the sites primarily in the form of flakes and finished tools, or that primary reduction was an insignificant reduction activity at these sites. Rather, the scarcity of raw material has probably contributed strongly to the characteristics of the collection by creating a situation in which larger pieces of lithic material, mainly primary reduction products, were either intensively reduced or removed from the sites, leaving mostly the smaller unwanted products of secondary and primary reduction.

To some extent, the predominating evidence of secondary reduction at AZ CC:10:6 may also reflect the availability of raw material and the nature of the occupation. That the site may represent a relatively long, perhaps seasonal occupation is suggested by the presence of substantial quantities of ground stone implements, and subsurface remains, and by the large size of the site. If the occupation was long or intense, the lack of naturally occurring raw material on the site may have resulted in thorough reduction, thereby contributing to evidence of secondary reduction, and obscuring evidence of primary reduction.

In general, however, the area in which AZ CC:10:6 is located is richer in raw material than the areas around AZ CC:13:6 and AZ CC:9:2. Further, the comparatively low artifact density at AZ CC:10:6 suggests that this site may represent the least intensive occupation of the three sites. Further studies to clarify the nature of the occupations and the proximity of raw material sources should indicate that AZ CC:10:6 was the least intensively or permanently occupied, and that it is located in the region of greatest raw material abundance. One might postulate that the need to intensively reduce lithic material was not as great at AZ CC:10:6 as it was at the other two sites. This would suggest that the strong representation of secondary reduction and the paucity of evidence for primary reduction at AZ CC:10:6 may be more strongly related to the form in which lithic material was brought to the site than it is at AZ CC:9:2 or AZ CC:13:6. For example, more flakes than cores may have been brought to AZ CC:10:6 and reduced. Assuming that hammerstones were more often used in primary reduction than secondary reduction, the absence of these items at AZ CC:10:6, and their presence at both AZ CC:9:2 and AZ CC:13:6 further suggests that primary reduction was not as important at AZ CC:10:6 as it was at the other two sites.

Besides breaking rocks into small pieces to make tools, what else can be said about the activities in which the inhabitants of these sites engaged? At all three sites, the presence of projectile points suggests hunting (assuming that these artifacts are indeed projectile points, and not hafted tools having some other function). The majority of the points are fragmentary, most often having broken tips. Breakage could have occurred during the final stages of manufacture, as a result of postdepositional destructive forces such as cattle grazing, or as a result of use. Three of the points from AZ CC:10:6 and one from AZ CC:9:2 show fracture morphologies suggesting that damage was a result of use. The tips of these points, rather than having been cleanly snapped off, are crushed. In all cases, a flake scar, resembling an attempt at intentional fluting but originating from the tip rather than the base, extends parallel to the long axis of the point, down one face. On the point from AZ CC:9:2, the force producing this flake scar turned inward, and severed the point's base. It is likely that these points were damaged when they hit a hard object.

If this assumption is correct, the presence of these points at AZ CC:9:2 and AZ CC:10:6 suggests that hunting occurred at the sites. On the other hand, these projectiles may have been used elsewhere, were damaged, then recovered and brought back to the sites for refurbishing. Points that were not seriously damaged could have been reworked, or if too badly broken, they may have been discarded. One can further postulate that some of the other retouched pieces from these sites, such as scrapers, were used to process game.

The presence of ground stone implements at AZ CC:9:2, AZ CC:10:6, and AZ CC:13:6 indicates that plant material was processed. It is possible that, in addition to grinding, plant materials such as leaves, bark and wood were worked with the use of chipped stone tools as well. Perhaps the denticulates from AZ CC:10:6 and AZ CC:9:2, and the heavy unifaces from AZ CC:10:6 and AZ CC:13:6 were used to shred plant fibers, leaves, and bark. Heavy unifaces, scrapers, notches and graver/perforators may also reflect wood working.

To summarize, the collections from AZ CC:10:6, AZ CC:9:2, and AZ CC:13:6 reflect the intensive reduction of materials obtained from offsite sources. Evidence of secondary reduction predominates; the role of primary reduction at the sites is not known for certain. At AZ CC:9:2 and AZ CC:13:6, the scarcity of raw material and the nature of the occupations suggests a need to use lithic material to its fullest potential. As a result, larger primary reduction products were probably intensively reduced or removed from the sites. At AZ CC:10:6, raw material appears to be more plentiful in the surrounding area, suggesting that the strong representation of secondary reduction may be more related to the intensity of the occupation or the form in which lithic material was brought to the site. Thus, three factors which must be considered in attempting to explain the intensity of reduction at all three sites are (1) the scarcity of raw material, (2) the length or intensity of occupation, (3) the form in which lithic material was brought to the sites. To clarify the role of each of these factors in determining the characteristics of the collections, further studies of the sites and their surrounding areas would be necessary. An analysis designed to determine tool function would be required to clarify the tasks performed although it is relatively safe to say that a wide variety of natural resources obtained from the surrounding areas were brought to these sites for processing and use.

Numerous projectile points and point fragments were collected from AZ CC:10:6 and AZ CC:9:2. Several of these exhibit attributes that are stylistically significant. Eight projectile points collected from AZ CC:10:6 have retained enough characteristics to be of diagnostic value. Three basic categories are recognizable and each of these can be related to diagnostic point types from preceramic sites elsewhere in the Southwest.

The first is a shallow side-notched, convex-based point (see Figure 92h). The type has been found at Ventana Cave (Haury 1950) and at the Fairchild Site in the Sulphur Spring Valley (Windmiller 1973); it is characteristic of the San Pedro stage Cochise. The second point type (Figure 92a-e) is side-notched with a straight or concave base. One of these has serrated edges, which is characteristic of the Pinto Basin type from the Mohave Desert in California (Campbell and Campbell 1935). These concave-based points also were found at Ventana Cave, and Haury (1950:Plate 22) places them within the Chiricahua-Amargosa II time period. The third type (Figure 92f,g) has an unstemmed triangular blade with a concave base. Haury (1950:275) notes that at Ventana Cave, triangular blades are common and appear to be a late development from the earlier leaf-shaped blades. Further, he notes that triangular blades are absent in the California desert cultures and the first two stages of the Cochise culture. Thus, these triangular points probably date no earlier than the San Pedro stage.

Projectile points from AZ CC:9:2 are more numerous and varied, and the collection exhibits a few striking differences when compared to AZ CC:10:6. Points with contracting stems (Figure 93a-e) and small triangular blade stemmed points (Figure 93f-i) occur at AZ CC:9:2, but are absent at AZ CC:10:6. Contracting stem points were first described for Gypsum Cave, Nevada (Harrington 1933), and appear to be commonly distributed throughout the Southwest. Huckell (1973:191) has summarized this information as follows:

> In Arizona this point style, or at least styles quite similar to it, has been recovered from the San Pedro River valley (Agenbroad 1970), the Papago Reservation (Haury 1950), along the Colorado River and into the Mohave Desert (Rogers 1939), near the Grand Canyon (McNutt and Euler 1966), and in the east central part of the state near Concho (Wendorf 1951). In addition, at least two areas in the central New Mexico area have yielded contracting stemmed points: Bat Cave (Dick 1965) in the San Augustin Plains area and the Artrisco sites in the middle Rio Grande Valley (Campbell and Ellis 1952). Scattered examples of the same style are also known from northern and central Mexico, Utah (Jennings 1957), California (Rogers 1939), and Texas. Thus the idea of a point with a contracting stem seems to have been widely spread over the Southwest and the western part of North America in general.

Parallel stemmed points have been found in the midden level at Ventana Cave, to which the AEPCO points bear resemblance (Haury 1950:281-2). Based on the stratigraphic distribution of the Ventana examples, these points would probably fit within the Chiricahua-Amargosa II period.

Shallow side-notched concave-based points (Figure 93 j, k) are similar to Ventana examples of the Chiricahua-Amargosa II period, and those with convex bases (Figure 93 n,o) are typical San Pedro stage examples. One ovate unstemmed type is not diagnostic; two examples are shown in Figure 93 l, m. The last point illustrated has a triangular blade with a poorly defined stem, but a pronounced basal notch (Figure 93p), suggesting a possible Pinto Basin style (Campbell and Campbell 1935). Huckell (1973:191) found a Pinto point at the Hardt Creek site south of Payson. Pinto Basin points have also been reported from several other locales in Arizona:

> Agenbroad (1970) recovered Pinto points from the Lone Hill site in the San Pedro Valley near Readington, as did Haury at Ventana Cave (Haury 1950). Other Arizona sites producing Pinto Basin points include the Red Butte sites (McNutt and Euler 1966) and scattered sites in the vicinity of Concho (Wendorf and Thomas 1951).

Although the projectile points from AZ CC:9:2 and AZ CC:10:6 are significant, allowing us to postulate probable cultural and temporal affiliations of the sites, they are of limited use in attempting to correlate site activities with specific time periods. This is because their surface context has exposed them to postfabrication movement or reuse by later populations. Collection biases also affect comparative type frequencies. Since one cannot control these factors, only a few general statements about the cultural significance of the points can be made. These are discussed in Chapter 8.

AZ CC:9:2 (subsurface), AZ CC:13:11, and AZ CC:13:14

The collections from these sites are very similar to one another, and share many characteristics with the collections from AZ CC:9:2 (surface), AZ CC:13:6, and AZ CC:10:6. Heterogeneous raw material, small flake size, lack of cortex on flakes, high frequencies of small, noncortical fragments, low frequencies of cores, complete flakes, and retouched pieces are common to all six collections. However, the materials from AZ CC:9:2 (subsurface), AZ CC:13:11, and 14 are distinguished from the other three on the basis of the frequency and size of the fragments. While the frequency of fragments is high (63 to 68 percent) at AZ CC:9:2 (surface), AZ CC:13:6, and AZ CC:10:6, it is even higher (80 to 91 percent) at AZ CC:9:2 (subsurface), AZ CC:13:11, and 14. Conversely, the collections from AZ CC:9:2 (subsurface), AZ CC:13:11, and AZ CC:13:14 show slightly lower frequencies of cores, unretouched complete flakes, and retouched pieces than do the collections from the other three sites. Fragments not only make up a greater percentage of the artifacts from AZ CC:9:2 (subsurface), AZ CC:13:11, and AZ CC:13:14, but they also tend to be smaller (mean weight = 1.9 to 2.8 g) than those of the other three collections (mean weight = 3.8 to 7.7 g).

AZ CC:9:2 (subsurface). The difference between the surface and subsurface collections from AZ CC:9:2 in terms of the frequency and size of unretouched fragments can possibly be related to (1) differences in the kind and intensity of lithic reduction between earlier and latter occupations, (2) natural processes, and (3) differences in the methods by which artifacts were recovered from the surface and subsurface units.

In comparison to the surface collection, the higher frequency of smaller noncortical fragments of the subsurface collection suggests that secondary reduction debris is even more prevalent beneath the surface than on the surface. This could be interpreted as reflecting a shift from more to less intensive lithic reduction through time. One might further postulate that such a shift is related to changes in the intensity of the occupation(s), or perhaps changes in the specific reduction activities which occurred at particular loci within the site.

In view of the likelihood that natural processes have altered the surface distribution of artifacts since the time of their deposition, however, it is doubtful that the differences between the surface and subsurface collections can be attributed solely to changes in reduction activities. Sheetwash erosion may have transported smaller surface artifacts into the small, shallow drainages which pass through the site. Because of vegetation change resulting, in part, from cattle grazing, the effect of sheetwash erosion on the surface distribution of artifacts has probably been more pronounced during recent times than previously. Thus, the higher frequency of smaller fragments in the subsurface collection may be partially explained by better preservation conditions.

Collection methods also contributed to the differences between the surface and subsurface in terms of the frequency and size of unretouched fragments. All soil from the excavated units was passed through 1/8 inch screen, while surface units were collected by simple inspection. Because screening is a more efficient means of recovering very small artifacts, more small artifacts would be recovered from the fill than the surface.

The collections from the surface and subsurface differ with respect to raw material texture, as well as in the size and frequency of unretouched fragments. Although the very fine and coarse texture classes are about equally represented in both collections, the fine class is more strongly represented in the subsurface material than it is in the surface collection. Conversely, the medium texture class is more strongly represented in the surface material than it is in the subsurface collection. Earlier in this chapter, it was demonstrated that smaller flakes tend to be made of finer-textured materials and larger flakes to be of coarser materials. If this relationship between raw material texture and size is also characteristic of flake fragments and shatter, the tendency of subsurface artifacts to be made of finer textured materials than those on the surface probably reflects the higher frequency of smaller fragments in the subsurface sample. Since differences between the samples in terms of fragment size and frequency are probably related to natural processes and collection methods, these factors probably contributed directly to differences between the collections with respect to raw material texture.

In summary, the major differences between the surface and subsurface artifacts from AZ CC:9:2 are most likely the result of natural processes and collection methods, and cannot be attributed to change in reduction activities through time. While this interpretation does not negate the possibility that such changes may have occurred, it is clear that further study to define the effects of erosion and deposition on artifact distribution would be necessary to demonstrate that interstrata variation could have been caused by different kinds of lithic reduction.

AZ CC:13:11. AZ CC:13:11 is located on a large sand dune about 6.75 km northeast of the Willcox Playa. As is the case at AZ CC:13:6, raw material for lithic reduction is completely absent in the vicinity of the site. All of the materials from which the artifacts are made were brought to the site in one form or another, and the heterogeneous raw material composition of the collection suggests that raw material was obtained from several sources, possibly located in the upper bajadas and foothills of the Dos Cabezas Mountains.

In evaluating the significance of evidence for different reduction activities at AZ CC:13:11, it is important to note that approximately 80 percent of the artifacts analyzed were recovered from subsurface levels. Further, the vast majority of subsurface artifacts came from only six of the twelve 2.5 m^2 excavated units. Even though the horizontal extent of subsurface archaeological remains has been partially defined by test excavations, only a small percentage of the known extent of the deposit was excavated. Unless it is assumed that artifacts produced by different kinds of reduction are present in the same proportions throughout the deposit, the following interpretation must allow for the possibility that the artifacts analyzed may not be entirely representative of the full range of lithic manufacture which occurred at AZ CC:13:11, or accurately reflect the importance of different kinds of reduction in relationship to each other. Further discussion of this problem will follow the interpretation of the evidence for different reduction activities.

Like AZ CC:9:2, AZ CC:13:6, and AZ CC:10:6, evidence of primary reduction, tool manufacture, and tool use can be seen in the data from AZ CC:13:11. Again, however, most of the artifacts are probably debris produced by secondary reduction. This interpretation is supported by the very high frequency of very small, noncortical fragments, the low frequencies of cores, complete flakes, and retouched pieces, and the fact that complete flakes also tend to be small and show little or no cortex. Very strong evidence for tool manufacture at the site came from one of the excavated units (25N 15W NE). Here, 53 of the 80 lithics recovered from all levels consist of small pieces of jasper, including one uniface fragment. With the exception of this fragment which weighs about 5 g, none of the jasper artifacts weighs less than 1.5 g. The morphology of the complete flakes and many of the proximal flake fragments suggests that direct percussion was the method by which these artifacts were produced. Many of the other unretouched fragments, however, consist of pieces of very small, long, thin flakes having parallel sides. This suggests that both direct percussion and pressure flaking were part of the manufacturing sequence. The single retouched fragment is probably a piece of a tool which broke during manufacture. Although no attempt was made to physically reconstruct the jasper artifacts, it is possible that this material represents only one or two episodes of secondary reduction (tool manufacture).

Although most of the artifacts from AZ CC:13:11 are probably secondary reduction debris, evidence for primary reduction is seen by the presence of eight cores. It is important to note that four of these cores are core tools (heavy unifaces on cobbles), one of which exhibits pronounced rounding of the working edge and polishing on the striking platform. Since these artifacts may have been manufactured elsewhere, their presence at AZ CC:13:11 as an indicator of primary reduction at the site is not conclusive. However, the forms of the other four cores suggest that their primary purpose was to provide a source of flakes. Conclusive evidence that one of these cores, (recovered from 10N 15W NE, Level IV), was reduced at the site, is that two of the flakes and a small fragment which were struck from this core were collected from Levels II, III, and V of the same unit. Less direct evidence of primary reduction is the relatively small nubmer of larger, more cortical flakes and fragments in the material collected from throughout the site. Also, the presence of hammerstones suggests that primary reduction was done.

The discrete episodes of lithic reduction identified in two of the excavated units suggest that further excavation of the site could produce evidence of other task specific activity loci. The proportion of primary reduction to secondary reduction, however, cannot be conclusively demonstrated. The predominance of secondary reduction debris could be a function of the sampling methods used in site testing; that is excavation units were placed over discrete task areas. The extent to which chance circumstances of sampling have contributed to the strong representation of secondary reduction could be conclusively demonstrated only if more thorough excavations were to be conducted.

In view of the absence of raw material in the vicinity of the site, and the little that is known about the nature of the occupation(s), however, it is unlikely that further excavation would produce abundant evidence of primary reduction in the form of concentrations of cores and large cortical flakes and fragments. Although the known horizontal extent of artfacts at AZ CC:13:11 is small in comparison to AZ CC:9:2, AZ CC:13:6 and AZ CC:10:6, the high artifact density both on and below the surface in the vicinity of Feature 1, and the presence of significant quantities of subsurface ground stone tools, sherds, and animal bone suggests that AZ CC:13:11 represents an intense, perhaps semipermanent or permanent occupation. As is the case at AZ CC:9:2, AZ CC:13:6, and AZ CC:10:6, one can expect at AZ CC:13:11 that the relatively great demand for raw material in an area of low availability created a need to use lithic resources to their fullest potential. Consequently, larger primary reduction products were probably either intensively reduced or removed from the site for use elsewhere. Since it is likely that the need for intensive reduction was "site-wide," one can expect that the analyzed artifact sample (consisting of a high frequency of small noncortical fragments, low frequency of cores, and small flakes) reflects the lithic assemblage at AZ CC:13:11 in general.

The problem of why unretouched fragments are both smaller and more frequent at AZ CC:13:11 than at either AZ CC:13:6, AZ CC:9:2 (surface), or AZ CC:10:6 deserves careful study to determine if this variation is a result of prehistoric behavior or other factors. The data could indicate that more secondary reduction was done or that reduction was more intensive at AZ CC:13:11. It was demonstrated that the differences between the surface and subsurface lithics at AZ CC:9:2 (in terms of the size and frequency of fragments) may be related more to natural processes and field recovery methods. These factors must also be considered in explaining why fragments tend to be smaller and more numerous at AZ CC:13:11. At this site the recovery of artifacts produced during the same reduction episode from a single 2.5 m^2 test pit suggests that horizontal movement of smaller artifacts by sheetwash erosion has been minimal, although the distribution of these items throughout different levels of the excavated unit shows that some natural processes have caused vertical displacement of the artifacts. Thus the higher frequency of small fragments at AZ CC:13:11 could be a result of less sheetwash erosion than occurred at the other sites. Field recovery methods are another reason for the high number of small fragments. Eighty percent of all artifacts from AZ CC:13:11 were recovered from screened subsurface levels. Conversely, a much smaller percentage of all artifacts from AZ CC:10:6 were recovered by screening, and none at all from AZ CC:13:6. Thus, in comparing lithic collections from the sites under consideration, the high frequency of small fragments at AZ CC:13:11 does not necessarily mean that reduction was more intensive here than at the other sites. The purpose of the foregoing discussion is to point out the need to consider all factors of site disturbance when attempting to determine the significance of different artifact frequencies.

Of the 614 artifacts analyzed, only 16 were classified as tools, including the eight hammerstones, four heavy unifaces, and the uniface fragment already mentioned. The remaining three tools are a notch, a denticulate, and a tabular piece of schist which appears to have been shaped by flaking.

On the basis of such limited evidence, it is impossible to determine the importance of different tasks associated with the processing of various natural resources. However, the presence of ground stone tools, sherds and large quantities of animal bone suggests that a wide range of tasks involving both animal and vegetable materials may have been performed. Possibly, some of the unretouched flakes were used to butcher small game. Although no projectile points were found, one might postulate that the jasper debitage from 25N 15W NE was produced during projectile point manufacture. The heavy unifaces, including the one of basalt which shows extensive use-wear, suggest that heavy scraping or planing was done. Conceivably, this could reflect wood working, hide preparation, or plant fiber processing. The notch and denticulate may also have been used to work vegetable material.

To summarize, the collection from AZ CC:13:11 is similar to those from AZ CC:9:2, AZ CC:10:6, and AZ CC:13:6 in that it reflects the intensive reduction of lithic materials obtained from offsite sources. Primary reduction, secondary reduction (tool manufacture), and tool use occurred, but most of the artifacts appear to be secondary reduction debris. As is the case at the other three sites, raw material scarcity and intensive or long occupation have been identified as factors contributing to the intensity of lithic reduction at AZ CC:13:11. Because larger primary reduction products were probably further reduced or removed from the site, the extent of primary reduction in manufacturing sequences at the site is uncertain. Unretouched fragments tend to be smaller and more frequent at AZ CC:13:11 than they are at AZ CC:10:6, AZ CC:13:6, or in the surface collection from AZ CC:9:2. The cause of this difference is not entirely clear, but it may be a result of archaeological recovery methods. At least one, and probably two, discrete episodes of reduction were identified. The recovery of artifacts produced by the same reduction episode in one 2.5 m^2 unit suggests that sheetwash erosion has not significantly contributed to the horizontal displacement of smaller artifacts at AZ CC:13:11. Differences among the sites, in terms of fragment size and frequency may thus be related to unequal effects of sheetwashing. On the basis of the presence of ground stone tools, sherds, and large quantities of animal bone, it is postulated that chipped stone tools were used for a wide variety of tasks, involving both animal and plant materials. Excavation of the site to obtain a larger sample of tools, to further define task specific activity loci, and to determine the effect of natural processes on the artifact distribution could provide much information relevant to the resolution of so far unanswered questions about the activities that occurred.

AZ CC:13:14. AZ CC:13:14 is located 1.4 km east of the Willcox Playa, in a region which was once inundated by Pleistocene Lake Cochise. There is no naturally occurring lithic raw material on or near the site. As is the case at AZ CC:13:6, AZ CC:9:2, and AZ CC:13:11, the lack of raw material has probably been an important factor contributing to the nature of the collection from AZ CC:13:14. Again, the very high frequency of small noncortical fragments and the fact that complete flakes also tend to be small and noncortical indicate that reduction was intensive, and that most of the artifacts were probably produced by secondary reduction. More direct evidence of secondary reduction at the sites is that seven of the 16 tools are uniface fragments. These are probably pieces of tools which broke during manufacture or possibly during modification after use.

Although the collection from AZ CC:13:14 is very similar to that from AZ CC:9:2 (surface), AZ CC:13:6, AZ CC:10:6, and especially AZ CC:9:2 (subsurface), and AZ CC:13:11 with respect to fragment size and frequency, it is unique in that it contains no direct evidence of primary reduction in the form of cores.(Cores were recovered from subsurface units at AZ CC:9:2, but they are absent in the random sample which was selected for analysis.) The absence of hammerstones further distinguishes AZ CC:13:14 from AZ CC:9:2, AZ CC:13:6, and AZ CC:13:11. Because test excavations indicated that there were no subsurface archaeological remains, and because a 100 percent surface collection was conducted, one can assume that there were no cores or hammerstones at the site when the AEPCO field crew arrived.

One explanation for the absence of these artifacts is that primary reduction did not occur at AZ CC:13:14, and that all material for reduction was imported in the form of selected products of primary and secondary reductions which occurred elsewhere. Thus, the inclusion of some larger cortical flakes and fragments in the collection does not necessarily indicate that primary reduction was done at the site.

Another explanation for the absence of cores and hammerstones is that primary reduction was done, producing some of the larger flakes and fragments, but the cores and hammerstones were removed for use elsewhere. In view of the lack of lithic raw material in the area surrounding the site this is a more realistic explanation.

If one assumes that primary reduction was done at the site, and that the lack of raw material in the surrounding area resulted in removing cores for use elsewhere, one must explain why cores and hammerstones were found at sites located in areas which are also devoid of naturally occurring raw material. For instance, raw material is no more abundant at AZ CC:13:6, and 11, and yet hammerstones and cores were found at both these sites. Here, a comparison of the sites with respect to the nature of the occupations may provide an answer. That AZ CC:13:6 and 11 probably represent relatively long, semipermanent or permanent occupations has already been mentioned. At AZ CC:13:14, the presence of some ground stone tools and the high artifact density at Feature 1 suggests that the occupation may have been intense, but, the small size of the site and the lack of subsurface artifacts indicate that AZ CC:13:14 represents a shorter occupation than either AZ CC:13:6, 11, or AZ CC:9:2. One might postulate that the remains at AZ CC:13:14 could have been produced by 10 to 20 individuals during a day or two, or perhaps by a smaller group over a matter of weeks or months.

Assuming that AZ CC:13:14 represents a much shorter occupation than either AZ CC:13:6, 11, or AZ CC:9:2, it is possible that cores were not found because people were not at the site long enough to exhaust, and subsequently discard their cores. In contrast, because AZ CC:13:6, 11, and AZ CC:9:2 were probably occupied longer than AZ CC:13:14, one would expect exhausted cores to accumulate at these sites.

As a result of the apparent brief occupation, of all the collections from sites located in regions of little or no raw material, the artifacts from AZ CC:13:14 may be the least representative of the entire range of activities that occurred. This problem not only has implications for the interpretation of reduction activities, but must be considered in evaluating evidence of tool use, as well. Sixteen tools, including three scrapers, three small irregularly retouched pieces, three denticulates, and the seven uniface fragments already mentioned were recovered from AZ CC:13:14. Although the uniface fragments may be unfinished tools, the other implements were probably used and discarded at the site. Because of the small tool sample size, strong statements as to differences between AZ CC:13:14 and other sites cannot be made in terms of tool frequencey. Of all the sites located in regions lacking in raw material, however, AZ CC:13:14 yielded the smallest number of types. Furthermore, the types present are basically very similar to each other in gross form. For example, the one end scraper is essentially the same as the two side scrapers except for the location of the retouch, the denticulates are little more than scrapers with more jagged edges, and the uniface fragments may well be pieces of scrapers that broke during manufacture or modification. Generally, the tools from AZ CC:13:6, 11, and especially AZ CC:9:2 are more formally diverse than the types represented at AZ CC:13:14, as they include scrapers, denticulates, notches, heavy unifaces, small bifaces, and projectile points.

At first glance, the lack of tool diversity at AZ CC:13:14 suggests that the range of tasks performed was more limited than it was at AZ CC:13:6, 11, or AZ CC:9:2, and one might postulate on the basis of the presence of ground stone that plant processing was the principal activity at AZ CC:13:14. But because of the possibility that evidence of other activities may have been removed from the site, the lack of tool diversity cannot be used to infer that AZ CC:13:14 represents a specialized activity sites. AZ CC:13:14 was probably occupied for a shorter time than AZ CC:13:6, 11, or AZ CC:9:2, so one might expect that tools representing the full range of activities did not accumulate as they might have had the occupation been longer.

Assuming that AZ CC:13:14 was occupied for only a short time, and that its inhabitants took almost everything that could be of further use when they left, it is likely that cores, larger flakes and fragments, and unbroken and unexhausted tools were taken. The removal of these artifacts may explain in part the very high frequency of small, noncortical fragments.

To summarize, it is clear that lithic reduction was intensive at AZ CC:13:14 and that secondary reduction and tool use occurred. Of all the collections from sites located in areas devoid of raw material, the artifacts from AZ CC:13:14 may be the least representative of the entire range of activities that occurred because of the apparent briefness of the occupation. As a result, it cannot be demonstrated that primary reduction either did or did not take place. The size of the site, and the lack of tool diversity suggests that a relatively narrow range of tasks was performed, but tools used in a greater variety of activities may have been removed from the site.

AZ CC:10:13 and AZ CC:10:14

AZ CC:10:13 and 14 are located on the southeastern bajada of the Pinaleño Mountains, 1.4 km from each other, on separate, west-to-east trending ridges. Lithic raw material is abundant at both sites and in the surrounding area. Predominantly medium-textured rhyolitic gravels and cobbles occur on the ridge tops and in the washes immediately to the north and south of each site. Cobbles as large as 30 to 40 cm occur in the washes, but tend to be smaller on the ridge tops. Small cobbles and pebbles of chalcedony are comparatively scarce. Because the sites are located in very similar environments, and because the collections are also very similar to each other, the sites are discussed together. Relatively minor differences between the collections will then be identified and discussed.

The analysis indicates that raw material procurement, primary reduction, secondary reduction (tool manufacture), and tool use occurred at AZ CC:10:13 and 14, and that most of the artifacts are primary reduction products.

Both collections have relatively homogeneous raw material compositions in which rhyolite predominates (about 85 percent), with chalcedony making up most of the remainder. This indicates that the vast majority of the artifacts are made of materials which were obtained either at or in the immediate vicinity of the sites.

The strongest evidence for primary reduction is the presence of cores, and the form of the unretouched complete flakes and unretouched fragments. Cores vary greatly in size, but tend to be much larger than those from any of the other AEPCO II sites. This reflects the availability of large pieces of raw material. Approximately 65 percent of the cores have cortex covering 50 percent or more of their exterior surfaces, nearly half are unidirectional, and the modal number of flake scars is one. These data indicate that primary reduction was not intensive in most cases. That reduction often did not proceed beyond the removal of a few flakes may mean that many of the cores are tested and rejected pieces. With the exception of a few cores of coarse materials, most are made of medium-textured, structurally homogeneous rocks, suitable for lithic manufacture. The lack of advanced core reduction may be related to the abundance of raw material and the nature of the occupations. The low artifact density in most portions of the sites, the absence of sherds, and habitation features suggest that AZ CC:10:13 and 14 represent temporary, nonintensive occupations. If this is correct, it is likely that the demand for raw material was never very great in relation to the supply. It is possible that many cores were not fully reduced because of the low need for flakes. A second possibility is that the abundance of raw material permitted greater selectivity of materials for manufacture. Thus, cores which appear to be suitable for reduction, may have been simply rejected by the knapper because they were unsuitable for the particular task at hand.

Complete flakes are also the largest of any in the AEPCO II collections. In comparison to flakes from sites in the Sulphur Spring Valley, flakes from AZ CC:10:13 and 41 are more cortical. Thus, it is likely that nearly all of the flakes were produced by primary reduction. Similarly, unretouched fragments tend to be large and cortical. Although weight and cortex were the attributes recorded, it was noted that most of the artifacts from the Sulphur Spring Valley sites are small flake fragments. In contrast, unretouched fragments from AZ CC:10:13 and 14 are characteristic of primary reduction debris, including pieces of shattered platforms and cones, large flake fragments, and large, irregularly shaped chunks.

Both sites yielded a number of small bifaces, most of which are broken or appear to represent unsuccessful attempts at bifacial thinning. Assuming that these are unfinished tools and that unfinished tools were discarded where last reduced, one can conclude that secondary reduction (tool manufacture) occurred at AZ CC:10:13 and 14. A wide variety of other retouched pieces, many of which are probably finished tools, indicate that tool use also occurred.

From the foregoing, it is apparent that the cores and the vast majority of the unretouched flakes and fragments are primary reduction products. With the exception of a few smaller flakes and fragments, the only artifacts that can be positively identified as secondary reduction products are retouched pieces. Although primary reduction products are more numerous than secondary reduction products, it is important to note that retouched pieces are roughly three times more abundant than cores. In terms of the number of episodes, then, secondary reduction probably occurred more often than primary reduction.

If this assumption is correct, one would expect that sizable quantities of small, noncortical flakes and fragments would have been produced. Yet, secondary reduction debris is almost completely absent in the collections from AZ CC:10·13 and 14. A number of explanations can account for this. First, most of the retouched pieces could have been manufactured elsewhere and brought to the site. The extent to which this may have happened is unknown, but considering the abundance of raw material on and near the site, it was probably not necessary to transport tools for any great distance.

An alternative explanation is that secondary reduction debris was present, but was generally not collected. Although a few small bifaces were found, many of the retouched pieces, such as notches, denticulates, and irregularly retouched flakes represent a much less intensive kind of secondary reduction than biface manufacture. In all likelihood, the flakes and fragments produced in the manufacture of these implements were very small. Because they were made of rhyolitic materials and were lying on a surface strewn with small rhyolitic gravels, it is likely that many of these artifacts were not seen, even though collections were made by systematic examination of grid squares.

A third explanation for the lack of secondary reduction debris deals with natural processes. Both sites are located along the tops and slopes of high, narrow ridges. It is possible that very small artifacts, such as the by-products of secondary reduction, were washed downslope, out of the grid layout. The lack of secondary reduction debris could be a function of the interaction of all three factors, so there is no reason to assume that tool manufacture did not occur at the sites.

In terms of the range of activities involving lithic artifacts, then, AZ CC:10:13 and 14 bear a gross resemblance to sites in the Sulphur Spring Valley, in that primary reduction, tool manufacture, and tool use occurred. It is clear, however, that differences with respect to artifact form are strongly related to differences in the availability of raw material. In the Sulphur Spring Valley, the scarcity of raw material created a need to use available materials to their fullest potential. As a result, large pieces of material were intensively reduced, leaving mostly small noncortical flakes and fragments. In contrast, the abundance of raw material at AZ CC:10:13 and 14 meant reduction did not have to be intensive. Thus, larger, more cortical flakes and fragments escaped reduction.

Differences in terms of artifact frequencies can also be related to the availability of raw materials. In comparison to the collections from AZ CC:9:2, AZ CC:13:6, AZ CC:13:11, and AZ CC:13:14, those from AZ CC:10:13 and 14 show higher frequencies of cores, complete flakes, and retouched pieces, and lower numbers of unretouched fragments. To some extent, differences in fragment frequency may reflect the relative visibility of these artifacts at different sites, or the extent to which sheetwash erosion has affected their spatial distribution. That these factors may have resulted in low numbers of unretouched fragments at AZ CC:10:13 and 14 has already been mentioned. In contrast, the sites in the Sulphur Spring Valley are situated on more level ground, and so erosion may not have moved small artifacts as much as it has at AZ CC:10:13 and 14. Additionally, the substrate at most of the sites in the Sulphur Spring Valley is light colored and free of small gravels. Thus, more small artifacts may have been collected from these sites because they were more visible than at AZ CC:10:13 or 14. However, because the abundance of raw material at AZ CC:10:13 and 14 alleviated the need for intensive reduction, the lower frequencies of unretouched fragments were expected. The higher frequencies of cores, retouched pieces, and complete flakes in the collections from AZ CC:10:13 and 14 can thus be viewed as the statistical product of lower frequencies of unretouched fragments. One might also expect that cores, complete flakes, and retouched pieces are more frequent in the collections from AZ CC:10:13 and 14 because the abundance of material in the surrounding area made it unnecessary to remove these items from the site for use elsewhere.

Considering AZ CC:10:13 specifically, it should be noted that 146 (about 43 percent) of the 340 artifacts analyzed were collected at three distinct concentrations (Features 1 - 3). Preliminary examination of these materials suggested that they represent individual reduction episodes, and cores were successfully reconstructed. No detailed discussion of the significance of these reconstructions is provided, but a description of the contents of each of the features is given below.

Feature 1 yielded 76 artifacts, 48 of which were produced from the same cobble of yellow, banded, coarse-textured rhyolitic tuff. These artifacts include one core, nine unretouched complete flakes, 35 unretouched fragments, two irregularly retouched flakes, and one irregularly shaped heavy biface. The presence of retouched pieces indicates that, in addition to primary reduction, tools were manufactured at Feature 1. Assemblage of these artifacts yielded only a partial reconstruction, estimated to represent 50 to 75 percent of the original cobble volume. Although incomplete, the reconstruction indicates that the cobble was greater than 15 cm long, and that flakes were detached multidirectionally in an unsystematic fashion. The absence of some of the artifacts struck from the cobble, both at Feature 1 and in the surrounding grid suggests either that some reduction occurred outside the collected area, or that artifacts were taken elsewhere for use. Although some smaller fragments were found, none of these could be fitted to flake scars on the retouched pieces. No secondary reduction debris appears therefore to have been recovered.

Nineteen of the artifacts from Feature 1 are of a fine-textured, red, porphyritic rhyolite, including six unretouched flakes. Most of the artifacts articulate with each other, having been struck from the same platform. The core from which the artifacts were produced was not found within the grid system. Two explanations can account for its absence. First, core reduction may have occurred at another location within the site and the artifacts brought to Feature 1, implying that they are the selected products of reduction. Second, reduction may have occurred at the feature's locus and the core subsequently taken to another location. The second interpretation is favored because it seems unlikely that small primary fragments would have been selected for use and brought to Feature 1. Flakes removed from the two retouched pieces were not recovered.

Also present at Feature 1 was a large rhyolite cobble (15 cm), one end of which was rounded by pronounced battering. Two small pieces of shatter were fitted to shallow flake scars originating from the battered portion of the cobble. It is likely that the pieces of shatter were unintentionally detached from the cobble during its use as a hammerstone.

The remaining artifacts from Feature 1 include a smaller battered core which is also probably a hammerstone, three small chalcedony flakes, a flaked chunk, and a large unidirectional core. The significance of these artifacts with respect to the two partial reconstructions is uncertain.

Feature 2 produced a total of 31 artifacts. Twenty-three of these (one core, seven unretouched complete flakes, and 15 unretouched fragments) were assembled to produce a large, globular core, about 13 cm in diameter. The only pieces missing from the cobble are three large flakes that were probably completely cortical and a few small fragments. This suggests that either the initial stages of reduction occurred outside the grid system, or the flakes were taken elsewhere. The former interpretation is favored because it seems unlikely that reduction would have continued if the knapper only wanted the now-missing flakes.

In addition to six small fragments which appear to be only coincidentally present, the only other artifacts collected from Feature 2 are a relatively small cobble with one flake scar and the corresponding flake. This cobble is probably a tested and rejected core.

Feature 3 contained 39 artifacts, 27 of which were assembled to form a nearly complete cobble about 14 cm long. The only items missing are one completely cortical flake and a few small pieces. The cortical flake was not found in the general grid collection, suggesting that the initial stages of reduction occurred outside the grid system. Four notches, two irregularly retouched pieces, one side scraper, and one graver/perforator indicate that tool manufacture and, (if these are finished tools) tool use, occurred at this locus. None of the secondary reduction debris produced in the manufacture of the retouched pieces was recovered.

The remaining 12 artifacts from Feature 3 include one core, five unretouched complete flakes, and six unretouched fragments. When assembled, these artifacts yield only a partial reconstruction, too incomplete to indicate the size of the original cobble.

At AZ CC:10:14, 56 (about 38 percent) of the 150 artifacts analyzed were collected in five separate concentrations (Features 1 through 5). The contents of the features with respect to reduction product categories are given in Table 34.

Table 34. Reduction product categories at Features 1 to 5, AZ CC:10:14.

	Cores	Unretouched complete flakes	Retouched pieces	Unretouched fragments	Total
Feature 1	0	2	2	1	5
Feature 2	0	3	3	3	9
Feature 3	2	8	3	9	22
Feature 4	1	2	7	5	15
Feature 5	0	3	1	1	5
Total	3	17	16	20	56

Although the artifacts contained in Feature 1 could have come from the same core, as suggested by the similarity of raw material types, none of the artifacts articulate with each other.

Similarly, none of the artifacts collected from Feature 2 fit together. However, one core and three flakes from grid squares adjacent to Feature 2 (35N 55W, 30N 55W, and 30N 40W) create a partial core reconstruction. One flake collected in Feature 2 articulates with this reconstruction, and other artifacts collected as part of the feature also appear to have come from the same core.

None of the artifacts from Feature 3 could be fitted together, and variation with respect to color, texture, inclusion, and so forth suggest that most of the artifacts originated from different cores. However, one flake from Feature 3 articulates with a retouched piece collected at 10S 5E, approximately 40 m away, and one flake from the general grid collection (25N 45E), fits with one of the cores from Feature 3.

Artifacts from Feature 4 also show considerable variation in raw material type and none were reconstructable. Three flakes collected in Feature 5 articulate with each other and with two flakes from the general grid collection. One of these was collected north and downslope from Feature 5 at 50N 5W, and the other was found south and upslope from Feature 5 in 20N 0E. The large size of the flakes (maximum length = 111 mm) and the fact that the first flake of the series to be struck was completely cortical suggest that this partial reconstruction represents the initial stages of the reduction of a large cobble. Interestingly enough, the first flake of the series to be struck was collected the farthest downslope. The second, third, and fourth flakes struck were collected further upslope at Feature 5, and the last piece flaked was found the farthest upslope, near the top of the ridge. The distribution of the artifacts suggests that reduction occurred as the cobble was carried to the ridge top. No trace of the core from which the flakes were struck was found in the rest of the collection.

Of all the features at AZ CC:10:14, Feature 2 is the most similar to Features 1 through 3 at AZ CC:10:13 in that it appears to be largely composed of artifacts produced by the reduction of a single core. However, Features 1, 3, 4, and 5 at AZ CC:10:14 do not represent "chipping stations" in the same sense this term might be applied to Features 1 to 3 at AZ CC:10:13. While the reduction activities which produced the artifacts at AZ CC:10:14 Features 2 and 5, and AZ CC:10:13 Features 1 to 3 are very clear, the significance of Features 1, 3, 4 at AZ CC:10:14 is uncertain. Conceivably the concentrations may represent chance accumulations of artifacts, or perhaps activity areas where artifacts manufactured in other parts of the site were used for specific tasks and subsequently discarded.

While there is no doubt that reduction was much less intensive at AZ CC:10:13 and 14 than it was at any of the sites in the Sulphur Spring Valley, differences between the collections from AZ CC:10:13 and 14 suggest that reduction may have been more intensive at AZ CC:10:13 than at AZ CC:10:14. In comparison to the collection from AZ CC:10:14, that from AZ CC:10:13 shows a higher frequency of unretouched fragments and slightly lower frequencies of cores, unretouched flakes, and retouched pieces. Unretouched fragments also tend to be somewhat smaller and less frequently cortical at AZ CC:10:13 than they are at AZ CC:10:14. Further, complete flakes from AZ CC:10:13 are, on the whole, less cortical than those from AZ CC:10:14. These differences may reflect the presence of comparatively complete primary reduction episodes at AZ CC:10:13 (Features 1 to 3), and with the exception of Feature 2, a general lack of similar manifestations at AZ CC:10:14. This explanation for the differences between the collections would be supported if further analysis showed that the general grid collection from AZ CC:10:13, excluding artifacts from the features, was more similar to the collection from AZ CC:10:14. Flakes from both sites are about the same size, and yet those from AZ CC:10:13 are less cortical than those from AZ CC:10:14. This may indicate that the initial stages of primary reduction at AZ CC:10:13 may have occurred more often outside the grid system (possibly near the washes).

The tool assemblages from AZ CC:10:13 and 14 are similar in that they both contain a wide variety of types, including scrapers, notches, irregularly retouched pieces, denticulates, small bifaces, and heavy unifaces. Although no projectile points were found, the presence of unfinished small bifaces suggests that other small bifaces may have been finished into projectile points and removed from the sites. The tasks for which the tools were used are unknown. Heavy unifaces and notches suggest that woodworking may have been done. However, the significance of the notches and other artifacts which show irregular and discontinuous retouch, such as denticulates and irregularly retouched pieces, is open to question. While these artifacts may represent finished tools used for specific tasks, it should be noted that both sites have been subjected to cattle grazing and were also disturbed by previous tower construction. In additon, AZ CC:10:13 was traversed by a D-8 Caterpillar. If postdepositional destructive forces have caused retouch on a significant number of artifacts the collections may reflect more tool manufacture and use than actually occurred. But, the extent to which such destructive forces may have contributed to the high frequencies of retouched pieces is unknown.

To summarize, AZ CC:10:13 and 14 represent nonintensive occupations involving raw material procurement, primary reduction, secondary reduction (tool manufacture), and tool use. Most of the artifacts are primary reduction products reflecting the reduction of large rhyolitic cobbles which were obtained either on or in close proximity to the sites. Retouched pieces are more numerous than cores, suggesting that more secondary than primary reduction episodes may have occurred. Secondary reduction debris is largely absent from the collections probably because of its poor visibility, or perhaps because it may have been washed outside the collected grids. In most cases, primary reduction was not done intensively. Because of the apparent temporary nature of the occupations and the abundance of raw material, there was no need to use lithic resources to their fullest potential. Partial and complete core reductions demonstrate that Features 1 to 3 at AZ CC:10:13 were each produced by the reduction of two cobbles. At AZ CC:10:14, Feature 2 contained material which is associated with a partial core reconstruction obtained from nearby grid squares, and three of the artifacts collected at Feature 5 are associated with what appears to be initial primary reduction, done as the cobble was being transported. The significance of Features 1, 3, and 4 is uncertain, but it is clear that they do not represent individual episodes of primary reduction as do Features 1 to 3 at AZ CC:10:13. Differences between the collections from AZ CC:10:13 and 14 may thus be related to differences in the nature of the features. Further analysis treating the artifacts from the features as separate collections may clarify the activities of which these features are a result and may help explain differences between the sites.

AZ CC:10:11—Locus 1, Locus 2, and Sample 2

AZ CC:10:11 is located in the Pinaleño upper bajadas, about 4 km north of AZ CC:10:13. Lithic raw material occurs abundantly at Locus 1 in the form of gravels and cobbles of a brown, fine-grained, igneous rock, seldom exceeding 10 cm in length. Although this material was originally identified as rhyolite and recorded as such during the analysis, under microscopic examination, crystals of its mineral components could not be identified. So instead, the term "felsite" was applied, generally referring to dense, cryptocrystalline, igneous rocks which are presumably rich in silica and feldspar. Although fine-grained and abundant at Locus 1, cobbles of this material commonly contain numerous fissures and irregular flow surfaces.

At Locus 2, angular chunks of fine-textured, light gray rhyolite have weathered out from outcrops at the northern end of the grid column and to the west of the R-O-W. At the extreme southern extent of the grid column, small nodules and chunks of chalcedony are plentiful. Between the northern and southern extremes of the grid, raw material occurs principally in the form of scattered, small, angular fragments of fine-textured, light gray rhyolite. For the remainder of this discussion, "Locus 1" will refer to AZ CC:10:11 Locus 1, and "Locus 2" to AZ CC:10:11 Locus 2

In comparison to collections from the Sulphur Spring Valley, those from Loci 1 and 2 both show lower frequencies of unretouched fragments and higher frequencies of cores, complete flakes, and retouched pieces. Both complete flakes and unretouched fragments tend to be larger and more cortical, and their raw material composition more homogeneous. Thus, of all the AEPCO II collections, Locus 1 and 2 most closely resemble AZ CC:10:13 and 14 and generally appear to represent similar activities involving raw material procurement, primary reduction, tool manufacture, and use. The similarities among Locus 1, Locus 2, AZ CC:10:13, and AZ CC:10:14, and the basic dissimilarity of these four collections with those from the Sulphur Spring Valley, are related to raw material distribution. Whereas the Sulphur Spring Valley collections represent the intensive reduction of materials obtained from offsite sources, less intensive reduction of locally available materials is characteristic of Locus 1 and 2, as well as AZ CC:10:13 and 14. The availability of raw material in contributing to differences between the collections from the Sulphur Spring Valley and those from AZ CC:10:13 and 14 can also explain the major differences between the Sulphur Spring Valley collections and those from Locus 1 and 2. The following discussion will focus on the significance of some of the other differences between AZ CC:10:13 and 14 on the one hand, and Locus 1 and 2 on the other. Differences between the two loci will then be addressed.

Locus 1 and Locus 2 in relation to AZ CC:10:13 and AZ CC:10:14. Although these collections have many characteristics in common when contrasted to those from the Sulphur Spring Valley, differences can nonetheless be identified.

With respect to reduction product frequencies, both Locus 1 and 2 show lower frequencies of retouched pieces and higher frequencies of cores than either AZ CC:10:13 or 14. While one might argue that the higher frequencies of retouched pieces at AZ CC:10:13 and 14 could be due to more extensive cattle grazing at these sites, this is clearly not the case. Because a stock tank is located within the R-O-W between Locus 1 and 2, the extent to which livestock have caused retouch is, if anything, probably greater at Loci 1 and 2. Thus, the significance of some of the retouched pieces, as they may relate to tool manufacture and use, is open to serious question. For example, notches and irregularly retouched pieces account for 35 and 43 percent, respectively, of the retouched pieces from Locus 1 and 2. Because many of these items may have been modified through post-depositional destructive forces, one might suspect that the overall frequencies of retouched pieces at Locus 1 and 2 misrepresents the role of tool manufacure and use, implying that these activities occurred more often than they did.

Miscellaneous flakes and chunks account for about 25 percent of the retouch pieces at Locus 1 and Locus 2. As was mentioned earlier, it is likely that these retouched pieces are secondary cores, rather than tools. If this assumption is correct, the percentage of retouched pieces from Loci 1 and 2 which reflects tool manufacture and use is even lower. In comparison to AZ CC:10:13 and 14, then, the collections from Loci 1 and 2 not only show lower frequencies of retouched pieces, but probably contain more retouched pieces which are unrelated to tool manufacture and use.

One interpretation of the differencec between the sites with respect to the frequency of retouched pieces is that reduction activities at Loci 1 and 2 focused more on the production of flakes for use elsewhere (raw material extraction), rather than on the production of tools for use at the site.

Because of its enormous size and the spectacular raw material density in many portions of its known extent, AZ CC:10:11 may have been well-known to the inhabitants of the surrounding area for its abundance of lithic raw material. Possibly, the site was visited intermittently over a long period of time by people whose principal concern was the acquisition of lithic material, rather than the collecting or processing of biotic resources available on or in close proximity to the site. But, while raw material procurement was undoubtedly an integral part of the activities at AZ CC:10:13 and 14, the comparatively high frequency of retouched pieces, many of which may be finished tools, suggest that these sites were visited not only to obtain lithic material, but also to gather, and possibly process certain biotic resources.

An alternative interpretation of the differences between the sites with respect to the frequence of retouched pieces deals with raw material limitations. At AZ CC:10:13 and 14 raw material is large, abundant, and generally free of structural flaws. As a result, large flakes could be easily produced and shaped to meet the requirements of a particular task at hand. At Loci 1 and 2, however, raw material, though abundant and fine-textured, is smaller and commonly flawed by numerous fissures and irregular flow surfaces. Because the raw material was smaller and less predictable, it is likely that larger flakes suitable for tool manufacture could not be produced as easily. In response to raw material limitations, tool manufacturing at Loci 1 and 2 may have, thus, consisted of breaking cobbles apart to produce quantities of sharp pieces from which one best suited to the task was selected and used without further shaping.

The different implications of these two interpretations are by no means trivial. While the former suggests that raw material procurement and primary reduction were the principal activities, and that tool manufacture and use were relatively insignificant, the latter suggests that tool use may have been an important activity. On the basis of this analysis, however, the problem cannot be conclusively resolved. Like many problems of interpretation, it is likely that the solution does not lie entirely with either one or the other explanation. One might expect that the relatively low frequency of retouched pieces at Loci 1 and 2 is related to both the site's function as a source of raw material and the limitations of the raw material for tool manufacture.

Locus 1 and Locus 2 differ from AZ CC:10:13 and AZ CC:10:14 not only in terms of reduction product frequencies but in artifact form as well. Complete flakes from Locus 1 and 2 tend to be smaller than those from AZ CC:10:13 and 14. This probably reflects differences with respect to raw material size. However, another factor which must be considered is the intensity of primary reduction. In comparison to cores from AZ CC:10:13 and 14, those from Locus 1 are less cortical and are less frequently unidirectional and more frequently bidirectional. This suggests that primary reduction was more thorough at Locus 1 than at AZ CC:10:13 and 14. Although only 20 cores were recovered from Locus 2, the data on cortex and direction of flaking indicate that primary reduction was also more intensive at Locus 2 than at AZ CC:10:13 and 14. Whereas cores showing cortex on 50 to 90 percent of their surfaces are the most frequent at AZ CC:10:13 and 14, those of the 10 to 50 percent cortex class are the most frequent at Locus 2, as well as at Locus 1. Cores from Locus 2 also tend to be more frequently bidirectional and less frequently unidirectional than those from AZ CC:10:13 and 14. Thus flakes from Locus 1 and 2 are smaller than those from AZ CC:10:13 and 14, not only because the pieces of raw material were smaller, but also because primary reduction was more thorough.

Why was primary reduction more intensive at Locus 1 and 2 than at AZ CC:10:13 and 14? As is the case with reduction product frequencies, differences between the sites with respect to the intensity of primary reduction might also be related to the nature and purpose of the occupations, or qualitative differences in the raw materials.

With regard to the first possibility, one might expect primary reduction to have been more intensive at sites which were visited intermittently over a long time by people interested primarily in producing quantities of flakes for use elsewhere. In contrast, primary reduction may have been less intensive at sites which were occupied only once for a short time, and where the object of reduction was to produce tools for immediate use.

However, assuming that tool use was an important activity at Locus 1 and 2, that the limitations of the raw material necessitated that the tool manufacturing strategy be different than that at AZ CC:10:13 and 14, one might expect that primary reduction was more thorough at Loci 1 and 2 because, in order to obtain enough sharp pieces to accomplish a particular task, cores had to be more completely reduced.

Differences between Locus 1 and Locus 2. An obvious difference between these collections is raw material composition. While the Locus 1 artifacts are nearly all made of brown felsite, the Locus 2 collection is more heterogeneous, being predominantly composed of light gray rhyolite with chalcedony making up the remainder. A few pieces of brown felsite were also collected. Differences with respect to raw material composition merely reflect the differential occurrence of the raw material types at the two loci.

More provocative variation can be seen in reduction product frequencies. In comparison to Locus 1, Locus 2 is lower in cores and unretouched fragments and is higher in unretouched complete flakes and retouched pieces. Possibly, these differences could reflect slightly more tool use and less primary reduction at Locus 1. However, it is also possible that the higher frequency of retouched pieces at Locus 2 may be related to raw material variability. While in comparison to AZ CC:10:13 and 14, raw material is smaller and more often contains structural flaws at Locus 1 and Locus 2, it is possible that the light gray rhyolite occurs in larger pieces which tend to be less seriously flawed than the brown felsite at Locus 1. If this is the case, rhyolite at Locus 2 may have been more suitable for producing larger flakes which could be more easily shaped into tools. Another factor which must be considered is the proximity of the collected areas to the stock tank. Because Locus 2 is closer, it is possible that the higher frequency of retouched pieces reflects more extensive cattle disturbance. Thus, the three factors which may account for differences between the reduction product frequencies at Locus 1 and 2 are (1) the extent to which tool use may have occurred in relation to primary reduction, (2) tool form as dictated by limitations of the raw materials, and (3) the extent to which cattle may have caused retouch. The relative contribution of each of these factors is, however, unknown.

Although both complete flakes and unretouched fragments are about the same size in both collections, those from Locus 1 are more cortical. The significance of this as it might be related to reduction processes is not clear. One possible explanation has to do with raw material cortex characteristics. Cortex on the brown felsite cobbles at Locus 1 consists of a very light colored, weathered layer that is easily recognized against the generally much darker color of fractured surfaces. Cortical surfaces on the rhyolite artifacts from Locus 2 are also very light colored, but since they do not contrast sharply with the light color of the fractured surfaces, cortex on rhyolite artifacts from Locus 2 may have gone unrecognized, and hence unrecorded, more often than at Locus 1.

Another possibility is that rhyolite flakes from Locus 2 were struck from pieces of material which were not completely cortical to begin with. Angular chunks of rhyolite, whose surfaces are formed by planes of natural fracture, may have been collected at, or physically extracted from, outcrops at the northern end of the grid column. It is likely that these chunks were not exposed long enough to develop a layer of weathering thick enough to be recognized as cortex.

At Locus 1, artifacts appeared to be densely and uniformly distributed throughout the entire extent of the collected area, and no discrete concentrations were observed. The overall artifact density at Locus 2 is much lower than at Locus 1, but four concentrations were collected as features.

Features at Locus 2. Feature 1 was located at the northern end of the grid (55S 15W) a few meters away from a rhyolite outcrop. Forty-nine artifacts were recovered, including three cores, 20 unretouched complete flakes, two retouched pieces, and 24 unretouched fragments, all made of rhyolite. Attempts to reconstruct the cores resulted in only a few pieces being fitted to the cores from which they were struck. This suggests that Feature 2 represents the primary reduction of pieces of rhyolite, probably obtained from the outcrop, but that many of the flakes produced were removed for use elsewhere. The presence of one notch and a graver/perforator suggests that tool use may have occurred at the locus of reduction.

Feature 4 (224S10W) consisted of approximately 125 small angular fragments of light gray rhyolite. The morphology of the surfaces of these items suggests that none was produced by intentional flaking. The significance of this feature is not entirely clear. One possibility is that it represents the remains of a chunk which broke apart as a result of natural processes such as thermal weathering, or perhaps it was run over by heavy equipment. In view of the isolation of this feature with respect to rhyolite outcrops to the north, it is also possible that Feature 4 represents the remains of a chunk which was deliberately smashed against the ground in order to obtain a large quantity of sharp fragments.

Features 2 and 3 are located within a few meters of each other outside the grid, on a high knoll approximately 70 m west of the transmission line centerline. Rhyolite bedrock is exposed along the top of the knoll, and naturally occurring angular chunks are abundant. Feature 3 was found in a dense concentration of natural chunks. Feature 2 was situated at a slightly lower elevation a few meters to the southwest of Feature 3 in an area in which natural chunks of raw material are more dense.

Feature 2 yielded 234 artifacts, including 10 cores, 108 unretouched complete flakes, 107 unretouched fragments, and 9 retouched pieces. Twenty-five collected pieces are probably natural fragments. Feature 2 undoubtedly represents the reduction of several rhyolite chunks obtained at the outcrop. Although the retouched pieces suggest that tool use may also have occurred, their low frequency indicates that most of the artifacts represent primary reduction debris. Attempts at core reconstruction produced four nearly complete reduction sequences, each of which involved an angular chunk of rhyolite. Through further examination of these reconstructed chunks it was discovered that all four could be assembled into a single piece of material. This seems to indicate that the original piece of material broke along planes of natural fracture during the initial stages of reduction, and that the resulting chunks were then further reduced. It is also possible that the original piece of material was deliberately thrown against the ground in order to break it into smaller pieces more convenient for reduction. Although time did not permit reconstruction of the remaining artifacts from Feature 2, it is likely that they represent similar activities.

Feature 3 contained three cores, 20 unretouched complete flakes, 13 unretouched fragments, and no retouched pieces. With the exception of a few flakes which were found to articulate with each other, no reconstructable reduction episodes were found. Although the significance of Feature 3 in relation to Feature 2 is not certain, one hypothesis is that Feature 3 is primarily composed of flakes and cores which were produced by raw material testing, and that selected cores were removed to more level, less rocky ground at Feature 2 for further reduction.

Sample 2. Sample 2 was collected from a 5 m^2 surface unit situated on the top of the ridge to the west of Locus 1 and was characterized by an extremely high artifact density. In comparison to an overall artifact density of 0.3 artifacts per m^2 at Locus 1, for example, the artifact density at Sample 2 was 155 times greater (46.5 artifacts per m^2). Outcrops which served as the source of raw material are located within 2 m to the east and west of the collected area. Here medium textured granite and the same brown felsite common at Locus 1 are interbedded. Although the geological processes which resulted in the association of the felsite with the granite are not completely understood, it seems likely that the granite formed first and that some agent, possibly tectonic movement, caused fissures to form in the granite. As a result of later volcanism, faster cooling felsic magma was forced into the interstices. The felsite thus occurs in the form of veins of variable width in a granitic matrix. Weathering of the outcrops has produced angular chunks of material which may be either entirely composed of granite or felsite, or contain both rock types. Between the outcrops, pieces of material seldom exceed 15 cm in length, and the ground surface is littered with much smaller natural fragments. At the outcrops larger chunks, including boulder-sized pieces, are present. The analysis indicates that lithic reduction at Sample 2 focused primarily on the extraction of felsite, and that only a small percentage of the artifacts were produced by secondary reduction to shape tools.

In comparison to Loci 1 and 2, Sample 2 is lower in cores and retouched pieces, and is much higher in unretouched fragments. In terms of reduction product frequencies, then, Sample 2 strongly resembles AZ CC:9:2, AZ CC:10:16 and AZ CC:13:6. Since these three sites appear to represent more intensive reduction activities than Loci 1 or 2, the similarity between the reduction product frequencies of Sample 2 and AZ CC:9:2, AZ CC:13:6, and AZ CC:10:6 suggests that Sample 2 may also represent more intensive reduction than Loci 1 or 2. The underlying assumption is that more intensive reduction produces more unretouched fragments in relation to other kinds of artifacts.

Evidence which indicates that primary reduction was more thorough at Sample 2 than at any of the other sites which yielded core samples sufficiently large for comparative purposes can be seen in the data on cortex, direction of flaking, and number of flake scars. In comparison to Locus 1 for example, cores of the 0 percent and 0 to 10 percent cortex classes are strongly represented at Sample 2. While unidirectional cores are the most common type at Locus 1, bidirectional cores predominate at Sample 2. Cores showing three flake scars are the most frequent at Sample 2, while those showing only one flake scar are the most common at Locus 1.

A possible reason why primary reduction was more intensive at Sample 2 than at Locus 1 concerns the forms in which felsite occurs. Although small chunks and natural fragments composed entirely of felsite are present at Sample 2, large naturally occurring pieces composed entirely of felsite may be relatively uncommon. Instead, larger volumes of felsite probably occur most often as veins in larger chunks of granite.

Locus 1 is located on a terrace-like alluvial deposit containing gravels of materials presumably derived from the outcrops at Sample 2 and similar outcrops to the west and north of Sample 2. Because pieces of material at Locus 1 have been detached from their sources longer than those at Sample 2, one might expect that they have been subjected to more thorough natural reduction by thermal fracturing and abrasion. Consequently, one would expect that pieces of material at Locus 1 would show a less expansive size range and generally tend to be smaller and more rounded than the felsite-bearing granite chunks at Sample 2. More importantly, because material at Locus 1 has been more thoroughly reduced by natural processes, it is possible that individual pieces are more homogeneous with respect to the two rock types than pieces at Sample 2. If this is true, primary reduction may have been more intensive at Sample 2 because cores had to be more thoroughly reduced in order to get at felsite occurring in chunks that also contained a lot of granite. In contrast, intensive reduction to obtain felsite flakes may not have been necessary at Locus 1 if felsite cobbles relatively free of granite could be obtained.

Some evidence to support this interpretation can be seen in the raw material texture data. At Sample 2, about 20 percent of the artifacts analyzed were assigned to the mixed texture class, indicating that they were approximately equally composed of both felsite and granite. At Locus 1 less than 2 percent were assigned to the mixed texture class. This suggests that individual pieces of material reduced at Sample 2 may have been more heterogeneous with respect tothe two rock types than those at Locus 1.

It was also noted during the analysis that several cores from Sample 2 were almost entirely composed of granite, except for vestigial portions of felsite, sometimes showing evidence of bidirectional flake removal. Cores showing similar configurations of granite and felsite are absent in the collection from Locus 1.

Since primary reduction was more thorough at Sample 2, one might expect that flakes and fragments would be smaller than those from Locus 1. While the mean length, width, and thickness of flakes from Sample 2 are somewhat lower than the values obtained for flakes at Locus 1, the results of the analysis of variance suggests that flakes from the two collections cannot be distinguished with respect to size on the basis of the smaple sizes. Further, a comparison of the mean fragment weight suggests that the two collections are very similar to each other, and that fragments from Sample 2 may actually be slightly larger than those from Locus 1.

If, indeed, primary reduction was more intensive at Sample 2 than it was at Locus 1, why are flakes and fragments about the same size in both collections? A comparison of the mean core weights indicates that cores from Sample 2 tend to be larger than those from Locus 1. This suggests that even though reduction was more thorough at Sample 2, flakes and fragments may be about the same size in both collections because the pieces reduced were larger than those at Locus 1.

Although flakes and fragments are about the same size in all three collections from AZ CC:10:11, those from Sample 2 tend to be the least cortical. The difference between Sample 2 and Locus 1 in terms of cortex on flakes is probably a result of three factors. First, if the pieces of material reduced at Sample 2 were larger than those reduced at Locus 1, one would expect to find less cortex on Sample 2 flakes because the ratio of the surface area to volume for a larger piece of material is smaller than for a smaller piece of material. Second, since primary reduction was more thorough at Sample 2, a greater number of flakes with less cortex would have been produced in comparison to Locus 1, where reduction generally stopped sooner. And finally, flakes from Sample 2 may be less cortical than those from Locus 1 because the pieces of material may not have been completely cortical before flaking. As at Locus 2, chunks reduced at Sample 2 may not have been detached from the outcrop long enough to develop cortex on much of their surfaces.

In general, then, the major differences between Sample 2 and Locus 1 are probably attributable to the relative intensity of primary reduction as dictated by the form in which felsite occurs. Although this interpretation seems to provide adequate explanations for most of the variation, one unanswered question concerns flake size. If the pieces of material reduced at Sample 2 were larger than those at Locus 1, one might expect a greater range of flake sizes at Sample 2 even though primary reduction was more intensive. For example, the flakes produced by the initial stages of primary reduction should be larger than at Locus 1. Yet, not only do flakes from the two collections have similar mean thicknesses, they share the same thickness range as well. One possible explanation is that the initial stages of primary reduction focused on the removal of the granite matrix, and that this operation more often occurred closer to or on the outcrops. Pieces of material from which most of the granite had been removed may then have been brought to the area between the outcrops for more thorough reduction. As a result, larger flakes struck during the initial stages of primary reduction may not have been present within the collected area. It is also possible that large flakes which could have been struck during the initial stages of primary reduction were not produced because reduction focused on trimming away granite, rather than striking larger flakes composed of both materials. Further analysis focusing on the raw material composition of individual artifacts with respect to reduction product categories might clarify explanations for variation between Sample 2 and Locus 1; it may be related to different raw material extraction strategies.

The presence of retouched pieces, accounting for 6 percent of the artifacts from Sample 2, indicates that secondary reduction as well as primary reduction occurred. As is the case at Locus 1 and Locus 2, flaked chunks which are probably secondary cores were collected at Sample 2. While notches, the most abundant type, and irregularly retouched pieces may have been produced by deliberate secondary reduction, it is also possible that the retouch was caused by postdepositional destructive forces. Because of the extremely high artifact density, the likelihood that Sample 2 was either occupied intensively for a short time or intermittently for a long time, and the likelihood that its inhabitants dropped sizable pieces of rock in the collected area, the significance of the notches and irregularly retouched pieces is unclear.

The presence of scrapers, denticulates, graver/perforators, heavy unifaces, and two burins suggest that tools were not only manufactured at the locus of Sample 2, but that they were used and discarded there as well. This range of tool types suggests that a variety of tasks relating to processing biotic resources was also carried out here.

AZ CC:13:15

This site is located 1.3 km east of the southern tip of Willcox Playa in an area once inundated by Pleistocene Lake Cochise. Lithic raw material is virtually nonexistent in the sandy loam substrate, either on the site or in the surrounding area.

The artifact assemblage from AZ CC:13:15 is composed almost entirely of potsherds; only seven nonground stone items were collected. Two of these are small, flat pebbles of basalt and possibly silicified wood, measuring 21 and 14 mm, respectively. The surfaces of both pebbles are polished, but microscopic examination revealed no evidence of use. These pebbles are thus assumed to have occurred naturally at the site.

Three small, angular chunks of basalt, collected from 5S 5E, were assembled to form a partial reconstruction of an angular pebble which could have been no larger than 30 mm. Since the fractured surfaces of the individual chunks are planes of natural fracture, it is impossible to determine if the pebble broke apart during a deliberate attempt at reduction, or as the result of natural processes. This pebble also shows polished surfaces, but no clear evidence of use was revealed under microscopic examination.

A small, discoidal rhyolite fragment, 13 mm long, was collected from 45N 10W and is probably a thermal spall, possibly originating from a larger artifact which was not found.

The only artifact from AZ CC:13:15 which can be positively identified as being the result of intentional lithic reduction is a small proximal flake fragment of basalt measuring about 26 mm. The exterior surface is noncortical, but the platform appears to be a polished cortical surface which contrasts sharply with the texture of the interior and exterior surfaces. Microscopic examination of the platform showed no clear evidence of use in the form of striations, but the edge formed by the intersection of the platform and the exterior surface is markedly rounded in comparison to other edges. This flake fragment was probably produced by tool resharpening after use.

The lack of lithic artifacts at AZ CC:13:15 indicates that material was brought to the site in the form of finished tools which were used, sometimes modified, and then removed for use elsewhere. While the evidence for tool modification consists solely of the above-described flake fragment, it is possible that the debris produced by tool refurbishing was usually very small and thus not recovered by the AEPCO field crew. The extent to which this factor may have contributed to the absence of evidence for activities involving lithic artifacts is, however, unknown.

Another explanation is that the activities which occurred at AZ CC:13:15 did not require the use of stone tools. One might suspect that the implements used to collect or harvest certain plant materials, such as leguminous seed pods, berries, roots, tubers, and so forth, may have been more often made of wood rather than stone.

The absence of chipped stone at AZ CC:13:15 may be related to a combination of both the explanations outlined above. The major activities performed may not have required chipped stone tools, and those few tools which were brought to the site and used may have been removed for use elsewhere.

AZ CC:13:16

AZ CC:13:16 is located south of AZ CC:13:15 on a sand dune along an extinct lake margin, 0.8 km east of the Willcox Playa. Naturally occurring lithic raw material is almost completely absent on and near the site.

Fifty-nine nonground lithics were collected, only eight of which can be positively identified as the products of intentional reduction. They include one heavy uniface, one projectile point, two unretouched complete flakes, and four unretouched fragments.

The heavy uniface is a plane made on a cobble of coarse-textured basalt, and measures 80 mm in length and 52 mm from the planar surface to the highest point on the convex surface. The working edge is irregularly convex in outline and is very steep angled, nearly 90 degrees along much of the perimeter. Many portions of the working edge are well rounded, and high spots on the planar surface exhibit a pronounced polish which is not characteristic of most other surfaces. Microscopic examination of the planar surface revealed striations generally oriented perpendicular to the working edge. This indicates that the implement was used in a planing fashion, with the worked material frequently in contact with the planar surface of the tool. The steep edge angle, rounded working edge, and the presence of striations all suggest that this implement was intensively used and probably modified several times before being exhausted and discarded.

The projectile point is broken and therefore consists of only the basal portion of a side-notched point of rhyolite. The surfaces are so deeply weathered that all traces of retouch flake scars have been obliterated.

With the exception of an unretouched quartz flake fragment, the remaining flakes and fragments are all made of basalt. These artifacts may possibly represent debris produced by the reduction of cores which were subsequently removed from the site, or perhaps debris which resulted from the modification of implements similar to the heavy uniface that was collected.

Twenty-nine of the remaining 51 lithics from AZ CC:13:6 are small, angular chunks of pink limestone, collected in two small concentrations. The chunks from each of these concentrations can be assembled to form a larger angular piece of limestone. From these reconstructions it is evident that the chunks broke apart along planes of natural fracture, and there are no features which could have only resulted from percussion. Thus, it is impossible to determine if these chunks broke apart as a result of deliberate reduction or natural processes.

Also collected from AZ CC:13:16 were 22 miscellaneous pieces of rock. For the most part, these are small pebbles and chunks of quartz, basalt, rhyolite, and possibly silicified wood. While some of these may be pieces of ground stone implements, it is likely that most occurred naturally.

As is the case at AZ CC:13:15, the lack of lithic artifacts at AZ CC:13:16 may indicate that the tasks performed did not frequently require the use of chipped stone tools and that most of the implements used at this site were removed for use elsewhere. The presence of ground stone implements indicates that plant processing occurred. Possibly the heavy uniface was used to work wood or prepare plant fiber. The projectile point suggests that hunting was done, but its temporal relationship to the other archaeological remains is uncertain. The absence of secondary reduction debris suggests that the point was not manufactured at the site, and it is possible that it was present long before the occupation of the site when the other artifacts were deposited.

Problems and Discussion

Generally speaking, the reduction activity model discussed earlier has been useful as a framework for formulating the characteristics of collections produced by different kinds of reduction and for interpreting the analysis results. Nevertheless, a number of problems with the application of the model can be identified.

In terms of its implication for the preceding interpretations, the most serious problem concerns distinguishing primary and secondary reduction when both occurred at the same locus, especially when there is reason to suspect that primary reduction was intensive. In such situations, intensive primary reduction would have produced more smaller, less cortical primary flakes and fragments than if primary reduction were not as thorough. As a result, the range of variation of size and cortex for primary flakes and fragments may more completely overlap with that for secondary flakes and fragments than if primary reduction were less intensive. Rather than trying to make statements about the relative importance of specific reduction activities, it is more realistic, on the basis of the attributes examined, to discuss intersite variation resulting from these activities within the broader context of reduction intensity.

In the future, it may be possible to make stronger statements about the prevalence of particular activities by analyzing other formal attributes in addition to size and cortex. Primary flakes may tend to be thicker in relation to length and width than secondary flakes, regardless of absolute size. Comparisons of flake samples with respect to an index of relative thickness may therefore help distinguish primary and secondary products. The angle formed by the platform and the interior surface may tend to be steeper on primary flakes than on secondary flakes. Platform angle could thus be a useful attribute for distinguishing primary and secondary reduction.

The unretouched fragment category used in this analysis is a gross artifact class that includes flake fragments and angular, irregular pieces which are very diverse in size. Since primary reduction may produce more angular fragments than secondary reduction, and secondary reduction may produce more flake fragments than angular fragments, distinctions between primary and secondary reduction might be clarified if the unretouched fragment category were split into more formally specific categories such as "flake fragments," "chunks," "shatter," and so forth.

Further studies to distinguish primary and secondary reduction on the basis of relative flake thickness, platform angle, and the frequency of different kinds of fragments could all be strengthened with comparative experimental studies focusing on formal variation in primary and secondary products.

Another problem in the application of the reduction activity model concerns modification reduction. Because modification is defined as the reduction of a tool after use, its visibility in the archaeological record depends on the identification of use-wear. The small size of the collections from AZ CC:13:15 and 16 permitted careful microscopic examination that revealed some evidence that tool refurbishing occurred at these sites. Because the analysis did not attempt to identify use-wear in any systematic fashion, however, the importance of modification in the other collections is uncertain.

This problem suggests a hypothesis which could be tested by further research. The form and frequency of the various reduction products indicate that reduction was more intensive at AZ CC:10:6, AZ CC:9:2, AZ CC:13:6, 11, and 14 than it was at the other sites. If the need for intensive reduction was stimulated by a raw material scarcity at these sites, then one would expect to find more evidence of modification than at sites where raw material was abundant.

One problem not directly related to the application of the reduction activity model is that cores and hammerstones are not mutually exclusive categories. Cores showing battering are hammerstones and cores at the same time. By classifying these artifacts as hammerstones rather than cores, core frequencies are depressed. Conceivably, this problem could have implications for the comparison of the Sulphur Spring Valley sites with other sites in terms of core frequency. Because cores were classified as hammerstones only if they showed battering over 50 percent or more of their surfaces and because cores may have been more intensively used as hammerstones in areas scarce in raw material, it is likely that relatively fewer battered cores would be classified as hammerstones in regions rich in raw material. In general, it was noted that cores were more extensively battered at AZ CC:9:2 and AZ CC:13:11 than at sites located outside the Sulphur Spring Valley. An extreme case of intensive core use can be seen in two artifacts form AZ CC:9:2; these are exhausted cores which apparently broke during use as hammerstones. When the breakage resulted in a platform from which flakes could be struck, the cores were further reduced. Such intensive use is not surprising considering the scarcity of raw material and the nature of the occupation at AZ CC:9:2.

While relatively more battered cores were probably classified as hammerstones in the Sulphur Spring Valley than elsewhere,thus depressing core frequencies at AZ CC:9:2 and AZ CC:13:11, the increase in core frequency obtained by combining cores and hammerstones is only slight, and does not seriously affect the interpretation of the reduction product frequencies.

Turning to problems of a more practical nature, a comparison of Tables 36 and 46 of Appendix III indicates discrepancies between the absolute frequencies of retouched pieces and tools. In some cases, the tool count is higher than the retouched piece count. This is expectable because the tool count includes core tools and hammerstones which were not classified as retouched pieces for the purposes of determining reduction product frequencies. In some collections, however, the absolute tool frequency is less than the retouched piece frequency. This arose when artifacts classified as retouched pieces during the initial rough sorting into the reduction product categories later proved to be unretouched under closer inspection during attribute recording. In all collections where the retouched piece frequency exceeds the tool frequency, the difference between the two counts is less than 2 percent of the sample size. These discrepancies are regrettable, but do not seriously affect the interpretations.

A more serious problem concerns the analysis of variance performed on flake thickness data. The valid application of this statistical procedure rests on two assumptions. First, the data must be normally distributed, and second, the variance of the distributions being compared must be the same (Blalock 1972). Inspection of the flake thickness histograms shows that neither of these assumptions can be made for most of the collections. It is clear, for example, that distribution from AZ CC:10:6 is so skewed that it is not even approximately normal, and the variance of the distributions from AZ CC:10:11 is obviously less than that at AZ CC:10:13. While assumptions of normality and homogeneity of variance could be relaxed if the sample sizes are very large, the flake sample sizes in the AEPCO II collections are small. This suggests that a nonparametric statistical technique may be more appropriate for the purposes of identifying significant intersite variation with respect to flake thickness.

AT AZ CC:9:2 appriximately 30 percent of all artifacts recovered in a certain portion of the site were selected for analysis by using a table of random numbers. This sampling method permitted a determination of reduction product frequencies without having to sort the entire collection from the site. If, however, the entire collection had been sorted into the reduction product categories, and random samples taken within the categories, enough cores could have been selected to enable the comparison of AZ CC:9:2 with other sites with respect to cortex, direction of flaking, number of flake scars, and weight of cores. The interpretation that reduction was more intensive at AZ CC:9:2 than at sites where raw material was more plentiful would be strengthened if further study indicated that cores tend to be smaller, less cortical, show more flake scars, and are more often multidirectional at AZ CC:9:2 than at AZ CC:10:11, 13, and 14.

Synthesis

Conceivably, the Sulphur Spring Valley sites may differ from each other in age, cultural affiliation, and occupation length, periodicity, and intensity. Yet, these collections are basically very similar to each other. In comparison to most of the sites north of Willcox Playa, the Sulphur Spring Valley collections are poor in cores, complete flakes, and retouched pieces; they are rich in unretouched fragments, and have smaller, less cortical flakes and fragments, and more heterogeneous raw material compositions. These characteristics have been interpreted as reflections of more intensive reduction of imported materials at the Sulphur Spring Valley sites, in contrast to the less intensive reduction of immediately available materials at most of the sites to the north of the valley.

Raw material scarcity, by creating a need to use lithic resources to their fullest potential, was probably an important factor contributing to the intensity of reduction at the Sulphur Spring Valley sites. Because the collections are composed chiefly of the end products of intensive reduction, one can be certain that the entire range of lithic manufacture is not represented. As a result, intersite variation possibly caused by specific reduction activities, raw material size differences, and other factors is generally not observable.

Although the Sulphur Spring Valley collections are basically very similar to one another, comparatively minor intersite variation was identified in reduction product frequencies (some collections are slightly richer in cores, complete flakes, retouched pieces, and lower in unretouched fragments), and the frequency of particular raw material types. The reduction product frequency differences are probably the result of site formation processes and collection methods, and most likely do not represent differences in the nature of lithic reduction. Variation in the raw material compositions may reflect the proximity of the sites to different raw material sources. But if artifacts were nonrandomly distributed with respect to raw material type at individual sites, differences among the collections could have been produced by chance, depending on which portions of the sites were crossed by the AEPCO transmission line.

Most of the collections from sites north of the Sulphur Spring Valley not only reflect less intensive reduction than those from the Sulphur Spring Valley, but also exhibit greater variability among themselves. To a great extent, this variability reflects the primary reduction of raw materials occurring abundantly in different forms. For example, raw material procurement and primary reduction are strongly represented at AZ CC:6:3 and AZ CC:10:13. Because the pieces of material reduced at AZ CC:6:3 were smaller, the flakes tend to be smaller and more cortical than those from AZ CC:10:13, where raw material was larger. Although reduction was less intensive at more sites in the Pinaleño Mountains than it was in the Sulphur Spring Valley, different degrees of reduction intensity are nonetheless discernible. The form of the cores, for instance, suggests that primary reduction was more intensive at AZ CC:10:11 Locus 1 than at AZ CC:10:13 and 14. This could be related to differences in the nature of the occupations or possibly in manufacturing strategies as dictated by certain raw material limitations at AZ CC:10:11 Locus 1.

One characteristic common to most of the sites located outside the Sulphur Spring Valley is that raw material procurement, primary reduction, secondary reduction (tool manufacture), tool use, and tool discard all occurred. There are no sites which were exclusively devoted to either tool manufacture or use. There is, however, some evidence suggesting that the sites may differ with respect to the relative importance of tool manufacture and use. For instance, AZ CC:10:13 is lower in cores and higher in retouched pieces than is AZ CC:10:11 Locus 1. Tool use may thus have been more prevalent at AZ CC:10:13 than at AZ CC:10:11 Locus 1.

Generally speaking, most of the collections from the Pinaleño Mountains bajadas sites represent the nonintensive reduction of materials occurring abundantly on or in close proximity to the sites, and are probably associated with the collection or processing of biotic resources.

Two collections do not conform to this pattern: AZ CC:10:11 Sample 2 and AZ CC:10:6. Core attributes indicate that, of all the sites having collections which contain enough cores for statistical comparisons, primary reduction was the most intensive at AZ CC:10:11 Sample 2. The reduction product frequencies in this collection strongly resemble those characteristic of the Sulphur Spring Valley sites. This further suggests that reduction was intensive. The unusual intensity of reduction has largely been attributed to the necessity of first extracting workable material from veins in a granitic matrix.

Like AZ CC:10:11 Sample 2, AZ CC:10:6 is lower in cores, retouched pieces, and complete flakes, and richer in unretouched fragments. Both flakes and fragments are smaller and less cortical than those from any other sites outside the Sulphur Spring Valley, and the raw material composition is heterogeneous. In short, AZ CC:10:6 is completely typical of the collections from the Sulphur Spring Valley, reflecting intensive reduction of material which was largely obtained from offsite sources.

To some extent, the characteristics of the collection from AZ CC:10:6 may be related to raw material availability. Of all the sites located in the Pinaleño upper bajadas, raw material appears to be the least plentiful at AZ CC:10:6. The scarcity of raw material on the site may thus have contributed to the intensity of the reduction by creating a need to more fully use lithic material. Unlike the Sulphur Spring Valley sites, however, where raw material is not only scarce on the sites, but in the surrounding regions as well, raw material is plentiful in the areas around AZ CC:10:6. Hence, raw material availability is not a completely adequate explanation for variation between AZ CC:10:6 and other sites outside the Sulphur Spring Valley.

An alternative explanation concerns the function of individual sites as components of broader subsistence systems. It is possible that AZ CC:10:11 13, 14, and AZ CC:6:3 represent sites which were devoted to the procurement of biotic and abiotic resources, or perhaps were temporary camps associated with extractive activities carried out nearby. In contrast, AZ CC:10:6 may be a more permanently occupied base camp where the processing and the use of biotic and abiotic resources collected from the surrounding areas were the principal activities involving chipped stone tools.

Differences between the lithic collections from base camps and extractive sites can be expected. Because base camps should contain artifacts made of materials obtained from different sources in the surrounding areas, one would expect heterogeneous raw material composition. In contrast, people engaged in collecting biotic resources at extractive sites probably used whatever lithic raw materials were immediately available. Depending on the variety of rock types present, raw material compositions at extractive sites may thus be either heterogeneous or homogeneous.

Because base camps were most likely occupied for longer periods of time than work camps, one would expect the products of previous reductions to be subjected to further reduction and reuse more often at a base camp. As a result, the form and frequency of reduction products may indicate more intensive reduction at base camps. If lithic material was often brought to base camps in the form of flakes and finished tools, rather than cores, one might also expect to find less evidence of primary reduction than at extractive sites.

The characteristics of the collections from AZ CC:10:6 support the interpretation that this site was a base camp, and that the other sites located in the Pinaleño Mountains bajadas represent impermanent occupations devoted to the procurement of natural resources. If one accepts the differences in reduction intensity between AZ CC:10:6 and the other sites in the Pinaleño upper bajadas as being the result of differences in site function (for example base camp versus extractive sites), one must also consider the possibility that site function, rather than raw material availability, is the primary cause of differences in reduction intensity which can be seen when comparing the Sulphur Spring Valley sites (AZ CC:13:11, AZ CC:9:2, AZ CC:13:14) to the Pinaleño upper bajada sites. In other words, perhaps reduction intensity at the Sulphur Spring Valley sites is more strongly related to their function as base camps than to the raw material scarcity.

Indeed, there is evidence suggesting that AZ CC:9:2, AZ CC:13:6 and AZ CC:13:11 were relatively permanent occupations, involving the processing of what may have been diverse natural resources, and that they may be interpreted as base camps. While it is reasonable to assume that site function, length and intensity of occupation, and raw material scarcity interacted to produce reduction intensity, and that these factors may have contributed unequally to reduction intensity at different sites, no precise statement of the importance of these factors in relation to each other can be made for any particular sites.

At AZ CC:13:14, the importance of raw material scarcity in comparison to site function in causing intensive reduction is more certain. Its small size and lack of depth suggest that this site was occupied for a much shorter time than either AZ CC:10:16, AZ CC:9:2, AZ CC:13:6, or AZ CC:13:11, and cannot be classified as a base camp in the same sense as the above sites. At best, it might be postulated that AZ CC:13:14 represents a very brief occupation, perhaps no longer than a day or two, during which only limited processing of natural resources occurred. As such, lithic raw material scarcity, rather than occupation length or intensity, is viewed as the primary cause of reduction intensity. It is further suggested that the lithic collection from this site would look very different had the same task been performed in an area of abundant raw material.

Sites devoted to the extraction of lithic raw material are absent in the Sulphur Spring Valley. But, sites at which biotic resources were collected, because of the temporary nature of their occupation and the need to conserve lithic material, may yield little or no lithic artifacts, even though chipped stone tools were used. AZ CC:13:15 and 16 may thus be the typical expression of primary extractive, rather than processing sites, in the Sulphur Spring Valley.

Attempts to identify significant intersite variation in terms of tool type frequencies met with only limited success because of small tool sample sizes in most of the collections. Nonetheless, very general differences between the Sulphur Spring Valley collections, and the collections from the Pinaleño bajadas were identified with respect to a few tool types. Uniface fragments are generally more frequent in the Sulphur Spring Valley, suggesting retouched pieces are not only less abundant than they are elsewhere, but that the also tend to be more fragmentary. This would not be surprising considering the differences between the sites of the two regions with respect to the intensity of lithic use.

Notches, irregularly retouched pieces, and denticulates generally seem to be more abundant in the collections from outside the Sulphur Spring Valley. This trend might also be related to variation in the intensity of reduction. Because reduction was intensive at the Sulphur Spring Valley sites, tools showing only a limited amount of retouch such as notches, irregularly retouched pieces, and denticulates, may have been modified to such an extent that their original forms are no longer recognizable. Because reduction was less intensive at most sites outside the Sulphur Spring Valley, notches, irregularly retouched pieces, and denticulates may have more often escaped further reduction after use. Comparison of the collections with respect to tool weight and edge angle might provide further indications of the effects of different degrees of reduction intensity on tool form. Additional study might find lower mean tool weights and steeper edge angles where reduction was more intensive.

In conclusion, one aspect of the study found to be of particular interest will be briefly mentioned. The core reconstructions from AZ CC:10:11, 13, 14, and AZ CC:6:3 have provided very specific information about some of the reduction activities that occurred at these sites. Casual inspection of these core reconstructions indicated that variation exists in the degree to which the method of reduction was patterned. At one end of the spectrum, reduction was completely random, suggesting little if any concern for the production of regularly sized and shaped flakes. At the other extreme, some examples exhibit highly systematized reduction methods, involving platform preparation and the consistent repetition of flake removal around the core. Conceivably, differences in the degree to which reduction methods were patterned, and the patterns themselves, could be related to raw material variability, the purposes for which the flakes were intended, cultural traditions, or idiosyncratic preferences held by individual knappers. Further studies of the AEPCO II core reconstructions, and others like them, could provide valuable information about the role of the abovementioned factors in contributing to technological variability.

CHAPTER 8

SUMMARY AND DISCUSSION

Summary of Research Goals, Data Recovery and Analysis Results

In this final chapter research goals are briefly summarized and analysis results are evaluated and discussed. The AEPCO II data analysis was intended to clearly describe and analyze the composition of both small and large surface lithic scatter sites, which had rarely been studied. Although much material was collected and the analysis designed to be as comprehensive as possible, not all goals could be fully realized. The AEPCO II study, however, has provided some substantial data regarding site-specific activity in the AEPCO II project area. The special emphasis given to analyzing the chipped stone assemblages has shown that numerous variables affect archaeological surface remains, and these must be carefully considered in any interpretation of site function.

Chapters on the ceramic, ground stone, and chipped stone have answered most of the AEPCO II research questions regarding natural resource exploitation in the general study area. Differences and similarities among the sites with respect to their artifact assemblages and environmental context have been discussed. Furthermore, initial comparisons have been made between the AEPCO II cultural resources and those investigated elsewhere in the region. In the following summary, each site (ordered by environmental strata) is discussed briefly, with more consideration given to the significance of the AEPCO II project in the general prehistory of the region.

The basic hypothesis guiding the AEPCO II study is that sites are located with respect to the availability of certain natural resources and that analysis of archaeological remains will identify the specific activities conducted at sites. It was hoped that identification of these activities could provide a data base for making inferences about prehistoric land use. This study attempted to answer questions about lithic raw material procurement, tool manufacture, tool use and discard, how these particular activities contributed to site composition, and what particular subsistence and settlement practices could be identified from site characteristics. Most of the questions regarding lithic exploitation were answered; problems of general subsistence pursuits and settlement proved to be more difficult to answer.

An examination of the results of several other investigations at Archaic sites in southeastern Arizona (Huckell 1973; Windmiller 1973; Whalen 1971) shows that many small surface or shallow sites reflect an emphasis on hunting and gathering. Whalen (1971), using a model developed by Binford and Binford (1969), divides such nonagricultural sites into two basic types: work camp and base camp. The former reflects specific "extractive" activities, such as lithic reduction, food gathering, hunting, or some combination of these. Resources were brought into a base camp where further extractive tasks and "maintenance" tasks were done, such as tool manufacture and refurbishing, food preparation, and food consumption or storage.

Goodyear and Dittert (1973:80) describe a base camp in the Papaguería as "a site of demonstrable varied activities of a kin group or by both sexes." Such sites contain large quantities of both sherds and lithics, and the artifact inventory as a rule is more complex than that of simple gathering sites.

There may or may not be evidence for domiciliary structures, such as ramadas; it is unlikely that remains of such features constructed during the Archaic period would survive in the archaeological record. Features such as roasting pits and storage pits also aid in determining the relative length of occupation that would verify the hypothesis that a site is a base camp.

Stewart and Teague (1974) developed a set of criteria to determine if large artifact scatters in the Vekol Mountains area of the Papaguería were base camps. These criteria are:

(1) Sites are situated so as to provide the most efficient utilization of nearby biotic and/or abiotic resources.

(2) Base camps are centrally located in terms of their relationship to all gathering site groups.

(3) Tool assemblages at base camps are related to multiple sets of activities which suggest more processing activities than occur at gathering sites.

(4) Base camps vary through time.

The general criteria used in these studies served as a comparative basis for determining the function of the larger AEPCO II sites, as will be seen below.

Corridor environmental strata were set up in the AEPCO I study for ordering sites to test general ideas about prehistoric land use (Simpson and Westfall 1978).This was continued in the AEPCO II study. Due to the low number of sites in any one stratum in the AEPCO II study, however, no substantial statements about general patterns of land use in certain microenvironments can be made. The study has shown, however, that sites do differ at a grosser level of environmental variability, such as the desert grassland area encompassing the Dos Cabezas lower bajadas, Willcox Playa dunes, and Sulphur Spring Valley on the one hand and the woody plant zones of the Pinaleño upper bajadas on the other.

Because no detailed biological studies were made during th AEPCO II project, and only one investigated site yielded faunal remains, little can be said about prehistoric diet. The necessary information is not available to identify changes in patterns of food procurement through time and to determine the degree of seasonality or permanence of site occupation. A few sites do, however, contain culturally diagnostic artifacts which can be used to tentatively place them into a cultural-temporal framework.

1. San Simon Basin/Pinaleño Mountains Lower Bajadas Transition Zone

AZ CC:6:3 is distinct from the other AEPCO II sites in its relative isolation and its artifact assemblage. Primary reduction of pebbles and small cobbles obtained from desert pavement was a dominant activity, and many of the reduction products were probably used as tools with a minimum of modification. A single cordmarked rim sherd found at the site has a late date of A.D. 1100 to 1300 (Breternitz 1966), but it is not known if the sherd is contemporaneous with the lithic material. No diagnostic lithic pieces were found, and the cultural and temporal affiliation of the site remains tentative.

Seven reconstructible lithic reduction episodes were identified which show that pebbles were reduced, tools were made for expedient use, and then were discarded on the spot. The small size of the tools found at AZ CC:6:3 is, at least in part, a result of small raw material size; the functional implications, if any, of these diminutive tools are not clear.

The sherd, the single mano fragment, and the site's location all suggest this site is probably associated with the prehistoric occupation of the Safford Valley. Another possible relationship is with sites in the Foote Wash-No Name Wash drainage to the west (Fitting 1977). As is the case with surface sites in general, however, such suggestions about associations can only be tentative.

2. Pinaleño Mountains Upper Bajadas

Of the 12 sites recorded in this zone, four were investigated, which are believed to be fairly representative of the range of site types encountered in this zone, except for the possible village sites AZ CC:6:6 and 7. Sites AZ CC:10:13 and 14, on ridge crests, appear to be loci where activities related to hunting and plant gathering and initial processing were carried out. Tool types at these sites include scrapers, notched flakes, denticulates, heavy unifaces, and small bifaces. Heavy unifaces and notches may suggest that wood working or plant processing were done, while the small bifaces suggest projectile point manufacture indicating hunting. Analysis of reduction product frequencies shows that primary reduction, secondary reduction (tool manufacture) and tool use all occurred at AZ CC:10:13 and 14. Raw material procurement for chipped stone tools was then probably coincident with biotic resource procurement and processing at these two sites.

The enormous size of the site and high raw material and debitage density at AZ CC:10:11 indicate that quarrying was an important concern at this site. The existence of retouched pieces indicates that procurement and processing of biotic resources also was an important activity. In contract to AZ CC:10:13 and 14, however the relative frequency of retouched pieces at AZ CC:10:11 (Loci 1 and 2) is low. This may be due to the abundance of raw material, whereby the need for tools was reduced, since a sharp edged flake could be easily and quickly obtained. It was also pointed out, however, that structural flaws in the raw material at AZ CC:10:11 may have contributed to the low number of retouched pieces. The implication is that limitations inherent in raw material effectively preclude stylized tool manufacture, such that flakes showing little or no further modification may have been used as tools. This creates problems in determining whether reduction was done primarily to obtain raw material or to produce tools. The problem cannot be conclusively resolved on either point at this time.

AZ CC:10:6 differs from the three sites discussed above in its diversity of artifacts and the existence of cultural depth. The ground and chipped stone artifacts indicate the activities included seed grinding, general plant processing, hunting and game processing, and chipped stone tool manufacture, use, and refurbishing. These indications of multipurpose use and occupational depth suggest that the site functioned as a base camp, in contrast to AC CC:10:11, 13, and 14, which appear to have been work camps.

The nearness of Dial Wash may have been an important factor in site location. While mesquite and acacia are abundant on the bajada, the wash contains denser growths of these, in addition to desert willow, walnut, and hackberry, which are not available in the drier areas. The wash, then, provides favorable habitat as well as abundant biotic resources necessary to maintain existence for a length of time.

It is no coincidence that the two other major sites in this zone, AZ CC:66:6 and 7 just to the north of AZ CC:10:6, also are situated adjacent to major drainages that are fed by numerous deep arroyos from the Pinaleño Mountains. AZ CC:6:6 is similar to AZ CC:10:6 in having a dense scatter of chipped and ground stone, but no pottery. In contrast to AZ CC:10:6, however, backhoe testing revealed cultural deposits at AZ CC:6:6 to a minimum depth of 60 cm, indicating a much longer occupation. AZ CC:6:7 is different from the other two sites in that plainware pottery is abundant on the surface. Testing at this site also revealed dense material to a depth of 1 m and exposed a possible stone wall. It is unfortunate that more information is not available from AZ CC:6:6 and 7, as well as from the outlying areas of AZ CC:10:6, which could answer numerous questions about prehistoric occupation of this area.

The area of AZ CC:6:6, AZ CC:6:7 and AZ CC:10:6 is peppered with numerous granite bedrock outcrops. These served as a source of bedrock mortars, and by their number and depth, appear to have been used over a long period of time. Such outcrops do not occur elsewhere in the path of the transmission line, although it is expected that other sites with bedrock mortars may be found in an areal survey. The availability of bedrock for mortars may also have been a factor in deciding site location. They are known to have been used by the Papago for processing mesquite bean pods (Doelle 1976). No direct evidence exists from the site for mesquite or other leguminous plant processing, and available pollen data from AZ CC:10:6 are scant in leguminous plant pollen. Nevertheless, the likelihood is strong that mesquite or some other seed was processed in the mortars at these sites. Because these sites may be base camps (or long-term habitation at AZ CC:6:7), it is possible that there may be outlying gathering stations where vegetal materials were obtained and brought in for processing.

AZ CC:10:6 may have been occupied at one time by Cochise culture groups during the late Chiricahua and San Pedro stages. There is also evidence for occupation by Amargosa-like groups. These suggestions are based on ground stone characteristics and projectile point styles. The site is distinctive in having one of the highest frequencies of projectile points (mostly broken, however) and high frequencies of small bifaces and small retouched pieces. This could be taken to mean that hunting was more important at this site than at others, or simply that it was an important activity in itself, although its importance in relation to plant food gathering cannot be determined. As pointed out earlier, the relative frequencies of ground versus chipped stone from site surfaces are not meaningful because of the high likelihood of artifact removal from the sites. This problem prevents determination of a site's cultural and temporal affiliation on the basis of differing subsistence strategies.

AZ CC:10:6 is very similar to two other sites in the Sulphur Spring Basin, AZ CC:9:2 and CC:13:6, both of which may be large base camps. The relationship of these large sites to each other, however, cannot be positively determined beyond finding similarities in their respective chipped stone assemblages because not enough supporting data are available.

3. Dos Cabezas Lower Bajadas

The two prehistoric sites recorded in this zone (AZ CC:9:2 and 3) contain the best evidence for a desert Archaic occupation on the basis of diagnostic artifact types. Both are extensive artifact scatters with discrete artifact concentrations that may indicate specific activity areas. AZ CC:9:3 was avoided by AEPCO and therefore not investigated; AZ CC:9:2 was investigated where the R-O-W crossed the western periphery of the site.

AZ CC:9:2 has numerous characteristics in common with AZ CC:10:6 in the Pinaleño bajadas to the north, and with AZ CC:13:6 in the sand dunes to the south. These include large site size, diversity of artifacts, and similarity to their respective artifact assemblages. Like the other two sites, AZ CC:9:2 is probably a base camp, where the prehistoric inhabitants took advantage of a variety of accessible biotic resources in the Dos Cabezas upper and lower bajadas and the desert grasslands of the Sulphur Spring Valley.

The artifacts recovered from AZ CC:9:2 range from implements connected with hunting and gathering to those associated with resource processing. No information exists to determine specifically what was obtained and processed, but it can be assumed that many of the resources available were used. The lithic data indicate that the majority of raw material was brought in from elsewhere to be worked into tools. Tools themselves were also brought into the site. This suggests that extractive tasks, such as obtaining lithic raw meterial, plant and animal foods, and other basic necessities were conducted in areas away from the site, and brought to AZ CC:9:2 to be further processed and possibly consumed. The presence of pestles indicates that the mortar and pestle were part of the food processing tool kit. Leguminous plant products as well as other grassland resources may have also been obtained and processed by the site inhabitants. The mortar and pestle combination suggests some affinities with AZ CC:10:6 to the north where bedrock mortars are found nearby.

AZ CC:9:2 is similar to AZ CC:10:6 in terms of tool form and frequency; however, the stylistic attributes of several artifacts suggest that the initial occupation of AZ CC:9:2 was earlier. The slab and shallow basin metates, for example, are typical Chiricahua stage types, as are the one-hand manos dominating the ground stone inventory. The projectile points, while difficult to assign to a cultural group, nevertheless display characteristics described for California desert cultures. Only a very small number have attributes typical for Chiricahua or San Pedro Cochise. The majority resemble Pinto Basin and Gypsum Cave types, which may be subsumed under Amargosa II, dated 3000 to 2500 B.C. (Rogers 1966). AZ CC:10:6, on the other hand, has more characteristics typical of the San Pedro stage (1000 B.C. to A.D. 1), although several Pinto type points at AZ CC:10:6 suggest a late Amargosa II date preceding the San Pedro stage occupation. The pestles found at AZ CC:9:2 are not particularly useful for dating purposes, although some points regarding their occurrence are noteworthy. Haury (1950:324) noted that a pestle was found at a Sulphur Spring stage site at Double Adobe in the Sulphur Spring Valley. Sayles and others (n.d.) state that while pestles do occur in the Chiricahua stage, only in the San Pedro stage are the mortar and pestle found as fully developed implements. Additionally, the largest pestle found at AZ CC:9:2 resembles one found at San Simon Village (Sayles 1945:Plate XXXIV), which is an early Mogollon site. The presence of the pestles at AZ CC:9:2 could indicate relationships either with San Simon Village or earlier Cochise groups, but this may never be determined given the surface context of these artifacts.

4. Willcox Playa Dunes

The two sites investigated in this zone--AZ CC:13:6 and 6--differ from sites in the mountainous areas, having a more mixed artifact assemblage and evidence of continuous, sustained use.

AZ CC:13:11, Locus 1 yielded much subsurface material, yet the data are difficult to interpret. One reason is the site's location in a sand dune area resulted in poorly preserved stratigraphy. Testing revealed the occurrence of artifacts to a maximum depth of 60 cm, but occupation levels could not be defined either by changes in the artifact assemblages, or change in soil color. No architectural features or occupation surfaces were defined. It is probable that the unstabilized nature of the dune surface, combined with natural erosion and animal burrowing, have destroyed such recognizable features.

Analysis of the lithics at Locus 1 has shown that lithic reduction activity was particularly intensive, especially secondary reduction, presumably because of the raw material scarcity. Few tools were recovered; this was surprising in view of the apparent heavy use of the site, but they may have been removed from the site. While no projectile points were found, hunting and butchering are amply documented by the quantity and variety of burned bone that was recovered. The remains of small birds, cotton tail rabbit, jackrabbit, badger, box turtle, and mud turtle were found. No larger mammal remains were encountered; whether this is a result of sampling bias or simply that large mammals were not brought in to the site is not known.

Five one-hand manos, one possible slab metate, and two possible shallow basin metates were recovered. A single pollen sample from one mano revealed a high count of ragweed-type pollen; however, this is consistent with modern pollen rain and the economic significance of this is consequently lessened.

The site yielded sherds attributed to the Mimbres and San Simon branch Mogollon, as well as the Tucson Basin Hohokam (see Chapter 5, Table 24). Two discrete, but overlapping phases are represented by the sherd types: A.D. 650 to 950 and A.D. 900 to 1100. The cultural affiliation of the groups using the sites, however, cannot be confidently inferred, because the status of the San Simon branch and its relationship to the Mimbes branch Mogollon is not clear. Tucson Basin pottery types have been found in the San Pedro Valley to the west, beyond the Dragoon Mountains, and their occurrence at this site extends the range further east. Analysis of the plainware pottery has shown that it strongly resembles the plainware from San Simon Village and the AEPCO I sites in the Safford Valley. The functional analysis shows that most of the sherds are jar fragments with a high porosity index, suggesting that they are parts of ollas. Together with the decorated pottery, these data strongly point to use of this site by early Mogollon or Hohokam groups. The lithic and ground stone artifacts, however, are not markedly distinct from the other investigated sites. This factor raises the problem of determining whether other AEPCO I lithic sites are of preceramic or ceramic age. It is only because pottery was found with lithics at AZ CC:13:11 that we can say that this site may have once been occupied by the Mogollon. The problem is exacerbated by the lack of diagnostic tool types.

Locus 2, east of the site may be a separate occupation area, but it is not known whether it is contemporaneous with Locus 1. Due to its distance from the R-O-W, it was not in the impact zone, and therefore was not investigated. The 11 concentrations of ground stone fragments, lithic tools and debitage, and sherds appear to be distinct task areas. Other than making an inventory of artifacts, however, detailed *in situ* study of these concentrations could not be done.

The evidence from AZ CC:13:11 provides no clearcut picture of the site's occupation. The ground stone strongly resembles types described for the Chiricahua stage Cochise and Chiricahua-Amargosa II at Ventana Cave (Haury 1950), and are typical of the ground stone tool forms found at other sites in the AEPCO corridor. But, the pottery is decidedly from a later time. It is possible that pottery-using people reused artifacts at AZ CC:13:11 left by earlier groups, not an uncommon practice.

As noted in Chapter 4, investigations at AZ CC:13:6 were restricted to the eastern edge of the site where the R-O-W corridor crossed the base of the high sand dune. Compared to the situation at AZ CC:13:11, this dune, one of the highest and most massive in the area, is more stable and thus less prone to deposition-erosion patterns. The true function of AZ CC:13:6 remains uncertain, since the major portion of the site on the dune crest was only recorded by surface observation. Nevertheless, the number and diversity of artifact clusters strongly indicate a site of varied activities typical of a base camp as defined by Whalen (1971). Like AZ CC:13:11, this site reveals the presence of possibly two cultural groups--Archaic and early Mogollon--on the basis of distinctive ground stone tool types, projectile point style, and Mimbres pottery. The data on ground stone and lithics show a fairly high degree of artifact recycling and intensive lithic reduction. Again, this may be attributed to raw material scarcity, intensive use of the site, or both.

A minimum of 27 artifact concentrations was recorded on the dune's southern crest. (The northwestern portion of the dune was not examined due to its distance beyond the R-O-W, but more material may be present.) For ease in recording, these were designated as features, although many may not be true task areas as the name implies. The features represent grinding, primary and secondary lithic reduction to form tools, and tool use. Several brown plainware sherds occur within several features, undoubtedly the remnants of containers, but their cultural type is unknown.

Although the dune rises above what was once a well-watered area (several small dry playas are within 3 km to the east), as yet no evidence for agriculture has been found. Because of previous heavy disturbance of the R-O-W, no pollen washing was done on the recovered ground stone. It was felt that future research in the main site areas on the dune crest would yield more complete information on the question of agriculture in this area.

In summary, these two sand dune sites have created more problems than answers to questions; each is in need of additional work, as large portions of each remain uninvestigated. With respect to an examination of all the sites investigated within the AEPCO R-O-W, however, they are useful for making some suggestions about prehistoric land use, as will be seen below.

5. Sulphur Spring Basin

The three sites investigated in this zone (AZ CC:13:14, 15, and 16 are all situated close to the edge of Willcox Playa; their location appears to be a result of utilization of the Sulphur Spring Valley grassland environment.

Two of the sites (AZ CC:13:15 and 16) contained plainware sherds, the majority of which occurred at AZ CC:13:15, the only completely investigated sherd scatter site. The ceramic analysis showed that for both AZ CC:13:15 and 16, the majority of sherds have low porosities. These have been interpreted as being from water containers (as opposed to dry material storage vessels.) The sherds were too fragmentary to determine vessel shape in relation to these characteristics, but it may be assumed they were jars if they held water. Interestingly, the sherds at AZ CC:13:15 and 16 do not bear any strong resemblance to those from San Simon Village, the AEPCO I sites or AZ CC:13:11. This could represent a difference in cultural traditions, but a more plausible explanation is that the pottery reflects local manufacture, and functional differences.

No ground stone and only five lithic debitage pieces were recovered at AZ CC:13:15. Nothing is known of lithic tool use at the site; tools were probably removed when the site was abandoned. Two mano fragments and a pecked cobble were found, but no metates. The most that can be said about site function is that AZ CC:13:15 was probably a gathering station, with a minimum of initial plant processing carried out.

AZ CC:13:14, situated just northeast of AZ CC:13:15 contained a scatter of lithic debitage flakes and a concentration of ground stone and broken rock (Feature 1). Its proximity to AZ CC:13:15 suggests that plant products could have been brought here for processing, but this cannot be positively determined. The ground stone artifacts do, however, indicate plant processing was an important activity. Results of the pollen analysis for this site show that an extremely high frequency of grass pollen was present on one of the metates; this is the best evidence obtained that grass seeds were ground on these metates. The tools (uniface fragments, denticulates, and scrapers) appear to be components of a plant gathering and processing tool kit. A reconstruction of the ground stone shows that one unifacial and two bifacial metates were in use here; no manos could be found. Several pieces of metate were absent; they may have been removed for reuse elsewhere.

AZ CC:13:16 combines aspects of both AZ CC:13:14 and 15. Sherds, lithic tools and debitage, and ground stone all indicate plant gathering and processing. The brown plainware pottery is essentially similar to that at AZ CC:13:15, and the two metates are the typical slab and shallow basin types. Two chipped stone tools were recovered: an unidentified rhyolite projectile point and a large uniface showing heavy use, possibly as a pulping or planing tool. Again, the low tool number suggests that tools were brought into the sites by hunters and gatherers while they obtained grassland resources in the Sulphur Spring Basin, and were then removed.

Discussion

In summing up site activities in the AEPCO II project area, the data tend to support the interpretation of the sites as base camps and work camps. From the evidence, it appears that the larger investigated AEPCO II sites, AZ CC:10:6, AZ CC:9:2, AZ CC:13:6, and 11 were at least seasonally occupied camps where many diverse activities were carried out. The first three are roughly coeval in time and on the basis of diagnostic artifacts, were probably occupied primarily during the Chiricahua-Amargosa II time span. Although diagnostic pottery was found at AZ CC:13:11, the poor stratigraphic preservation of the site clouds its temporal significance. AZ CC:13:11 was occupied by early Mogollon or Hohokam groups, and the site therefore could be related to the occupation of San Simon Village a few kilometers to the northwest. An earlier Archaic occupation of the site, however, cannot be positively determined.

If AZ CC:9:2, AZ CC:10:6, AZ CC:13:6 and 11 are base camps, then the smaller sites could represent work camps where various procurement tasks were conducted. This function is suggested for AZ CC:6:3, AZ CC:10:11, 13, and 14 in the Pinaleño bajadas. These may represent temporarily occupied sites devoted to the procurement of lithic resources and food as well. Sites AZ CC:10:6, and AZ CC:6:6 and 7 functioning as base camps, could have been the focal point for further processing of biotic resources collected from the smaller work camps.

In the Sulphur Spring Valley, sites AZ CC:13:14, 15, and 16 may represent gathering stations, where a limited amount of processing also occurred. Some limited hunting is also indicated. The plainware pottery from AZ CC:13:15 and 16 is different from that recovered from AZ CC:13:11 and San Simon Village, but these differences may be related to the functional purpose of the vessels or their locus of manufacture, rather than to culturally determined differences. Regardless, a strong case cannot be made for drawing relationships between these gathering stations and the larger base camp/habitation sites north of the Playa since their contemporaneity cannot be established.

One goal of the AEPCO II study was to place the sites into a chronological position relative to known preceramic and early ceramic cultures. The lack of suitable materials makes absolute dating impossible; thus relative dating, using diagnostic attributes, was the only method available for placing the sites into some temporal framework. Where preceramic or ceramic sites are being dealt with and no radiometric dating is possible, projectile points may be the best index for discovering local variation in time and cultural affiliation. The presence of Pinto, Amargosa, Chiricahua, and San Pedro points enable one to assign some sites to the Chiricahua-Amargosa II and San Pedro occupation of southeastern Arizona. From a cultural perspective, the stone artifacts contain attributes similar to those described for Amargosa and Cochise sites, as well as those at Ventana Cave where artifacts attributed to both Amargosa and Cochise occur in the same stratigraphic context. While Haury and Sayles maintain an essential distinction between Cochise and Amargosa; recent researchers (Huckell 1973; Windmiller 1973) prefer to discuss sites in terms of time periods rather than as the remains of specific cultural groups. Hence, one cannot confidently assign the AEPCO sites to Amargosa or Cochise, since surface or shallow sites without diagnostic artifacts are nearly indistinguishable with respect to more generalized artifact types.

The problem of whether the AEPCO II sites were occupied by Amargosa or Cochise as distinct cultural groups cannot therefore be resolved with the data at hand. One can only demonstrate that such groups existed in the study area, and that the sites as a whole reflect discontinuous occupation from middle Archaic to early Mogollon times. Site and artifact variation appear to be related more to the availability of certain resources and procurement and processing methods than to cultural or temporal factors. In this respect, the AEPCO II sites are quite similar to other widespread desert Archaic sites, where variations on a basic, simple tool kit are perhaps best explained as a result of different adaptational strategies to certain microenvironments in the Southwest.

APPENDIX I

FAUNAL IDENTIFICATION
by
Jon S. Czaplicki

The author would like to thank Stanley J. Olsen, zooarchaeologist at the Arizona State Museum, and members of his 1977-78 zooarchaeology laboratory class who rough-sorted much of the identifiable material from the mass of small bone fragments recovered during the excavation of 11 sites. Also, Walter Birkby and Jeff Shipman of the Human Osteology Laboratory, Department of Anthropology, University of Arizona, provided identification of the human bone fragments.

AZ CC:9:2

The faunal remains from this site consisted of small, fragmented bits and pieces of bone, some of which were burned. Only one piece was identifiable.

	Right	Left	Indet.*	MNI**
Class Mammalia				
Order Lagomorpha				
Family Leporidae				
Lepus californicus (jackrabbit)				1
scapula, proximal	1			

AZ CC:13:11

Essentially all identifiable faunal material from AEPCO II came from this site. The material consisted of highly fragmented pieces and slivers of bone, almost all of which could not be identified. Many of these small bone pieces were burned. Sixteen complete and partial elements were identified, and pieces of turtle carapace were recognized, but identification could only be made to the Family level. One upper molar and several cranial fragments were identified as human, although the latter were not absolute identifications.

	Right	Left	Indet.	MNI
Class Reptilia				
Family Chelydridae				
Kinosternon sp. (mud turtle)				1
carapace fragment			1	
Family Testudinidae (box turtle)				1
genus and species indeterminate				
carapace fragments	1			

*Indet. = indeterminate; **MNI = minimum number individuals

	Right	Left	Indet.	MNI
Class Aves				
Family Fringillidae				
Pipilo sp. (?) (towhee-sized bird)				1
humerus, complete		1		
Class Mammalia				
Order Lagomorpha				
Family Leporidae				
Silvilagus auduboni (cottontail)				1
humerus, distal end	1			
innominate	1			
lumbar vertebrae (2), proximal end	1			
Lepus californicus (jackrabbit)				1
phalange			1	
metatarsal, proximal end			1	
femur, head	1			
Order Carnivora				
Family Mustelidae				
Taxidea taxus (badger)				1
femur, proximal half		1		
Order Perissodactyla				
Family Equidae				
Equus caballus (domestic horse)				1
first phalanx, distal end, burned			1	
metacarpal, proximal end	1			
second phalanx (?), proximal end, burned			1	
(caudal vertebra, distal end--compare *E. caballus*)				
(thoracic vertebrae (2),--compare *E. caballus*)				
Order Artiodactyla(?)				
genus and species indeterminate				1
rib facet			1	
Order Hominoidea				
Family Hominidae				
Homo sapiens				1
upper molar, burned			1	
occipital fragment	1?			
cranial fragments (possibly human)			4	

APPENDIX II

POLLEN ANALYSIS OF SURFACE-RECOVERED GROUND STONE ARTIFACTS

by

Gerald K. Kelso

Laboratory of Paleoenvironmental Studies
University of Arizona

Objectives

Analysis of washings from ground stone artifacts has been a standard feature of archaeological pollen studies for a number of years. At least one investigator (Bohrer 1972:24) has reported good results. Ethnobotanical evidence is rarely preserved in shallow archaeological sites. This study of pollen from metates and manos found on the surface in the area between Willcox and Safford, Arizona was undertaken to determine if such pollen sources will provide data concerning the plants utilized by the inhabitants of such sites.

Methods

The analysis was performed at the Laboratory of Paleoenvironmental Studies, University of Arizona. Ten whole and fragmentary milling stones found with their grinding surfaces down and one found with its grinding surface up, taken to provide comparative data, were sealed in plastic bags immediately upon being collected. Samples of the soil in immediate contact with the under surface of each artifact and a general surface sample from each investigated site were taken for comparative purposes.

All visible soil was removed from the artifacts in the laboratory and discarded. The face of each artifact which had been turned to the soil was moistened with distilled water and thoroughly rinsed with hydrochloric acid to dislodge the sediments trapped in the cracks and crevices of the stone. The resulting pollen matrices were dried and weighed. They, along with the comparative soil samples, were processed according to Mehringer's (1967) mechanical/chemical method.

Pollen residues were mounted in glycerol for viewing. Fifty to two hundred pollen grains were tabulated (Table 35) for each sample, depending upon the density of pollen in the sample, with a compound transmitted-light microscope at 400X. Problematical pollen grains were examined under oil emersion at 1000X. Identification of pollen types is based on the pollen reference collection of the Laboratory. Terminology follows Mehringer (1967) except that "Ambrosia-type" and "other-Compositae" categories have been substituted for his "low-spine" Compositae groupings.

Absolute pollen sums were computed (Table 35, Figure 106) by Benninghoff's (1962) exotic pollen addition method to determine if the samples contained quantities of pollen comparable to those of undegraded soil samples and could therefore be confidently interpreted. The data for individual pollen types are, however, presented in terms of relative pollen frequencies. Absolute pollen frequencies are of limited value in the absence of information concerning the rate at which the pollen matrices accumulated.

Results

All of the AEPCO II samples contained sufficient pollen to warrant analysis. Absolute sums, however varied considerably. It is notable that the washings from the grinding stones contained larger quantities of pollen per gram (Figure 106, Table 35) than did the corresponding soil samples. This is probably a function of the protection against oxidization afforded the pollen grains by the fissures in the metates and manos. It could also be partially due to concentration of pollen from plant materials ground on the milling stones.

The residue from the under side of the artifact found with its grinding surface up (Mano 6A) contained only perfectly preserved pollen grains which took stain like modern pollen. This mano had probably been recently turned over and therefore its pollen spectra reflects the current pollen rain on AZ CC:9:2.

Arboreal Pollen Types

Pinus. Pine (Pinus) pollen was not a major element in the AEPCO Phase II pollen spectra and, with one exception, the pine pollen counts of the artifacts differed from those of their respective soil samples by only a few percent. Most (94.5 percent) of these pollen grains were of a size (Figures 107 and 108) consistent with the range (bladder length of 40 microns or less) which Martin (1963:Figure 9) defined for the piñons, smallest of the pine pollen types. Seventy percent, sample 12A excluded, of the well-preserved pine pollen grains also displayed the gemmae (belly-warts) in the vicinity of the germinal colpus which are characteristic of the Haploxlon pine subgenus to which the piñons belong.

Sample 12A from AZ CC:13:16 is unique. The pine pollen frequency from this metate comprised 23 percent of the sample sum, while the pines contributed only 2.5 percent of the pollen in the soil in contact with the metate grinding surface. No other arboreal pollen frequency from any of the AEPCO II sites even approaches that of sample 12A. The pine pollen bladder length histogram

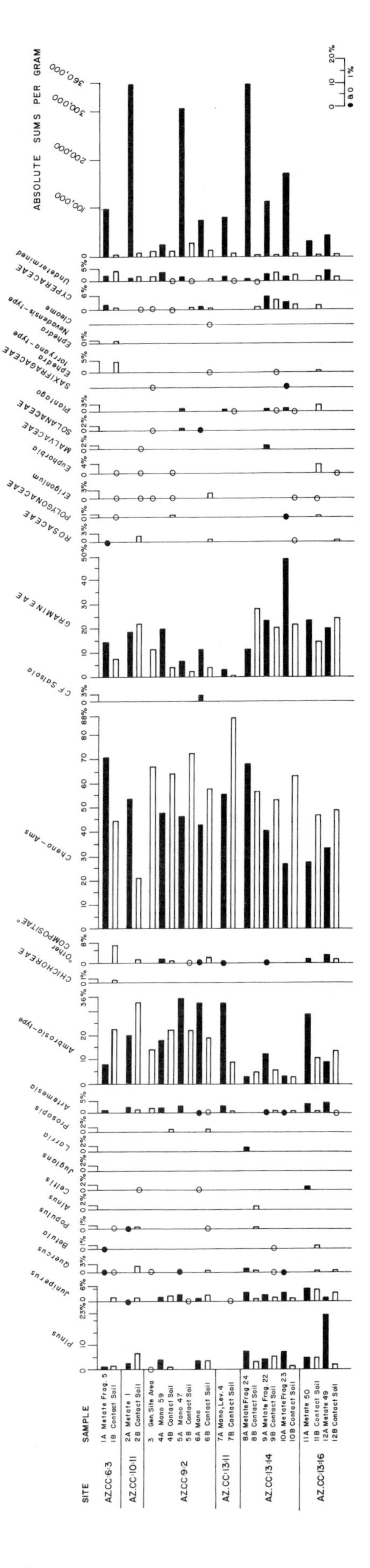

Figure 106. AEPCO II pollen sums.

Table 35. AEPCO II pollen counts.

Site	Sample	Pinus	Juniperus	Quercus	Betula	Populus	Alnus	Celtis	Juglans	Larria	Prosopis	Artemesia	Ambrosia-type	CHICHOREAE	Other COMPOSITAE	Cheno-Ams	CF Salsola	GRAMINEAE	ROSACEAE	POLYGONACEAE	Erigonium	Euphorbia	MALVACEAE	SOLANACEAE	Plantago	SAXIFRAGACEAE	Ephedra torryana-type	Ephedra Nevadensis-type	Cleome	CYPERACEAE	Undetermined	Raw Sums	Absolute sums per gram
AZ CC:6:3	1A Metate, Frag. 5	2	-	1	1	-	-	-	-	-	-	2	16	-	-	142	-	29	1	-	-	-	-	-	-	-	-	-	-	4	2	200	96,786
	1B Contact Soil under 1A	3	4	1	-	1	-	-	-	-	-	-	45	2	15	90	-	15	-	1	1	1	-	-	-	-	9	2	-	2	8	200	4,552
AZ CC:10:11	2A Metate 1, Feat. 1	5	1	-	-	1	-	-	-	-	-	5	40	-	-	107	-	38	-	-	-	-	-	-	-	-	-	-	-	-	3	200	358,879
	2B Contact Soil under 2A	14	3	6	-	2	1	1	-	-	-	3	67	-	3	42	-	44	5	-	1	1	1	-	-	-	-	-	-	1	5	200	7,766
AZ CC:9:2	3 General Site area	1	-	1	-	-	-	-	-	-	-	4	29	-	-	135	-	22	-	-	1	-	-	1	-	1	-	-	-	1	4	200	10,757
	4A Mano 1A 59	2	1	-	-	-	-	-	-	-	-	1	9	-	1	24	-	10	-	-	-	-	-	-	-	-	-	-	-	-	2	50	24,574
	4B Contact Soil under 4A	2	5	-	-	-	-	-	-	-	3	-	45	-	2	129	-	8	-	2	1	1	-	-	-	-	-	-	-	1	1	200	10,757
	5A Mano 1A 47	-	2	-	-	-	-	-	-	-	-	2	24	-	-	32	-	5	-	-	-	-	-	1	1	-	-	-	-	-	1	68	308,544
	5B Contact Soil under 5B	-	1	1	-	-	-	-	-	-	-	-	44	-	1	145		5	-	-	-	-	-	-	-	-	-	-	-	2	1	200	28,429
	6A Mano (grinding surface rep.)	5	2	-	-	-	-	1	-	-	-	1	44	-	1	57	3	15	-	-	-	-	-	1	-	-	-	-	-	2	-	132	76,342
	6B Contact Soil under 6A	7	6	2	-	1	-	-	-	-	3	1	38	-	5	116	-	8	2	-	5	-	-	-	-	-	1	-	1	2	2	200	12,061
AZ CC:13:11	7A Mano, Level 4	-	-	-	-	-	-	-	-	-	-	3	34	-	1	56	-	3	-	-	-	-	-	-	1	-	-	-	-	-	2	100	82,671
	7B Contact Soil under 7A	-	1	-	-	-	-	-	-	-	-	2	18	-	-	175	1	2	-	-	-	-	-	-	1	-	-	-	-	-	1	200	8,468

Table 35. AEPCO II pollen counts (continued).

Site	Sample	Pinus	Juniperus	Quercus	Betula	Populus	Alnus	Celtis	Juglans	Larria	Prosopis	Artemesia	Ambrosia-type	CHICHOREAE	Other COMPOSITAE	Cheno-Ams	CF Salsola	GRAMINEAE	ROSACEAE	POLYGONACEAE	Erigonium	Euphorbia	MALVACEAE	SOLANACEAE	Plantago	SAXIFRAGACEAE	Ephedra torryana-type	Ephedra Nevadensis-type	Cleome	CYPERACEAE	Undetermined	Raw Sums	Absolute sums per gram
AZ CC:13:14	8A Metate Frag.24, Feature 1	8	4	2	-	-	-	-	-	2	-	-	3	-	-	68	-	12	-	-	-	-	-	-	-	-	-	-	-	-	1	100	358,878
	8B Contact Soil under 8A	7	2	2	-	2	3	-	-	-	-	-	10	-	-	113	-	57	-	-	-	-	-	-	-	-	-	-	-	3	1	200	3,433
	9A Metate Frag.22, Feature 1	9	6	-	-	-	-	-	-	-	-	1	25	-	1	81	-	53	-	-	-	-	4	-	2	-	-	-	-	12	6	200	115,317
	9B Contact Soil under 8A	12	4	1	1	-	-	-	-	-	-	2	12		-	107	-	42	-	-	-	-	-	-	1	-	1	-	-	9	8	200	4,916
	10A Metate Frag.23, Feature 1	15	8	1	-	-	-	-	-	-	-	1	7	-	-	54	-	99	-	1	-	-	-	-	3	1	-	-	-	7	3	200	173,390
	10B Contact Soil under 10A	4	3	-	-	-	-	-	1	-	-	2	6	1	1	127	-	44	1	-	1	-	-	-	1	-	-	-	-	5	5	200	7,623
AZ CC:13:16	11A Metate IA 50	3	3	-	-	-	-	1	-	-	-	2	16	-	1	15	-	13	-	-	-	-	-	-	-	-	-	-	-	-	-	54	32,827
	11B Contact Soil under 11A	5	5	1	1	-	-	-	-	-	-	1	11	-	-	47	-	15	-	1	1	4	-	-	3	-	1	-	-	2	2	100	2,095
	12A Metate IA 49	46	4	-	-	-	-	-	-	-	-	9	17	-	7	67	-	41	-	-	-	-	-	-	-	-	-	-	-	-	9	200	43,384
	12B Contact Soil under 12A	5	8	2	-	-	-	-	-	-	-	1	27	-	3	99	-	49	2	-	-	1	-	-	-	-	-	-	-	-	3	200	5,452

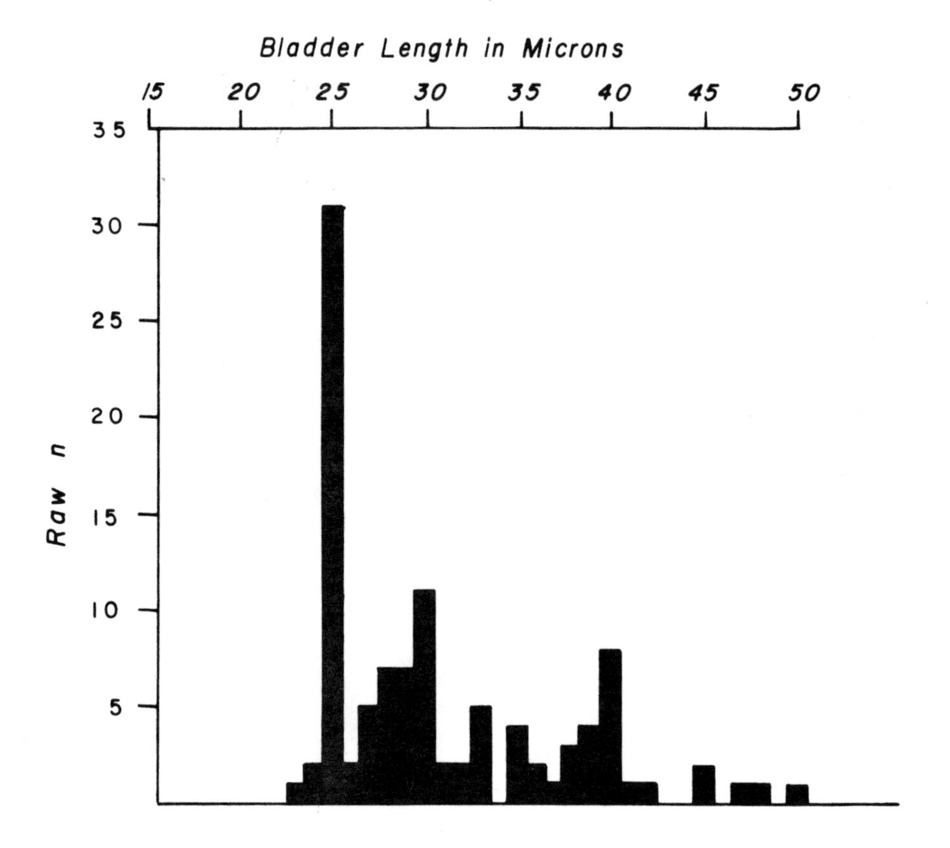

Figure 107. Pine pollen bladder lengths; all samples except 12A, based on raw sums.

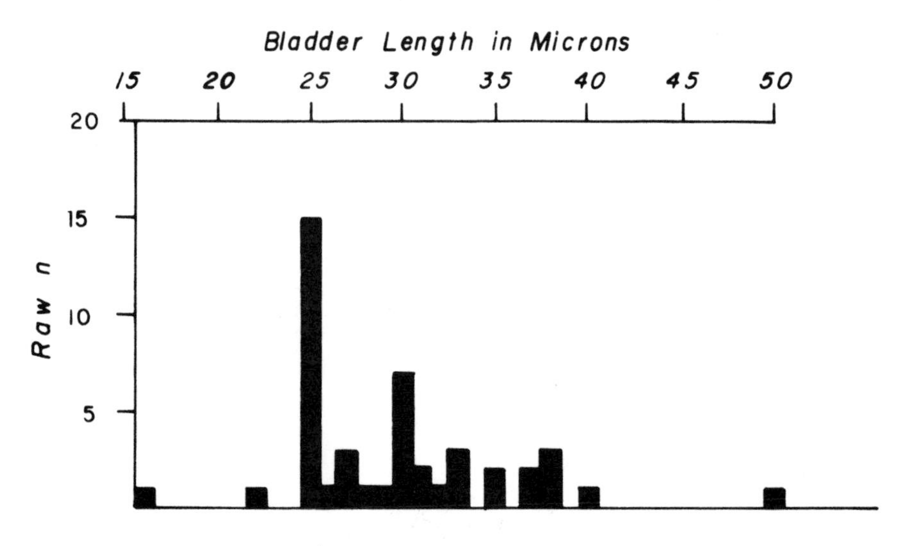

Figure 108. Pine pollen bladder lengths; Sample 12A, based on raw sums.

(Figure 108) for this sample closely resembles that for the other pine pollen spectra of the AEPCO Phase II sites, but "belly-warts" were absent on 83 percent of the sample 12A pollen grains in which this characteristic could be observed.

The sample 12A pine pollen percentage is probably not a function of statistical constraint. If if were the result of a reduction in the pollen contribution of some other plant, the rest of the pollen types in sample 12A should have gained proportionately as well. Some unusual circumstance, whether natural or cultural, was certainly in operation. Perhaps this metate was placed in the face down position during the peak of the pine anthesis period. It is also possible that the count reflects a human activity involving some portion of a pine tree which was heavily laden with pollen.

It is unlikely that the high pine pollen frequency of metate 12A is a function of the milling of piñon nuts. These were a popular wild food with all aboriginal southwestern peoples in the areas where piñon pines grew, but pollen does not adhere to such seeds (Bohrer 1972:Table 7). The native inhabitants of the Southwest during the ethnographic present do not appear to have extensively consumed the green portions of pine trees. Young buds and shoots of yellow and piñon pines were eaten by members of the Great Fire Fraternity at Zuni (Stevenson 1915:96) in efforts to influence the sex of unborn children, and pine needles are consumed by inhabitants of the same pueblo (Stevenson 1915:57) as part of the treatment for venereal disease. The Navajo use pine pollen ritually (Vestal 1952:13), but the literature seems to contain no evidence for this practice among the historic pueblos.

Other Arboreal Pollen Types. Varying quantities of pollen from nine other trees and shrubs were found in the AEPCO II pollen spectra. Seven of these, juniper (*Juniperus*), oak (*Quercus*), birch (*Betula*), cottonwood (*Populus*), alder (*Alnus*), hackberry (*Celtis*) and walnut (*Juglans*) are wind-dispersed pollen types. The other two, creosote bush (*Larrea*) and mesquite (*Prosopis*), are adapted to insect transportation. Of these nine pollen types, only juniper was found with any reqularity on the milling stones, and there is too little difference between the counts from the milling stones and those from the contact soil samples to suggest that the metates and manos were employed in grinding products from these trees.

Wind-pollinated Herbs

Artemisia. Sagebrush (*Artemisia*) leaves and flowers were eaten by the prehistoric Great Basin Shoshoni (Fry 1969:8) and portions of these plants appear in the dietary and medical inventory of the historic Hopi (Whiting 1939:94) and Zuni (Stevenson 1915:94). Sagebrush pollen was present on 10 of the 11 AEPCO II milling stones. Some of the metate and mano sagebrush pollen percentages are higher than those of the corresponding soil samples. None of the milling stone counts, however, exceeded 5 percent and differences between such small sums of a wind-dispersed pollen type cannot be reliably attributed to economic factors.

Ambrosia-type. Comparatively high percentages of ragweed-type (Ambrosia-type) pollen appeared on four (5A, 6A, 7A and 12A) of the eleven AEPCO II milling stones. These frequencies were notably larger than those of the corresponding soil samples, suggesting that they are a function of plant material processed with these artifacts. Dicoria seeds and flowers were consumed by the Hopi (Whiting 1939:96) and Martin and Sharrock (1964:175) suggest, from coprolite evidence, that the prehistoric inhabitants of the Glen Canyon, Utah area ate Oxytenia.

Mano 6A, however, contained only pollen representative of the very recent pollen rain on AZ CC:9:2. The ragweed-type pollen percentage of this sample is virtually identical to the other three outstanding ragweed-type pollen frequencies. The differences between the proportions of this pollen type on the milling stones and in the comparative pollen matrices may be a function of statistical constraint due to the proportions of Cheno-am pollen in these samples.

Cheno-ams. Pollen contributed by the Chenopodiaceae (goosefoot) family and the genus Amaranthus (pigweed), which cannot be reliably differentiated, was prominent in all of the AEPCO II samples. For the most part there was more of this pollen type in the soil samples than on the milling stones. Washings from three of the metates (1A, 2A, and 8A) did produce higher Cheno-am pollen percentages than did the respective soil samples. In two of these, samples 1A and 2A, the difference is notable and could have resulted from the processing of some portion of the parent plant. Neither of these pollen frequencies is, however, conspicuously higher than the majority of those from the comparative samples taken under the other AEPCO II artifacts. They cannot be firmly assigned an economic origin.

The consumption of plants producing Cheno-am-type pollen is well documented for the historic Zuni, Hopi, Navajo and Tewa-speaking pueblos (Stevenson 1915:66; Whiting 1939:73-74; Elmore 1944:45-6; Robbins, Harrington and Freire-Marco 1916:53) and seeds of plants producing this pollen type have been recovered from human feces found in several southwestern archaeological sites (Callen and Martin 1969:329; Kelso 1976:97-8). Pollen in moderate to abundant quantities has been found adhering to the winnowed seed of species of Chenopodium and Amaranthus (Bohrer 1972:Table 7).

Gramineae. The grass (Gramineae) pollen frequencies of the majority of the AEPCO II milling stones were higher than those of the matching soil samples. For the most part the differences were not striking. Two of the milling stone grass counts (4A and 10A) do, however, seem sufficiently prominent to appear significant. These two counts could be the statistical product of the somewhat lower percentages of Cheno-am and Ambrosia-type pollen in their respective samples. They could also have resulted from the milling of grass seed.

The metate 10A grass pollen count is especially notable. The percentages of this pollen type in the three soil samples from site AZ CC:13:14 in which this metate was found are quite uniform and are very likely representative of the local pollen rain. The metate 10A grass pollen frequency stands out sharply from these samples and from all other AEPCO II grass pollen spectra.

The seeds of a number of grasses were collected by the Hopi (Whiting 1939:64-7). The use of at least one variety is recorded for the Zuni (Stevenson 1915:67). Bohrer (1972) found evidence for the prehistoric processing of grass seed in the washings from a metate found in the Hay Hollow Site.

Minor Wind-pollinated Herbs. Wind-transported pollen assignable to the sedges (Cyperaceae) and Russian thistle (Salsola) as well as two morphological varieties of Mormon tea (Ephedra) appeared in the AEPCO II pollen spectra. Sedge pollen is the most prominent of these, but it reaches only 6 percent (Sample 9A) of one sum, and there is little to distinguish the milling stone sedge counts from those of the corresponding soil samples. Mormon tea pollen appears only in the soil samples. The dominance of Ephedra-torryana-type over E.-nevadensis-type is consistent with the present distribution of these pollen types in southwestern soils (Martin 1963:Figure 31).

Russian thistle (tumbleweed) is a recent introduction to the Western Hemisphere. Its pollen is distinguished from that of other genera of the Chenopodiaceae family by its small number of comparatively large pores. The presence of this pollen type only in the washings from mano 6A supports the interpretation that the pollen spectra of the artifact is modern.

Insect-pollinated Herbs

Varying quantities of 11 zoophilous pollen types; Chicory subfamily of the Chenopodiaceae (Chicoreae), sunflower ("other-Compositae"), rose family (Rosaceae), buckwheat family (Polygonaceae), wild buckwheat (Erigonium), spurge (Euphorbia), mallow family (Maivaceae), nightshade family (Solanaceae), plantain (Plantago), saxifrage family (Saxifragaceae) and Rocky Mountain beeweed (Cleome) were present in the AEPCO II pollen counts. Such pollen is generally rare in natural deposits, as the resins and sticky oils by means of which the pollen is transferred to the insect vector also hold it firmly in the flower. Any amount of such pollen in a soil sample indicates that the parent plants were growing nearby. A large amount of it in any pollen matrix must reflect some unusual circumstance.

Five of the 11 insect-transported pollen types recorded in the AEPCO II pollen spectra were found only in the soil samples. Most of the remaining six zoophilous pollen types are from plants which were utilized, in one way or another, by southwestern aboriginal groups during the ethnographic present. Only one of these, "other-Compositae" appeared in the washings from a majority of the artifacts. Its contribution does not exceed 3.5 percent (Sample 12A) and it is unlikely that this count, or any other percentage among the insect-transported pollen types, reflects the milling of plant products.

Summary and Conclusions

All of the pollen types which appear in the AEPCO II pollen spectra are produced by plants currently growing in the Willcox/Safford area. The majority of the individual pollen frequencies from the metates and manos are lower than or indistinguishable from their corresponding counts from the comparative soil samples.

The ragweed-type pollen spectra of ground stone Samples 5A, 7A, and 11A; the Cheno-am pollen frequencies of ground stone Samples 1A and 2A and the grass pollen percentage of ground stone sample 4A are, however, noticeably higher than their respective soil samples. Plants producing all three pollen types are known to have been consumed by southwestern aboriginal peoples during the ethnographic present, but one cannot firmly assign an economic origin to these counts. Each frequency is either matched or exceeded by those of the same pollen type in the soil samples from under other milling stones, or in the case of the ragweed-type counts, by the modern pollen rain recorded in the washing from mano 6A.

The pine pollen count from metate 12A (AZ CC:13:16) and the grass pollen frequency from metate 10A (AZ CC:13:14) are distinctive and must reflect some special circumstance. The grass pollen contribution to metate 10A is notably higher than all of the rather uniform grass percentages of the soil samples from the site (AZ CC:13:14) in which the metate was found. It is also higher than any other grass pollen frequency from the AEPCO II sites. This count probably reflects the milling of grass seed.

The pine pollen frequency of metate 12A is less easily explained. The pine pollen on this artifact, like that from the rest of the AEPCO II samples, is of a size which strongly suggests that it is derived from piñon pines. This high percentage of pine pollen does not appear to be a function of statistical constraint and it is possible that it could be due to the season in which the metate was turned face down. This would not, however, account for the absence of morphological features characteristic of piñon pine pollen grains from the vast majority of the pine pollen grains from metate 12A. It is also possible that the unique pine pollen count of metate 12A is the surviving evidence of some human activity involving some portion of one or more pine trees. The ethnographic literature does not, unfortunately, seem to contain any record of a practice to which this pollen frequency could be attributed.

APPENDIX III

TABULATED LITHIC DATA

by
Kenneth Rozen

Table 36. Artifact frequency by stage of reduction.

Location	Cores	Unretouched Complete Flakes	Retouched Pieces	Unretouched Fragments	Other	Total
AZ CC:6:3	65	31	12	25	0	133 Absolute
	48.9	23.3	9.0	18.8		100 Percent
AZ CC:10:6	7	91	51	320	0	469
	1.5	19.4	10.8	68.2	0.0	99.9
AZ CC:10:11 Locus 1	92	292	122	551	0	1057
	8.7	27.6	11.6	52.1	0.0	100
AZ CC:10:11 Locus 2	20	81	41	107	1	250
	8.0	32.4	16.4	42.8	0.4	100
AZ CC:10:11 Sample 2	38	305	70	751	1	1165
	3.3	26.2	6.0	64.5	0.0	100
AZ CC:10:13	24	85	73	158	0**	340
	7.1	25.0	21.4	46.5	0.0	100
AZ CC:10:14	11	44	42	53	0	150
	7.3	29.3	28.3	35.3	0.0	99.9
AZ CC:9:2* Surface	9	148	59	428	6	650
	1.4	22.8	9.1	65.8	0.9	100
AZ CC:9:2* Subsurface	0	50	14	253	0	317
	0.0	15.8	4.4	79.8	0.0	100
AZ CC:13:11	8	33	5	559	9	614
	1.3	5.4	0.8	91.0	1.5	100
AZ CC:13:6	4	41	18	105	0	168
	2.4	24.4	10.7	62.5	0.0	100
AZ CC:13:14	0	45	16	356	0	417
	0.0	10.8	3.8	85.4	0.0	100

* Sampled; ** Two artifacts originally classified as cores are probably sheared hammerstones.

Table 37. Absolute frequencies of flakes by thickness.

Thickness (mm)	AZ CC:6:3	AZ CC:10:6	AZ CC:10:11* Locus 1	AZ CC:10:11 Locus 2	AZ CC:10:11* Sample 2	AZ CC:10:13	AZ CC:10:14	AZ CC:9:2* Surface	AZ CC:9:2* Subsurface	AZ CC:13:11	AZ CC:13:6	AZ CC:13:14	
1	0	0	1	0	1	0	0	3	6	5	0	4	
2	1	18	1	2	2	1	0	22	5	4	7	6	
3	1	13	2	4	10	1	0	16	12	3	7	6	
4	2	12	8	7	6	0	2	16	6	6	6	5	
5	5	10	11	13	12	8	2	20	8	4	6	6	
6	2	11	14	10	10	4	1	17	3	1	2	3	
7	4	6	15	7	12	3	4	18	1	1	4	5	
8	3	8	11	9	18	6	6	6	2	2	5	5	
9	6	6	5	6	9	11	3	7	0	2	1	1	
10	3	4	9	6	6	12	2	6	2	3	1	3	
11	1	1	4	2	5	6	2	2	2	0	1	1	
12	1	1	6	4	3	6	7	5	0	1	1	1	
13	2	2	3	3	4	6	5	3	0	0	0	0	
14	1	1	2	3	1	6	6	2	1	0	0	0	
15	1	0	1	1	1	5	3	0	2	0	0	1	
16	1	1	1	3	2	3	1	2	0	1	1		
17	0	1	2	0	0	4	2	2	1				
18	0	0	1	1	1	2	2	0	0				
19	0	1	0	1	0	2	0	0	0				
20	0		1	1	2	3	0	1	1				
21	1					1	0						
22						4	2						
23						1	0						
24						0	0						
25						2	1						
26						1							
	35	96	98	83	105	98	51	148	52	33	42	47	Totals

* Sampled

Table 38. Relative frequencies of flakes by thickness.

Thickness (mm)	AZ CC:6:3	AZ CC:10:6	AZ CC:10:11 * Locus 1	AZ CC:10:11 Locus 2	AZ CC:10:11* Sample 2	AZ CC:10:13	AZ CC:10:14	AZ CC:9:2 * Surface	AZ CC:9:2 * Subsurface	AZ CC:13:11	AZ CC:13:6	AZ CC:13:14
1			1.0		1.0			2.0	11.5	15.2		8.5
2	2.9	18.8	1.0	2.4	1.9	1.0		14.9	9.6	12.1	16.7	12.8
3	2.9	13.5	2.0	4.8	9.5	1.0		10.8	23.1	9.1	16.7	12.8
4	5.7	12.5	8.2	8.4	5.7		3.9	10.8	11.5	18.2	14.3	10.6
5	14.3	10.4	11.2	15.7	11.4	8.2	3.9	13.5	15.4	12.1	14.3	12.8
6	5.7	11.5	14.3	12.0	9.5	4.1	2.0	11.5	5.8	3.0	4.8	6.4
7	11.4	6.3	15.3	8.4	11.4	3.1	7.8	12.2	1.9	3.0	9.5	10.6
8	8.6	8.3	11.2	10.8	17.1	6.1	11.8	4.1	3.9	6.1	11.9	10.6
9	17.1	6.3	5.1	7.2	8.6	11.2	5.9	4.7		6.1	2.4	2.1
10	8.6	4.2	9.2	7.2	5.7	12.2	3.9	4.1	3.9	9.1	2.4	6.4
11	2.9	1.0	4.1	2.4	4.8	6.1	3.9	1.4	3.9		2.4	2.1
12	2.9	1.0	6.1	4.8	2.9	6.1	13.7	3.4		3.0	2.4	2.1
13	5.7	2.1	3.1	3.6	3.8	6.1	9.8	2.0				
14	2.9	1.0	2.0	3.6	1.0	6.1	11.8	1.4	1.9			
15	2.9		1.0	1.2	1.0	5.1	5.9		3.9			2.1
16	2.9	1.0	1.0	3.6	1.9	3.1	2.0	1.4		3.0	2.4	
17		1.0	2.1			4.1	3.9	1.4	1.9			
18			1.0	1.2	1.0	2.0	3.9					
19		1.0		1.2		2.0						
20			1.0	1.2	1.9	3.1		0.7	1.9			
21	2.9					1.0						
22						4.1	3.9					
23						1.0						
24												
25						2.0	2.0					
26						1.0						

* Sampled

Table 39. Absolute and relative frequencies of flakes by cortex class.

	Cortex Classes						
	0	1	2	3	4	5	
AZ CC:6:3	3 8.6	0 0.0	10 28.6	13 37.1	3 8.6	6 17.1	n = 35
AZ CC:10:6	61 63.5	9 9.4	15 15.6	8 8.3	3 3.1	0 0.0	n = 96
AZ CC:10:11 Locus 1	11 11.2	13 13.3	25 25.5	23 23.5	15 15.3	11 11.2	n = 98
AZ CC:10:11 Locus 2	21 25.3	19 22.9	22 26.5	11 13.3	3 3.6	7 8.4	n = 83
AZ CC:10:11 Sample 2	55 52.4	9 8.6	23 21.9	13 12.4	5 4.8	0 0.0	n =105
AZ CC:10:13	22 22.4	8 8.2	29 29.6	21 21.4	11 11.2	7 7.1	n = 98
AZ CC:10:14	9 17.6	2 3.9	18 35.3	16 31.4	3 5.9	3 5.9	n = 51
AZ CC:9:2 Surface	97 65.5	9 6.1	32 21.6	5 3.4	5 3.4	0 0.0	n =148
AZ CC:9:2 Subsurface	38 73.1	4 7.7	7 13.5	2 3.8	0 0.0	1 1.9	n = 52
AZ CC:13:11	17 51.5	2 6.1	6 18.2	5 15.2	2 6.1	1 3.0	n = 33
AZ CC:13:6	27 64.3	2 4.8	9 21.4	3 7.1	1 2.4	0 0.0	n = 42
AZ CC:13:14	37 78.7	0 0.0	6 12.8	4 8.5	0 0.0	0 0.0	n = 47

Table 40. Absolute and relative frequencies of cores by cortex class and direction of flaking.

	Cortex Classes						Direction of Flaking Classes			
	0	1	2	3	4	n	1	2	3	n
AZ CC:6:3	0 0.0	1 1.5	8 12.3	45 69.2	11 16.9	65	37 57.8	16 25.0	11 17.2	64
AZ CC:10:6	2 28.6	1 14.3	3 42.9	0 0.0	1 14.3	7	3 42.9	2 28.6	2 28.6	7
AZ CC:10:11 Locus 1	1 1.1	1 1.1	45 49.5	38 41.8	6 6.6	91	32 37.2	30 34.9	24 27.9	86
AZ CC:10:11 Locus 2	0 0.0	4 21.1	8 42.1	6 31.6	1 5.3	19	7 35.0	7 35.0	6 30.0	20
AZ CC:10:11 Sample 2	3 7.9	8 21.1	14 36.8	9 23.7	4 10.5	38	10 29.4	15 44.1	9 26.5	34
AZ CC:10:13	0 0.0	1 4.2	6 25.0	12 50.0	5 20.8	24	13 56.5	6 26.1	4 17.4	23
AZ CC:10:14	0 0.0	2 18.2	3 27.3	6 54.5	0 0.0	11	3 27.3	3 27.3	5 45.5	11
AZ CC:9:2 Surface	3 33.3	3 33.3	3 33.3	0 0.0	0 0.0	9	4 50.0	1 12.5	3 37.5	8
AZ CC:9:2 Subsurface	. . . . No Cores									
AZ CC:13:11	0 0.0	3 37.5	2 25.0	1 12.5	1 12.5	8	5 71.4	1 14.3	1 14.3	7
AZ CC:13:6	0 0.0	3 75.0	1 25.0	0 0.0	0 0.0	4	1 33.3	0 0.0	2 66.7	3
AZ CC:13:14	. . . . No Cores									

Table 41. Absolute and relative frequencies of cores by number of flake scars.

	n	1	2	3	4	5	6	7	8	9	10	11
		Number of Flake Scars										
AZ CC:6:3	61	16	15	13	9	4	4	0	0	0	0	0
		26.2	24.6	21.3	14.8	6.5	6.5	0.0	0.0	0.0	0.0	0.0
AZ CC:10:6	6	0	0	1	0	0	1	3	0	1	0	0
		0.0	0.0	16.7	0.0	0.0	16.7	50.0	0.0	16.7	0.0	0.0
AZ CC:10:11	78	17	9	16	10	8	4	4	7	2	0	1
Locus 1		21.8	11.5	20.5	12.8	10.3	5.1	5.1	9.0	2.6	0.0	1.3
AZ CC:10:11	16	1	4	1	3	4	1	2	0	0	0	0
		6.3	25.0	6.3	18.8	25.0	6.3	12.5	0.0	0.0	0.0	0.0
AZ CC:10:11	30	1	8	9	5	4	3	0	0	0	0	0
Sample 2		3.3	26.7	30.0	16.7	13.3	10.0	0.0	0.0	0.0	0.0	0.0
AZ CC:10:13	23	6	2	4	4	4	1	0	1	0	0	1
		26.1	8.7	17.4	17.4	17.4	4.3	0.0	4.3	0.0	0.0	4.3
AZ CC:10:14	11	1	1	2	2	2	0	2	1	0	0	0
		9.1	9.1	18.2	18.2	18.2	0.0	18.2	9.1	0.0	0.0	0.0
AZ CC:9:2*	5	0	0	0	2	2	0	1	0	0	0	0
Surface		0.0	0.0	0.0	40.0	40.0	0.0	0.0	20.0	0.0	0.0	0.0
AZ CC:9:2* Subsurface		No Cores										
AZ CC:13:11	2	0	0	0	0	1	0	0	0	0	0	1
		0.0	0.0	0.0	0.0	50.0	0.0	0.0	0.0	0.0	0.0	50.0
AZ CC:13:6	1	0	0	0	0	0	0	0	0	1	0	0
		0.0	0.0	0.0	0.0	0.0	0.0	0.0	100.0	0.0	0.0	0.0
AZ CC:13:14		No Cores										

* Sampled

Table 42. Presence and absence of cortex (absolute and relative frequencies), mean, maximum, minimum weight frequency distributions for fragments.

	n	Cortex +	Cortex -	Weight Mean	Weight Maximum	Weight Minimum
AZ CC:10:6	320	111 34.7	209 65.3	3.8	91	0.5
AZ CC:10:11* Locus 1	100	77 77.0	23 23.0	10.3	112	0.5
AZ CC:10:11 Locus 2	107	60 56.0	47 44.0	9.3	135	0.5
AZ CC:10:11* Sample	100	27 27.0	73 73.0	11.4	155	0.5
AZ CC:10:13	158	103 65.2	55 34.8	20.6	205	1
AZ CC:10:14	53	37 69.8	16 30.2	34.9	272	1
AZ CC:9:2* Surface	428	113 26.4	315 73.6	4.7	139	0.5
AZ CC:9:2* Subsurface	253	58 23.0	195 77.0	2.5	46	0.5
AZ CC:13:11	559	99 17.7	460 82.3	1.9	71	0.5
AZ CC:13:6	105	36 34.3	69 65.7	7.7	95	0.5
AZ CC:13:14	356	89 25.0	267 75.0	2.8	27	0.5

* Sampled

Table 43. Absolute and relative frequencies of artifacts by texture class.

	Texture Classes						
	1	3	3	4	5	6	n
AZ CC:6:3	66 50.0	38 28.8	20 15.2	6 4.5	2 1.5	0 0.0	132
AZ CC:10:6	117 24.9	165 35.2	139 29.6	43 9.2	5 1.1	0 0.0	469
AZ CC:10:11 Locus 1	114 28.5	199 48.9	47 11.5	25 6.1	8 2.0	7 1.7	400
AZ CC:10:11 Locus 2	43 17.2	149 59.6	44 17.6	8 3.2	0 0.0	6 2.4	250
AZ CC:10:11 Sample 2	134 44.5	93 30.9	10 3.3	3 1.0	0 0.0	61 20.3	301
AZ CC:10:13	2 0.6	131 38.9	166 49.3	35 10.4	3 0.9	0 0.0	337
AZ CC:10:14	1 0.7	53 35.3	77 51.3	19 12.7	0 0.0	0 0.0	150
AZ CC:9:2 Surface	70 10.8	209 32.2	330 50.8	41 6.3	0 0.0	0 0.0	650
AZ CC:9:2 Subsurface	39 12.3	128 40.5	131 41.5	18 5.7	0 0.0	0 0.0	316
AZ CC:13:11	113 18.7	176 29.2	262 43.4	46 7.6	6 1.0	0 0.0	603
AZ CC:13:6	19 11.3	76 45.2	64 38.1	8 4.8	1 0.6	0 0.0	168
AZ CC:13:14	22 5.3	204 48.9	116 27.8	65 15.6	10 2.4	0 0.0	417

Table 44. Absolute and relative frequencies of raw material types.

Raw Material	AZ CC:6:3	AZ CC:10:6	AZ CC:10:11* Locus 1	AZ CC:10:11 Locus 2	AZ CC:10:13	AZ CC:10:14	AZ CC:9:2* Surface	AZ CC:9:2 Subsurface	AZ CC:13:11	AZ CC:13:6	AZ CC:13:14
Rhyolite = 1	49	269	388	157	291	128	95	59	3	14	114
	36.8	54.7	95.3	62.8	86.1	85.3	14.6	18.6	0.5	8.3	27.3
Chert = 2	35	14	0	2	1	1	7	2	0	6	4
	26.3	3.0	0.0	0.8	0.3	0.7	1.1	0.6	0.0	3.6	1.0
Chalcedony = 3	9	72	19	90	44	17	16	8	0	9	10
	6.8	15.4	4.7	36.0	12.9	11.3	2.5	2.5	0.0	5.4	2.4
Jasper = 4	3	5	0	0	0	0	31	7	76	6	3
	2.3	1.1	0.0	0.0	0.0	0.0	4.8	2.2	12.4	3.6	0.7
Obsidian = 5	0	4	0	0	0	0	6	4	0	0	4
	0.0	0.9	0.0	0.0	0.0	0.0	0.9	1.3	0.0	0.0	1.0
Quartzite = 6	12	11	0	0	0	3	136	81	279	62	102
	9.0	2.3	0.0	0.0	0.0	2.0	20.9	25.6	45.4	36.9	24.5
Quartz = 7	1	22	0	0	0	0	4	3	49	5	0
	0.8	4.7	0.0	0.0	0.0	0.0	0.6	0.9	8.0	3.0	0.0
Andesite = 8	3	15	0	0	0	0	1	0	0	0	5
	2.3	3.2	0.0	0.0	0.0	0.0	0.2	0.0	0.0	0.0	1.2
Basalt = 9	6	33	0	1	1	0	301	143	123	47	50
	4.5	7.0	0.0	0.4	0.3	0.0	46.3	45.1	20.0	28.0	12.0
Vesicular basalt = 10	0	0	0	0	0	0	0	0	0	0	0
	0.0	0.0	0.0	0.0	0.0	0.0	0.0	0.0	0.0	0.0	0.0
Schist =11	0	0	0	0	0	0	0	3	2	0	0
	0.0	0.0	0.0	0.0	0.0	0.0	0.0	0.9	0.3	0.0	0.0
Shale =12	2	0	0	0	0	0	1	0	0	0	0
	1.5	0.0	0.0	0.0	0.0	0.0	0.2	0.0	0.0	0.0	0.0
Gneiss =13	1	0	0	0	0	0	0	0	1	0	0
	0.8	0.0	0.0	0.0	0.0	0.0	0.0	0.0	0.2	0.0	0.0
Hematite =14	0	0	0	0	0	0	0	0	0	1	0
	0.0	0.0	0.0	0.0	0.0	0.0	0.0	0.0	0.0	0.6	0.0
Unknown metamorphic =15	0	0	0	0	0	0	0	0	0	0	0
	0.0	0.0	0.0	0.0	0.0	0.0	0.0	0.0	0.0	0.0	0.0
Unknown sedentary =16	2	0	0	0	0	0	0	0	11	0	0
	1.5	0.0	0.0	0.0	0.0	0.0	0.0	0.0	1.8	0.0	0.0
Unknown igneous =17	10	24	0	0	0	0	52	7	66	17	125
	7.5	5.1	0.0	0.0	0.0	0.0	8.0	2.2	10.7	10.1	30.0
Limestone =18	0	0	0	0	1	1	0	0	0	1	0
	0.0	0.0	0.0	0.0	0.3	0.7	0.0	0.0	0.0	0.6	0.0
Granite +19	0	0	0	0	0	0	0	0	3	0	0
	0.0	0.0	0.0	0.0	0.0	0.0	0.0	0.0	0.5	0.0	0.0
N	133	469	407	250	338**	150	650	317	614**	168	417

AZ CC:10:11 Sample 2 not shown

* Sampled ; ** Missing observations

Table 45. Sample size, mean, standard deviation, and the 95 percent confidence interval for mean flake thickness.

	n	Mean	Standard Deviation	95 Percent Confidence Interval for Mean
AZ CC:6:3	35	8.6	4.02	7.27 to 9.93
AZ CC:10:6	96	5.76	3.61	5.02 to 6.49
AZ CC:10:11 Locus 1	98	8.10	3.62	7.38 to 8.83
AZ CC:10:11 Locus 2	83	8.25	4.08	7.36 to 9.14
AZ CC:10:11 Sample 2	105	7.73	3.74	7.00 to 8.46
AZ CC:10:13	98	12.14	5.33	11.07 to 13.21
AZ CC:10:14	51	11.90	4.92	10.52 to 13.29
AZ CC:9:2 Surface	148	6.03	3.69	5.43 to 6.63
AZ CC:9:2 Subsurface	52	5.38	4.39	4.16 to 6.61
AZ CC:13:11	33	5.18	3.68	3.88 to 6.49
AZ CC:13:6	42	5.40	3.12	4.43 to 6.38
AZ CC:13:14	47	5.40	3.24	4.45 to 6.36

Table 46. Absolute frequencies of tool types.

	AZ CC:6:3	AZ CC:10:6	AZ CC:10:11 Locus 1	AZ CC:10:11 Locus 2	AZ CC:10:11 Sample 2	AZ CC:10:13	AZ CC:10:14	AZ CC:9:2 Surface	AZ CC:9:2 Subsurface	AZ CC:13:11	AZ CC:13:6	AZ CC:13:14	AZ CC:13:15	Total
End scrapers	4	4	7	1	0	3	0	12	0	0	2	1	0	34
Side scrapers	2	6	12	3	7	1	3	8	1	0	0	2	0	45
Multi-side scrapers	0	0	3	1	3	1	3	3	1	0	0	0	0	15
Denticulates	1	2	6	1	2	6	2	4	0	1	0	3	0	28
Notches	4	2	14	11	13	11	11	6	0	1	1	0	0	74
Irreg. retouched (large)	0	1	11	3	4	17	5	2	2	0	1	0	0	46
Irreg. retouched (small)	0	7	16	5	6	2	2	0	2	0	0	3	0	43
Burins	0	0	0	0	2	0	0	2	0	0	0	0	0	4
Graver/perforators	1	2	1	1	3	1	0	2	0	0	0	0	0	11
Misc. unifacial fragments	0	8	7	1	4	3	1	11	2	1	7	7	0	52
Small bifaces	1	8	5	2	1	4	5	8	1	0	1	0	0	36
Projectile points	0	11	1	1	0	0	0	3	1	0	4	0	1	22
Heavy unifaces	0	1	0	1	2	7	4	0	0	4	1	0	1	21
Heavy bifaces	0	0	0	0	0	3	0	0	0	0	1	0	0	4
Misc. flaked chunks	0	0	30	11	7	1	2	0	0	0	1	0	0	52
Pebble tools	17	0	4	2	0	5	1	0	0	0	0	0	0	29
Hammerstones	0	0	0	0	1	2	0	5	0	8	3	0	0	19
Shaped schist	0	0	0	0	0	0	0	1	0	1	0	0	0	2
Total	30	52	117	44	55	67	39	67	10	16	22	16	2	537

Table 47. Sample size (n), mean, standard deviation, and 95 percent confidence interval for flake thickness by texture class.

Texture Class	n	Mean Flake Thickness	Standard Deviation	95 Percent Confidence Interval
1 very fine	166	5.78	3.22	5.28 to 6.27
2 fine	347	7.08	4.30	6.62 to 7.53
3 medium	296	8.41	4.81	7.86 to 8.96
4 coarse	55	11.76	5.63	10.24 to 13.29
5 very coarse	4	13.00	5.48	4.28 to 21.72

REFERENCES

Agenbroad, Larry D.
1970 Cultural implications from the statistical analysis of a prehistoric lithic site in Arizona. MS. Master's thesis, The University of Arizona, Tucson.

Antevs, Ernst V.
1955 Geologic-climatic dating in the West. _American Antiquity_ 20::317-355.

Arizona Bureau of Mines
1958 Geologic map of Graham and Greelee counties, Arizona

1959 Geologic map of Cochise County, Arizona.

1969 Mineral and water resources of Arizona. _Arizona Bureau of Mines Bulletin_ 180.

Basso, Keith H.
1971 _Western Apache raiding and warfare_. The University of Arizona Press, Tucson.

Bennett, M. Ann
1974 Basic ceramic analysis. _Eastern New Mexico University Contributions in Anthropology 6(1); San Juan Valley Archaeological Project Technical Series 1._

Benninghoff, W. S.
1962 Calculation of pollen and spores density in sediments by addition of exotic pollen in known quantities. _Pollen et Spores_ 6(2): 332-333.

Binford, Lewis R.
1962 Archaeology as anthropology. _American Antiquity_ 28:217-225.

Binford, Lewis A. and Sally R. Binford (editors)
1969 _New perspectives in archaeology_. Aldine Publishing Co., Chicago.

Blalock, Hubert M., Jr.
1972 _Social statisitics_, (second ed.). McGraw Hill Company, New York.

Bohrer, Vorsila L.
1972 Paleoecology of the Hay Hollow Site, Arizona. _Fieldiana--Anthropology_ 63(1):1-30.

Bradfield, Wesley
1931 Cameron Creek Village, a site in the Mimbres area in Grant County, New Mexico. Monographs of the School of American Research 1.

Breternitz, David A.
1966 An appraisal of tree-ring dated pottery in the Southwest. Anthropological Papers of the University of Arizona 10.

Brown, David E.
1973 The natural vegetative communities of Arizona (map). Arizona Resources Information System.

Brown, Jeffery L.
1973 The origin and nature of Salado evidence from the Safford Valley, Arizona. Unpublished Ph.D. dissertation, Department of Anthropology, the University of Arizona.

Brugge, David
1964 Navajo ceramic practices. Southwestern Lore 30(3): 37-46.

Bryan, Kirk
1925 Date of channel trenching (arroyo cutting) in the arid southwest. Science 62:338-44.

Bryan, Kirk and J. H. Toulouse, Jr.
1943 The San José non-ceramic culture and its relation to a Puebloan culture in New Mexico. American Antiquity 8:269-280.

Bullard, William R., Jr.
1962 The Cerro Colorado Site and pithouse architecture in the southwestern Untied States prior to A.D. 900. Papers of the Peabody Museum of American Archaeology and Ethnology 44(2).

Burkham, D. E.
1972 Channel changes of the Gila River in Safford Valley, Arizona 1846-1970. United States Geological Survey Professional Paper 655-G.

Burns and McDonnel Engineering Company
1974 Report on the environmental analysis for Apache Electric Units No. 2 and No. 3 and related transmission for Arizona Electric Power Cooperative. Kansas City.

Callen, Eric O. and Paul S. Martin
1969 Plant remains in some coprolites from Utah. American Antiquity 34:329-331.

Campbell, Elizabeth C. and William H. Campbell
1935 The Pinto Basin Site. Southwest Museum Papers 9.

Campbell, J. M. and Florence H. Ellis
1952 Cochise manifestations in the middle Rio Grande Valley. American Antiquity 17:211-221.

Canouts, Veletta (assembler)
1975 An archaeological survey of the Orme Reservoir. Arizona State Museum Archaeological Series 92.

Cochran, W. G.
1953 Sampling Techniques. John Wiley and Sons, New York.

Coe, Carol N.
1977 Recommendations for site protection and research, Dos Condado to Apache Segment. Prepared for Arizona Electric Power Cooperative, Inc., Benson. MS, on file at Arizona State Museum, Cultural Resource Management Section, Tucson.

Collins, Michael B.
1975 Lithic technology as means of processual inference. In Lithic technology; making and using stone tools, edited by Earl Swanson, pp. 15-34. Mouton, The Hague.

Colton, Harold S.
1953 Potsherds, an introduction to the study of prehistoric Southwestern ceramics and their use in historic reconstruction. Museum of Northern Arizona Bulletin 25.

1955 A checklist of Southwestern pottery types. Museum of Northern Arizona Ceramic Series 2.

1958 Pottery types of the Southwest. Museum of Northern Arizona Ceramic Series 3D.

Cooper, John R.
1960 Reconnaissance map of the Willcox, Fisher Hills, Cochise, and Dos Cabezas quadrangles, Cochise and Graham counties, Arizona. United States Geological Survey, Mineral Investigations Map MF-321.

Cosgrove, H. S. and C. B. Cosgrove
1932 The Swarts Ruin: A typical Mimbres site in southwestern New Mexico. Papers of the Peabody Museum of American Archaeology and Ethnology 15(1).

Danson, Edward B.
1957 Pottery type descriptions. In "Excavations, 1940, at University Indian Ruin, Tucson, Arizona," by Julian D. Hayden pp. 219-231. Southwestern Monuments Association Technical Series 5.

David, Nicholas and Hilke Hennig
1972 The ethnography of pottery: A Fulani case seen in archaeological perspective. McCalab Module in Anthropology 21.

Davis, Goode P.
1973 Man and wildlife in Arizona. The pre-settlement era, 1823-64. Master's thesis, The University of Arizona, Tucson.

Debowski, Sharon, Anique George, Richard Goddard, and Deborah Mullon
1976 An archaeological survey of the Buttes Reservoir. Arizona State Museum Archaeological Series 93(1).

Dick, Herbert W.
1965 Bat Cave. The School of American Research Monograph 27.

Dick-Peddie, S.
1976 Changes in grass cover and desert rodent fauna following habitat perturbation. Journal of the Arizona Academy of Science 11:23.

DiPeso, Charles C.
1951 The Babocomari Village site on the Babocomari River, southeastern Arizona. The Amerind Foundation 5.

1956 The upper Pima of San Cayetano de Tumacacori. The Amerind Foundation 7.

1958 The Reeve Ruin of southeastern Arizona. The Amerind Foundation 8.

1974 Casas Grandes: A fallen trading center of the Gran Chichimeca (Vol. 1-3). The Amerind Foundation 9.

Dobyns, Henry F.
1956 Prehistoric Indian occupation within the eastern area of the Yuman complex. Master's thesis, The University of Arizona, Tucson.

Doelle, William Harper
1976 Desert resources and Hohokam subsistence: The Conoco Florence Project. Arizona State Museum Archaeological Series 103.

Doyel, David E.
1972 An archaeological survey of the San Juan-Vail 345 kV power transmission line, Clifton-Vail section. Arizona State Museum Archaeological Series 15.

1974 Excavations in the Escalante Ruin group, southern Arizona. Arizona State Museum Archaeological Series 37.

Doyel, David E.
1977 Excavations in the middle Santa Cruz River Valley, southeastern Arizona. _Arizona State Museum Contribution to Highway Salvage Archaeology_ 44.

Elmore, F. W.
1944 _Ethnobotany of the Navajo_. University of New Mexico Press, Albuquerque.

Emory, Lieut. Col. William H.
1848 Notes of a military reconnaissance from Fort Leavenworth in Missouri to San Diego in California. U.S. Congress Senate, Executive Document 41, 30th Congress, 1st Session.

Enlows, H. E.
1939 Geology and ore deposits of the Little Dragoon Mountains. Unpublished Ph.D. dissertation, The University of Arizona, Tucson.

Faulk, Odie B.
1973 _Destiny road: The Gila trail and the opening of the Southwest_. Oxford University Press, New York.

Fewkes, Jesse W.
1909 Prehistoric ruins of the Gila Valley. _Smithsonian Institution Miscellaneous Collections_ 52(4):403-436.

Fish, Paul R.
1978 Consistency in archaeological measurement and classification: A pilot study. _American Antiquity_ 43:86-89.

Fitting, James E.
1977 _Mitigation of adverse effects to archaeological resources on the Foote Wash conservation and development project_. Commonwealth Associates, Inc. , Jackson, Michigan.

Folk, Robert L.
1951 A comparison chart for visual percentage estimation. _Journal of Sedimentary Petrology_ 21(1):32-33.

Fontana, Bernard L., William J. Robinson, C. W. Cormack and E. E. Leavitt, Jr.
1962 _Papago Indian Pottery_. University of Washington Press, Seattle.

Fry, Gary
1969 Preliminary analysis of the Hogup Cave coprolites. Paper presented at the 34th Annual Meeting of the Society for American Archaeology, Milwaukee.

Fulton, William S.
1934-38 Archaeological notes in Texas Canyon, Arizona. _Contributions from the Museum of the American Indian Heye Foundation_ 12:1-3.

Fulton, William S. and Carr Tuthill
1940 An archaeological site near Gleeson, Arizona. The Amerind Foundation 1.

Gelderman, Frederick W.
1970 Soil survey of the Safford area, Arizona. USDA Soil Conservation Service.

Gifford, E. W.
1932 The southeastern Yavapai. University of California Publications in American Archaeology and Ethnology 29(3).

Gifford, James C. (editor)
1953 A guide to the description of pottery types in the Southwest. MS, on file at Arizona State Museum, Tucson.

1957 Archaeological exploration in caves of the Point of Pines region. Master's thesis, The University of Arizona, Tucson.

Gillerman, Elliot
1958 Geology of the central Peloncillo Mountains, Hidalgo County, New Mexico, and Cochise County, Arizona. New Mexico State Bureau of Mines and Mineral Resources Bulletin 57.

Gilluly, James
1956 General geology of central Cochise County, Arizona. United States Geological Survey Professional Paper 281.

Gilluly, James, John R. Cooper and James S. Williams
1954 Late Paleozoic stratigraphy of central Cochise County, Arizona. United States Geological Survey Professional Paper 266.

Gladwin, Harold S.
1957 A history of the ancient Southwest. Bond-Wheelwright, Portland.

Gladwin, Harold S., Emil W. Haury, E. B. Sayles, and Nora Gladwin
1937 Excavations at Snaketown, material culture. Medallion Papers 25.

Gladwin, Winifred and H. S. Gladwin
1935 The eastern range of the red-on-buff culture. Medallion Papers 16.

Goodyear, Albert C. III
1975 Hecla II and III: An interpretive study of archaeological remains from the Lakeshore Project, Papago Reservation, southcentral Arizona. Arizona State University Anthropological Research Paper 9.

Goodyear, Albert C. and Alfred E. Dittert
1973 Hecla I: A preliminary report on the archaeological investigations at the Lakeshore Project, Papago Indian Reservation, southcentral Arizona. _Arizona State University Anthropological Research Paper_ 4.

Greenleaf, J. Cameron
1975 Excavations at Punta de Agua in the Santa Cruz River Basin, southeastern Arizona. _Anthropological Papers of the University of Arizona_ 26.

Gumerman, George J. (editor)
1971 The distribution of prehistoric population aggregates. _Prescott College Anthropological Papers_ 1.

Hargrave, Lyndon L.
1932 Guide to forty pottery types from the Hopi country and San Francisco mountains, Arizona. _Museum of Northern Arizona Bulletin_ 1.

Harrington, Mark
1933 Gypsum Cave, Nevada. _Southwest Museum Papers_ 8.

Hastings, James R.
1959 Vegetation change and arroyo cutting in southeastern Arizona during the past century: A historical review. _The University of Arizona, Arid Lands Colloquia_, 1958-59:24-39.

Hastings, James R. and Raymond M. Turner
1965 _The Changing Mile_. The University of Arizona Press, Tucson.

Haury, Emil W.
1936a Some southwestern pottery types: Series IV. _Medallion Papers_ 19.

1936b The Mogollon culture of southwestern New Mexico. _Medallion Papers_ 20.

1945 The excavation of Los Muertos and neighboring ruins in the Salt River Valley, southern Arizona. _Papers of the Peabody Museum of American Archaeology and Ethnology_ 24(1).

1950 _The stratigraphy and archaeology of Ventana Cave_. University of Arizona Press and University of New Mexico Press, Tucson and Albuquerque.

1953 Artifacts with mammoth remains, Naco, Arizona. _American Antiquity_ 19:1-24.

1962 The greater American Southwest. In "Courses toward Urban Life," pp. 106-31, edited by R. J. Braidwood and G.R. Willey. _Viking Fund Publications_ 32.

Haury, Emil W.
1976 The Hohokam; desert farmers and craftsmen. The University of Arizona Press, Tucson.

Haury, Emil W., E. B. Sayles, and William W. Wasley
1959 The Lehner site, southeastern Arizona. American Antiquity 25:2-30.

Hayden, Julian D.
1970 Of Hohokam origins and other matters. American Antiquity 35:87-93.

Haynes, C. Vance, Jr.
1966 Elephant hunting in North America. Scientific American 214(3):104-112.

Haynes, C. Vance, Jr., and E. Thomas Hemmings
1968 Mammoth bone shaft wrench from Murray Springs, Arizona. Science 159:186-187.

Heizer, Robert F.
1966 General comments. In The current status of anthropological research in the Great Basin: 1964. Warren L. d'Azevedo and others (editors). Desert Research Institute, Reno.

Hemmings, E. Thomas
1968 Preliminary archaeological report on the Murray Springs Clovis site, Arizona. Paper presented at the 33rd Annual Meeting of the Society for American Archaeology, Santa Fe, New Mexico.

Hevly, Richard H.
1964 Pollen analysis of Quaternary archaeological and lacustrine sediments on the Colorado Plateau. Unpublished Ph.D. dissertation, The University of Arizona.

Hole, Frank and Robert F. Heizer
1965 An introduction to prehistoric archaeology. Holt, Rinehart, and Winston, New York.

Hough, Walter
1907 Antiquities of the upper Gila and Salt River valleys in Arizona and New Mexico. Bureau of American Ethnology, Bulletin 35.

Huckell, Bruce B.
1973 The Gold Gulch Site: A specialized Cochise site near Bowie, Arizona. The Kiva 39:105-130.

Humphrey, Robert R.
1958 The desert grassland: A history of vegetational change and analysis of causes. University of Arizona Agricultural Experiment Station, Bulletin 299.

Irwin-Williams, Cynthia
1967 Picosa: The elementary Southwestern culture. American Antiquity 32:441-457.

n.d. Paleo-Indian and Archaic cultural systems in the southwestern United States. MS, on file, Department of Anthropology, Eastern New Mexico University.

Jahn, L. R. and J. B. Trefethen
1972 Placing channel modifications in perspective. In Watersheds in transition, pp. 15-21. American Water Resources Association and Colorado State University Symposium.

James, Kathleen G.
1974 Analysis of potsherds and ceramic wares. In "Excavation of main pueblo at Fitzmaurice Ruin," by Franklin Barnett, pp. 106-129. Museum of Northern Arizona Special Publication.

Jelinek, Arthur J.
1976 Form, function and style in lithic analysis. In Cultural change and continuity: Essays in honor of James Bennett Griffin, edited by Charles E. Cleland, pp. 19-34. Acedemic Press, New York.

Jennings, Jesse D.
1957 Danger Cave. University of Utah Anthropological Papers 27.

1973 The short useful life of a simple hypothesis. Tebiwa 16:1-9.

Johnson, Alfred E.
1965 The development of Western Pueblo culture. Unpublished Ph.D. dissertation, Department of Anthropology, The University of Arizona.

Johnson Alfred E. and William W. Wasley
1966 Archaeological excavations near Bylas, Arizona. The Kiva 31:205-253.

Karlstrom, T.N.V., George J. Gumerman, and Robert C. Euler
1976 Paleoenvironmental and cultural correlates in the Black Mesa region. In Papers on the Archaeology of Black Mesa, Arizona, edited by George J. Gumerman and Robert C. Euler, pp. 149-161. Southern Illinois University Press, Carbondale.

Kayser, David W. and Donald C. Fiero
1970 Pipeline salvage near Willcox, Arizona. The Kiva 35:131-137.

Kelly, Isabel
1978 The Hodges Ruin: A Hohokam community in the Tucson Basin. Anthropological Papers of the University of Arizona 30.

Kelso, Gerald K.
1976 Absolute pollen frequencies applied to the interpretation of human activities in northern Arizona. Unpublished Ph.D. dissertation. The University of Arizona, Tucson.

Kendeigh, C. S.
1964 Animal ecology. Prentice Hall, Englewood Cliffs.

Kinkade, Gay M.
1975 Foote Wash--No Name Wash project. Arizona State Museum Archaeological Series 67.

Knechtel, Maxwell N.
1936 Geological relations of Gila conglomerate. American Journal Science 31:80-92.

1938 Geology and ground water resources of the valley of Gila River and San Simon Creek, Graham County, Arizona. United States Geological Survey Water Supply Paper 796-F.

Lance, J. F.
1959 Faunal remains from the Lehner Mammoth site. American Antiquity 25:35-39.

LeBlanc, Steven and Ben Nelson
1976 The Salado in southwestern New Mexico. The Kiva 42:71-80.

Leone, Mark P.
1968 Economic autonomy and social distance: Archaeological evidence. Unpublished Ph.D. disseratation. Department of Anthropology, The University of Arizona.

Lindsay, Alexander J., Jr. and Calvin H. Jennings
1968 Salado redware conference: Ninth southwestern ceramic seminar. Museum of Northern Arizona Ceramic Series 4.

Long, Austin
1966 Late Pleistocene and recent chronologies of playa lakes in Arizona and New Mexico. Unpublished Ph.D. dissertation, The University of Arizona.

Loose, Richard W.
1977 Appendix VII. Petrographic notes on selected lithics and ceramic materials. In Settlement and subsistence along the Lower Chaco River, edited by C. A. Reher, pp. 567-571. The University of New Mexico Press, Albuquerque.

Lowe, Charles H.
1959 Contemporary biota of the Sonoran Desert: Problems. University of Arizona, Arid Lands Colloquia, 1958-59, pp. 54-74.

1964 Arizona's natural environment. University of Arizona Press, Tucson.

Lowe, Charles H. and David E. Brown
1973 The natural vegetation of Arizona. Arizona Resources Information System, Cooperative Publication 2. Arizona Game and Fish Department.

Martin, Paul Schultz
1963 The last 10,000 years. The University of Arizona Press, Tucson.

Martin, Paul S. and Ernst Antevs
1949 Cochise and Mogollon sites, Pine Lawn Valley, western New Mexico. Fieldiana: Anthropology 38(1).

Martin, Paul S. and Fred Plog
1973 The Archaeology of Arizona. Doubleday Natural History Press, New York.

Martin Paul S. and F. W. Sharrock
1964 Pollen analysis of prehistoric human feces: A new approach to ethnobotany. American Antiquity 30:168-180.

Martin Paul S., J. B. Rinaldo, Elaine Bluhm, H. C. Cutler, and Roger Granger, Jr.
1952 Mogollon cultural continuity and change: The stratigraphic analysis of Tularosa and Cordova caves. Fieldiana: Anthropology 40.

McClellan, Carole
1976 Archaeological Survey of Vail-Bicknell Transmission Line. Arizona State Museum Archaeological Series 97.

McDonald, James E.
1956 Variability of precipitation in an arid region: A survey of characteristics for Arizona. University of Arizona Institute of Atmospheric Physics, Technical Reports on the Meteorology and Climatology of Arid Lands 1.

McGregor, John
1965 Southwestern archaeology (second edition.) University of Illinois Press, Urbana.

McKinley, W. L.
1973 Fishes of Arizona. Arizona State Fish and Game Department, Phoenix.

McNutt, Charles H. and Robert C. Euler
1966 The Red Butte lithic sites near Grand Canyon, Arizona. American Antiquity 31:410-419.

Mehringer, Peter, J., Jr.
1967 Pollen analysis of the Tule Springs area, Nevada. In "Pleistocene studies in southern Nevada," edited by H. M. Wormington and D. Ellis, pp. 120-200. Nevada State Museum Anthropological Papers 13(3).

Mehringer, Peter J., Jr. and C. Vance Haynes, Jr.
1965 The pollen evidence for the environment of early man and extinct mammals at the Lehner Mammoth Site, southeastern Arizona. American Antiquity 31:17-23.

Meigs, Peveril
1953 World distribution of arid and semi-arid homoclimates. Reviews of Research on Arid Zone Hydrology, Arid Zone Program 1:203-210.

Meinzer, O. E. and F. C. Kelton
1913 Geology and water resources of Sulphur Spring Valley, Arizona. United States Geological Survey Water Supply Paper 320.

Miller, J. P.
1958 Problems of the Pleistocene in cordilleran North American, as related to reconstruction of environmental changes that affected Early Man. In Climate and Man in the Southwest, edited by T. L. Smiley, pp. 19-49. University of Arizona Press, Tucson.

Mills, Jack P. and Vera M. Mills
1969 The Kuykendall Site: A pre-historic Salado Village in southeastern Arizona. El Paso Archaeological Society Special Report 6.

Myrick, David F.
1975 Railroads of Arizona (Vol. 1, The southern roads). Howell-North Books, Berkeley, California.

National Cooperative Soil Survey
1972 Atascosa Series.

Nesbitt, Paul H.
1938 The Starkweather Ruin, a Mogollon pueblo site in the upper Gila area of New Mexico. Logan Museum Publications in Anthropology Bulletin 6.

Nichol, Andrew Alexander
1952 The natural vegetation of Arizona (Revised by W. S. Phillips). University of Arizona, Agricultural Experiment Station, Technical Bulletin 127:185-231.

Nicklin, Keith
1971 Stability and innovation in pottery manufacture. World Archaeology 3:13-48.

Nie, H. Norman, C. Hadlai Hull, Jean G. Jenkins, Karl Steinbrenner, and Dale H. Bent
1975 Statistical package for the social sciences (second edition). McGraw Hill Company, New York.

Pattie, James O.
1930 The personal narrative of James O. Pattie of Kentucky. Lakeside Press, Chicago.

Pettijohn, F. J.
1957 Sedimentary rocks (second edition). Harper and Brothers, New York.

Pettijohn, F. J., P. E. Potter and R. Siever
1972 Sand and sandstone. Springer-Verlag, New York.

Pine, Gordon L.
1963 Sedimentation studies in the vicinity of Willcox Playa, Cochise County, Arizona. Master's thesis, The University of Arizona, Tucson.

Pipkin, Bernard
1964 Clay mineralogy of Willcox Playa and its drainage basin, Cochise County, Arizona. Ph.D. dissertation, The University of Arizona, Tucson.

Plog, Fred T.
1974 The study of prehistoric change. Academic Press, New York.

Plog, Stephan E.
1976 A multivariate approach to the explanation of ceramic design variation. Unpublished Ph.D. dissertation, University of Michigan.

Poulson, E. N. and F. O. Youngs
1938 Soil survey of the upper Gila Valley area, Arizona. U.S. Department of Agriculture, Bureau of Chemistry and Soils Series 1933(15).

Quaide, W. L.
1951 Geology of Central Peloncillo Mountains, Hidalgo County, New Mexico. Unpublished thesis, University of California.

Quinn, Kathleen H. and John Roney
1973 Archaeological resources of the San Simon and Vulture units of the Bureau of Land Management. Arizona State Museum Archaeological Series 34.

Raab, L. Mark
1973 AZ AA:5:2: A prehistoric cactus camp in the Papaguería. Journal of the Arizona Academy of Science 8:116-118.

1974 Archaeological investigations for the Santa Rosa Wash project, Phase I, preliminary report. Arizona State Museum Archaeological Series 60.

Rice, Prudence
1976 Rethinking the ware concept. American Antiquity 41:538-543.

Richmond, Davie L.
1976 Soil survey of the Willcox area, Arizona. United States Department of Agriculture Soil Conservation Service.

Rinaldo, John B. and Elaine A. Bluhm
1956 Late Mogollon pottery types of the Reserve area. Fieldiana: Anthropology 36(7).

Robbins, W. W., J. P. Harrington, and B. Freire-Marreco
1916 Ethnobotany of the Tewa Indians. Bureau of American Ethnology Bulletin 55.

Rogers, Malcolm J.
1936 Yuman pottery making. San Diego Museum Papers 2.

1939 Early lithic industries of the lower basin of the Colorado River and adjacent desert areas. San Diego Museum Papers 3.

1958 San Dieguito implements from the terraces of the Rincon-Pantano and Rillito drainage system. The Kiva 24:1-22.

1966 Ancient hunters of the Far West, edited by Richard F. Pourade. Union-Tribune Publishing Co., San Diego.

Rye, Owen S. and Clifford Evans
1976 Traditional pottery techniques of Pakistan, Smithsonian Contributions to Anthropology 21.

Sabins, Floyd F., Jr.
1957 Stratigraphic relations in Chiricahua and Dos Cabezas mountains, Arizona. American Association of Petroleum Geologists Bulletin 41(3).

Sackett, James R.
1977 The meaning of style in archaeology: A general model. American Antiquity 42:369-380.

Sauer, Carl and Donald Brand
1930 Pueblo sites in southeastern Arizona. University of California Publications in Geography 3(7).

Sayles, E. B.
1945 The San Simon branch, excavations at Cave Creek and in the San Simon Valley (Vol I: Material culture.) Medallion Papers 34.

Sayles, E. B. and Ernst Antevs
1941 The Cochise culture. Medallion Papers 29.

Sayles, E. B., E. Antevs, T. L. Smiley, W. W. Wasley, and R. H. Thompson
n.d. The Cochise gathering culture of southeastern Arizona. MS, on file, Arizona State Museum.

Schiffer, Michael B.
1976 Behavioral archaeology. Academic Press, New York.

Schoenwetter, James and Alfred E. Dittert, Jr.
1968 An ecological interpretation of Anasazi settlement patterns. In Anthropological Archaeology in the Americas, edited by Betty J. Meggars, pp. 41-66. Anthropological Society of Washington, Washington, D.C.

Schroeder, Albert H.
1958 Lower Colorado Buff ware. In "Pottery types of the Southwest, wares 14, 15, 16, 17, 18," edited by Harold S. Colton. Museum of Northern Arizona Ceramic Series 3D.

Schultz, Vernon B.
1964 Southwestern town: The story of Willcox, Arizona. The University of Arizona Press, Tucson.

Schwennesen, A. T.
1917 Ground water in San Simon Valley, Arizona and New Mexico. United States Geological Survey Water-Supply Paper 425.

Scovill, Douglas, Garland J. Gordan and Keith M. Anderson
1972 Guidelines for the preparation of statements of environmental impact on archaeological resources. Arizona Archaeological Center, National Park Service.

Sellers, William D. and R. H. Hill (editors)
1974 Arizona climate 1931-1972 (Revised, second edition) University Press, Tucson.

Shepard, Anna O.
1956 Ceramics for the archaeologist. Carnegie Institution of Washington Publication 609.

Shreve, F.
1915 The vegetation of a desert mountain range as conditioned by climatic factors. Carnegie Institution of Washington Publication 217.

1951 Vegetation and flora of the Sonoran Desert (Vol. I, Vegetation). Carnegie Institution of Washington Publication 591.

Simpson, Kay and Deborah Westfall
1978 The AEPCO Project. Volume I: Greenlee to Dos Condado survey and data recovery of archaeological resources. Arizona State Museum Archaeological Series 117.

Simpson, Kay, Carol Coe, Carole McClellan, and Kathryn Ann Kamp
1978 The AEPCO Project. Volume III: Greenlee to Apache site descriptions. Arizona State Museum Archaeological Series 117.

Spicer, Edward
1962 Cycles of conquest; the impact of Spain, Mexico, and the United States on the Indians of the Southwest 1533-1960. The University of Arizona Press, Tucson.

Stevenson, Matilda Coxe
1915 Ethnobotany of the Zuni Indians. Thirtieth Annual Report of the Bureau of American Ethnology 1908-1909, pp. 35-102.

Stewart, Yvonne G. and Lynn S. Teague
1974 An ethnoarchaeological study of the Vekol Copper Mining Project. Arizona State Museum Archaeological Series 49.

Swanson, Earl H., Jr.
1951 An archaeological survey of the Empire Valley, Arizona. MS. Department of Anthropology, The University of Arizona.

1966 The geographic foundations of the Desert culture. In The Current Status of Anthropological Research in the Great Basin: 1964 Edited by Warren L. d'Azevedo and others. Desert Research Institute, Reno.

Teague, George A.
1975 Foote Wash-No Name Wash F.R.S. archaeological studies research design. MS, on file, Cultural Resource Management Section, Arizona State Museum.

Teague, Lynn S.
1974 Winkleman and Black Hills unit, Bureau of Land Management. Arizona State Museum Archaeological Series 47.

Thompson, Raymond H.
1958 Modern Yucatecan Maya pottery making. Society for American Archaeology, Memoir 15.

Travis, Russel B.
1955 Classification of rocks. Quarterly of the Colorado School of Mines 50(1).

Tringham, Ruth, Glen Cooper, George Odell, Barbara Voytek, and Anne Whitman
1974 Experimentation in the formation of edge damage: A new approach to lithic analysis. Journal of Field Archaeology 1:171-196.

Tuan, Yi-Fu
1959 Pediments in southeastern Arizona. University of California Publications in Geography 13.

Tuohy, Donald R.
1960 Archaeological survey and excavation in the Gila River channel between Earven Dam Site and Buttes Reservoir Site, Arizona. MS, on file, Arizona State Museum.

Tuthill, Carr
1947 The Tres Alamos Site on the San Pedro River, southeastern Arizona. Amerind Foundation Publication 4.

1950 Notes on the Dragoon Comples. In For the Dean, pp. 51-57. Hohokam Museum Association, Tucson, and Southwestern Monuments Assoc., Santa Fe.

Udden, J. A.
1914 Mechanical composition of clastic sediments. Bulletin of the Geological Society of America 25:655-714.

United States Department of Agriculture (USDA), Soil Conservation Service
1973 Coronado resource conservation and development project-program of action.

United States Department of Interior, Bureau of Land Management
1978 Upper Gila-San Simon livestock grazing environmental statement.

United States Department of the Interior, National Park Service, Advisory Council on Historic Preservation
1974 Procedures for the Protection of Historical and Cultural Properties. Federal Register 39:18, part II, 36CFR 800.10, pg.3369.

Van Devender, Thomas
1977 Holocene woodlands in the Southwestern deserts. Science 198:189-192.

Vestal, Paul A.
1952 Ethnobotany of the Ramah Navajo. Peabody Museum of American Archaeology and Ethnology, Report of the Ramah Project 4.

Vivian, R. Gwinn
1970 Archaeological resources of the Corps of Engineers' channel improvement project area in the upper Gila. Arizona State Museum Archaeological Series 2.

Wagner, Jay J.
1952 History of the cattle industry in southern Arizona, 1540-1940. University of Arizona Social Science Bulletin 20.

1975 Early Arizona: Prehistory to Civil War. The University of Arizona Press, Tucson.

Wasley, William W.
1966 Classic period Hohokam. Paper presented at the 31st annual meeting of the Society for American Archaeology, Reno.

Weaver, Donald E., Jr.
1972 Investigations concerning the Hohokam Classic period in the lower Salt River Valley, Arizona. Unpublished Master's thesis, Department of Anthropology, Arizona State University.

1976 Salado influences in the lower Salt River Valley. The Kiva 42:17-26.

Wendorf, Fred
1950 A report on the excavation of a small ruin near Point of Pines, east central Arizona. University of Arizona, Social Science Bulletin 19.

Wendorf, Fred, and Tully Thomas
1951 Early man sites near Concho, Arizona. American Antiquity 17:107-114.

Wentworth, C. K.
1922 A scale of grade and class terms for clastic sediments. Journal of Geology 30:377-392.

Westfall, Deborah A.
1978 Appendix II: Ceramics. In "The AEPCO Project: Volume I. Greenlee to Dos Condado survey and data recovery of archaeological resources," by Kay Simpson and Deborah A. Westfall. Arizona State Museum Archaeological Series 117.

Whalen, Norman M.
1971 Cochise culture sites in the San Pedro drainage. Unpublished Ph.D. dissertation. Department of Anthropology, The University of Arizona.

Wheat, Joe Ben
1955 Mogollon culture prior to A.D. 1000. Society for American Archaeology, Memoir 10.

Whiting, Alfred F.
1939 Ethnobotany of the Hopi. Museum of Northern Arizona Bulletin 15.

Whittaker, Robert H.
1953 A consideration of climax theory: The climax as a population and pattern. Ecological Monographs 23:41-78.

Wilcox, David R.
n.d. The entry of Athapaskans into the American Southwest: The problem today. MS, on file at the Arizona State Museum, University of Arizona, Tucson.

Williams, D. A.
1937 Settlement and growth of the Gila Valley as a Mormon colony, 1879-1900. Unpublished Master's thesis, University of Arizona.

Wilson, Eldred D.
1962 A resumé of the geology of Arizona. Arizona Bureau of Mines Bulletin 171.

Windes, T. C.
1977 Typology and technology of Anasazi ceramics. In Settlement and subsistence along the lower Chaco River, edited by Charles A. Reher, pp. 279-370. The University of New Mexico Press, Albuquerque.

Windmiller, Ric
1971 Early hunters and gatherers in southeastern Arizona. The Cochise Quarterly 1(2).

1973 The late Cochise culture in the Sulphur Spring Valley, southeastern Arizona: Archaeology of the Fairchild site. The Kiva 39:131-170.

Yang, T. W. and Charles H. Lowe, Jr.
1956 Correlation of major vegetation climates with soil characteristics in the Sonoran desert. Science 123:542.

Young, Jon N.
1967 The Salado culture in southwestern prehistory. Unpublished Ph.D. dissertation, Department of Anthropology, The University of Arizona.